Pigskin Warriors

Pigskin Warriors

140 Years of College Football's Greatest Traditions, Games, and Stars

Steven Travers

TAYLOR TRADE PUBLISHING
Lanham • New York • Boulder • Toronto • Plymouth, UK

To my great friend Jake Downey

Published by Taylor Trade Publishing
An imprint of The Rowman & Littlefield Publishing Group, Inc.
4501 Forbes Boulevard, Suite 200, Lanham, Maryland 20706
http://www.rlpgtrade.com

Estover Road, Plymouth PL6 7PY, United Kingdom

Distributed by National Book Network

British Library Cataloguing in Publication Information Available

Library of Congress Cataloging-in-Publication Data

Travers, Steven.
  Pigskin warriors : 140 years of college football's greatest traditions, games, and stars /
Steven Travers.
    p. cm.
  Includes index.
  ISBN 978-1-58979-333-0 (cloth : alk. paper) — ISBN 978-1-58979-458-0 (electronic)
  1. Football—United States—History. 2. Football—Social aspects—United States—History. I. Title.
  GV950.T72 2009
  796.332'63--dc22
  [B]
                                                                        2009015455

Printed in the United States of America

Contents

Part III: THE BEST OF THE BEST

College Football's All–Time Top 25 Traditions

1. Southern California Trojans
2. Notre Dame Fighting Irish
3. Alabama Crimson Tide
4. Oklahoma Sooners
5. Ohio State Buckeyes
6. Nebraska Cornhuskers
7. Miami Hurricanes
8. Texas Longhorns
9. Michigan Wolverines
10. Penn State Nittany Lions
11. Florida State Seminoles
12. Florida Gators
13. Louisiana State Tigers
14. Tennessee Volunteers
15. Auburn Tigers
16. Georgia Bulldogs
17. UCLA Bruins
18. Pittsburgh Panthers
19. Minnesota Golden Gophers
20. California Golden Bears
21. Army Black Knights
22. Washington Huskies
23. Michigan State Spartans
24. Stanford Indians/Cardinal
25. Georgia Tech Yellow Jackets

Others receiving "votes": Arizona State, Arkansas, Brigham Young, Clemson, Colorado, Illinois, Iowa, Maryland, Mississippi, Princeton, Syracuse, Texas A&M, Texas Christian, West Virginia, Wisconsin, Yale

The Quest

Recognition, Legitimacy, and Historical Revisionism

ON JANUARY 1, 2007, I was fulfilling family tradition.

My father, Donald E. Travers, used to sit in the sunshine of Pasadena, California, watching the Rose Bowl when I was little more than a gleam in his eye. When I started to come of age, he began to take me to the Rose Bowl. As a lifelong fan, student, and alum of the University of Southern California, I came to regard the Arroyo Seco as our "winter residence." Eventually, I began to take my daughter, Elizabeth, to Rose Bowl games. So, we were carrying on a family tradition on January 1, 2007, watching Southern California defeat Michigan. We are big on tradition.

Sitting a few rows in front of me was a man wearing a Michigan T-shirt. The back of his shirt read, "MICHIGAN: 11 NATIONAL CHAMPIONSHIPS." Hmm, eleven national titles, huh? Well, there was that co-national title they shared with Nebraska in 1997, the one that inspired the Bowl Championship Series and was supposed to end the awarding of *co* championships.

Okay, there was 1997. There was 1948. Then there was . . . there was . . . wait, there must be . . . more? Well, yes. There was 1918, 1923, and 1933. That was five. But where were the other six? Had they won six before World War I?

Then the public address announcer asked the mammoth throng to provide a "moment of silence" for recently deceased president Gerald Ford, "an All-American on Michigan's national championship teams of 1932–1933."

After that, I turned to the guy next to me, a USC man, and said, "Now that's funny. How could Michigan have been the national champion of 1932 if USC was the national champion of 1932?" He was not exactly a historian, but he had certainly seen enough Trojan propaganda to possess at least vague knowledge that in 1932 Southern Cal coach Howard "Head Man" Jones led the greatest of his Thundering Herd teams to an unbeaten, untied season, something like nine shutouts (eight, actually, and only thirteen points allowed all year; including a 35–0 Rose Bowl victory over Jock Sutherland's national powerhouse Pitt Panthers), and the *national championship of college football!*

Well, the truth is in 1932 there were more organizations awarding national championships than there were lobbyists in Washington, D.C. At least it seems that way. In almost any given year between 1920 and 1945, a host of polls, organizations, and computer systems ranging from the respected to the obscure were awarding "national champion-ships" to various college football teams. Any team that might be considered among the top five, or even the top ten, could find a friendly group proclaiming them the nation's best team of the year. It was like politics, baseline federal budgeting, debating, editorials. All you needed to do was spin the facts, the figures, the story; shroud it in a little mystery; hope the audience did not know all the details; and put forth the proposition that this university or that was "number one"!

In 2006 I wrote *The USC Trojans: College Football's All-Time Greatest Dynasty*. As the title suggests, this book carried the premise that Southern California was a champion for the ages above all other dynasties, East, West, North, or South. In the back of that book I list all the national championships won between 1869 and 2005. As I investigated a little further, I came to realize that I like so many others had been bamboozled by some of the illegitimate "national championship" claims of various programs over the years. As we approach the 140th anniversary of college football (1869–2009), I decided there needed to be a book unshrouding the mystery once and for all. Here you have a work that de-scribes every national champion, legit or not; peels away the façade of championship status from the undeserving (read: those unfortunate teams that lost their bowl games after being awarded premature national titles); and in the end allows you to decide.

This is not revisionist history. Every title is listed. There is no attempt to hide the past in the manner of Joseph Stalin murdering the census takers who described the failures of Communism. I have listed the Associated Press winners, the United Press In-ternational winners, the consensus champs, the cochamps, the winners of "other" polls, the teams that lost bowl games, the teams that did not play in bowl games, and even the "revised" winners who, if logic had ruled their respective days, would have been able to call themselves champions.

What is fascinating about college football is that it is one of the most popular forms of entertainment in American society, a true culture in and of itself. Despite the impor-tance we place on it, and the rabid yearly battles to determine who is "number one," a true way of deciding this very thing has never really been arrived at.

We have had systems, rankings, polls, computer analysis, multiple polling, and now the BCS (Bowl Championship Series). We have never had a true play-off, such as basket-ball's March Madness, the College World Series, or the NFL play-offs leading to a Super Bowl. Most of the time, people arrive at the conclusion that the team awarded the na-

Did You Know . . .

That Yale coach Walter Camp is considered the "father of college football"? He began the naming of yearly All-American teams in the nineteenth century, which led to the popularization of the game and the countrywide desire to determine the "best," whether players, teams, or eventually national champions. All-American teams are now named in every men's and women's college and high school sport, plus other athletic endeavors. Furthermore, the term All-American has come to connote a certain kind of wholesomeness, unique to this nation's character and indicative of our quest for excellence.

tional championship is indeed the best of the best. Some years, this is debated. In other years, gross injustice is done. Passions are inflamed. Anger is stirred.

The current system has its critics and its defenders. Many state that a play-off would award a hot team at the end of the season, which certainly has explained more than its share of upset winners in other sports. College football fans seem to place more value on nonconference games and early-season records than any other sports supporters do. The BCS undoubtedly keeps people interested and talking. It has arguably produced some great nonchampionship bowl games that some say would not have been so exciting had they been part of a play-off format (in particular the 2007 Boise State-Oklahoma Fiesta Bowl). Even its greatest "failure," the co-national championships won by USC and LSU in 2003, satisfied some who liked the fact the Trojans were able to win their title in the traditional manner of all previous USC titles—victory in the Rose Bowl over a Big 10 opponent—without denying the Tigers their deserving shot.

Over the years, determining the national champion has at times made the 2000 Florida presidential recount look uncomplicated. Anybody can award a title. Some guy with a computer and some letterhead can claim this authority. If the Touchdown Club of Columbus decides the Ohio State Buckeyes are that season's national champions, even if they got smoked in the Rose Bowl, then by golly who is to stop them? Some titles are seemingly awarded in a manner almost as secret as a Mossad assassination order. To publicize it at the time is to open the award to scorn and derision.

Then one day a few years or decades later a T-shirt is made, a media guide is published, a press release is produced, claiming this "national championship." The unsuspecting fan reads it and is duly impressed that this school or that school has won a slew of such things and therefore is worthy of great imprimatur as a grid tradition.

These championships go forth, like toothpaste squeezed out of the tube, synapses in the air, words in the wind, sticking like graffiti or hot dog wrappers against the wall. There are no asterisks, nobody attaching caveats to Alabama's claim that they were the "national champions of 1973," or Texas's proud assertion that 1970 was *their year*, despite the fact that in both of these cases the season ended in abject bowl defeat at the hands of the victorious Notre Dame Fighting Irish!

Until now!

Some claims are more outrageous than others. Ohio State's media guide carries a section on Buckeye "national champions." One of these is of the 1970 team, complete with a team photo and the assertion that in that year the team was named national champs by the National Football Foundation, or that the 1961 Bucks won the "football writer's" version. How misleading. Were these "titles" awarded in a dark room disclosed to nobody? The 1961 "football writer's" title, for instance, leaves the impression that they

Did You Know . . .

That due to 18 deaths and 159 serious injuries in 1905, President Theodore Roosevelt created rule changes, allowing for a "more open game," including the establishment of a neutral zone along the line of scrimmage and creation of the forward pass?

were the AP champs, a perfectly legitimate title, albeit one that came with a *co* attached to it if the UPI had not seen it that way.

But what the Ohio State guide fails to mention (oh, let's face it, they did not fail to mention it, they just plain do not want you to get the right idea) is that Alabama was the consensus 1961 champion, an unbeaten team that won their bowl game and captured the AP *and* UPI championships, while Ohio State was saddled by a tie while not even *playing* in a bowl. (Not only did they not play in a bowl, they *turned down* an invitation to the Rose Bowl, theoretically because if they played and lost they could not claim this "title.") So who are the "football writers"? Traditionally, the AP (consisting of the media as opposed to the UPI "coaches poll") make up the football writers, but not in this case. So who were they?

Well, apparently some football writers. They awarded something called the MacArthur Trophy, and in fairness it was a fairly prestigious honor, but one can take the term *football writers* and use it as broadly or as narrowly as you like. Ohio State is happy to take it, leading unsuspecting, unknowing members of the media and fandom into hearing it, repeating it in stories about their cherished history, to be further repeated and made into T-shirts, coffee mugs, hats. . . .

Not on my watch.

College football, we are told, was begun in 1869 by Rutgers University in New Jersey. Two teams, Princeton and Yale, quickly dominated it. Other schools played football. It became more and more popular. By the 1890s, most colleges fielded a team, but Princeton and Yale were almost without exception the best.

By the 1900s, the game had spread and was being played well throughout the country. However, it was a dangerous sport. The so-called "Yale wedge" and the "flying wedge" caused serious injuries, even deaths. President Theodore Roosevelt got involved, and legislation was passed to effectuate safety measures.

Over the next decade or so, the game was an irregular affair. Some schools took to playing rugby instead of real football. World War I reduced the number of students, players, and games. It is for these and other reasons that judging college football history must be done by separating the "modern" era, which begins after the soldiers came home from the Great War with the 1919 season, and the fifty years that came before that.

In the Roaring '20s, everything changed in America. Sports craze enveloped the country. Babe Ruth and the Yankees dominated baseball. Huge arenas were built, great throngs filling them up. Radio brought these events to coast-to-coast audiences. Football went pro, college fans thrilling to the exploits of Red Grange; to the Four Horsemen of Notre Dame; and to the first great rivalry.

Did You Know . . .

That the first major football stadium was Harvard's 42,000-seat stadium, built in 1903 on the shores of the Charles River in Boston?

When Notre Dame and Southern California began to play each other, in combination with the annual Rose Bowl in Pasadena, the sporting public looked at the landscape of college football and asked itself, "Who really is number one?" These two teams represented the gritty Midwest and the growing, sun-splashed golden West. Regional pride shadowed the assertions that "Eastern football" was or was not better than what was played in Dixie or out on the coast.

With this came the ranking systems, which in essence were mathematical formulas looking at a team's strength of schedule, the scores of its games, and other factors, in order to determine the national champion. The most respected of these was the Dickinson System, begun in 1926. This was the first and most widely reported, but it was followed up by the Houlgate System (1927), the Dunkel Index (1929), the Boand System (1930), the Williamson System (1932), the Poling System (1935), the DeVold System (1945), and others.

In the late 1920s, these systems began to assert that there were national champions of each season. They were irregular, sometimes arriving at more or less of a consensus (as in 1927, when Illinois was number one), other times not so clear-cut (as in 1930, when Notre Dame and Alabama "shared" the honor). In any given year, three or four schools might claim the title from *somebody*.

Notre Dame coach Knute Rockne thought the system created by Frank Dickinson, an economics professor at the University of Illinois, was the most accurate. Rockne knew that the term *national champion* carried great weight. He realized that the concept of tradition, or great past performance, worked in his team's favor. It helped recruiting, ticket sales, and the school's image.

Rockne asked Professor Dickinson to gather the data of past football seasons, arriving at a list of national champions. Of course, Rockne knew that his Irish would be awarded the lion's share of these championships, thus increasing his and his program's growing national prestige. While it may be easy to say that Rockne instituted this backdating process to assure a favorable outcome for Notre Dame, the truth is it was generally fair.

After Rockne's death following the 1930 season, the Dickinson System came to be known as the Dickinson/Rockne System. After the AP poll began in 1936, it was for about eight years the only system other than the AP that was considered valid and, therefore, worthy if it happened to produce a champion other than the poll, which did happen in 1939. Over time, as the other systems were instituted, history has accorded national championships going all the way back to that first season, 1869. Naturally, since college football supremacy generally rested on who won the Princeton-Yale game most of the years between then and 1900, the national champions were most often . . . Princeton or Yale.

Truth be told, these programs were competitive on a national basis into the 1930s. Harvard even won the 1919 national title and as recently as 1951 Princeton produced the Heisman Trophy winner, Dick Kazmaier. If an alien were to come to this country (think Spock from *Star Trek*) and be asked to determine the "greatest of all college football traditions," a look at the raw numbers may well determine that in this person's logical mind

Princeton, winner of twenty national champions, or Yale (with twelve) is the answer to this question.

Logic and historical perspective, however, tell us that neither of these teams has maintained in the modern era the remotest amount of success, in comparison to the great programs that have withstood the test of time since the boys came home from World War I. Only baseball allows the historian to go back before the war—which lasted from 1914 to 1918, reshaped Europe, and transformed America from a modern power into a superpower—and make legitimate comparisons with today's teams and superstars. Baseball's nature, rules, dimensions, and schedule permit some commonality of comparison. Despite the obvious differences between Barry Bonds's seventy-three home runs in 2001 and Frank "Home Run" Baker's twelve in 1913, between George Brett's .390 in 1980 and Ty Cobb's .420 in 1911, and between Roger Clemens's 24–4 of 1986 versus Walter Johnson's 36–7 of 1913, mentioning Christy Mathewson in the same breath with Greg Maddux, or Honus Wagner alongside Cal Ripken, is a fairly easy concept. With the possible lone exception of the legendary Jim Thorpe, football players of the early century are regarded as an entirely different breed, almost a separate species from the Lawrence Taylors and Joe Montanas of recent memory.

Before 1920 there was no NFL, no NBA, and for that matter no NCAA. College football had evolved from a club sport of sorts into an Ivy League preoccupation for the "bowler hat and raccoon coat" crowd, but it was not until the 1920s that it caught on as an American craze. California became the first team to really recruit football players. Coach Andy Smith established a pipeline through his assistant, Nibs Price, a former San Diego high school coach with strong Southland connections. He picked off top players who otherwise might have gone to Southern California and even "stole" some of the Trojans, who transferred to Berkeley and helped the Wonder Teams become the first dynasty of the modern era.

The names became established in the national mind: the Irish, the Trojans, the Fighting Illini, the Wolverines . . . and the alumni, the public imagination, wrapped itself around these new heroes. Today the exploits of their predecessors still resonate when trying to understand the tradition of college football on dozens of campuses, where the school never relocates and the players are not lost to free agency, by the way. Even a school like the University of California, which deemphasized football in the 1960s when Berkeley allowed itself to become the de facto staging grounds of American Communism, still clings to the ancient glories of Brick Muller and Pappy Waldorf in hopes that whatever magic there was, there might still be enough stardust by the bay to bring back one more national title.

In the 1920s and 1930s, in particular, the varying systems—Dickinson, Houlgate, the National Football Research organization, the Helms Athletic Foundation, and others—awarded enough titles to go around. In 1936, the Associated Press began to conduct their poll, but they made the grave error of awarding the regular season winner championships before the bowl games were played. The UPI came into being in 1950. Instead of learning from the AP's mistake, they also awarded their winner before the bowl games. This caused immediate embarrassment when in 1950 Oklahoma was awarded a "consensus" title before losing to Kentucky in the Sugar Bowl; in 1951 Tennessee screwed it up for everybody by getting waxed by Maryland in the Sugar Bowl; and in 1953 Maryland lost to the Sooners in the Orange Bowl.

In the first eleven years of the AP and UPI polls, there were only four truly "legitimate" champions. Michigan State won both polls in 1952, but they did not play in the Rose Bowl. In 1954, the Pacific Coast Conference's no-repeat rule either saved the day or ruined it. The AP already decided Ohio State was number one. The UPI said it was UCLA. But the Bruins never made the half-hour drive to Pasadena, where the Buckeyes pasted USC instead while settling for a "tie" with UCLA.

Oklahoma left no doubt, going unbeaten with a bowl win (1955), then going unbeaten again in 1956 (without a bowl due to their conference's no-repeat rule). In 1957 Ohio State and Auburn split the polls. The fact that they were awarded prior to the bowls too often destroyed the credibility of the two polls and the teams that wore their championships. In 1958 and 1959, Louisiana State and Syracuse were legitimate national champions, but in 1960 Minnesota won both polls only to lose to Washington in the Rose Bowl.

Alabama would like everybody to believe that they are the national champions of 1964, and of course if the Associated Press and United Press International are to be believed and respected, they are. Tell that to their quarterback, Joe Willie Namath, who to this day states that his most disappointing moment in sports was January 1, 1965, when he left the Orange Bowl field on the losing end of a 21–17 heartbreaker with Texas. Pictures of his long, tear-stained face *are not* pictures of that year's national champion, regardless of what any plaque, list, or proclamation might state.

The AP seemed to come to their senses in time to award Alabama the 1965 title *after* beating Nebraska in the Orange Bowl. The UPI looked stupid when Michigan State's upset at the hands of UCLA illegitimatized their "title." The question is asked, *What were they thinking?* in reference to the AP's inexplicable decision to revert *back* to the prebowl award between 1966 and 1967 (finally awarding the national championship once and for all *after* Ohio State beat USC in the 1969 Rose Bowl, continuing the practice henceforth). The UPI stuck to its dumbbellionite practice right through the 1973 season, by which point two of the all-time bad polling blunders ever perpetrated had happened. On January 1, 1971, UPI "champion" Texas lost to Notre Dame in the Cotton Bowl, and on December 31, 1973, Alabama lost a true national championship battle with unbeaten, untied Notre Dame in the Sugar Bowl. *Again,* the Crimson Tide walked off the field in abject New Year's (Eve) defeat, their UPI title clinging to their necks in infamous mockery (none of which stops them from promoting 1973 as one of 'Bama's "twelve national championships"; they have nine legit championships at best). This is done in the hope that lack of knowledge will attach greater prestige to their program. In the meantime, while Notre Dame of course was the AP winner in '73, they are not allowed to call themselves a consensus champ, as if beating Bear Bryant's squad in a contest that was closer to war than football was some kind of exhibition game.

The fact that "anybody" can award a title did not end with the UPI poll. Historians recognized several years in between 1936 and the end of World War II in which a team other than the AP champion was at least worthy of legitimate co-national championship status. The systems usually tended to award a national championship after bowl games, which made sense. Notre Dame and Michigan dominated the years between the war and the UPI, although the difference between them was at times so razor thin that controversy continued to reign.

Since Maryland's loss in the 1954 Orange Bowl, at least the two polls produced one legitimate winner with the exception of 1960 and 1964. While the two services awarded bogus titles to Minnesota and 'Bama, there were still in existence rating systems left over from the pre-AP era that were broken out of mothballs. This allowed the true 1960 and 1964 champions—Mississippi and unbeaten, untied Cotton Bowl winner Arkansas, respectively—to be given the title and the historically "revised" championship of that season.

At least in 1965, 1970, and 1973, enough changes had been made to award one legitimate titleholder in each of those years (Alabama '65, Nebraska '70, Notre Dame '73). The UPI finally came to their senses, and in all the years since, they and their successors (*USA Today*/ESPN, the BCS, and others) have named their champions when the bowl dust cleared. There continue to be disputes and co-national champions, but no illegitimate ones.

The continued existence and creation of ranking systems other than the human polls have continued, with the Sagarin System being the most well known, but these computers have in the BCS era (1998–present) demonstrated a shocking lack of common sense. They have rated one-loss teams ranked seventh or eighth ahead of unbeaten juggernauts. The fact that anybody can award a title has allowed some schools to pad their statistics.

Most egregious examples include the aforementioned Ohio State claim to the 1961 and even 1970 championships (the latter most laughable in light of the Buckeyes' 27–17 loss to Stanford in the Rose Bowl). The Big 10, once the premiere football conference, lost year after year after year to Pacific-8 and Pacific-10 Rose Bowl opponents. Michigan, like Ohio State, tried to hide all their Pasadena misery, using their conference titles, their great pipeline to the pros, and their all-time victory mark (much of it achieved while other schools were still playing rugby, were small time, or were not even in existence yet) to spin their history in a desperate attempt to hold themselves up as a tradition on par

Best College Football Movies	Other Football-Themed Movies
Knute Rockne: All-American (1940)	*All the Right Moves* (1982)
Something for Joey (1977)	*Varsity Blues* (1997)
Everybody's All-American (1988)	*Friday Night Lights* (2004)
Triumph of the Heart: The Ricky Bell Story (1991)	
Necessary Roughness (1991)	
Rudy (1993)	
The Program (1993)	
The Waterboy (1998)	
The Junction Boys (2002)	

with the USCs, the Notre Dames, the Alabamas—to no avail. Their media guide states that they have won eleven national titles. They have won seven (1901, 1902, 1918, 1923, 1933, 1947, and 1997). A fair historical analysis concludes that their claims to the 1903 (Princeton), 1904 (Minnesota), 1932 (Southern Cal), and 1947 (Notre Dame) national championships are just words on paper. Fairness is not always part of the equation; their 1947 team was unbeaten with a 49–0 pasting of USC in the Rose Bowl, but that year's Notre Dame team is viewed as one of the five best teams ever assembled. Even without playing a bowl game, they were the legit consensus national champions of 1947.

The fairness angle works for and against most everybody. Notre Dame may well have been the AP's only "three-peat" champion in 1948, but the voters this time went for Michigan, even though they played no bowl game due to the no-repeat rule. The 1966 Alabama Crimson Tide was unbeaten, untied, and a Sugar Bowl winner over Nebraska but denied the national title that was so ridiculously awarded them two years earlier. It is believed to this day that disgust not only over that 1964 ranking but their segregationist status in 1966 cost them against Notre Dame's "Catholic vote."

The argument that social pathos dominated voting motivations, however, does not hold up, particularly in light of the fact that Texas, the last all-white national champions, was awarded the 1969 championship ahead of an unbeaten, untied, integrated Penn State team that had neither lost nor tied a game in two years. No less an authority than President Richard Nixon declared Darrell Royal's Longhorns to be number one. Everybody was happy to honor another segregated Texas team in 1970, at least until Notre Dame beat them in the Cotton Bowl.

As for Alabama, things turned around on their behalf twelve years after the 1966 "Catholic vote." In 1978, Alabama was once beaten with a Sugar Bowl win over number one Penn State. USC was once beaten with another in a seemingly endless list of Rose Bowl triumphs over Michigan. The split decision of the AP (Alabama) and UPI (USC) seemed logical, except in consideration of the fact that in September of that very season the Trojans had traveled to Legion Field in Birmingham, pasting the Tide 24–14. The rare opportunity of the voters to decide between two close contenders in favor of the team that beat the other in an actual head-to-head matchup on the other team's field did not result in the correct vote. The AP (writers) now saw Bear Bryant as a sympathetic legend, in part for finally integrating his team, which now looked like everybody else but played better. Their vote reflected this.

The Alabama media guide informs the readers that their beloved Tide has won twelve national championships. At least one 'Bama website lists thirteen. In the section detailing their national champions, no mention of the January 1, 1965, Orange Bowl or December 31, 1973, Sugar Bowl losses are made to provide the right idea. Minnesota, unbeaten with Heisman winner Bruce Smith, was the consensus 1941 (AP) champ. This does not stop 'Bama from calling the 9–2 Tide (who did not even win the Southeastern Conference championship captured by Mississippi State) the 1941 winners.

They do list the fact that Michigan, Ohio State, and Oklahoma were the "other" 1973 national champions according to sources that never even made the newspaper (National Championship Foundation, Poling, FACT, Billingsley, DeVold, Dunkel, Sagarin). The only reason for doing this would seem to be to dilute the impact of Notre Dame's legitimate title, coming on the strength of victory over the Tide. It is as if by opening a "can of worms" in the form of different champions it makes their bogus UPI award look . . . legit.

In truth, Alabama has won nine deserving national championships (1925, 1926, 1930, 1934, 1961, 1965, 1978, 1979, 1992). What goes around comes around. The two il-legitimates (1964, 1973) are matched by unbeaten seasons (1945 and 1966) in which the Tide was denied titles that they well could have deserved but did not win. So it goes.

Oklahoma may be the most irresponsible. Their media guide lists no less than *sixteen national championships!* Somebody needs to tell the 1949 Notre Dame Fighting Irish, the 1957 Ohio State Buckeyes and Auburn Tigers, the 1967 USC Trojans, the 1973 Irish, the 1978 Trojans and Alabama Crimson Tide, the 1980 Georgia Bulldogs, the 1986 Penn State Nittany Lions, the 2003 Trojans, and even the LSU Tigers (who beat OU in the '03 BCS title game) that, like a politician who is losing a campaign but manipulates the polls to create the appearance of winning, the Sooners were number, uh, well . . . one?

Oh, and get this. In any given year from 1950 to 1995, in which there existed both the AP and the UPI polls, and in which OU won both polls, they count that (when they think they can get away with it) as *two national championships.* As in 1975, for instance, when they were a legitimate consensus winner of both polls, but they would have you read it as two titles in a single year. Slick work. The way they do it is to create columns. Column A contains AP titles. Column B contains UPI titles. Throw in a little deception, and then they list "TOTALS." This is especially rich considering the 1950 season, the first year of the UPI in which the Sooners won both prebowl polls only to lose their bowl game. The Sooners' legitimate national championships? 1954, 1955, 1956, 1974, 1975, 1985, and 2000. They also can make a solid claim on the 1915 title, but Washington State's Rose Bowl win over Brown gives the unbeaten Cougars claim to that season's actual national championship.

Oklahoma's incredible series of streaks, which mark the Bud Wilkinson 1950s, the Barry Switzer 1970s and 1980s, and later the Bob Stoops 2000s, combined with a long list of Heisman, Outland, Lombardi, and other award winners, tells the story of excel-lence personified, but this excellence is also pockmarked by NCAA probation.

Various schools promote their legacy as "eight-time Associated Press national champions," or some such variation on the theme, but most avoid real scrutiny of their national titles, because to do so leaves the diligent researcher with knowledge that the number of titles claimed is greater than the number of titles really earned. The AP is a fine organization. The great majority of championships under their banner are legitimate and worthy. But there are enough exceptions to lump AP championship status with the Nobel Peace Prize or the Academy Awards. If terrorists can win the Nobel, if clowns can claim Oscars, if tyrants can be named *Time*'s "Man of the Year," then the AP can list their share of mistaken "winners," too.

A close reading of the top college football schools demonstrates that the two programs that in the end stand out above the rest—ancient rivals Southern California and Notre Dame—are the most honest in their respective assessment of themselves. I mentioned the forthrightness of Notre Dame's description of its rich history to a close Catholic friend of mine.

"That's because they're Catholic," he stated, and he was not kidding. Belief in God does indeed keep one honest. Perhaps because USC was once considered a Methodist school before becoming a private, nondenominational institution, their history is not filled with falsehoods, misinformation, and outright lies. The fact of the matter is that *some* system named the Trojans national champions of 1929, 1933, 1976, 1979, and 2002, but instead of counting these and calling themselves the "sixteen-time national champion Men of Troy," USC like Notre Dame dutifully states that these are not recognized titles, that *they* do not recognize them, and so they do not count.

Notre Dame provides a very helpful historical analysis of all the years in which they won national championships or came close. History considers them consensus champions in 1924 and 1929 and cochampion with Alabama in 1930, and of course they have eight AP titles (1943, 1946, 1947, 1949, 1966, 1973, 1977, 1988). Their media guide carefully lists "other" national champions in the years in which the Irish won (Penn in 1924; Pitt and USC in 1929; a tie with 'Bama in the 1930 Parker H. Davis Ratings). However, Notre Dame notes that in 1919, 1920, 1927, and 1938 (and later years after the AP), while they "won" titles according to the Davis, the National Championship Foundation, and other systems, these are not "qualified" title teams. In 1919 and 1920, Notre Dame dutifully does not claim titles that, upon historical retrospect, they could claim. They were unbeaten both seasons, but in 1919 Harvard's win in the Rose Bowl made them a consensus winner. In 1920, the first of Cal's Wonder Teams was unbeaten, won the Rose Bowl, was into a 50-game unbeaten skein, and in fact is considered a three-time champion (1920–22). Notre Dame might have tried to sneak the 1926 Irish in as a national champion on the strength of their 9–1 record, their 13–12 win at USC, and the subsequent tie between unbeatens Alabama and Stanford in the Rose Bowl, but they do not. The eleven titles they claim are the real deal.

USC also has eleven actual national championships. They are tied with Notre Dame but have some strong arguments in their favor. For one, nine of their championships came in years in which they won in the Rose Bowl, either against a sterling Big 10 foe or a great Eastern or Southern team prior to the conference arrangement. One came in the BCS Orange Bowl against Oklahoma (2004 season). None are marred by defeat. While Notre Dame never slipped in the "back door" with a bowl loss, seven of their eleven titles came in years in which school policy prevented them from playing in a bowl game. USC was their last game almost every year until the South Bend contest was switched to October in 1961. The "Trojan wars" were thought of as their "bowl game." Logic stands to reason that had they played in bowl games, in at least one or two of those seven years some opponent would have beaten them. That said, they earned two national championships (1973, 1977) when they beat the prior number one team in a bowl game.

USC also has the modern edge. Seven of their eleven championships come from 1962 on—all within the period that is considered modern, integrated, an era of national TV, scholarships, refined recruiting, training, and equipment. All seven of their Heisman Trophies are from this era. Seven of Notre Dame's national championships and five of their seven Heisman winners are products of the "leather helmet" or "no face mask era" that, in retrospect, is just that: retro.

The reason some schools fudge their facts a little bit in order to create the illusion of more national championships than they deserve may very well come down to how very difficult it is to win the darn things. It could be easy to say that Notre Dame has an advantage because they are a "national school," benefiting from the "Catholic vote," or that USC has the edge because they are in the media capital of the world.

The truth is, the national championship of college football is an elusive goal. There is probably nothing harder to win, at least among sports that are played every year. Obviously, an Olympic gold medal or a soccer World Cup is up for grabs only every four years. But in college football *every single game* is for the national title. A nonconference loss in September has the immediate effect of possibly knocking a team out of the hunt. Certainly they are no longer in control of their own destiny. If the teams ahead of them stay unbeaten until the end, forget about it.

The BCS has created a scramble for number one like never before. Under unusual circumstances, a team might be able to grab the AP co-national championship, but it is not likely. The necessities of going unbeaten with a bowl win, which has been the requirement in seven of nine BCS seasons between 1998 and 2005, creates an atmosphere of pressure and alumni expectations that is greater even than professional sports, with very few if any exceptions. It has come to the point where the expectations at a Miami, an Oklahoma, a Notre Dame, a USC are as great as those placed upon Yankee managers by George Steinbrenner.

Compare and contrast the Yankees with Notre Dame and USC. The Yankees won their first World Series in 1923, the year that Yankee Stadium was built and the Trojans moved into the L.A. Memorial Coliseum. It was a demarcation point in American sports. In the state of California, Stanford Stadium, Memorial Stadium in Berkeley, and the

Rose Bowl in Pasadena were all built within a few years of the Coliseum's erection (which drew the 1932 Olympics nine years later).

Yale's 64,000-seat Yale Bowl, built in 1914, had once been the largest of all football arenas, but after World War I huge stadiums went up throughout the country, leading to the Orange, Sugar, and Cotton Bowls. Football became spectacle, America the new Rome, these grid warriors the new gladiators of the twentieth century. In 1924, the Irish legend was made when they defeated Army at the sold-out Polo Grounds, prompting New York sports columnist Grantland Rice to dub their backfield the Four Horsemen of Notre Dame.

In 1927, 120,000 fans crowded Soldier Field in Chicago to watch Notre Dame beat Southern California. Two years later another 112,000 came to see the same two teams in the same stadium. Crowds of close to 80,000 watched the Irish and Trojans play in Los Angeles. Between 1924 and 1931, "the Big House" was built in Ann Arbor, Michigan; "the Horse Shoe" in Columbus, Ohio; "the Swamp" in Gainesville, Florida; "Death Valley" in Baton Rouge, Louisiana; and finally Notre Dame Stadium in South Bend, Indiana. After years forced to play many games as a "barnstorming team" on the road, the Irish finally met the attendance needs of their adoring public with a home field.

While Babe Ruth's New York Yankees won the 1923 World Series, and Knute Rockne's Irish captured their first national title in 1924, the respective feats apparently were much easier accomplished by the pinstripers. They won world championships in 1927, 1928, 1932, 1936, 1937, 1938, 1939, 1941, 1943, 1947, 1949, 1950, 1951, 1952, 1953, 1956, 1958, 1961, 1962, 1977, 1978, 1996, 1998, 1999, and 2000. They have twenty-six overall world championships and have come very close on numerous other occasions, compared to eleven for Notre Dame and USC apiece.

The Boston Celtics sport seventeen NBA crowns. Between 1972 and 2002, the Lakers won almost as many titles (nine) as USC football has won since 1888. In the first six years the Dodgers played in Los Angeles, they won three World Series to quickly close the gap with USC, who by 1965 had won only five national championships. To this day, true Los Angeles sports loyalty is reserved not for the Lakers, Clippers, Angels, Bruins, Kings, Ducks, or the since-displaced Rams and Raiders, but for the Dodgers and Trojans.

At the collegiate level, other sports appear much easier to win. A hot team can get on a streak and not be stopped. USC's track team was once so dominant it appeared there were rules for them, then rules for everybody else (twenty-six national championships). The U.S. Olympic teams of the 1920s, '30s, '40s, and '50s looked like the Trojans in red, white, and blue uniforms. The Trojans captured seventeen NCAA tennis championships, but whether they or Stanford is the most dominant historical program is not as clear cut. Rod Dedeaux's USC baseball team made it look easy, winning every College World Series between 1970 and 1974.

Over in Westwood, John Wooden's Bruin basketball team won seven straight and ten of twelve NCAA titles between 1964 and 1975, although historically it would appear that going all the way is as tough on the hardwood as it is on the gridiron. The Trojans and Irish have equaled UCLA's eleven overall championships, but of course the NCAA Tournament only goes back to 1939. The UCLA volleyball team has been even more dominant than Bruins hoops, with nineteen NCAA banners through 2006. California's De La Salle High School once won 151 consecutive football games in what may be the most impressive streak in sports history.

Texas is a sport where football is king, but while the Longhorns parse out rare titles (three in forty-three years), their baseball team is more regular about it: 1949, 1950, 1975, 1983, 2002, and 2005. LSU similarly worships the god of football, but the Eisenhower, Kennedy, Johnson, Nixon, Ford, Carter, Reagan, Bush, Clinton, and Bush administrations separate their first two titles, the second a shared championship (plus a highly questionable two-loss championship in 2007). In the meantime, Tiger baseball coach Skip Bertman took his team to the promised land four times in the 1990s. Multiple and repeat champions in other sports have been relatively frequent, but until USC fell nineteen seconds shy of a third straight crown in 2005, it was treated like the quest for the Holy Grail. Not only had it never been done in the AP era, but none had come quite as close at season's end. Only California (1920–1922) and Minnesota (1934–1936) had done it since World War I.

Because winning the national championship is so difficult in college football, when it actually comes around, it is bigger than most. Reverence for past championship seasons reaches religious fervor. College kids playing for scholarship money, legends of the green plains, purists who, in the imagination at least, are in it out of love of the game, not padding their stats in a free-agent year.

*   *   *

One might say, who really cares? Does it truly matter if a few college football programs fudge the numbers a little bit to make themselves look better? Probably not. Nobody is really getting hurt by it. This is all ancient history anyway, right? As a Christian, I am compelled to address my own part in this research and attention to college football history. In a world in which so many problems exist, am I really serving humanity by spending all this time and energy just trying to determine who college football's all-time top 25 traditions really are? Who is *number one*? Why one team is in the top ten and another is not?

Well, I do know this. Man does not live by bread alone. We love our sports. Furthermore, sport is more than just fun 'n' games. Athletics have been a vehicle for great social change. Great black athletes toiling at Columbia and other Northern schools in the early part of the twentieth century helped to set an example. The sight of integrated USC and UCLA teams (with the great Jackie Robinson and Kenny Washington) toiling before crowds of close to 100,000 in the L.A. Coliseum of the 1930s was a visual statement about what this country could be. Integrated Southern California, Penn State, Navy, and Pittsburgh teams playing in the South of the 1950s helped forge progress. When the Trojans brought Sam "Bam" Cunningham into Alabama in 1970, it proved to be the final nail in the coffin of segregation.

Steven R. Travers
USCSTEVE1@aol.com
(415) 455-5971

PART I

The Elite Ten

Chapter 1

Southern California Trojans

U SC HAS BEEN CREDITED with sixteen national championships in its history. Unlike most other programs, they do not count all of them; they only count the legitimate eleven that they have earned. They do not try to say that the 1929, 1933, 1976, 1979, or 2002 Trojans were that year's best, even though some organization or service did see fit to declare them just that. They do not use the perverse logic that a "national championship" can be awarded prior to a bowl loss, which if they did would theoretically let them print T-shirts proclaiming that in 1968 or 2005, for instance, well by gum the Trojans were "national champs." Their eleven national titles tie them with Notre Dame, who also do not claim some of the national titles they could because they are not, as is the case with USC's extra five, historically recognized as legitimate.

University of Southern California
Los Angeles, California
Founded: 1880
Enrollment: 16,500
Colors: Cardinal and gold
Nickname: Trojans
Stadium: Los Angeles Memorial Coliseum (opened: 1923; capacity: 92,000)
All-time record (1888–2008): 766-303-54
All-time bowl record: 31–16 (through 2009 bowls)
National championships: 1928, 1931, 1932, 1939, 1962, 1967, 1972, 1974, 1978, 2003, 2004
Pacific Coast-AAWU-Pacific-8/10 Conference championships: 38 (through 2008)
Heisman Trophies: Mike Garrett (1965), O. J. Simpson (1968), Charles White (1979), Marcus Allen (1981), Carson Palmer (2002), Matt Leinart (2004), Reggie Bush (2005)
Outland Trophies: Ron Yary (1967)
Consensus All-Americans: 84 (through 2008)

First-round NFL draftees: 74 (through 2009)

Website: www.usctrojans.com

Notable alumni: First man on the moon, Neil Armstrong; astronaut Wally Schirra; Academy Award-winning actor John "Duke" Wayne; actors Robert Stack, Ward Bond, Marlo Thomas, Henry Winkler, John Ritter, Ally Sheedy, John Berardino, Tom Selleck, Forrest Whittaker, and Will Ferrell; *Star Wars* director George Lucas; Academy Award-winning directors Ron Howard, Robert Zemeckis, and Steven Spielberg; directors John Singleton and Paul Mazursky; producers Kerry McCluggage, David L. Wolper, and Barney Rosenzweig; *Dirty Harry* screenwriter John Milius; Academy Award-winning composer John Williams; *The OC* creator Josh Schwartz; theatre producer Darren Lee Cole; author Steven Travers; Secretary of State Warren Christopher; California Attorney General Dan Lungren; California Assembly Speaker Jesse Unruh; Securities and Exchange Commission Chairman Christopher Cox; U.S. Congressman Dana Rohrabacher; California Supreme Court Justice Malcolm Lucas; Los Angeles police chief Daryl Gates; Watergate figures Donald Segretti and H. R. Haldeman; White House aide Dwight Chapin; First Lady Patricia Nixon; U.S. Senator John McCain's wife, Cynthia McCain; General Norman Schwarzkopf; syndicated columnist Art Buchwald; sports columnist Mal Florence; public relations executive Carl Terzian; political consultant Joseph Cerrell; architect Frank Gehry; Public Storage founder Wayne Hughes; Coca-Cola/North America president Terry Marks; Flour Corporation founder Robert Flour; Dart Corporation president Justin Dart; Los Angeles Lakers' owner Dr. Jerry Buss; opera star Marilyn Horne; singer Macy Gray; musicians Herb Alpert and Lionel Hampton; secret service agent Bill Bordley; newscasters Sam Donaldson and Kathleen Sullivan; Christian minister John Werhas; sports announcer Petros Papadakis; restaurateur John Papadakis; attorney Robert Kardashian; Hall of Fame baseball player Tom Seaver; baseball players Bill Lee, Dave Kingman, Fred Lynn, Mark McGwire, Randy Johnson, Bret Barberie, Jim Barr, Barry Zito, Don Buford, Steve Busby, Rich Dauer, Dave Engle, Seth Etherton, Ron Fairly, Randy Flores, Eric Munson, Dave Hostetler, Tom House, Geoff Jenkins, Jacque Jones, Steve Kemp, Marcel Lachemann, Ray Lamb, Jason Lane, Bob Lillis, Pete Redfern, Tom Satriano, Bob Skube, Roy Smalley, Brent Strom, Gary Sutherland, Tim Tolman, Dave Van Gorder, Bret Boone, Aaron Boone, Jeff Cirillo, Morgan Ensberg, and Mark Prior; USC baseball coach Rod Dedeaux; baseball general manager Pat Gillick; baseball manager Rene Lachemann; Hall of Fame basketball player Bill Sharman; Hall of Fame basketball coach Alex Hannum; basketball players Paul Westphal, John Block, Mack Calvin, Sam Clancy, Bill Hewitt, Bo Kimble, Hank Gathers, John Lambert, Dennis Layton, Harold Miner, Robert Pack, Cliff Robinson, Brian Scalabrine, and Gus Williams; basketball coach Tex Winter; Olympians Charlie Paddock, Mel Patton, Frank Wykoff, Johnny Weissmuller, Parry O'Brien, Bob Seagren, John Naber, Cheryl Miller, Pam McGee, Cynthia Cooper, Dan Jorgensen, Mike O'Brien, Lenny Krayzelburg, Steve Timmons, Lisa Leslie, Bruce Furniss, Lennox Miller, Don Quarrie, Randy Williams, Fred Kelly, Sammy Lee, and Angela Williams; tennis players Stan Smith, Luke Jensen, Murphy Jensen, Rick Leach, and Dennis Ralston; golfer Craig Stadler; sports agents Lon Rosen, Mike Trope, and Ed Hookstratten; Hollywood agents Lloyd Robinson and Adam Novak; USC film school professor Andrew Casper; real estate executives Ed Roski, Jeffrey Cole, and James Connor; reinsurance executive Peter Cooper; financial adviser Len Gabrielson

Other programs count "national championships" from every Podunk "service" imaginable. They count those won when bowls were lost after the polls were closed; those won when they were on probation, and—perhaps the most rich of all—a consensus Associated Press and United Press International national title in a single season as *two titles*! Check the media guides and see for yourself.

None of USC's titles were won in years in which they failed to win a bowl game. Each bowl victory was a major confrontation with a powerhouse from the Big 10, or in the early days with a powerhouse from the East or the South—always the very best that America had to offer. The challenge was met each time. In the years when bowl defeat against a worthy foe came the Trojans' way, national championship glory did not. There is one exception to the Rose Bowl gauntlet; the 2005 55–24 BCS Orange Bowl victory over Oklahoma, which, by the way, was referred to by longtime college football observer Lee Corso as "the greatest game I ever saw any team play."

If there is a single piece of evidence that nudges Southern California over Notre Dame for ultimate historical supremacy, it is the fact that their national championships came with the price tag of bowl victory while seven of the Irish titles did not. From 1925 to 1968, Notre Dame were the champions of 1929, 1930, 1943, 1946, 1947, 1949, and 1966. Their "bowl game" was always against USC. USC, champions in 1928, 1931, 1932, 1939, 1962, 1967, 1972, 1974, 2003, and 2004, always had to beat not just Notre Dame in Los Angeles and South Bend but UCLA, too. No bowl defeats mar their national title record.

The second factor favoring Southern California is the commonsensical notion that greater credence be placed on modern events as opposed to "ancient history." There is no question that Notre Dame is the *Rock* that college football is built on, but much of that foundation is the sturdy rivalry with the Trojans that, along with the Rose Bowl, nationalized the game.

USC has the edge in that they were a power in the early years after World War I (the best record in the nation, 1920s; three national titles, 1930s); a steady power in the 1940s and 1950s; the greatest dynasty ever in the 1960s and 1970s; usually a top twenty-five, bowl-bound team in the 1980s and 1990s; and now the champions of the twenty-first century (2000s). They are not a nineteenth-century Ivy League relic, nor do they build their record on the backs of championships won in the rugby era (1900s, 1910s). They earned four national championships to Notre Dame's three prior to World War II. In the decade in which Knute Rockne reigned supreme, it was the Trojans who actually had a better record than the Irish.

Notre Dame won four in a decade (1940s) dominated by war, leather helmets, no facemasks, and almost no blacks. The great demarcation point of college football

National Champions—Legitimate and Historically Revised

1. Southern California (7 Heismans)   11 legitimate
   1928, 1931, 1932, 1939, 1962, 1967, 1972, 1974, 1978, 2003, 2004
2. Notre Dame (7 Heismans)   11 legitimate
   1924, 1929, 1930, 1943, 1946, 1947, 1949, 1966, 1973, 1977, 1988
3. Alabama   9 legitimate
   1925, 1926, 1930, 1934, 1961, 1965, 1978, 1979, 1992
4. Oklahoma (5 Heismans)   6 legitimate
   1955, 1956, 1974, 1975, 1985, 2000
5. Ohio State (7 Heismans)   5 legitimate
   1942, 1954, 1957, 1968, 2002
6. Nebraska (3 Heismans)   5 legitimate
   1970, 1971, 1994, 1995, 1997
7. Miami (2 Heismans)   5 legitimate
   1983, 1987, 1989, 1991, 2001
8. Minnesota (1 Heisman)   5 legitimate
   1934, 1935, 1936, 1940, 1941
9. Michigan (3 Heismans)   4 legitimate
   1923, 1933, 1948, 1997
10. California   4 legitimate
    1920, 1921, 1922, 1937
11. Florida (3 Heismans)   3 legitimate
    1996, 2006, 2008
11. Texas (2 Heismans)   3 legitimate
    1963, 1969, 2005
11. Louisiana State (1 Heisman)   3 legitimate
    1958, 2003, 2007
12. Army (3 Heismans)   2 legitimate
    1944, 1945
13. Florida State (2 Heismans)   2 legitimate
    1993, 1999
15. Penn State (1 Heisman)   2 legitimate
    1982, 1986
15. Pittsburgh (1 Heisman)   2 legitimate
    1937, 1976
15. Stanford (1 Heisman)   2 legitimate
    1926, 1940
20. Georgia (2 Heismans)   1 legitimate
    1980

20. Auburn (2 Heismans)		1 legitimate
1957		
22. Brigham Young (1 Heisman)		1 legitimate
1984		
22. Syracuse (1 Heisman)		1 legitimate
1959		
22. UCLA (1 Heisman)		1 legitimate
1954		
22. Texas A&M (1 Heisman)		1 legitimate
1939		
22. Texas Christian (1 Heisman)		1 legitimate
1938		
22. Princeton (1 Heisman)		1 legitimate
1919		
22. Colorado (1 Heisman)		1 legitimate
1990		
22. Harvard		1 legitimate
1919		
29. Tennessee		1 legitimate
1998		
30. Michigan State		1 legitimate
1952		
30. Clemson		1 legitimate
1981		
30. Illinois		1 legitimate
1927		
30. Washington		1 legitimate
1991		
30. Georgia Tech		1 legitimate
1990		
35. Maryland		1 illegitimate
1953		
36. Arkansas		1 revised
1964		

divides itself in 1960, which aside from being a nice round number separates the old days from the modern era. When John McKay took over at Southern California that year, the Trojans were still stuck on four national championships to Notre Dame's seven. The Irish boasted five Heisman Trophy winners to USC's grand total of zero. Somehow, Princeton's Dick Kazmaier was deemed a more worthy recipient of the 1951 Heisman than USC's Frank Gifford. In 1956, Notre Dame's Paul Hornung won it when USC's "Jaguar Jon" Arnett was forced to sit out half the season because of NCAA penalties.

National Champions—Chronological Order, 1919–2008 (Modern Era)

1919   Harvard 9–0

Beat Oregon, 7–6/Rose Bowl; unanimous

> *Other: *Notre Dame (Davis: tie, NCF: tie), *Illinois 6–1 (Davis: tie, FR: tie, Boand),*
> **Texas A&M 10–0 (NCF: tie)*

1920   California

Beat Ohio State, 28–0/Rose Bowl; Helms, FR, Houlgate, NCF

> *Other: *Notre Dame 9–0 (Davis: tie), *Princeton 6–0–1 (Davis: tie, Boand: tie), *Harvard 8–0–1 (Boand: tie)*

1921   California 9–0–1

Tied Washington & Jefferson, 0–0/Rose Bowl

1922   *California 9–0

First Rose Bowl played in Rose Bowl Stadium January 1, 1923 (Southern California defeated Penn State, 14–3); various other regional bowls played in 1920s

1923   *Michigan 8–0

1924   Notre Dame 10–0

Beat Stanford, 27–10/Rose Bowl

> *Other: *Pennsylvania 9–1–1 (Davis)*

1925   Alabama 10–0

Beat Washington, 20–19/Rose Bowl; Helms, Billingsley, Boand, FR, Houlgate, NCF, Poling

> *Other: *Dartmouth 8–0*

1926   Stanford 10–0–1, Alabama 9–0–1 (co-national champions)

Stanford tied Alabama, 7–7/Rose Bowl; split – Billingsley, FR, Helms, NCF, Poling

1927   *Illinois 7–0–1

DS, Davis, Helms, NCF

> *Other: *Yale 7–1 (FR), *Notre Dame 7–1–1 (Houlgate), *Georgia 9–1 (Boand, Poling)*

1928   *Southern California 9–0–1, Georgia Tech 10–0 (co-national champions)

Southern California (Dick/Rissman)

Georgia Tech beat California, 8–7/Rose Bowl

1929   *Notre Dame 9–0

Bill, DS, Dunkel, Boand, Helms, FR, NCF, Poling

> *Other: Southern California 10–2 (beat Pittsburgh, 47–14/Rose Bowl; Houlgate, Thes),*
> *Pittsburgh 9–1 (lost Southern California, 47–14/Rose Bowl; Davis)*

1930   *Notre Dame 10–0, Alabama 10–0 (co-national champions)

Notre Dame; all but FR, tie/Davis

Alabama beat Washington State, 24–0/Rose Bowl; tie/Davis, FR)

1931   Southern California 10–1

Beat Tulane, 21–12/Rose Bowl; Dick/Rockne, Dunkel, Ann, Helms, Thes, Wms, FBR, NCF, Poling, Bill, Mas

1932   Southern California 10–0

Beat Pittsburgh, 35–0/Rose Bowl; Ann, Dunk, Thes, Helms, Wms, Davis/Co, FBR, NCF, Poling, Bill, Mas

   *Other: *Michigan 8–0*

1933   *Michigan 7–0–1

   *Other: *Southern California 10–1–1 (Wms)*

1934   *Minnesota 8–0, Alabama 10–0 (co-national champions)

Alabama beat Stanford, 29–13/Rose Bowl; Dunkel, Houlgate, Poling, Williamson; Sugar, Orange Bowls first played January 1, 1935; Cotton Bowl first played January 1, 1937

1935   *Minnesota 8–0

Associated Press poll begins, 1936–2008

Final rankings prior to bowls, 1936–64**

1936   *Minnesota 7–1 (AP)

1937   *Pittsburgh 9–0–1, California 10–0–1 (co-national champions)

Pittsburgh; AP

California beat Alabama, 13–0/Rose Bowl

1938   Texas Christian 11–0

Texas Christian beat Carnegie Tech, 15–7/Sugar Bowl; AP, WS, Helms, NCF; Heisman: Davey O'Brien

   *Other: Tennessee 11–0 (beat Oklahoma, 7–0/Orange Bowl; Bill, Dunkel, LS, Board, Houlgate, FR, Poling, Sagarin), *Notre Dame 8–1 (DS)*

1939   Southern California 8–0–2, Texas A&M 11–0 (co-national champions)

Southern California beat Tennessee, 14–0/Rose Bowl; Dick/Rockne

Texas A&M beat Tulane, 14–13/Sugar Bowl; AP

1940   *Minnesota, Stanford (co-national champions)

Minnesota (AP)

Stanford beat Nebraska, 21–13/Rose Bowl

1941   *Minnesota 8–0 (AP)

Heisman: Bruce Smith

1942   *Ohio State 9–1 (AP)

   Other: Georgia 11–1 (beat UCLA, 9–0/Rose Bowl)

1943   *Notre Dame 9–1 (AP)

Heisman: Angelo Bertelli

1944   *Army 9–0 (AP)

1945   *Army 9–0 (AP)

Heisman: Doc Blanchard

1946   *Notre Dame 8–0–1 (AP)

1947   *Notre Dame 9–0 (AP)

Heisman: John Lujack

(continues)

National Champions (*continued*)

1948   *Michigan 9–0 (AP)

1949   *Notre Dame 10–0 (AP)

      Heisman: Leon Hart

United Press International poll begins, 1950–95
Final rankings prior to bowls, 1950–73**

1950   Oklahoma 10–1 **ILLEGITIMATE**

      Oklahoma lost to Kentucky, 13–7/Sugar Bowl; AP, UPI

        REVISED: *Tennessee 11–1 (beat Texas, 20–14/Cotton Bowl)*

1951   Tennessee 10–1 **ILLEGITIMATE**

      Tennessee lost to Maryland, 28–13/Sugar Bowl; AP, UPI

        REVISED: *Maryland 10–0 (beat Tennessee, 28–13/Sugar Bowl)*

1952   *Michigan State 9–0 (AP, UPI)

1953   Maryland **ILLEGITIMATE**

      Maryland lost to Oklahoma, 7–0/Orange Bowl; AP, UPI

        REVISED: *Michigan State 9–1 (beat UCLA 28–20/Rose Bowl)*

        Other: **Notre Dame 8–0–1 (FRI, INS, Berry; Heisman: John Lattner), Oklahoma 9–1–1 (beat*

           Maryland 7–0/Orange Bowl; FR, Berry)

1954   *UCLA 9–0, Ohio State 10–0 (co-national champions)

      UCLA; UPI

      Ohio State beat Southern California, 20–7/Rose Bowl; AP

1955   Oklahoma 11–0 (AP, UPI)

      Beat Maryland, 20–6/Orange Bowl

1956   *Oklahoma 10–0 (AP/UPI)

1957   Ohio State 8–1, *Auburn 10–0 (co-national champions)

      Ohio State beat Oregon, 10–7/Rose Bowl; UPI

      Auburn; AP

1958   Louisiana State 11–0 (AP, UPI)

      Beat Clemson, 7–0/Sugar Bowl

1959   Syracuse 11–0 (AP, UPI)

      Beat Texas, 23–14/Cotton Bowl

1960   Minnesota 8–2 (AP, UPI) **ILLEGITIMATE**

      Lost to Washington, 17–7/Rose Bowl

        REVISED: *Mississippi 10–0–1 (beat Rice, 14–6/Sugar Bowl)*

1961   Alabama 11–0 (AP, UPI)

      Beat Arkansas, 10–3/Sugar Bowl

Associated Press—Top 10, 1962–67

1962 Southern California 11–0 (AP, UPI)
Beat Wisconsin, 42–37/Rose Bowl)
1963 Texas 11–0 (AP, UPI)
Beat Navy, 28–6/Cotton Bowl
1964 Alabama 10–1 **ILLEGITIMATE**
Alabama lost to Texas, 21–17/Orange Bowl; AP, UPI
    *REVISED: Arkansas 11–0 (beat Nebraska, 10–7/Cotton Bowl; Billingsley, FR,
    Football Writers, Helms, Poling, NCF)*

Associated Press poll
Final rankings after bowl, 1965

1965 Alabama 9–1–1
Michigan State 10–1 (UPI) **ILLEGITIMATE** (co-national champions)
Alabama beat Nebraska, 39–28/Orange Bowl; AP
Michigan State lost to UCLA, 14–12; UPI

Associated Press poll
Final rankings before bowls, 1966–67**

1966 *Notre Dame 9–0–1 (AP, UPI)
1967 Southern California 10–1 (AP, UPI)
Beat Indiana, 14–3/Rose Bowl

Associated Press—Top 20, 1968–88
Final rankings after bowls, 1968–2008

1968 Ohio State 10–0 (AP, UPI)
Beat Southern California, 27–16/Rose Bowl
1969 Texas 11–0 (AP, UPI)
Beat Notre Dame, 21–17/Cotton Bowl
1970 Nebraska 11–0–1
Texas 10–1 **ILLEGITIMATE** (co-national champions)
Nebraska beat Louisiana State, 17–12/Orange Bowl; AP
Texas lost to Notre Dame, 24–11/Cotton Bowl; UPI
1971 Nebraska 13–0 (AP, UPI)
Beat Alabama, 38–6/Orange Bowl
1972 Southern California 12–0 (AP, UPI)
Beat Ohio State, 42–17/Rose Bowl

(continues)

National Champions (*continued*)

1973 Notre Dame 11–0

Alabama 11–1 **ILLEGITIMATE** (co-national champions)

Notre Dame beat Alabama, 24–23/Sugar Bowl; AP

Alabama lost to Notre Dame, 24–23/Sugar Bowl; UPI

United Press International poll

Final rankings after bowls, 1974–95

1974 Southern California 10–1–1, *Oklahoma 11–0 (co-national champions)

Southern California beat Ohio State, 18–17/Rose Bowl; UPI

Oklahoma on NCAA probation; AP

1975 Oklahoma 11–1 (AP, UPI)

Beat Michigan, 14–6/Orange Bowl

1976 Pittsburgh 12–0 (AP, UPI)

Beat Georgia, 27–3/Sugar Bowl; Heisman: Tony Dorsett

1977 Notre Dame 11–1 (AP, UPI)

Beat Texas, 38–10/Cotton Bowl

1978 Southern California 12–1, Alabama 11–1 (co-national champions)

Southern California beat Alabama, 24–14, on 9–23–78 @ Legion Field, Birmingham, Ala.; beat
Michigan 17–10/Rose Bowl; UPI

Alabama lost to Southern California, 24–14, on 9–23–78 @ Legion Field, Birmingham, Ala.; beat
Penn State, 14–7/Sugar Bowl; AP

1979 Alabama 12–0 (AP, UPI)

Beat Arkansas, 24–9/Sugar Bowl

1980 Georgia 12–0 (AP, UPI)

Beat Notre Dame, 17–10/Sugar Bowl

1981 Clemson 12–0 (AP, UPI)

Beat Nebraska, 22–15/Orange Bowl

USA Today *poll begins, 1982–2008*

1982 Penn State 11–1 (AP, UPI, *USA Today*)

Beat Penn State, 27–23/Sugar Bowl

1983 Miami 11–1 (AP, UPI, *USA Today*)

Beat Nebraska, 31–30/Orange Bowl

1984 Brigham Young 13–0 (AP, UPI, *USA Today*)

Beat Michigan, 24–17/Holiday Bowl

1985 Oklahoma 11–1 (AP, UPI, *USA Today*)

Beat Penn State, 25–10/Orange Bowl

1986 Penn State 12–0 (AP, UPI, *USA Today*)

Beat Miami, 14–10/Fiesta Bowl

1987   Miami 12–0 (AP, UPI, *USA Today*)
       Beat Oklahoma, 20–14/Orange Bowl
1988   Notre Dame 12–0 (AP, UPI, *USA Today*)
       Beat West Virginia, 34–21/Fiesta Bowl

Associated Press—Top 25, 1989–2008

1989   Miami 11–1 (AP, UPI, *USA Today*)
       Beat Alabama, 33–25/Sugar Bowl
1990   Colorado 11–1–1, Georgia Tech 11–0–1 (co-national champions)
       Colorado beat Notre Dame, 10–9/Orange Bowl; AP, USA Today
       Georgia Tech beat Nebraska, 45–21/Citrus Bowl; UPI
1991   Washington 12–0, Miami 12–0 (co-national champions)
       Washington beat Michigan, 34–14/Rose Bowl; UPI, USA Today
       Miami beat Nebraska, 22–0/Orange Bowl; AP
1992   Alabama 13–0 (AP, UPI, *USA Today*)
       Beat Miami, 34–13/Sugar Bowl

USA Today *Hall of Fame poll begins, 1993–1996*

1993   Florida State 12–1 (AP, UPI, *USA Today*, Hall of Fame)
       Beat Nebraska, 18–16/Orange Bowl; Heisman: Charlie Ward
1994   Nebraska 13–0 (AP, UPI, *USA Today*, Hall of Fame)
       Beat Miami, 24–17/Orange Bowl
1995   Nebraska 12–0 (AP, UPI, *USA Today*, Hall of Fame)
       Beat Florida, 62–24/Fiesta Bowl

United Press International poll discontinued, 1996

1996   Florida 12–1 (AP, *USA Today*, Hall of Fame)
       Beat Florida State, 52–20/Sugar Bowl; Heisman: Danny Wuerffel)

USA Today *Hall of Fame poll discontinued, 1997*

1997   Michigan 12–0, Nebraska 13–0 (co-national champions)
       Michigan beat Washington State, 21–16/Rose Bowl; AP; Heisman: Charles Woodson
       Nebraska beat Tennessee, 42–17/Orange Bowl; USA Today

Bowl Championship Series (USA Today poll) begins, 1998–2008

1998   Tennessee 13–0 (AP, BCS/*USA Today*)
       Beat Florida State, 23–16/Fiesta Bowl

(*continues*)

National Champions (*continued*)

1999   Florida State 12–0 (AP, BCS/*USA Today*)

      Beat Virginia Tech, 46–29/Sugar Bowl

2000   Oklahoma 13–0 (AP, BCS/*USA Today*)

      Beat Florida State, 13–2/Orange Bowl

2001   Miami 12–0 (AP, BCS/*USA Today*)

      Beat Nebraska, 37–14/Rose Bowl

2002   Ohio State 14–0 (AP, BCS/*USA Today*)

      Beat Miami, 31–24/Fiesta Bowl

2003   Southern California 12–1, Louisiana State 13–1 (co-national champions)

      Southern California beat Michigan, 28–14/Rose Bowl; AP

      Louisiana State beat Oklahoma, 21–14/Sugar Bowl; BCS/USA Today

2004   Southern California 13–0 (AP, BCS/*USA Today*)

      Beat Oklahoma, 55–19/Orange Bowl; Heisman: Matt Leinart

2005   Texas 13–0 (AP, BCS/*USA Today*)

      Beat Southern California, 41–38/Rose Bowl

      Bowl Championship Series championship game separates from traditional bowls, 2006

      Bowl Championship Series game stands alone from other bowls, 2006–2008

2006   Florida 13–1 (AP, BCS/*USA Today*)

      Beat Ohio State, 41–14/BCS (Glendale, AR)

2007   Louisiana State 13–1 (*AP, BCS/USA Today*)

      Beat Ohio State, 38–24/BCS (New Orleans, LA)

2008   Florida 13–1 (*AP, BCS/USA Today*)

      Beat Oklahoma, 24–14 (Miami, FL)

*No bowl

**National champions were selected prior to bowl games: AP (1936–1964, 1966–1967); UPI (1950–1973)

When the landscape of college football tightened up beginning in the 1960s—color TV, big-time recruiting, big-time money, integration, wide-open offenses, modern equipment, diet, and coaching—in other words, when parity reared its head, when winning became a harder thing to achieve, winning was precisely what USC started to do more of than anybody.

Since 1962, USC has won seven national titles to Notre Dame's four. When John Huarte won Notre Dame's sixth Heisman Trophy in 1964, USC still had zero. Since then, Southern California has had seven Heisman winners to one for the Irish. A review of the Heisman winners from USC, Notre Dame, and Ohio State (all with seven total) reveals that the "Trojan seven" is the most impressive of the bunch. They include:

1965   Mike Garrett set the NCAA career rushing record. He was a top pro running back on two Kansas City Chief Super Bowl teams, including the 1969 world champions.

1968   O. J. Simpson set the NCAA single-season rushing record as a senior. He should have won the award as a junior (1967), when he led Troy to a national title. They just missed a repeat in 1968. O. J. was the first pick of the 1969 draft. He became the all-time single-season NFL rushing leader with Buffalo when, in 1973, he became the first to break the 2,000-yard mark in a 14-game season. O. J. is a member of the Pro Football Hall of Fame.

1979   Charles White finished as the NCAA's second all-time rusher with 5,598 yards. White could have won the award in 1978 when he led USC to the national championship.

1981   Marcus Allen set or tied sixteen NCAA records, including most yards in a season (2,342) and most yards per game (212.9). The first pick of the Raiders, Allen led Los Angeles to the 1983 world championship and is a member of the Pro Football Hall of Fame.

2002   Carson Palmer was the first pick of the 2003 NFL Draft by Cincinnati and is currently a pro superstar.

2004   Matt Leinart was a three-time All-American, considered by many to be the greatest player in the history of college football. A first-round draft pick of the Arizona Cardinals in 2006, he was a starter, holds the promise of becoming a superstar and was a member of Arizona's 2009 Super Bowl team.

2005   Reggie Bush, a junior winner and two-time Heisman finalist, was the first pick of the New Orleans Saints in 2006. As a rookie, he led New Orleans to the NFC championship game for the first time in club history.

Notre Dame's seven Heisman winners do include Paul Hornung (1956), who was a legend at Green Bay, and Tim Brown (1987), a surefire Pro Football Hall of Famer after a great career with the Raiders. But Angelo Bertelli (1943), Johnny Lujack (1946), John Lattner (1953), and John Huarte (1964) did not impact the professional game very much. Lujack was a particular legend for tackling Army's Doc Blanchard in the open field of the famed 0–0 game in 1946. None of the others went on to the kind of pro fame as Simpson, Allen, or Palmer (or for that manner, the kind Leinart and Bush promise to achieve).

Ohio State's seven winners are also, uh, a bit long in the tooth. They include Les Horvath (1944), Vic Janowicz (1950), Howard "Hopalong" Cassady (1955), Archie Griffin (1974–75), Eddie George (1995), and Troy Smith (2006). Cassady was a big name best remembered because he was "saddled" with the same moniker as a cowboy movie star. Griffin had a career like few others, but his 1974 Heisman should have gone to USC's

USC versus Conferences (through 2008)

Atlantic Coast (11–6), Big 10 (66–27–2), Big 12 (29–9–2), Big East (9–4), Big Sky/Mountain West (21–6–1), Pacific-10 (405–58–29), Southeastern (17–10–1), Western Athletic (27–1), Independents (117–62–13)

Elite Ten by the Numbers
United Press International national championships (1950–95), coaches poll

1. Southern California   5
2. Oklahoma   5   *
3. Alabama   5   @
4. Miami   4
5. Texas   4   #
6. Ohio State   3
7. Nebraska   3
8. Notre Dame   3   +
9. Penn State   2
10. Michigan   0

*1 lost bowl, 1 no bowl
@2 lost bowls
#1 lost bowl
+1 no bowl

Alabama (5): 1961, *1964 (split/Arkansas – Billingsley, Football Research, Football Writers, Helms, Poling, National Championship Foundation), @1973 (split/Notre Dame – UPI), 1979, 1992
  *Lost Orange Bowl
  @Lost Sugar Bowl
Miami (4): 1983, 1987, 1989, 2001
Michigan (0)
Nebraska (3): 1971, 1994, 1995
Notre Dame (3): *1966, 1977, 1988
  *No bowl
Ohio State (3): *1957 (split/Auburn – AP), 1968, 2002
  *No bowl
Oklahoma (5): *1950, 1955, @1956, 1975, 1985
  *Lost Sugar Bowl
  @No bowl
Penn State (2): 1982, 1986
Southern California (5): 1962, 1967, 1972, 1974 (split/Oklahoma on probation/no bowl – AP), 1978 (split/Alabama – AP)
Texas (4): 1963, 1969, *1970, 2005
  *Lost Cotton Bowl

Anthony Davis. Davis led USC to one of the most extraordinary victories of all time, a 55-point comeback over Notre Dame *after the ballots were mailed in*. Griffin was a solid pro. George was the real deal in college and the NFL. If any Heisman winner ever looked worse than Troy Smith against Florida in the 2007 BCS championship game, I am un-aware of it.

Finally, there are the national championships. Forget the no-bowl titles of Notre Dame's salad days. In the late 1980s and early 1990s under Lou Holtz, the Irish bid for a return to greatness, perhaps beyond their best previous years. In the end they captured only the 1988 title, then went into a period of some funk. Under Charlie Weis they ap-peared to be contenders in a new football reality more Darwinian than any previously imagined. The masters of this new jungle: Pete Carroll's Trojans.

One decade into the BCS era, the Trojans have firmly established themselves as the "new centurions." Never has it been harder to win national championships, to maintain consistent excellence, than in this era. Since the initiation of the BCS, old champions Nebraska and Florida State have withered away. Miami was unable to sustain its run. Tennessee was a one-shot wonder. Oklahoma under Bob Stoops might have ascended to the top, but Carroll's Trojans told them there was no room in the penthouse for two kings. Jim Tressel and Ohio State were thinking "Team of the 2000s" until Florida and LSU embarrassed them in the 2007 and 2008 title games. Texas sunk under the weight of *all that pressure*.

In the midst of this maelstrom of Hollywood attention and high expectations; when the best juniors leave for the NFL (USC always has the best juniors, or in the case of Mike Williams in 2003, the best sophomores); when a title must be earned in the BCS world with multimillions at stake; when every game is televised and every move scrutinized—the clear winner is Southern California.

In the pre-BCS days, there would have been *no possibility* that LSU would have snagged that split title with USC in 2003. In 2005, USC would have gone to the Rose Bowl, beaten Penn State 60–2 while Texas beat somebody by a similar score in the Or-ange or Fiesta Bowl, then taken a national-title plaque back to Heritage Hall amid great howls of indignant complaint from Austin (just like Ann Arbor '47, Tuscaloosa '66, State College '94 . . .). In 2002, had there been a play-off, pundits agree that the best team in the nation at season's end was the Carson Palmer-led Trojans, who killed Iowa in the Orange Bowl to finish fourth while Ohio State won a close but basically lackluster BCS Fiesta Bowl game over injured Miami.

Elite Ten by the Numbers

Pro Bowl selections (through 2005)

1. Southern California		198
2. Notre Dame		135
3. Ohio State		122
4. Michigan		75

USC started playing football in 1888, but by 1919 they were at best the sixth best team on the Pacific Coast. Washington, Washington State, Oregon, California, and Stanford were all teams with national or budding national reputations. USC did play Stanford until 1905 and California starting in 1915. The Big Game between California and Stanford was the "big story." Rivalries such as Washington-Washington State and the "civil war" between Oregon and Oregon State were already under way. UCLA did not even open its doors until 1919. USC was mostly reduced to playing small colleges in California's Southland.

For various reasons, the top high school players were in the Seattle, Washington, area. USC went after the best coach in Seattle, Elmer "Gloomy Gus" Henderson. He brought with him to Los Angeles the best players from the Pacific Northwest. This immediately turned the Trojans into a "player." From 1919 to 1924, Henderson's teams were 45-7 (.865). They entered the Pacific Coast Conference in 1922. On January 1, 1923, USC defeated Penn State 14-3 in the first game ever played at the Rose Bowl Stadium. One of those Seattle-bred players, Brice Taylor, became USC's first All-American in 1925. Taylor was a symbol of the new America, embodied by the West. He was of both African and Cherokee descent and had only one hand. End Red Badgro became a Pro Football Hall of Famer with the New York Giants. Henderson was fired, however, because he could not beat Andy Smith and California's Wonder Teams, who lost to *nobody* for a 50-game stretch between 1920 and 1925.

Despise his "failure," Henderson elevated USC football to a higher stage. His tenure was a very important one. In 1921, Stanford built Stanford Stadium. Shortly thereafter, California's Memorial Stadium went up. Stanford bid hard for the Rose Bowl to be moved up north. The city of Pasadena stepped up, building the famed Rose Bowl Stadium in the Arroyo Seco. One year later, the Los Angeles Memorial Coliseum was erected across the street from the USC campus. The Rose Bowl and the Coliseum had the effect of elevating USC while turning the city of Los Angeles and the state of California into the sports capital of the world. Nine years after the Coliseum was built, the Olympics were held there. USC served as the Olympic village.

On January 1, 1925, Notre Dame's Four Horsemen defeated coach Pop Warner, running back Ernie Nevers, and Stanford, 27-10 in the Rose Bowl. After the game Rockne made an offhand remark to the writers about "coming out here to California" and "teaching USC" how to be a champion. This could have been interpreted as inviting a rivalry with the Trojans, or inviting himself to become their coach in the wake of Henderson's firing.

Rockne's wife indeed had a fondness for southern California, and he did toy with serious offers from the USC administration. Notre Dame held his feet to the fire, however. He recommended Howard Jones, who had beaten him when Jones was at Iowa. Jones also won a national championship coaching at Yale almost two decades prior. He was hired. Jones then formalized the rivalry with Notre Dame, but not without a little help from Mrs. Rockne. She insisted that if Rock not move to the Golden State, he at least take his team there every two years, ostensibly so she could shop on Rodeo Drive.

The rivalry with Notre Dame started in 1926 (in the decade, USC's 88–13–2 record was better than Rockne's 81–12–4), with a brief interruption when the world went to war in the 1940s. It is the greatest in college sports history and perhaps the athletic world. The Ohio State-Michigan, Alabama-Auburn, Oklahoma-Nebraska, Army-Navy, California-Stanford, Notre Dame-Michigan, and even Southern Cal-UCLA rivalries all lack the kind of national prestige attached to the USC-Notre Dame event. Some are just regional. Some lack the tradition of eighty years. Some are played between teams that do not for the most part contend much. USC-Notre Dame has it all.

"It's like Nick Lachey eyeing Jessica Simpson, each from across a crowded room for the first time," said *Sports Illustrated* college football writer Austin Murphy in 2005.

"It's like the Republican National Convention," says J. Kevin McCormack, whose father graduated from Notre Dame, and who himself attended college there before transferring . . . to USC. "Private schools, lots of wealth, very classy, not a lot of swearing or class envy like UCLA or Cal; Democrat schools who hate USC instead of trying to upgrade themselves to that level of excellence. Obviously Notre Dame's Catholic and USC is 'Hollywood's school,' but it was originally a Methodist institution and remains a bastion of patriotism. Both schools are conservative by nature, a rare thing outside of the South. Both are mocked for it and remain above such unimpressiveness."

Few "football schools" have such mutual respect for each other as USC and Notre Dame. Michigan can't stand Ohio State; thinks the Buckeyes are lower class. Georgia fans think Florida graduates can use their degrees as handicap stickers. Nebraska and Oklahoma think of each other like Bosnians and Croats. Alabama and Auburn are like the Hatfields and the McCoys. UCLA is just plain teed off that Trojans respect Notre Dame more, and too often tend to own the corporations they toil for.

USC lost to Notre Dame 13–12 in front of 74,378 at the Coliseum in 1926, and 7–6 in front of an all-time record crowd of 120,000 at Chicago's Soldier Field in 1927. Southern California finally won a national championship in 1928 on the strength of a 27–14 victory over the Irish in front of 72,632 at the Coliseum. It was the equivalent then of Florida State finally getting one for Bobby Bowden in 1993, or Tom Osborne at Nebraska in 1994. At the time, many pundits felt the Trojans to be the greatest college team ever assembled. In 1929, 112,912 attended Notre Dame's 3–12 win over the USC at Soldier Field in a de facto national championship game. Also in 1929, USC destroyed UCLA 76–0 in the first meeting between the two schools. After a couple of games like that, the Bruins pulled out of the series in order to lick their wounds.

In 1931, Southern California traveled to the brand new Notre Dame Stadium. Trailing 14–0 entering the fourth quarter, they captured a thrilling a 16–14 comeback win on Johnny Baker's last-minute field goal. The game was broadcast nationally and made USC instant American heroes. At least 300,000 met the team upon their arrival by train in downtown Los Angeles. Jones's Thundering Herd captured back-to-back national championships in 1931 and 1932. The 1932 team was considered Jones's best, better even than the 1928 champions. Again, talk of "the best team ever" was entered into by pundits from coast to coast. USC football was doing as much or more to put their city and state on the map as Hollywood, or even the Olympics. Movie stars flocked to their games while writing fan letters to Jones. The film connection, started a few years earlier by ex-Trojan football player Marion Morrison, aka John "Duke" Wayne, was well under way.

Certainly until 1932, only Cal's Wonder Teams and Rockne's Four Horsemen of 1924 might have been considered as good. All-Americans of the 1920s and 1930s included Mort Kaer ("the Red Bluff Terror"), Jesse Hibbs, Morley Drury ("the Noblest Trojan of them all"), Erny Pinckert, Johnny Baker, Gus Shaver, Ernie Smith, Aaron Rosenberg, and Cotton Warburton. Rosenberg became one of Hollywood's most successful television producers.

In the mid-1930s, USC experienced a downturn. The UCLA series was resumed for good. It was an immediate bloodbath. The Trojans and Bruins twice battled to a tie: 7–7 in 1936 and 0–0 in 1939. But the impact of the series went beyond the ferocity of the competition. Huge throngs sat in the Coliseum watching integrated teams play each other. The Bruins in particular featured the likes of future baseball pioneer Jackie Robinson, Olympic sprinter Kenny Washington, and Woody Strode, the back gladiator who dies so that Kirk Douglas may live in the 1960 Stanley Kubrick classic *Spartacus* (another gladiator in that film was USC's Marv Goux).

On January 2, 1939, USC battled unbeaten, untied, unscored-on Duke in the Rose Bowl. Trailing 3–0 with mere minutes remaining, Jones inserted substitute quarterback Doyle Nave and backup end "Antelope Al" Krueger. They engineered the winning drive, 7–3, achieving sports notoriety that today might be compared to Tom Brady or Derek Jeter—love letters, publicity, and the like. An example of how different the world was then can be found a few years later. Nave found himself serving in the Navy alongside several of those Duke players during World War II.

In 1939, Jones's Trojans captured the last of his four national championships. They beat Notre Dame 20–12 at South Bend. Then they knocked off Bob Neyland's unbeaten, untied, and also unscored-on Tennessee Volunteers 14–3 in the Rose Bowl. Guard Harry Smith earned All-American honors.

Trojan consensus All-Americans of the 1940s and 1950s include Ralph Heywood, John Ferraro, Paul Cleary, Elmer Wilhoite, and Jim Sears. Ferraro (whose college career

The Howard Jones Era			
1925	11–2	1932	10–0
1926	8–2	1933	10–1–1
1927	8–1–1	1934	4–6–1
1928	9–0–1	1935	5–7
1929	10–2	1936	4–2–3
1930	8–2	1937	9–2
1931	10–1	1939	8–0–2

was interrupted by military service during the war) became a respected Los Angeles city councilman. The most famed player was the golden boy Frank Gifford. Gifford went on to a Pro Football Hall of Fame career, leading the New York Giants to glory. In the late 1940s and early 1950s, coach Pappy Waldorf's California Golden Bears went on a tremendous run, but in 1951 Gifford engineered a 21–14 upset victory at Berkeley.

In the two decades between Howard Jones and John McKay, USC won several conference championships. After the Rose Bowl was dominated by the Big 10 in the first six years of the arrangement, USC finally earned back some honor for the Pacific Coast Conference with a 7–0 triumph over Wisconsin on January 1, 1953. In 1954 an all-time college record fifteen Trojans were drafted by the NFL. In 1956, the Trojans traveled to Austin, Texas. USC's black running back, C. R. Roberts, led the 44–20 blowout win by rushing for 251 yards *in the first half.* This occurred after USC was forced to leave their hotel the night before because Roberts was not allowed to stay there. After the game, Longhorn players, who had baited and spit at Roberts at the beginning of the game, extended handshakes. As an athlete, Roberts had earned their respect. The fans, however, continued to catcall him. The time for major social progress was not yet at hand in the South.

USC's coach was Jess Hill, known as Mr. Trojan. Hill did it all at USC. He ran track and played football before embarking on a Major League career with the Philadelphia Athletics. After retiring, Hill coached track and football at his alma mater. He later became athletic director. Under his tenure in the 1960s and 1970s, the University of Southern California enjoyed the greatest run of sports success in all collegiate annals, before or since.

In the mid-1950s, a recruiting scandal hurt USC and the entire PCC. It ensnared Washington, UCLA, and California in a "rent payment" imbroglio. It came about when the cost of housing went up exponentially in Westwood, Berkeley, and other off-campus locations. It came to the NCAA's attention when Stanford, who was just as guilty, decided to "self-report" while turning their conference rivals in.

Willie Wood became the first major college black starting quarterback under coach Don Clark between 1957 and 1959. He went on to a Hall of Fame career playing defensive back for Vince Lombardi's Packer dynasty. All-American lineman Ron Mix became a Hall of Famer with San Diego. An assistant coach during that era, Al Davis became a Pro Football Hall of Famer as commissioner of the American Football League, coach, and owner of the Raiders.

Over the next two decades, relations between USC, Stanford, and California soured. When USC established dominance in the early 1930s, the northern universities accused USC of cheating and letting players into school with questionable academic credentials. Over the next years many of the "questionable" players went from football to successful careers as lawyers, writers, movie producers, architects, and like professions. This eliminated Cal and Stanford's argument, but they continued to argue it anyway.

In 1959, USC featured the Twin Holy Terrors of Mount Carmel, linemen Marlin and Mike McKeever. Unable to stop the McKeevers, California instead accused them of dirty play, even going so far as to sue USC when Mike's hard hit of a Bear player resulted in an

Elite Ten by the Numbers

First-round pro football draftees (through 2007)

1.	Southern California	74	6.	Michigan	40
2.	Ohio State	67	7.	Oklahoma	37
3.	Miami	59	8.	Penn State	35
4.	Notre Dame	58	9.	Alabama	33
5.	Texas	41	10.	Nebraska	32

injury. The case got big play in *Sports Illustrated*. Eventually, film was produced exonerating McKeever. California, exposed as a loser, decided that sports was not so important after all. They deemphasized athletics in the 1960s and 1970s. Their students, humiliated in yearly drubbings at the hands of Trojan powerhouses, took to dumbly waving credit cards because USC's students tended to come from wealth.

The term "University of Spoiled Children" emanated out of the political 1960s, when USC was a campus that actually rooted for America in its struggle with an ideology (Communism) responsible for the murder of 100 million human beings in the twentieth century. On the football field, the beatings went on with California and Stanford falling like Eastern Europe under Stalin. Humiliated by this fact, the supposedly enlightened Stanford student body took to running USC's players through a gauntlet when they made their way from the outside dressing rooms into Stanford Stadium. McKay and his great players, many of whom were black, were pelted with "the N word." McKay was called a "n----r lover."

"It made my blood boil," said McKay. "That's why I said I wanted to beat Stanford by two thousand points."

The Stanford student newspaper ran an editorial prior to the 1972 game stating that USC was a school that failed to learn how to put the game of football in proper perspective. The same old accusations—academic fraud, stupid athletes—was leveled at USC, as had been done in the 1930s. Over the years, when many members of *that* team became corporate attorneys, network broadcasters, schoolteachers, entrepreneurs, Christian ministers, and a Republican candidate for governor of Pennsylvania, it had the same effect as before, which was of no benefit to Stanford.

In 1960 McKay took over a program that was certainly one of the best in the nation but that had been underperforming. In 1962 USC went 11–0, defeating Notre Dame and UCLA, then Wisconsin in a wild Rose Bowl to capture the national championship. In 1963, Mel Hein, a Pro Football Hall of Fame center with the New York Giants, became an assistant coach at Southern California. In 1964, Ara Parseghian brought his first Notre Dame team into Los Angeles with an unbeaten record. Leading 17–0 at the half, he told his players they were "thirty minutes from the national championship." It seemed to have the effect of getting the Irish, as UCLA basketball coach John Wooden would put it, "playing not to win, but rather playing not to lose."

Number One versus Number Two

The Trojans are 3–3 in number one versus number two matchups through 2006.

USC has seven victories over number one-ranked opponents and has ended nine perfect seasons (through 2006).

USC battled back. Late in the fourth quarter, quarterback Craig Fertig hit receiver Rod Sherman on a clutch fourth-down pass called "84-Z delay," giving Troy the 20-17 upset victory.

In 1966, USC again opened the season at Texas. This time the focus was on former USC football star John "Duke" Wayne, who was filming *War Wagon* in the state at the time. Events of that weekend are momentous, probably enough for a book or a documentary. In a nutshell, Wayne, his Hollywood cohorts, sportswriters, and well-heeled USC alumni did a fair amount of drinkin'. There were fistfights, and Wayne's makeup man died of alcohol poisoning.

In the morning Fertig—now an assistant coach—was put in "charge" of Wayne, doing the job of the dead makeup man (although Wayne was not yet aware of his demise). Fertig dressed the Duke in a black business suit, white ten-gallon cowboy hat, and boots with spurs.

"I had him lookin' good," recalled Fertig.

Wayne was then brought before the USC football team to give them a pregame pep talk. According to legend, Wayne gave them a rip-roarin' exhortation filled with war references hinting at what America would do to the Communists in Vietnam, which was raging at the time. There are rumors that George C. Scott's speech at the beginning of *Patton* was patterned after Wayne's 1966 pregame talk in Austin. Wayne was then taken to the field, where he was hauled around in a golf cart driven by Fertig's father, Henry "Chief" Fertig, head of the Huntington Park, California (L.A. County), Police Department. Apparently still intoxicated from the night before—he slept little if at all and just kept drinkin'—Wayne was fortified by a clandestine whiskey bottle that Chief kept pouring from into a Dixie cup he drank out of. The Texas fans saw the Duke and cheered. Duke then gave 'em the "hook 'em, 'Horns" sign, but according to Fertig was saying the whole while, "F--k the 'Horns." USC won the game, 10-6. They never ever lost to Texas until the 2006 Rose Bowl game.

Later in 1966, Notre Dame was humbled by a 10-10 tie against Michigan State at East Lansing in which Ara Parseghian was disparaged for not going for the win late in the fourth quarter. The next week, the Irish played for "poll position" in a 51-0 drubbing of USC. The media prodded McKay in an attempt to get him to complain about Notre Dame running up the score. He was not of that bent. His contention was that it was USC's job to stop them. Besides, he said, "There's a billion Chinamen who could care less who won this game."

After the 51-0 loss to Notre Dame, McKay vowed "never to be beaten like that again." Over the course of the following sixteen years, USC under McKay and John Robinson lost just twice to the Irish. The Trojans' dominance inspired many to remember McKay saying "we'll never be beaten" by Notre Dame again. Close enough.

The comparison between McKay and Parseghian is best exemplified by events within less than two months of each other in 1966. Parseghian was derisively said to have "tied one for the Gipper" when he settled for the 10–10 tie in the "Game of the Century" against Michigan State. On January 2, 1966, USC trailed Purdue 14–7 in the Rose Bowl. Troy drove for a last-minute touchdown. The "gunslinger" McKay avoided playing for the tie. The 2-point try failed, giving victory to Bob Griese and the Boilermakers, respect for the men of Troy.

In the dressing room that day a young junior college recruit named O. J. Simpson told his future teammates, "Don't worry about it, we'll win the national championship next year." O. J. was attracted to USC by their famed white horse Traveler. He watched Traveler romp around the field on a color TV when USC beat Wisconsin in the 1963 Rose Bowl. O. J. immediately transformed Southern California from excellent to dominant. His two years at USC mark the dividing line between all that came before and all that came after.

When Simpson entered school in 1967, Notre Dame was the king of college football. The battle for "second" was an open war between USC, Oklahoma, and Alabama, which the Irish were happy to see fought, like the Romans encouraging skirmishes against Carthage so as to weaken their rivals. It is likely an exaggeration to say that USC was winning that "war."

O. J. started a period of Trojan success resulting in the school assessing, at the end of the 1982 season, whether they had caught Notre Dame for all-time collegiate football supremacy or were on the verge of doing so. Whether they did or not is immaterial, since over the next twenty years they fell well behind their rivals in the historical pantheon, but that is not for now.

The numbers are discussed in various sections of this book. Besides, football statistics do not resonate like, say, Barry Bonds hitting 73 homers, or Wilt Chamberlain averaging 50 points a game. Suffice to say that O. J. had the best season ever up until 1967. He was even better in 1968.

The junior transfer from City College of San Francisco announced his presence with authority when he led Troy first to a hard-fought 17–13 win over Texas. Then he and linebacker Adrian Young (who was born in Dublin, Ireland) starred in a huge 24–7 victory at Notre Dame. It was USC's first victory in South Bend since the 1939 national championship campaign.

In 1967 Southern California beat UCLA 21–20 at the Coliseum. There have been many incredible games over the years since then: the 1969 Texas-Arkansas, 1971 Nebraska-Oklahoma, and 1993 Notre Dame-Florida State battles. Only the 2006 USC-Texas Rose Bowl game seems to feature the hype, the matchups, and the ultimate result rivaling the 1967 "city game."

It was for the Rose Bowl and the national championship, no questions asked, played between two teams ten miles apart in the same city. Both wore their home jerseys in a stadium they shared. It was for the Heisman Trophy, too, which makes it very rare. Both UCLA's Gary Beban and USC's Simpson played their best games of the season. O. J.'s 64-yard run to win it late in the fourth quarter was pure magic. O. J. should have won the Heisman, but the senior Beban was so noble in the titanic struggle he ended up the winner.

In the 1950s, 1960s, and 1970s, the UCLA game was often more competitive than the Notre Dame battles. These were golden years at UCLA. First, there was the great Red Sanders, who said "the USC-UCLA game is not a matter of life or death; it's more important than that." Then there were Tommy Prothro and McKay, two Southerners from the old school who adjusted nicely to California sensibilities in the 1960s. McKay despised characterizations of Prothro outcoaching him. Later, Pepper Rodgers and Terry Donahue of UCLA, and John Robinson of USC, battled each other in fierce manner. Had USC not stood in their way, the Bruins may well have added national championships (to the one Sanders brought to Westwood in 1954) in 1967, 1969, 1972, and 1973.

O. J. led USC to a 14–3 victory over Indiana in the 1968 Rose Bowl, capping McKay's second national championship. When the season ended, a record five Trojans (Outland Trophy winner Ron Yary, Mike Taylor, Tim Rossovich, Mike Hull, Earl McCullough) were chosen in the first round of the NFL Draft. All-American linebacker Adrian Young was among the overall eleven USC players selected. Despite the talent drain, Southern California came back in 1968, challenging to be one of the great teams in history.

O. J. set the NCAA single-season rushing record with 1,880 and won the Heisman Trophy in a runaway. USC blasted through the season, but at the Rose Bowl met their match: a talent-laden group of Ohio State sophomores ended USC's bid for hegemony, 27–16. At that moment, Ohio State coach Woody Hayes was sitting on top of the world, with any talk of *hegemony* centered on the Buckeyes. In the next two years, his great teams somehow managed to get upset by Michigan 24–12 (1969) and Stanford 27–17 (1971 Rose Bowl). There would be no repeats or three-peats; in fact, mostly more disappointment in Pasadena. This served only to demonstrate just how darn hard it is to keep winning every year in college football.

O. J. was the first pick in the draft by the Buffalo Bills and the greatest pro football player of the 1970s. Many argued he had passed or was close to passing Cleveland's Jim Brown as the best running back—and football player—in history. Ultimately that would be an overstatement. O. J. was the leading commercial pitchman in the country for many years during and after his playing career. He was a member of the *Monday Night Football* broadcast crew, also working as an analyst and sideline reporter. O. J. enjoyed some success in Hollywood, most notably in *The Naked Gun* movies. In 1994, his wife, Nicole Brown Simpson, and her friend Ronald Goldman, were brutally stabbed to death in Los Angeles. O. J. was accused, tried, and found not guilty, but a civil trial found him liable. The overwhelming public sentiment is that he is guilty regardless of the verdict. He has been basically disowned by USC, a school he loved and who loved him back. In the 1990s, opponents taunted USC with placards featuring O. J.'s photo. In the Pete Carroll era, Trojan success has thankfully made the O. J. issue an old one despite subsequent legal trouble.

In 1969 USC did something few college teams are able to do. Despite losing their star player and most of his teammates, they reloaded and probably were better. Only a tie

Number One Overall Pro Football Draft Choices (through 2009 Draft)

1.	Southern California	5
2.	Notre Dame	5
3.	Alabama	5
4.	Miami	3
5.	Ohio State	3
6.	Oklahoma	3
7.	Nebraska	3
8.	Michigan	2

Alabama (5): Vaughn Mancha (Boston, 1947), Butch Avinger (Pittsburgh, 1951), Bobby Marlow (New York Giants, 1953), Lee Roy Jordan (Dallas, 1962), Joe Namath (St. Louis Cardinals NFL/New York Jets AFL, 1964)

Miami (3): Bernie Kosar (Cleveland, 1985), Vinny Testaverde (Tampa Bay, 1987), Russell Maryland (Dallas, 1991)

Michigan (2): Tom Harmon (Chicago, 1941), Jake Long (Miami, 2008)

Nebraska (3): Sam Francis (Philadelphia, 1937), Irving Fryar (New England, 1984), Mike Rozier (Houston, 1984 supplemental)

Notre Dame (5): Angelo Bertelli (Boston, 1944), Frank Dancewicz (Boston, 1946), Leon Hart (Detroit, 1950), Paul Hornung (Green Bay, 1957), Walt Patulski (Buffalo, 1972)

Ohio State (3): Tom Cousineau (Buffalo, 1979), Dan Wilkinson (Cincinnati, 1994), Orlando Pace (St. Louis Rams, 1997)

Oklahoma (3): Lee Roy Selmon (Tampa Bay, 1976), Billy Sims (Detroit, 1980), Brian Bosworth (Seattle, 1987)

Southern California (5): Ron Yary (Minnesota, 1968), O. J. Simpson (Buffalo, 1969), Ricky Bell (Tampa Bay, 1977), Keyshawn Johnson (New York Jets, 1996), Carson Palmer (Cincinnati, 2003)

with Notre Dame prevented Southern California from the national championship, or at least competing in an even struggle with Texas and Penn State for it. USC opened with a 31–21 win at Nebraska (a tie with USC in 1970 was the only blemish in the next thirty-two Cornhusker games). Last-minute thrillers over Stanford (26–24 on Ron Ayala's field goal) and UCLA (14–12 on a Jimmy Jones-to-Sam Dickerson touchdown pass) earned Southern California the moniker Cardiac Kids. The defensive line, featuring Al Cowlings, Tody Smith, and Charlie Weaver, was named after the Sam Peckinpah film *The Wild Bunch*. Michigan, fresh off a monumental 24–12 upset of Team of the Century Ohio State, was overwhelmed by the Wild Bunch in a 10–3 Rose Bowl loss to Southern Cal. The Trojans finished 10–0–1.

USC versus Their Biggest Rivals

Versus UCLA	43–28–7
Versus Notre Dame	33–42–5

Elite Ten by the Numbers
Bowl win-loss records

1. Southern California   31–16
2. Alabama   31–22–3
3. Penn State   26–13–2
4. Oklahoma   24–17–1
5. Texas   25–21–2
6. Miami   19–15
7. Nebraska   23–22
8. Michigan   19–20
9. Ohio State   18–22
10. Notre Dame   *14–15

*Holds NCAA record, most consecutive bowl losses (9), 1994–2006

Alabama: 31–22–3 (Sugar: 8–4, Orange: 4–4, Rose: 4–1–1, Cotton: 3–4)

Miami: 19–15 (Orange: 6–3, Sugar: 2–3, Rose: 1–1, Fiesta: 0–1)

Michigan: 19–20 (Rose: 8–12, Fiesta: 1–0, Orange: 1–1, Sugar: 0–1)

Nebraska: 23–22 (Orange: 8–9, Sugar: 3–1, Fiesta: 2–4, Cotton: 1–2, Rose: 0–2)

Notre Dame: 14–15 (Cotton: 5–2, Orange: 2–3, Sugar: 2–2, Fiesta: 1–3, Rose: 1–0)

Ohio State: 18–22 (Rose: 6–7, Fiesta: 4–2, Orange: 1–0, Sugar: 1–2, Cotton: 1–0, BCS: 0–2)

Oklahoma: 24–17–1 (Orange: 12–8, Sugar: 4–2, Fiesta: 1–3, Rose: 1–0, Cotton: 1–0, BCS: 0–1)

Penn State: 26–13–2 (Fiesta: 4–0, Orange: 4–1, Cotton: 2–0–1, Rose: 1–2, Sugar: 1–3)

Southern California: 31–16 (Rose: 24–9, Orange: 2–0, Cotton: 1–0, Fiesta: 2–1)

Texas: 25–21–2 (Cotton: 11–10–1, Sugar: 1–2, Rose: 2–0, Orange: 2–0, Fiesta: 1–1)

Consensus USC All-Americans of the 1960s include Hal Bedsole, Mike Garrett, Ron Yary, Nate Shaw, O. J. Simpson, Tim Rossovich, Adrian Young, and Jim Gunn. The 1970s promised more of the same. The first game of the new decade certainly portended greater glory than ever before. Indeed, that glory was attained, but there were obstacles to overcome. On September 12, 1970, McKay's fully integrated Trojans traveled to Birmingham, Alabama, to take on Bear Bryant's segregated Crimson Tide. Fourteen years after C. R. Roberts's game at Texas, it *was time* for social progress in the South. The game was planned by Bryant and McKay as a demonstration of sorts in front of the 'Bama faithful. The idea was to convince them that, in order to continue competing with the likes of USC on a national level, they would need to *look* more like USC.

Bryant had already recruited some black high school stars. He wanted to pave a smooth transition for them into the world of Alabama football and the Southeastern Conference. Sam "Bam" Cunningham, a black sophomore fullback from Santa Barbara,

USC versus the Elite Ten (71–68–8 through 2008)

Alabama (2–5), Miami (1–1), Michigan (6–4), Nebraska (3–0–1), Notre Dame (33–42–5), Ohio State (12–9–1), Oklahoma (6–2–1), Penn State (5–4), Texas (4–1)

California, ran for 135 yards and two touchdowns to key Troy's resounding 42–21 win in front of a stunned, silent Legion Field crowd. According to legend, after the game Bryant brought Cunningham into the silent Alabama dressing room, perched him atop a stool, and announced, "Gentlemen, this here's what a football player looks like." It is a great story, preached as Holy Writ at USC for years, but is apparently an exaggeration. Exactly what happened is still hazy, but the full Cunningham-in-the-locker story is fairly mythologized. Alabama assistant coach Jerry Claiborne did say, "Sam Cunningham did more for civil rights in sixty minutes than Martin Luther King did in twenty years."

The die was cast. White fans were heard exclaiming after the game, "Bear better get hisself a few of them nigra players." He did. The result was dominance in the 1970s at least at or maybe above USC's level.

Joe Gibbs, an assistant coach on the 1970 team, became the Super Bowl-winning coach of the Washington Redskins and a member of the Pro Football Hall of Fame. Filled with confidence after the Alabama game, the 1970 Trojans then experienced one of the all-time letdowns. It lasted for two 6–4–1 years. The irony is that while Alabama seamlessly transitioned black players into their system, going undefeated in the 1971 regular season and beyond, the *Trojans* were beset by racial tension. The bone of contention centered around black quarterback Jimmy Jones and his white backup, "blue-chip" recruit Mike Rae.

In 1971 USC was 2–4. McKay's shine was virtually gone. The week of the game at 6–0 Notre Dame, little-known offensive lineman Dave Brown approached McKay. He asked if he could bring in his friends from the Fellowship of Christian Athletes for a "demonstration." The Catholic McKay, probably figuring nothing could hurt at that point, agreed.

"A lot of guys accepted Christ that day," said Brown, who became a teacher and football coach at San Clemente High School in Orange County, south of Los Angeles. Several of the players, including All-American tight end Charles "Tree" Young, became Christian ministers later in life.

Fortified by The Word, Southern California marched into Notre Dame Stadium, ending Irish national title hopes, 28–14. That USC group never lost again. They remained unbeaten throughout the rest of the 1971 season. The 1972 Trojans are generally considered to be the greatest single-season team in history. They were unbeaten, ranked number one from the first poll until the last, and never were challenged despite playing a difficult schedule. After dismantling Ohio State 42–17 in the 1973 Rose Bowl, Southern California won McKay's third national championship.

Before starting his ministry, Young was a first-round draft choice of Philadelphia, then played on two Super Bowl teams (1979 Los Angeles Rams, 1981 San Francisco 49ers). He was a key member of the world champion 49ers, blocking for and catching

USC's College Hall of Famers (35)

Players				
		Jon Arnett	1954–1956
John Baker	1929–1931	Mike Garrett	1963–1965
Brad Budde	1976–1979	Frank Gifford	1949–1951
Mike McKeever	1958–1960	Mort Kaer	1924–1926
Aaron Rosenberg	1931–1933	Erny Pinckert	1929–1931
Harry Smith	1937–1939	O. J. Simpson	1967–1968
Tay Brown	1930–1932	Charles White	1976–1979
John Ferraro	1943–1947	Ronnie Lott	1977–1980
Dan McMillan	1917, 1919	Richard Wood	1972–1974
Marvin Powell	1974–1976		
Ernie Smith	1930–1932	*Coaches*	
Ron Yary	1965–1967	Bob Blackman	1939–1941
Paul Cleary	1946–1947	Don Coryell	1960 (assistant)
Charles Young	1970–1972	Mel Hein	1951–1965
Lynn Swann	1971–1973	Howard Jones	1926–1940
Morley Drury	1925–1927	John McKay	1960–1975
Cotton Warburton	1932–1934	John Robinson	1976–1982,
Marcus Allen	1978–1981		1993–1997
Ricky Bell	1973–1976	Ken O'Brien	1998 (assistant)
Anthony Davis	1972–1974	Mike McGee	1983–1993 (A.D.)

passes from the great Joe Montana. Quarterback Mike Rae played for the 1976 world champion Oakland Raiders. The All-American Cunningham was a first-round draft pick of New England (1973) and ran behind the blocking of Alabama's John Hannah with the Patriots. Lynn Swann was Pittsburgh's first draft pick (1974) and the most valuable player of the 1976 Super Bowl, when the Steelers beat the Dallas Cowboys, 21–17. He played on four Super Bowl winners in Pittsburgh. After retiring, he became a network sideline analyst. A College and Pro Football Hall of Famer, Swann ran as the Republican candidate for governor of Pennsylvania in 2006.

All-American defensive back Charles Phillips starred for the 1976 world champion Oakland Raiders. Three-time All-American linebacker Richard "Batman" Wood played for Tampa Bay. All-American guard Bill Bain played in the 1980 Super Bowl for the Los Angeles Rams. The Cleveland Browns drafted All-American offensive tackle Pete Adams in the first round.

All-American lineman John Grant played in Super Bowl XII for Denver. All-American lineman Booker Brown played for the Chargers. All-American safety Artimus Parker played for Philadelphia and the Jets. All-American offensive tackle Steve Riley was Minnesota's first-round draft choice and played in the 1977 Super Bowl.

Sophomore All-American running back Anthony "A. D." Davis scored six touchdowns in USC's 45–23 win over Notre Dame. That game is considered one of the finest, if not the finest, single-day performances in college football annals. Other all-time great individual games include Red Grange's performance for Illinois against Michigan in 1924 and Davis's repeat effort against Notre Dame in 1974. Davis went on to play for the Rams.

Backups on the 1972 team included receiver J. K. McKay (Buccaneers) and quarterback Pat Haden, who led the Rams to the 1976 NFC championship game. Haden also was a Rhodes Scholar, studying political science at Oxford College in England. He graduated from Loyola University Law School and became a corporate attorney in Los Angeles. Haden also went on to a long career as a college football network broadcaster. Interestingly, he became the "voice of the Irish," handling NBC's games as part of their national arrangement with Notre Dame.

Overall, the 1972 national champions produced ten seniors drafted in 1973; nine in 1974; and fourteen in 1975. The Trojans of the early 1970s made up a large portion of the two teams that met, appropriately enough, at the Rose Bowl to play the 1977 Super Bowl. Key Oakland Raiders included former USC All-Americans John Vella, Clarence Davis, Willie Hall, and Charles Phillips, plus Skip Thomas. Former USC Outland Trophy recipient Ron Yary, the first pick of the 1968 draft by Minnesota, was a Hall of Fame player for the Vikings. His teammate on the 1976 Vikings was Steve Riley. The Oakland Trojans, er, Raiders beat the Vikings, 32–14.

USC held the top spot in the Associated Press rankings for a then-record seventeen straight weeks between 1972 and 1973. Their unbeaten streak from 1971 to 1973 reached twenty-three until Notre Dame knocked them off at South Bend, the first Irish victory in seven years.

In 1974, USC beat Notre Dame in a game that defied description. Trailing 24–0, the Trojans scored *55 points in seventeen minutes* to annihilate the Irish before a disbelieving Coliseum throng. Davis again spearheaded the victory, which ranks along with his 1972 effort versus the Irish among the all-time individual performances ever. It also proved to be the impetus behind USC's second national championship in three years. Woody Hayes and Ohio State were waiting for them in the Rose Bowl. This time the Buckeyes did not get rolled like roadkill under a Mack truck.

Elite Ten by the Numbers
Super Bowl appearances (through 2005)

1. Southern California   98 (through 2009)
2. Miami   80
3. Michigan   62
4. Nebraska   58
5. Alabama   55

Trailing 17–10 late in the fourth quarter, Southern California drove the length of the field, with Pat Haden hitting J. K. McKay in the corner of the end zone for a touchdown. Coach McKay went for two, just as he had in the 1967 Rose Bowl versus Purdue, and as Parseghian had chosen not to do when the national title was also on the line. With everything riding on one play, Haden rolled to the right hoping to run it in. Met by a phalanx of Ohio State tacklers, he found Shelton Diggs "flashing" across the middle for the 2-pointer, giving them victory and glory.

The 1974 team was one of the most exciting teams ever. Between 1964 and 1982, in a series of comebacks against Notre Dame; against Ohio State twice in the Rose Bowl; against Oklahoma, Stanford, UCLA, and others, the Trojans thrilled their fans with improbable wins against all odds. A great program was elevated to legendary status during these years.

In 1975, USC was unbeaten, looking for a repeat national title when John McKay announced he was leaving at season's end to take over the expansion Tampa Bay Buccaneers. It took all the air out of the USC tires. They finished 8–4. New coach John Robinson led USC to an 11–1 record in 1976, complete with season-ending *conquests* of UCLA, Notre Dame, and Michigan in the Rose Bowl. Only a season-opening loss to Missouri prevented that team from capturing the national championship, which went to Tony Dorsett and Pittsburgh.

In 1978, USC made a return trip to Birmingham's Legion Field. The success of the 1970 "tackling segregation" victory over Alabama was apparent by what did *not* happen. Nobody who was there remembers anybody even bringing up the fact that Alabama's team was fully integrated, as was the coaching staff, the student body, the crowd, and much of the press corps. Unlike the civil rights struggles of the 1960s, Sam Cunningham's game in 1970 seemed to have changed hearts and minds in the most peaceful way possible. On the field, the result was similar. Charles White ran for 199 yards, spurring Troy to an enormous 24–14 victory over the number one-ranked Crimson Tide.

After dispatching with UCLA, USC faced Notre Dame at the Coliseum in a game with major national championship implications. Quarterback Paul McDonald and White keyed Troy to a 24–6 lead in the second half. Irish quarterback Joe Montana put on a comeback display for the ages. He led Notre Dame all the way back late in the fourth quarter, but their 2-point conversion try failed, leaving the score 25–24 Irish. Less than two minutes remained.

McDonald maneuvered USC into field goal range. Frank Jordan's 37-yard kick won the game 27–25, ensuring his immortality. USC took care of Michigan 17–10 in the Rose Bowl to give John Robinson what turned out to be his only national championship.

The 1979 Trojans entered the season ranked number one amid talk they might be the finest team ever assembled. A 17–12 comeback win at Louisiana State helped Troy start off 5–0. On October 13 they led Stanford 21–0 at halftime. Most of the USC student body repaired to the beer aisles to talk it over with the opposite sex. The frantic sounds of Stanford coming back to tie it drew them back in. Momentum was lost, resulting in a 21–21 deadlock.

Otherwise unbeaten, USC blasted all opposition, including Notre Dame on the road, 42–23, and UCLA at the Coliseum, 49–14. Entering the bowls, USC was only halfway in control of their destiny. Ohio State waited for them at the Rose Bowl. New coach Earle Bruce (whose coaching staff included young Pete Carroll) had the Buckeyes at 11–0, ranked first.

Alabama was also unbeaten and untied. USC needed to beat Ohio State while Arkansas upset 'Bama. The Trojans did their part. Trailing 16–10 with just minutes left, Charlie White spearheaded a ground-oriented attack, resulting in the winning touchdown, 17–16. Alabama beat Arkansas in the Sugar Bowl to capture Bear Bryant's last national championship. White won the Heisman Trophy.

Between 1978 and 1980, USC featured a 28-game unbeaten streak. Consensus USC All-Americans of the second half of the 1970s and early 1980s include Ricky Bell, Gary Jeter, Dennis Thurman, Pat Howell, Brad Budde, Keith Van Horne, Roy Foster, Don Mosebar, Bruce Matthews, George Achica, and Tony Slaton. Bell was the first pick of the 1976 NFL Draft (McKay's Buccaneers). Other first-round selections include Marvin Powell (Jets, 1977), Jeter (Giants, 1977), Clay Matthews (Cleveland, 1978), Anthony Munoz (Cincinnati, 1980), Budde (Kansas City, 1980), White (Cleveland, 1980), Ronnie Lott (San Francisco, 1981), Van Horne (Chicago, 1981), Dennis Smith (Denver, 1981), Chip Banks (Cleveland, 1982), Marcus Allen (Raiders, 1982), Foster (Miami, 1982), Bruce Matthews (Houston, 1983), Joey Browner (Minnesota, 1983), and Don Mosebar (Raiders, 1983).

Offensive lineman Anthony Munoz became a Hall of Famer with the Cincinnati Bengals. He played in two Super Bowls. Bruce Matthews of the Houston Oilers and Tennessee Titans was inducted into the Pro Football Hall of Fame in 2007. Hall of Fame defensive back Ronnie Lott is generally considered the greatest player ever to play his position in the NFL. He spearheaded the 49ers to four Super Bowl victories in the 1980s.

Defensive back Dennis Thurman starred for the Dallas Cowboys, playing in the 1979 Super Bowl. Lineman Brad Budde was a standout for Kansas City. Offensive lineman

Elite Ten by the Numbers
Pro Football Hall of Fame

Southern California	14 (11 players, 3 coaches through 2009)
Notre Dame	9
Michigan	8
Alabama	7
Ohio State	6
Penn State	5
Miami	3
Texas	3
Nebraska	3

Keith Van Horne was a mainstay of the 1985 world champion Bears. Don Mosebar was a key member of the Los Angeles Raiders, who beat Washington in the 1984 Super Bowl.

Vince Evans became a starting quarterback in Chicago and with the Los Angeles Raiders. Mosi Tatupu was a standout running back in New England. Rich Dimler played for Cleveland and Green Bay. Dennis Johnson enjoyed success in Minnesota. Sean Salisbury was a "bust" at USC but became a creditable quarterback with the Vikings before embarking on a successful career as an ESPN pro football analyst. Defensive back Jeff Fisher became the longtime head coach of the Tennessee Titans. All-American linebacker Jack Del Rio starred for the Saints, Chiefs, Cowboys, and Vikings before becoming the head coach of the Jacksonville Jaguars.

In 1981, running back Marcus Allen set the NCAA record with 2,427 yards (219 per game). It earned him USC's fourth Heisman Trophy. Allen went on to be the most valuable player of the Raiders' 38–9 1984 Super Bowl triumph over Washington; a perennial All-Pro, he eventually was elected into the Pro Football Hall of Fame.

In 1982, after USC beat Notre Dame for the fifth consecutive time, the all-time record between the two schools was virtually even. The Irish had beaten the Trojans only twice in sixteen years. In that time, Notre Dame won two national championships and zero Heisman Trophies. In the previous two decades, USC won five national championships and four Heisman Trophies. The twenty-year run under coaches John McKay and John Robinson stands out as not just the most dominant of any collegiate dynasty, but the most exciting and momentous by far. World-shaking regular season victories over Notre Dame, UCLA, Alabama, and Texas as well as Rose Bowl triumphs over Wisconsin, Michigan, and Ohio State had elevated Troy to myth status.

"It was a Camelot time at USC," was John Robinson's description of the era.

In the early-evening gloaming of November 27, 1982, the historically conscious USC fan, leaving the Coliseum after Southern California's 17–13 comeback win over Notre Dame, could not be blamed if he looked at the events of these two decades, especially the recent six-year run of John Robinson, and reached a few "conclusions." Troy had not missed a beat after McKay's departure. In comparing the program to Notre Dame, Alabama, Oklahoma, Nebraska—all the other giants of the college game—he concluded that maybe, just maybe, USC had ascended to a place where they could rightfully call themselves "college football's all-time greatest tradition."

Indeed, if this moment came, it also came to pass in what rocker Bruce Springsteen called "the twinkle of a young girl's eye." The "Glory Days" ended with a resounding thud when the NCAA leveled penalties on USC for ticket scalping. Robinson left for the Los Angeles Rams, bringing legendary assistant coach Marv Goux with him. The Trojans *lost to Notre Dame every single season from 1983 to 1993*! Oh, how the mighty had fallen,

Did You Know . . .

That Marcus Allen of Southern California set the NCAA record for single-season rushing with 2,427 yards in 1981, the year he was USC's fourth Heisman Trophy winner?

USC Coaches/Alumni Who Were Also Pro Football Coaches

Pete Carroll, John McKay, John Robinson (head coaches/USC-pro head coaches); Paul Hackett (head coach/USC-pro assistant); Jack Del Rio, Jim Fassel, Jeff Fisher, Mike Holmgren (players/USC-pro head coaches); Don Coryell, Norv Turner, Al Davis, Wayne Fontes, Joe Gibbs, Steve Mariucci, Dave Wannstedt, Lane Kiffin (assistant coaches/USC-pro head coaches); Jerry Attaway, Norm Chow, Mel Hein, Steve Sarkisian (assistant coaches/USC-pro assistants)

or as it says in the Bible of empires from the Babylonians, the Persians, the Greeks, the Romans to the . . . Trojans, "Pride goeth before the fall."

Like the 1940s and 1950s, USC football in the 1980s and 1990s was competitive, entertaining, and successful. It just did not reach the level of Miami, Oklahoma, Penn State, Notre Dame, Florida State, Nebraska, or the other programs ascending to college football's mountaintop over those years. USC won Rose Bowls in 1985, 1990, and 1996. They beat Texas Tech 55-14 in the 1995 Cotton Bowl. After finally ending the nightmare run against Notre Dame, they even managed to beat the Irish three straight years (1997-1999). In 1988, USC was unbeaten when they played UCLA at the Rose Bowl in a regular season game (reminiscent of the 1967 "city game") that promised to decide the Rose Bowl invite and, it was felt at the time, the Heisman Trophy and national championship. Trojan quarterback Rodney Peete outplayed Bruin quarterback Troy Aikman, apparently securing the Heisman for himself. But Notre Dame destroyed USC 27-10, ending Trojan national-title hopes (Lou Holtz's Irish won it) and Peete's Heisman campaign. He lost to Oklahoma State's Barry Sanders. It was the last gasp of a dying "empire," at least until Pete Carroll came along.

Nobody had an inkling of it in 1989, however. Succeeding Peete in that season was freshman quarterback Todd Marinovich. Marinovich was, quite simply, the most heralded high school football player who ever lived. He was to be a new "Trojan Moses," leading USC to the promised land. Marinovich's father, Marv, was the captain of USC's 1962 national championship team before playing for the Oakland Raiders. Marv's brother coached Bishop Amat High School in La Puente, California, the nation's best program in the 1960s. Out of Bishop Amat had come the likes of Pat Haden, J. K. Haden, Paul McDonald, and UCLA All-American John Sciarra.

Marv Marinovich married Craig Fertig's sister. Their son was Todd. He was raised by Marv to be, as the press dubbed him, Robo QB (from a film of the time, *Robo Cop*). He was groomed for greatness since the cradle. Despite being the most recruited player in history, young Marinovich's only choices were USC, SC, Southern California, or Southern Cal, take your pick.

Todd was a Freshman All-American in 1989, when he lived up to the promise by leading Troy to a 17-10 victory over Michigan in the Rose Bowl. In 1990 national championship fever swept through Heritage Hall. Marinovich led Southern California to a resounding 34-16 victory over Syracuse in the Kickoff Classic, played at Giants Stadium in

East Rutherford, New Jersey. There was also a dramatic 45–42 triumph over UCLA at the Rose Bowl. But All-American linebacker Junior Seau became one of the first players to take advantage of new rules, leaving school prior to his senior year. USC stumbled amid arguments between the hotshot quarterback and coach Larry Smith, who increasingly seemed to be in over his head. Marinovich left school early. Al Davis made him the Raiders' first pick of the 1991 draft. He failed in the NFL, ending up a repeat drug offender and symbol of lost potential. An eight-year losing streak to UCLA commenced after that year. Marinovich set USC back ten years, literally and figuratively. That was the time between his last season and the hiring of Pete Carroll in 2000.

Despite their worst two decades on the field, USC produced talent. Consensus All-Americans include Jeff Bregel, Dave Cadigan, Tim Ryan, and Johnnie Morton. Ricky Ervins went on to star for the Washington Redskins; Jason Sehorn with the New York Giants; Derrick Deese in San Francisco. Rob Johnson and Chad Morton were solid NFL players.

Mark Carrier won the 1989 Jim Thorpe Award. Tim McDonald was a star with the 49ers, credited with the famed *Jerry Maguire* saying, "Show me the money!" Chris Claiborne won the 1998 Butkus Award.

All-American wide receiver Keyshawn Johnson was the first pick of the 1996 draft by the Jets and became an NFL star. All-American lineman Tony Boselli, the second pick of the 1995 draft by Jacksonville, was a great pro player, too. Willie McGinest spearheaded New England's Super Bowl champions of the 2000s.

USC featured the most first-round draft picks of any college in the 1980s; the third-highest number of first-round picks in the 1990s. Year after year, USC produced the most players on pro rosters, the most Super Bowl players, and the most players on winning Super Bowl teams. In 1999, *SPORT* magazine did a study determining that USC had no fewer than fourteen players represented in the Pro Bowl (1990s).

The pattern was developed. USC's five first-round draft picks in 1968 had set the record for the most of any college. When Carson Palmer went number one in 2003, it marked the fifth time a Trojan had been chosen first (tied with Notre Dame). USC had three of the most highly drafted classes in history (1953, fifteen; 1975 and 1977, fourteen each). While records are somewhat sketchy, USC and Notre Dame easily had the most players drafted and the most players in the National Football League. Through the 2009 draft, USC's seventy-four first-round picks were the most of any school. Among the leaders in Super Bowl MVPs:

Elite Ten by the Numbers
Super Bowl-winning team (through 2005)

1. Southern California 45
2. Notre Dame 38
3. Penn State 35

USC's "Teammate Heismans"

1979	Charles White
1981	Marcus Allen
2002	Carson Palmer
2004	Matt Leinart
2004	Matt Leinart
2005	Reggie Bush

USC with two (Lynn Swann of the Steelers in 1976, Marcus Allen of the Raiders in 1984). NFL Players of the Year: two (O. J. Simpson of the Bills in 1973 and Marcus Allen of the Raiders, 1985). Pro Football Hall of Famers: Bruce Matthews became USC's fourteenth (the most of any school) in 2007.

That said, the "glittering statues that marked the historical lineage of Troy were beginning to fade," as was stated in *The History of USC Football* DVD (2005). Had the game passed them by? In the early 1990s, Dr. Steven Sample took over as USC's president. He hired Nobel Prize-winning faculty. Admissions standards were raised. By 2000, it was accepted as an article of faith among Trojan alumni that a great academic institution, which the University of Southern California had become, could not coincide with a great football program. A winning team, a solid program, maybe ranked in the Top 25 with a trip to the Rose Bowl here and there, but a dynasty? No. Whatever it was that Nebraska, Florida State, Miami, Oklahoma, and schools like that could do to make themselves dominant on the gridiron would no longer be expected of a school like USC.

In 2000, the *Time/Princeton Review College Guide* rated USC as College of the Year. The 2001 *Newsweek/Kaplan College Guide* named it one of America's nine "hottest schools." Its dental school was world class. Its film school was unsurpassed, its graduates now dominating nearby Hollywood. Federal research money poured in, its endowment coffers filling to the brim. Only "straight A" students need apply for admission. The alumni had accepted the fact that great academics did not mix with great athletics. They were okay with that.

After going 5–7 in 2000, coach Paul Hackett was fired. Athletic director Mike Garrett, whose own job hung precariously in the balance, went after the hot coaches of that year: Dennis Erickson, Mike Bellotti, and Mike Riley. The greatest job in college sports, or so it once seemed to be, was turned down by all of them. Then Pete Carroll walked into Garrett's office. The New England Patriots had fired Carroll after the 1999 season. The serendipity was almost too much to bear, at least in retrospect.

Carroll grew up in California. As a teenager at Redwood High School, he had attended the Diamond B Football Camp, where he slept in a cabin not far from where Bear Bryant and John McKay are rumored to have planned the 1970 USC-Alabama game, and therefore the full integration of Southern football. They were there as "guest coaches" at the camp, organized by Carroll's coach at Redwood, Bob Troppmann.

"I became a USC fan when Sam 'Bam' Cunningham integrated the South," Carroll told a sports reporter as far back as the 1980s.

Carroll, a Trojan fan, was in the Coliseum stands the day Jimmy Jones hit Sam Dickerson with a last-minute winning touchdown pass to beat UCLA 14–12 in 1969. He was an all-conference college player but not a professional. Carroll entered coaching and the nomadic life that goes with it. For twenty-five years Carroll coached from one end of America to another. Some jobs and cities were better than others. There were five years in New York, one of those as head coach of the Jets; two years in San Francisco; three in Boston where he was head coach of the Patriots. He took the team to the play-offs but not the Super Bowl.

In 2000, for the first time in his entire adult life, Carroll was not coaching football someplace. He and his wife, Glena, chose to move to Los Angeles. Glena had grown up in the South Bay area of Redondo and Palos Verdes Estates. Her father had graduated from USC. Carroll's daughter was a volleyball player at USC.

With time on his hands, Carroll was often on the USC campus, visiting with his daughter and watching her volleyball games. He often dropped in on the coaches and athletic staff at Heritage Hall—people he knew from his many years in football. Then the job opened up. Carroll let Garrett know he wanted it, but others were courted first. Carroll watched from the sideline while those deemed more attractive than he passed on the opportunity. Finally, Garrett went with Carroll. The enthusiasm level from USC alumni was none too great. No matter.

"Just days before Christmas in the year 2000," stated *The History of USC Football* DVD, "USC found its savior." Indeed, what Carroll did over the next years was nothing less than a football resurrection.

The program he took over that December day had slipped. If in fact they had "caught" Notre Dame at the end of the 1982 season, that short-lived stay was long forgotten. Little by little, USC's historical edge had begun to fade away. In 1985, a disappointing USC team met a disappointing Alabama team in an otherwise meaningless Aloha Bowl. However, when 'Bama polished off Troy 24–3, it had the effect of pushing the Crimson Tide over the Trojans for most all-time bowl victories, a record USC had held since its first Rose Bowl win in 1923.

In 1992, Alabama won the national championship, very likely passing USC into second place behind Notre Dame as the greatest tradition. In the 1990s, as USC lost year after year to Notre Dame and UCLA, the cracks in their "historical lineage" widened. When the New Millennium began on January 1, 2000, USC was not mentioned among the powers that made up the collegiate landscape. Notre Dame, by virtue of their great record, still clung to their all-time number one spot, but they too were struggling to maintain equal footing with the upstarts from Virginia Tech; Bobby Bowden's Florida State dynasty; juggernauts at Nebraska; and a Miami program that more resembled the National Football League than college ball.

Elite Ten by the Numbers

Pro football draft choices (through 2009 draft)

1.	Southern California	485 (457 NFL, 28 AFL)
2.	Notre Dame	464
3.	Oklahoma	334
4.	Alabama	304
5.	Ohio State	327
6.	Miami	291

Trojans on the Run

Year	Record	Run
1920	6–0	6–0 (1920)
1921	10–1	16–1 (1920–21)
1922	10–1	26–2 (1920–22)
1923	6–2	32–4 (1920–23)
1924	9–2	41–6 (1920–24)
1925	11–2	53–8 (1920–25)
		52–8 (1920–25) **60 games**
1926	8–2	61–10 (1920–26)
		59–11 (1920–26) **70 games**
1927	8–1–1 F/1–0	68–11–1 (1920–27)
		67–12–1 (1920–27) **80 games**
		1–0 (1927)
1928	9–0–1	77–11–1 (1920–28)
		76–12–2 (1920–28) **90 games**
		17–1–2 (1927–28)
		10–0–1 (1927–28)
1929	10–2 F/5–0	88–13–2 **(decade: 1920s)**
		85–13–2 (1920–29) **100 games**
		27–3–2 (1927–29)
		20–2–1 (1927–29)
1930	8–2	96–15–2 (1920–30)
		94–14–2 (1920–30) **110 games**
		35–5–2 (1927–30)
		28–4–1 (1927–30)
1931	10–1 F/10–0	107–16–2 (1920–31)
		113–15–2 (1920–31) **120 games**
		45–6–2 (1927–31)
		38–7–2 (1927–31)
		10–0 (1931)
1932	10–0	117–16–2 (1920–32)
		112–16–2 (1920–32) **130 games**
		55–6–2 (1927–32)
		48–7–2 (1927–32)
		20–0 (1931–32) **20 games**
1933	10–1–1 S/5–0, F/6–0–1	127–17–3 (1920–33) 147
		121–17–2 1920–33 **140 games**
		65–7–3 (1927–32)
		58–8–3 (1927–32)
		20–0 (1927–32) **20 games**
		25–0 (1931–33)
		27–0–1 (1931–33)

1934	4–6–1 S/3–0	131–23–4 (1920–34)
		130–17–3 (1920–34) **150 games**
		67–7–3 (1927–34)
		60–87–3 (1927–34)
1967	10–1	10–1 (1967)
1968	9–1–1	19–2–1 (1967–68)
1969	10–0–1	29–2–1 (1967–69)
1970	6–4–1 S/1–0, 3–0–1	30–2–1 (1967–70)
		33–2–2 (1967–70)
1971	6–4–1 F/4–0–1, 0–0–1	6–4–1 (1971)
		4–0–1 (1971)
		0–0–1 (1971)
1972	12–0	16–0–1 (1971–72)
		12–0 (1972)
1973	9–2–1 S/1–0, 5–0–1	21–2–1 (1972–73)
		21–0–2 (1971–73)
		13–0 (1972–73)
1974	10–1–1	31–3–2 (1972–74)
1975	8–4 S/7–0	39–7–2 (1972–74)
		38–3–2 (1972–74)
1976	11–1 F/11–0	50–8–2 (1972–76) **60 games**
		11–1 (1976)
		11–0 (1976)
1977	8–4	58–12–2 (1972–77)
		56–12–2 (1972–77) **70 games**
		19–5 (1976–77)
		19–4 (1976–77)
1978	12–1 F/8–0	70–12–2 (1972–77)
		66–12–2 (1972–77) **80 games**
		31–6 (1976–78)
		31–5 (1976–78)
		8–0 (1978)
1979	11–0–1	81–12–3 (1972–77)
		85–12–3 (1971–79) **100 games**
		75–12–3 (1972–77) **90 games**
		42–6–1 (1978–79)
		42–5–1 (1976–78)
		19–0–1 (1978–79)
1980	8–2–1 S/5–0, 7–0–1	89–14–4 (1972–80)
		88–12–4 (1972–80) **100 games**
		93–14–5 (1971–80)
		92–12–5 (1971–80) **100 games**
		24–0–1 (1978–80)
		26–0–2 (1978–80)

(*continues*)

Trojans on the Run (*continued*)

Year	Record	Run
2001	6–6 F/4–1	6–6 (2001)
		4–1 (2001)
2002	11–2 F/8–0	17–8 (2001–02)
		15–3 (2001–02)
		8–0 (2002)
		11–2 (2002)
2003	12–1 F/9–0	29–9 (2001–03)
		27–4 (2001–03)
		20–1 (2001–03)
		23–3 (2002–03)
		9–0 (2003)
2004	13–0	42–9 (2001–04)
		40–4 (2001–04)
		33–1 (2002–04)
		29–1 (2002–04) **30 games**
		36–3 (2002–03)
		29–1 (2002–03) **30 games**
		20–0 (2003–04) **20 games**
		22–0 (2003–04)
2005	12–1 S/12–0	54–10 (2001–05)
		54–9 (2001–05)
		50–10 (2001–05) **60 games**
		52–5 (2001–05)
		52–4 (2001–05)
		46–4 (2001–05) **50 games**
		35–2 (2002–05)
		29–1 (2002–05) **30 games**
		45–1 (2002–05)
		45–2 (2002–05)
		48–2 (2002–05) **50 games**
		48–3 (2002–05)
		47–3 (2002–05) **50 games**
		30–0 (2002–05) **30 games**
		34–0 (2003–06)
		34–1 (2003–06)
2006	11–2 S/6–0, 10–1	65–12 (2001–06)
		60–10 (2001–06) **70 games**
		64–11 (2001–05)
		63–7 (2001–06) **70 games**

		58–5 (2001–06)
		55–5 (2001–06) **60 games**
		62–6 (2001–06)
		46–4 (2002–06) **50 games**
		38–2 (2002–06) **50 games**
		41–2 (2002–06)
		45–2 (2002–06)
		56–4 (2002–06) **60 games**
		51–2 (2002–06)
		48–2 (2002–06) **50 games**
		55–3 (2002–06)
		58–5 (2002–06)
		55–5 (2002–06) **50 games**
		54–3 (2002–06)
		48–2 (2002–03) **50 games**
		58–4 (2002–06)
		56–4 (2002–06) **60 games**
2007	11-2 S/6-0, F/1-0	76-14 (2001-07) **90 games**
		71-12 (2001-07)
2008	12-1 S/2-0, F/9-0	88-15 (2001-08)
		85-15 (2001-08) **100 games**
		86-9 (2001-08)
		82-8 (2002-08)

S/start season; F/finish season

In 2000, the crack widened further at USC. While Hackett's team struggled to a losing record without a bowl invite, Oklahoma—a program that like USC had seen hard times—made their big comeback. When the Sooners captured the national championship, they could make a good argument that they too had passed poor old USC into third place in the historical pantheon. The Trojans could only hope to still call themselves an all-time top-five program. How could they, with a straight face, still claim a greater tradition than Nebraska, or even Miami and Florida State? These guys were the New Millennium, champions of the BCS era, winners of a long Darwinian struggle for supremacy in one of the most competitive arenas in American society. USC could offer only faded video of Anthony Davis in 1974, featuring crowd shots of fans with bad hair and flared pants.

But Hackett, to his credit, did not leave the cupboard bare. Quarterback Carson Palmer, the top high school recruit of 1997, had disappointed but had two more years of eligibility. Defensive back Troy Polamalu was a force. In 2001 under Carroll, USC started 2-5. They traveled to Arizona for a meaningless game in the excessive desert heat. Nobody cared. Trailing late, Kris Richard picked off a Wildcat pass, returning it for a touchdown to give USC the 41-34 victory. Carroll calls that the "turning point." They managed to shut out UCLA 27–0, and by the reduced standards of USC football at that time, the invite to the Las Vegas Bowl did not seem bad.

In 2002, USC rallied late but came up short at Kansas State, 27–20. Then they lost in overtime at Washington State when an extra point was missed. After that, USC was as dominant in the final eight games of the season as Carroll's subsequent teams. Their 2002 schedule was the toughest in the nation and one of the most competitive of all time. They annihilated UCLA 52–21 in one of the most impressive performances imaginable, then exploded past Notre Dame, 44–13. The co-Pacific-10 champions destroyed Iowa in the Orange Bowl to finish 11–2. Palmer won the Heisman Trophy. They were again a dominant program; could they be number one?

In 2003, the Trojans were just that when they went 12–1. They opened at Auburn, ranked number one in *Sports Illustrated*'s preseason poll. USC won 23–0. They destroyed Notre Dame at South Bend 45–14 and UCLA at the Coliseum 47–22. After polishing off Oregon State 52–28 while Oklahoma lost to Kansas State 35–7 in the Big 12 championship game, USC ascended to the top of all the polls. They defeated Michigan 28–14 in the Rose Bowl to capture their first national championship in twenty-five years.

Consensus All-Americans included wide receiver Mike Williams, offensive lineman Jacob Rogers, and defensive lineman Kenechi Udeze. Sophomore All-American quarterback Matt Leinart, the MVP of the Rose Bowl, led the team. Freshman running backs Reggie Bush and LenDale White were sensational. It was a young squad that promised to be the best in the nation not just for one more year, but for two more years at the least. Carroll got on a recruiting roll, bringing in classes that would be ranked number one in the nation by at least one service in 2003, 2004, 2005, 2006, and 2007.

In 2004, USC entered the season ranked number one by every preseason magazine as well as by the Associated Press. Leinart was the prohibitive Heisman favorite. The talk began.

Is this the greatest team of all time?

As the season played out, the answer to that question came back: *Probably not.* Number two, or three, or top five? Very likely. USC generally dominated but was pushed several times, unlike the 1972 Trojans who rolled through their entire schedule without a test. The 1995 Nebraska Cornhuskers did the same thing. Other great teams, such as Army (1945), Notre Dame (1947), Michigan (1948), and even the 1932 USC national champions won by more impressive margins.

That said, this was a new era—of parity, of the BCS, of big-time pressure. Notre Dame came to town but were no match for Leinart, who passed for more than 400 yards in the 41–10 drubbing. After beating UCLA at the Rose Bowl, Leinart won the Heisman in a New York ceremony featuring his teammate, Reggie Bush; Bush's teammate from Helix High School near San Diego, Alex Smith; and two players Troy

Elite Ten by the Numbers

National championships (1970–2008)

1. Southern California		5
2. Nebraska		5
3. Miami		5
4. Alabama		4
5. Oklahoma		4
6. Notre Dame		3

would face in the BCS Orange Bowl, quarterback Jason Smith and running back Adrian Peterson.

The Orange Bowl was the most hyped college game ever played up until that time. Aside from featuring four of the top five Heisman finalists (Smith was the NFL's number one draft pick when Leinart opted to return in 2005), the game matched teams that had been ranked one and two since the preseason. It was USC's shot at a repeat title. These were two of the most storied traditions.

When it was over, only one team was left standing. Leinart threw three touchdown passes and caught another in USC's 55–19 pounding of OU. ESPN's Lee Corso called it the finest game any college team had ever played. It certainly was up there with Nebraska's 62–24 pounding of Florida in the 1996 Fiesta Bowl, not to mention USC's 42–17 1973 Rose Bowl triumph over Ohio State, or that memorable 55–24 win over Notre Dame in 1974.

Leinart, the game's most valuable player, did something that Heisman winners rarely do: live up to their billing in a national championship bowl game. In so doing, he put himself in discussion for the "best single-season player ever" and, if he could do it again in 2005, the "best college player of all time."

Mel Kiper Jr. stated that Leinart would be the number one pick in the 2005 NFL Draft, but he decided to return for his senior year. The San Francisco 49ers chose Alex Smith first. There is virtually no possibility Smith would have been picked ahead of Leinart had the USC quarterback made himself eligible.

Shaun Cody and Matt Grootegoed were consensus All-Americans. Mike Williams (forced to sit out 2004 because he had tried to declare early) and Mike Patterson were both selected in the first round of the draft. Lofa Tatupu chose to leave school early. He immediately led the Seattle Seahawks, whose coach Mike Holmgren had been a backup USC quarterback, to the Super Bowl. They lost to Pittsburgh, led by Troy Polamalu.

Elite Ten by the Numbers

Bowl Championship Series national championships (1998–2008)

1. Southern California: 1, 2004 (1–1 in BCS championship games)
1. Miami: 1, 2001 (1–1 in BCS championship games)
3. Texas: 1, 2005 (1–0 in BCS championship games)
4. Ohio State: 1, 2002 (1–2 in BCS championship games)
4. Oklahoma: 1, 2000 (1–3 in BCS championship games)
6. Nebraska: 0 (0–1 in BCS championship games)
7. Alabama: 0
8. Michigan: 0
9. Notre Dame: 0
10. Penn State: 0

Elite Ten by the Numbers
Playboy Preseason All-Americans (through 2005)

1. Southern California	65 (2 Coach of Year, 1 Scholar-Athlete)
2. Michigan	46
3. Texas	45
4. Notre Dame	40 (1 Coach of Year)
5. Nebraska	33 (2 Coach of Year, 1 Scholar-Athlete)
6. Oklahoma	32 (2 Coach of Year)

Other stars included Tom Malone, LenDale White, Dwayne Jarrett, Taitusi Lutui, Darnell Bing, and Sam Baker.

In 2005, all bets were off. In the entire history of college athletics, no school ever achieved the kind of attention, notoriety, and celebrity status of Trojan football. It was all part of a growing trend extending beyond University Park. Once the sports capital of the world, Los Angeles had fallen on hard times in the 1980s and 1990s. The city's shine had tarnished in other ways, too. USC and UCLA once dominated California and Stanford, but a sense of parity had been achieved in the Pacific 10. The Dodgers no longer held the hammer over the Giants. The San Francisco 49ers had become a dynasty while the Los Angeles Rams had moved to St. Louis. The Los Angeles Raiders moved back to Oakland. The Lakers fell on hard times. Southern California was once a political juggernaut, producing presidents Richard Nixon and Ronald Reagan. In 1992's "year of the woman" elections, two liberal Jewish Democrats, Dianne Feinstein and Barbara Boxer of San Francisco, were elected to the U.S. Senate.

In 1991, video captured white LAPD officers beating black motorist Rodney King. In 1992, responding to their acquittal by a white jury in suburban Simi Valley, L.A.'s black neighborhoods exploded in riot. In 1994, an earthquake rocked the Los Angeles area. USC legend O. J. Simpson stood trial for murdering his wife. His acquittal created further racial divisions. A USC football player was grazed by a bullet during practice. Orange County declared bankruptcy. In the 1990s, the only championship won by a Los Angeles team was UCLA's 1995 NCAA basketball title. An accounting scandal cost coach Jim Harrick his job shortly thereafter.

But the city began a comeback in the late 1990s. After the fall of the USSR and America's victory in the Cold War, the defense industry had cut back drastically. This had an enormous effect on the Los Angeles economy, since much of the aerospace industry is centered along a corridor of the 405 Freeway between Los Angeles Airport and the Port of Long Beach. But many of these smart technological types "landed on their feet," fueling the Internet boom. Eventually, the "dot-bomb" disaster burst the techno-bubble, but in the wake of 9/11 a settled economy took shape, replacing the speculative nature of the 1990s stock market.

New regulations in industry, particularly auto emissions, created drastically cleaner air in the L.A. Basin. Fans in the 1970s could barely see the other side of the Coliseum. By the late 1990s, sitting high atop the stadium even in September, a fan could now see the Pacific Ocean and Palos Verdes Peninsula to the west; the Santa Monica Mountains, the Hollywood sign and Beverly Hills, the downtown skyline, and in the winter after rains, the snow-capped San Gabriel Mountain range to the east.

L.A. mayor Richard Riordan led a major gentrification project of downtown Los Angeles. New skyscrapers were built. Streets were cleaned up, neighborhoods revitalized, crime reduced. All of these events manifested themselves in a sports comeback. First, Staples Center was built in downtown L.A. The Lakers immediately won three consecutive NBA championships (2000–2002). The Angels captured the 2002 World Series.

The building of Staples had a big effect on USC. The overall work on the two-mile corridor between Staples and the USC campus resulted in a huge cleanup and building project, improving USC's surroundings. This helped to create a much more exciting football environment at the Coliseum, as well as the building of a gleaming on-campus basketball arena, the Galen Center.

Streaking Trojans in the Pete Carroll Era

15–3 (2001–02)	64–11 (2001–05)
27–4 (2001–03)	63–7 (2001–06) **70 games**
20–1 (2001–03)	58–5 (2001–06)
23–3 (2002–03)	55–5 (2001–06) **60 games**
40–4 (2001–04)	62–6 (2001–06)
33–1 (2002–04)	46–4 (2002–06) **50 games**
29–1 (2002–04) **30 games**	38–2 (2002–06) **50 games**
36–3 (2002–03)	41–2 (2002–06)
29–1 (2002–03) **30 games**	45–2 (2002–06)
22–0 (2003–04)	56–4 (2002–06) **60 games**
54–9 (2001–05)	51–2 (2002–06)
50–10 (2001–05) **60 games**	48–2 (2002–06) **50 games**
52–5 (2001–05)	55–3 (2002–06)
52–4 (2001–05)	58–5 (2002–06)
46–4 (2001–05) **50 games**	55–5 (2002–06) **50 games**
35–2 (2002–05)	54–3 (2002–06)
29–1 (2002–05) **30 games**	48–2 (2002–03) **50 games**
45–1 (2002–05)	58–4 (2002–06)
45–2 (2002–05)	56–4 (2002–06) **50 games**
48–2 (2002–05) **50 games**	71–12 (2001–07)
48–3 (2002–05)	76–14 (2001–07) **90 games**
47–3 (2002–05) **50 games**	88–15 (2001–08)
34–0 (2003–06)	85–15 (2001–08) **100 games**
34–1 (2003–06)	86–9 (2001–08)
65–12 (2001–06)	82–8 (2002–08) **90 games**
60–10 (2001–06) **70 games**	

By 2005, fans attending USC games at the Coliseum were stunned by what they saw. First, without an NFL team, USC had become "L.A.'s pro football franchise." Ninety thousand fans sold out the Coliseum for every game. The stadium was improved, modernized with a state-of-the-art scoreboard and sound system. The campus became a true celebration prior to games. Everything associated with USC seemed touched by gold.

Its marquee names were now bigger than Hollywood celebrities. Sportstalk radio featured USC football night and day. Pete Carroll was referred to as the "prince of the city." Matt Leinart was seen squiring hot starlets about town, his presence at parties and trendy clubs as requested as any actor.

Amid all of this hoopla, USC entered the 2005 campaign looking to do things nobody had ever done. Everybody ranked them number one. They were out to win a first-ever third straight AP national championship (oddly, USC was prohibited from marketing the appropriately named term "Three-*Pete*" because Lakers coach Pat Riley had actually *copyrighted* the term years earlier). The stars were aligned, all in their favor. The BCS national championship game was to be held at their longtime stomping grounds, the Rose Bowl. The Heisman seemed to be a fait accompli to be won either by Leinart or Reggie Bush, the greatest teammate combination since Army's Mr. Inside and Mr. Outside, Doc Blanchard and Glenn Davis.

The season seemed to play out according to form. The USC defense showed some vulnerability, but the offense was declared the best in history. Nobody really paid much attention to any flaws since USC averaged 50 points per game. Leinart was at least as good as he had been in his junior year, but Reggie Bush led the nation in all-purpose yards, ensuring the Heisman Trophy in his junior year. USC became just the second team ever to have back-to-back Heisman winners. The only other had been the aforementioned Army powerhouse of 1945–1946. The running back combination of Bush and White, known as "thunder and lightning," was as lethal as any the game had ever seen.

USC repeated the act of 2004, ranked number one in every poll from the preseason through the end of the regular season, thus setting an all-time record of thirty-three straight weeks at the top of the Associated Press rankings. They ran their winning streak to 34 games, tied for the second longest in the history of modern football (behind only Oklahoma's 47-game streak of 1953–1957). At South Bend, the Trojans rallied in one of the most intense environments imaginable to beat the Irish 34–31 in a game for the ages. Against Fresno State, Bush demonstrated moves reminiscent of O. J. Simpson in a Heisman-guarantee 50–42 USC win. He accumulated well over 200 first-half yards alone in USC's insane pounding of UCLA, 66–19.

The Heisman ceremony featured the victorious Bush winning over teammate Matt Leinart and Texas quarterback Vince Young. This set up a Rose Bowl showdown unlike anything yet seen. It overshadowed the hype of the previous year's Orange Bowl encounter. Aside from the Heisman matchups, the game featured four players who would be

The Four Horsemen of Southern California

Outlined against a blue, gray October sky the Four Horsemen rode again. In dramatic lore they are known as famine, pestilence, destruction and death. These are only aliases. Once named Stuhldreher, Miller, Crowley and Layden, the gladiators of the New Millennium are men of youth, color and American diversity. Their real names are: Leinart, Bush, Jarrett and White. These new Four Horsemen of Southern California came to the land of destiny riding their famed white steed Traveler, that dreaded Coliseum sight of Irish past. They relegated the old Notre Dame ghosts to their place and time, a time when the only color was white, myths were protected, lies told as Truths. They formed the crest of the South Bend cyclone before which another Fighting Irish team was swept over the precipice at Notre Dame Stadium on the afternoon of Saturday, October 15, 2005. 80,795 spectators peered down upon the bewildering panorama spread out upon the green plain below.

—Excerpted from *The USC Trojans: College Football's All-Time Greatest Dynasty* by Steven Travers, describing USC's 2005 victory over Notre Dame

chosen among the first ten picks of the 2006 draft: Bush (Saints), Leinart (Cardinals), Young (Titans), and his teammate Michael Huff (Raiders). It was again a game between two unbeatens averaging more than 50 points a game, who had held the number one and two spots since the preseason, which is completely rare. Its Rose Bowl location added to the sense of history, pomp, and circumstance. If that was not enough, it was the final game announced by the venerable Keith Jackson.

If a greater college football game has ever been played, I do not know of it. Considering first the pressure and expectations, then the performance of its stars—Leinart was spectacular, Young may have played the best game of all time—and the dramatic last-second comeback nature of Texas's 41–38 victory, the game must rank above all others. This includes 1967 USC-UCLA, 1971 Nebraska-Oklahoma, 1969 Texas-Arkansas, 1963 USC-Wisconsin, 1931 USC-Notre Dame, 1966 Notre Dame-Michigan State, and any other "Game of the Century" ever played.

Elite Ten by the Numbers

Heisman Trophy winners (through 2008)

1.	Southern California	7	6.	Michigan	2
1.	Notre Dame	7	6.	Texas	2
1.	Ohio State	7	6.	Miami	2
4.	Oklahoma	5	9.	Penn State	1
5.	Nebraska	3	10.	Alabama	0

In the end, what USC lost, aside from the 2005 national championship, was immeasurable. An enormous amount of history was taken from them when Young crossed the goal line with nineteen seconds left to play. USC lost its chance to:

- Pass Notre Dame to establish itself as the all-time leader with twelve national titles (not to mention passing UCLA's eleven in basketball and tying USC's twelve in baseball)
- Win a historic three straight national championships
- Earn the title "greatest college football team of all time" (which ESPN had already awarded them via a computerized pregame analysis)
- Go after Oklahoma's 47-game winning streak in 2006
- Add to their already-record thirty-three straight weeks atop the AP poll

Whether Leinart was the greatest player of all time now went from being accepted fact to a worthy debate. Whether the 2000s Trojan dynasty was better than Bud Wilkinson's Oklahoma Sooners (1950s), Frank Leahy's Notre Dame Fighting Irish (1940s), or Knute Rockne's Irish of the 1920s was now a much harder argument to make.

Bush and LenDale White both declared for the 2006 NFL Draft. This also cost them enormously in that, had either one returned, one of them probably would have won USC's third straight Heisman, fourth in three years, and an all-time most eighth overall in 2006. USC likely would have been ranked number one throughout the 2006 season on the way to its twelfth national title, thus increasing their AP streak to fifty. If they had beaten Texas, this would have meant their thirteenth national title and fourth straight (meaning seniors would have won each of their years at USC). In so doing, USC might have captured their forty-eighth straight victory, passing Oklahoma on the way to fifty and beyond.

The 2006 team, led by All-American receiver Dwayne Jarrett and quarterback John David Booty, still went 11–2 and beat Notre Dame and then Michigan in the Rose Bowl. But a stunning loss to UCLA denied them the national championship they probably would have won over highly overrated Troy Smith and Ohio State in the BCS title game played in Pac-10 friendly Glendale, Arizona.

There is no logical argument explaining why two-loss LSU or one-loss Florida won the 2007 and 2008 national championships instead of the better team both years (USC). Most commentary was that had USC played either team in the BCS title game, victory would likely have gone to the Trojans. If they had beaten Texas; if Bush, White, or both had returned (and possibly if Jets first-round pick Mark Sanchez returned in 2009); the team could have:

- Surpassed Washington's all-time record 63-game *unbeaten* streak (1907–17)
- Been ranked number one in the AP poll eighty straight weeks
- Won seven straight national championships
- Won their fifteenth national championship
- Won the Heisman three straight years, four of five, and ninth overall

These are accomplishments that no football team has ever approached. John Wooden and UCLA had this kind of run in basketball. USC under Rod Dedeaux and Dean

All-Time USC Team*

Pos.	First	*Honorable Mention*

OFFENSE

Pos.	First	Honorable Mention
QB	Matt Leinart	Pat Haden, Carson Palmer, Paul McDonald, Rodney Peete
TB	O. J. Simpson	Charles White, Mike Garrett, Ricky Bell, Frank Gifford
FB	Marcus Allen	Sam "Bam" Cunningham
WR	Lynn Swann	
WR	Mike Williams	Keyshawn Johnson, Erik Affholter, Bob Chandler, Dwayne Jarrett
TE	Charles "Tree" Young	
OT	Anthony Munoz	
OT	Ron Yary	Tony Boselli, Ernie Smith, Don Mosebar, Pete Adams, Keith Van Horne, John Vella
OG	Brad Budde	
OG	Bruce Matthews	Aaron Rosenberg, Roy Foster, Johnny Baker
C	Stan Williamson	Ryan Kalil

DEFENSE

Pos.	First	Honorable Mention
T	Marvin Powell	John Ferraro
DT	Shaun Cody	
DT	Ron Mix	Mike Patterson, Tim Ryan
DE	Tim Rossovich	
DE	Willie McGinest	Mike McKeever, Charles Weaver, Kenechi Udeze
LB	Junior Seau	
LB	Richard "Batman" Wood	
LB	Clay Matthews	Dennis Johnson, Chip Banks, Adrian Young, Charles Phillips, Chris Claiborne, Rey Maualuga
DB	Ronnie Lott	
DB	Tim McDonald	
DB	Troy Polamalu	Dennis Smith, Dennis Thurman, Joey Browner, Mark Carrier, Taylor Mays

SPECIAL TEAMS

Pos.	First	Honorable Mention
KR	Reggie Bush	Anthony Davis
P	Tom Malone	
PK	Frank Jordan	Ron Ayala

OFFENSIVE PLAYER	Matt Leinart
DEFENSIVE PLAYER	Ronnie Lott
COACH	John McKay
COACH, Honorable Mention	Pete Carroll, Howard Jones, John Robinson

*From *The USC Trojans: College Football's All-Time Greatest Dynasty* by Steven Travers

Cromwell had this kind of record in baseball and track, respectively. To do it in football, particularly in the BCS era, is somehow unthinkable. Still, some *do* think about it.

"I don't see any reason Pete Carroll can't win five or ten national championships," stated national sportstalk host Jim Rome.

These are the kinds of expectations the University of Southern California now deals with. As Carroll himself says of all "the hype, national championship talk, the Heismans; we embrace it."

It is why USC has surpassed Alabama, Oklahoma, and even Notre Dame in a 2000s stretch run firmly supporting the premise that they are now indeed college football's *all-time greatest dynasty*! USC has a tradition combining all the necessary elements. They have been a national power since the 1920s. They dominated the two decades prior to World II, the two decades of the 1960s and 1970s, and now the 2000s. Their down years were never really down; they always had many pro stars, won conference titles and Rose Bowls, even when times were tough. They have played as strong a schedule as any team, traveling east, west, north, and south to take on the best America has to offer. They have subjected themselves to eighty years of Notre Dame games and an almost equal number of "bloodlettings" versus UCLA.

No other conference features a single team that has dominated it as USC has the Pacific Coast, AAWU, Pac-8, and now Pac-10 Conference. It is historically the most successful football and overall athletic conference in the nation. The Trojans have dominated most all of the sports played in the Pac-10. The exceptions to that rule are schools that are number one among all collegiate programs: UCLA basketball and men's volleyball; maybe Stanford tennis. Outside of the Bruin basketball dynasty, in many cases the second greatest tradition in respective sports is USC's.

Southern California has established dominance of the very best bowl game—the Rose Bowl—against its most hallowed opponents (Ohio State's Woody Hayes, Michigan's Bo Schembechler, just to name two).

USC has always been an integrated program on the right side of history, walking proud with black players in the heart of Dixie. In viewing the ebb and tide of their history, they resemble in many ways a good baseball team that stays steady, winning six or seven of every 10 games to stay close even when opponents streak to ten straight, twenty straight, or more (think Oklahoma). When the others falter, the Trojans stay consistent, catch, and then pass them. On occasion, USC has long, wildly successful unbeaten streaks of their own (the Thundering Herd, McKay's champions of the early 1970s, Robinson's 28-game unbeaten 1978–80 teams, Carroll's recent 34-straight winners). In the end, the numbers add up in their favor: national titles, Heismans, pro stars. In no area of criteria do they trail by large margins. Michigan and Notre Dame have more all-time wins and higher winning percentages, but USC (who started playing later than those schools) hangs close to the top and is in the ultra-elite ".700 club."

All-Americans, college and pro Hall of Famers? USC is always right up there or ranked first. Certain statistics jump out, emphasizing the Trojans' status. Their bowl record, for instance, is impossible to dispute. While the Irish declined to accept the challenge year after year, the Trojans did and in so doing have put together the best bowl and Rose Bowl record in the country. Notre Dame is 14–15, having recently ended an embarrassing NCAA record for consecutive bowl defeats. Under Carroll, the Trojans have set NCAA records for most consecutive 11-win seasons (seven, 2002-2008); most consecutive BCS bowl appearances (seven, 2002-2008 seasons); best BCS bowl record (6-1); seven straight top five rankings; most consecutive weeks ranked number one in the AP (33, 2003-2006); and reached number one most atop the all-time AP polls (1936-2008, 90).

For all these reasons and more, USC is "college football's all-time greatest tradition!" May God bless America, and may the Trojans continue to . . . Fight On!

Did you know . . .

That USC has won more NCAA men's championships than any school, and their overall 121 national championships (through 2008–2009) are number one among all college sports programs? Furthermore, Pete Carroll's 88-15 record includes only one loss by more than a touchdown (in 2001 a late Irish score at South Bend made it 27-16). With a few breaks and bounces, his Trojans could be *102–1 with eight straight national titles*!

Consecutive Weeks Ranked Number 1 in the Associated Press Polls

Southern California	33 (2003–2006), 17 (1972–1973)
Miami	20 (2001–2002)
Notre Dame	19 (1988–1989)

Chapter 2

Notre Dame Fighting Irish

T HE *ESPN COLLEGE FOOTBALL ENCYCLOPEDIA* contains a chapter on every major college football program in the nation. The chapter on Notre Dame begins:

Every sport needs its kings. Kings define excellence and provide a standard for everyone else in the sport to measure themselves against. They are loved, hated, respected and feared, revered and reviled. They are royalty. Baseball has the Yankees, pro basketball the Celtics, pro hockey the Canadiens. And college football has Notre Dame.

University of Notre Dame
South Bend, Indiana
Founded: 1842
Colors: Blue and gold
Nickname: Fighting Irish
Stadium: Notre Dame Stadium (opened: 1930; capacity: 80,795)
All-time record (1887–2008): 831-284-42
All-time bowl record: 14–15 (through 2008)
National championships: 1924, 1929, 1930, 1943, 1946, 1947, 1949, 1966, 1973, 1977, 1988
Heisman Trophies: Angelo Bertelli (1943), John Lujack (1946), Leon Hart (1949), John Lattner (1953), Paul Hornung (1956), John Huarte (1964), Tim Brown (1987)
Outland Trophies: George Connor (1946), Bill Fischer (1948), Ross Browner (1946)
First-round NFL draftees: 58 (through 2009 draft)
Website: www.und.com
Notable alumni: Arizona governor Bruce Babbitt; television personalities Phil Donahue and Regis Philbin; Pulitzer Prize-winning sports columnist Red Smith; *Los Angeles Times* sports editor Bill Dwyre; Chicago *Tribune* sports editor Arch Ward; author Nicholas Sparks; newscaster Hannah Storm; Emmy Award-winning television

producers Don Ohlmeyer and Terry O'Neil; Nobel Prize-winning molecular biologist Eric Wieschaus; Notre Dame president Rev. Theodore Hesburgh; Congressional Gold Medal-winner Dr. Thomas Dooley; actor George Wendt; San Francisco 49ers' owner Eddie DeBartolo Jr.; Cleveland Indians' owner Larry Dolan; Golden State Warriors' owner James Fitzgerald; Tampa Bay Devil Rays' chairman Vince Naimoli; Oakland Athletics' President Michael Crowley; San Francisco 49ers' director John York; Arizona Diamondbacks' general manager Joe Garagiola Jr.; sportscasters Don Criqui and Ted Robinson; sportstalk host Bob Fitzgerald; ESPN sports personality Mike Golic; NFL vice president of public relations Greg Aiello; Ohio State athletic director Gene Smith; Hall of Fame baseball player Carl Yastrzemski; Hall of Fame basketball coach Ray Meyer; basketball players Adrian Dantley, Austin Carr, John Paxson, and Bill Laimbeer; Olympians Shannon Boxx and Jim Delaney

This is the general view of Notre Dame Fighting Irish football. Kings. Number one. The best of the best. If a vote were conducted, Notre Dame would probably be ranked number one. An online poll would likely result in the Irish winning. A discussion among the media would generally result in the same finding. If a vote were undertaken among *USC alumni*, the Fighting Irish would get a lot of, if not the most, votes.

In the late 1990s and 2000s, however, Notre Dame has not achieved the level of greatness emblematic of their glorious past. Their last national championship is a two-decade-old event. A best-selling book, *Under the Tarnished Dome* by Don Yaeger, revealed that former coach Lou Holtz reduced the traditional standards of Notre Dame excellence in order to achieve parity with the likes of Miami and Florida State. In the wake of the book's revelations, Holtz was gone and his successors, apparently trying to do it the "old way," have not measured up on the football field.

In the meanwhile USC, long considered the "football school" who could not compete with Notre Dame academically, did precisely that: compete with Notre Dame academically. At first it seemed that in so doing, USC had forfeited any chance of competing at the same level with the Irish, Hurricanes, Seminoles, Cornhuskers, and Sooners on the football field. Then along came Pete Carroll, and that concept no longer is a consideration.

Year by year in South Bend, it has been like being in a pot of water that rises to the boiling point slowly, but the individual never realizes what is happening until the steam overtakes him and it is too late. For college football fans, some time in the new century they looked up and examined the numbers, the statistics, the records, and increasingly the conclusion has been reached that under Pete Carroll, Southern California passed Notre Dame as the greatest of all collegiate football traditions.

The current era is not unlike the year 1982, however. That was the season in which USC beat the Irish for the fifth straight time. The all-time record between the two schools was then virtually even. The Irish had beaten USC only twice in sixteen years, and it took two of their greatest national championship teams to do it (1973, 1977). Since 1962, USC had won five national titles to three for Notre Dame. Since 1965, USC had won four Heisman Trophies to Notre Dame's one.

But time is not static. If indeed 1982 similarly marked the ascendance of USC to an equal place in history with the Irish, the following two decades completely reversed that course. Like the stock market reaching all-time highs before going into a prolonged "bear market," the Trojans fell far below their historical standards while Notre Dame embarked on a period of glory under Holtz.

The current claim that USC is the number one tradition for a New Millennium is of course not a static, unchangeable fact. All empires—the Babylonians, Persians, Greeks, Romans, French, and British—came and went. How long the "Trojan empire" can defend the Spartans and the Carthages of college football remains to be seen. But the change has come and it is upon us.

That said, Trojan superiority is not as clear-cut as some other sports empires. The Yankees, for instance, hold a position in baseball, and in all of athletics for that matter, that is unassailable and seems likely to be maintained for another century. UCLA's eleven NCAA basketball championships places it so far above Kentucky, Indiana, North Carolina, and Duke that it would require a run . . . like Pete Carroll's football Trojans of the 2000s . . . to challenge them.

Other dynasties are not as comfortable. Slowly but surely, the Los Angeles Lakers have built a pro basketball history that can be compared to the great Celtics, who have been mediocre for years now. If one compares the Minneapolis and Los Angeles franchises, then the Lakers are only a few NBA titles away from the seventeen won by Boston.

In pro football, there are no "traditional champions," really. The Green Bay Packers were a dominant NFL franchise prior to the creation of the Super Bowl. They won the first two and another in 1997, but in the modern era the Pack is not nearly as successful a franchise as Pittsburgh or Dallas. New England crashed the party with Tom Brady.

All that said, Notre Dame has a strong case. The argument saying Notre Dame is still the best is legitimate and worthy. The way it all started drips with history. University of

Elite Ten by the Numbers
College Football Hall of Fame (through 2009 induction)

1. Notre Dame — 48 (includes coaches)
2. Southern California — 36
3. Michigan — 30 (11 in Citizen Savings Football Hall of Fame)
4. Ohio State — 26 (8 coaches)
5. Oklahoma — 25 (includes coaches)
6. Alabama — 21
6. Penn State — 21
8. Texas — 15 (includes coaches)
9. Nebraska — 14
10. Miami — 6

Michigan students traveled by train to South Bend, Indiana, to engage in the first football game ever played by the University of Notre Dame.

In 1913, the Irish truly put themselves on the map when they went up against mighty Army. While the "forward pass" was not completely unknown, it was not considered a valid offensive weapon until Irish quarterback Gus Dorais and end Knute Rockne used it to spur a nation-shaking 35–13 triumph.

No team even comes close to shaping the college game as Notre Dame did in the 1920s. They were truly the right team at the right time. Its Catholic identity resonated with growing ethnic populaces in major cities like New York, Boston, Philadelphia, Pittsburgh, Chicago, and Los Angeles. The heavy European immigration flow of the early twentieth century was now Americanized with large, growing families. Many of them were Irish. They all *rooted* for the Irish.

Rockne's team dominated play on the field and in the sports psyche of a fascinated public in the 1920s. His untimely death in a plane crash in 1931 turned him into an iconic figure like James Dean or JFK. Under Frank Leahy in the 1940s, the Irish dominated the decade like no team has done in the modern era.

In 117 years of football, Notre Dame has had 110 winning years. They have featured twelve unbeaten, untied seasons and ten others in which they were unbeaten with a tie. In twenty-eight additional seasons they have suffered only one loss.

Notre Dame's 831–284–42 record (through 2008) ranks virtually tied with Michigan's (872–295–36) for the best all time. Their 831 wins (through 2008) is third behind Michigan and Texas. Perhaps Notre Dame's strongest argument that they remain superior to USC is their 42–33–5 record against the Trojans entering 2009 (though it includes seven straight losses to Troy). This includes one thirteen-year unbeaten run against them between 1983 and 1995.

Notre Dame is tied with USC for the most national titles with eleven. However, Notre Dame's eight Associated Press titles are the most of any program. None of their national championships are tainted by bowl defeat. Furthermore, the Irish easily could have been national champions in 1913, 1919, 1920, 1941, 1948, and 1953. Overall, there are at least nineteen seasons in which the Irish "qualified" to be the national champion by virtue of some rating service or historical analysis.

The Irish are tied with Southern California and Ohio State for the most Heisman Trophy winners (seven). They have the most consensus All-Americans with ninety-six (through 2008). Notre Dame's forty-two players and six coaches (through 2008) inducted into the National Football Foundation Hall of Fame are tied with Texas for the most of any institution. They are tied with Alabama and Michigan for the most Super Bowl MVP awards (Joe Montana with three). USC has two. Approximately 400 players have represented them in pro football, the second most of any college over the years (behind Southern California). An impressive 464 Irish players (slightly trailing USC's 486) have been drafted. They have five number one overall NFL draft picks, tied with USC for the most of any program. Notre Dame's five Associated Press Pro Football Players of the Year are the most from any college.

These are just numbers, and do not begin to explain the mystique, lore, and appeal of Notre Dame football. They are the only school with their own television deal (NBC).

Elite Ten by the Numbers
National championships (1869–1945)

Illustrated Football Annual (begun 1930)

Parker H. Davis Ratings (1889–1933)

Dickinson System (1924–40)

Dunkel System (begun in 1929)

Helms Athletic Foundation (begun in 1883)

The Football Thesaurus (begun in 1927)

Various other polling services

1. Notre Dame	8 (4, 1924–29–30–43/recognized historical national champs)
1. Michigan	8 (5, 1901–02–18–23–33/recognized historical national champs)
3. Southern California	5 (4, 1928–31–32–39/recognized historical national champs)
3. Alabama	5 (4, 1925–26–30–34/recognized historical national champs)
5. Oklahoma	1
6. Texas	1
7. Nebraska	0
8. Miami	0
9. Penn State	0
10. Ohio State	0

Alabama (5): 1925 (Helms, Billingsley, Board, FR, Houlgate, NCF, Poling; split/Dartmouth), 1926 (Billingsley, FR, Helms, NCF, Poling; split/Stanford), 1930 (FR, split/Notre Dame—Parke Davis), 1934 (Dunkel, Houlgate, Poling, Williamson, split/Minnesota), 1941 (Houlgate, split/Minnesota, Texas), 1926: Tied vs. Stanford, Rose Bowl

Miami: 0

Michigan (8): 1901, 1902, 1903, 1904, 1918, 1923, 1932, 1933: no bowls

Nebraska: 0

Notre Dame (8): 1919 (split/Illinois—Davis, split/Texas A&M—NCF, other/Harvard—unanimous, Illinois—Board), 1920 (split/Princeton—Davis, other/California—Helms, FR, Houlgate, NCF, Princeton/Harvard—Board), 1924 (Bill, DS, Helms, Board, FR, Houlgate, NCF, Poling, other/Pennsylvania—Davis), 1927 (Houlgate, other/Illinois—DS, Davis, Helms, NCF, Yale—FR, Georgia—Board, Poling), 1929 (Bill, DS, Dunkel, Board, Helms, FR, NCF, Poling, other/Pittsburgh—Davis, Southern California—Houlgate), 1930 (all but FR, split/Alabama—Davis, also FR), 1938 (DS, other/Tennessee—Bill, Dunkel, LS, Board, Houlgate, FR, Poling, Sagarin, Texas Christian—AP, WS, Helms, NCF), 1943 (unanimous including AP)

 1919, 1920, 1927, 1929, 1930, 1938,1943: no bowls

Fighting Irish on the Run

Year	Record	Run
1918	3–1–1 F/1–0–1	3–1–2 (1918)
		1–0–1 (1918)
1919	9–0	9–0 (1919)
1920	9–0	18–0 (1919–20)
1921	10–1	28–1 (1919–21)
1922	8–1–1	36–2–1 (1919–23)
1923	9–1	45–3–1 (1919–24)
1924	10–0	55–3–1 (1919–24)
1925	7–2–1	62–5–1 (1919–25)
1926	7–2–1	69–7–2 (1919–26)
1927	7–1–1	76–8–3 (1919–27)
1928	5–4 5–5 F/1–0	79–8–3 (1919–28) **90 games**
		83–11–3 (1919–28)
		1–0 (1928)
1929	9–0	90–12–4 (1919–29)
1930	10–0	96–11–3 (1919–30) **110 games**
		102–11–3 (1919–30)
		20–0 (1928–30)
1931	6–2–1 S/1–0, 6–0–1	105–11–4 (1919–31) **120 games**
		108–13–4 (1919–31)
		109–13–5 (1918–31)
		111–14–4 (1918–31)
1932	7–2	112–14–4 (1918–31) **130 games**
		112–13–5 (1918–32) **130**
1940	7–2	7–2 (1940)
1941	8–0–1	15–2–1 (1940–41)
1942	7–2–2	22–4–3 (1940–42)
1943	9–1	31–5–3 (1940–43)
1944	8–2	39–7–3 (1940–44)
1945	7–2–1 F/1–0	46–9–4 (1940–45)
1946	8–0–1 S/5–0, 5–0–1, F/3–0, 3–0–1	54–9–5 (1940–46)

(continues)

Fighting Irish on the Run (*continued*)

Year	Record	Run
1947	9–0	56–9–5 (1940–47) **70 games**
		63–9–5 (1940–47)
		12–0 (1946–47)
1948	9–0–1 S/9–0	66–9–5 1940–48 **80 games**
		72–9–6 (1940–48)
		19–0–1 (1946–48)
1949	10–0	75–9–6 (1940–48) **90 games**
		82–9–6 **(decade: 1940s)**
		29–0–1 (1946–49) **30 games**
1950	4–4–1 S/1–0	83–9–6 (1940–50)
		30–0–1 (1946–50)
		37–1–2 (1946–50) **40 games**
1951	7–2–1	85–9–6 (1940–51) **100 games**
		90–11–7 (1940–51)
1952	7–2–1	97–13–8 (1940–52) 118
		91–11–8 (1940–52) **110 games**
1953	9–0–1	99–13–8 (1940–53) **120 games**
		106–13–8 (1940–53)
1954	9–1	115–14–8 (1940–53)
		108–14–8 (1940–54) **130 games**
1955	8–2	123–16–6 (1940–55)
		118–14–8 (1940–55) **140 games**
1988	12–0	12–0 (1988)
1989	12–1	24–1 (1988–89)
1990	9–3	33–4 (1988–90)
1991	10–3	43–7 (1988–91) **50 games**
1992	10–1–1	51–8–1 (1988–92) **60 games**
		53–8–1 (1988–92)
1993	11–1	61–8–1 (1988–92) **70 games**
		64–9–1 (1988–93)
1994	6–5–1 S/1–0	65–9–1 (1988–94)
		68–11–1 (1988–94) **80 games**
		69–14–2 (1988–94)

S/start season; F/finish season

Perhaps as telling as any other statement is the fact that former USC quarterback Pat Haden is NBC's "voice of the Irish." Haden grew up Catholic. After starring at Bishop Amat High School in southern California, he chose USC mainly because in his senior year he *lived with coach John McKay*. His parents had moved to Walnut Creek (near San Francisco) due to a job transfer. McKay's son, J. K., was his receiver in high school and college. Recruiters from Notre Dame, Stanford, and other schools had to call on the McKay household in order to meet with Haden, who went on to lead USC to an astounding 55–24 win over the Irish in 1974. He set the all-time career record for touchdown passes against Notre Dame.

Elite Ten by the Numbers

Associated Press Pro Football Player of the Year (through 2008)

Notre Dame: 5

1961	Paul Hornung, Green Bay, HB
1971	Alan Page, Minnesota, DT
1983	Joe Theismann, Washington, QB
1989	Joe Montana, San Francisco, QB
1990	Joe Montana, San Francisco, QB

Alabama: 3

1966	Bart Starr, Green Bay, QB
1974	Ken Stabler, Oakland, QB
2005	Shaun Alexander, Seattle, RB

Southern California: 2

1973	O. J. Simpson, Buffalo, RB
1985	Marcus Allen, Los Angeles Raiders, RB

Texas: 1

1979	Earl Campbell, Houston, RB

Michigan: 1

2007	Tom Brady, New England, QB

Notre Dame versus Conferences (through 2005)

Atlantic Coast (72–27–2), Big East (56–20–1), Big 10 (213–106–15), Big 12 (37–18–2), Mountain West (26–7), Mid-American (4–0), Pacific-10 (74–39–6), Southeastern (21–12), Western Athletic (2–0)

Despite his USC pedigree Haden, who is also a corporate lawyer in the L.A. area, announces his games with the utmost admiration for Notre Dame. When the two teams play each other, there is no discernible bias favoring the Trojans; in fact it may be the other way around. The Haden-Notre Dame symbiosis is an example of what the late USC quarterback Craig Fertig calls "pure mutual respect" between the two schools.

Every even year in L.A., Fertig and Tommy Hawkins, a former Notre Dame basketball player who played for the Lakers, then became a media personality in L.A., emceed an event called The Game Is On. Much good-natured ribbing takes place, but the kind of humor and admiration the two schools openly express for each other and their respective heroes is genuine. This kind of thing certainly does not take place, at least to this extent, between California and Stanford; Nebraska and Oklahoma; Auburn and Alabama. When Auburn football coach Shug Jordan played golf with Alabama football coach Bear Bryant, he was careful to keep it a secret from his school's followers.

While much of the Notre Dame legend is built on "blarney" and "malarkey," it is nevertheless the stuff of great American mythology. Only true greatness shines forth in such a manner. The Four Horsemen of Notre Dame story may have been a media gambit, the "win one for the Gipper" story made up. No matter. They resonate with the populace. The love for Notre Dame is genuine and heartfelt. Notre Dame fans are the most intense, loyal, and regular in the nation. Certainly fans of Nebraska, Michigan, Ohio State, Louisiana State, and some other programs share the same kind of commitment, but the Notre Dame follower is sophisticated, is national, travels, and is enthusiastic at least on a level with all others.

The Notre Dame fan base is far more loyal than USC's, which for the most part is as dedicated as that of any other Los Angeles sports team but is still fickle in the notorious L.A. manner. When USC ventures into Notre Dame Stadium, they are a genuine road team facing every possible disadvantage. For years, when Notre Dame entered the Coliseum, perhaps 40 percent of the crowd rooted for them. In the Pete Carroll era, this has changed perceptibly, but it is still not nearly as fanatical in favor of the Trojans as vice versa in South Bend.

Notre Dame versus Biggest Rivals

Versus Southern California	42–33–5
Versus Michigan	15–20–1

The Gipper

I'm going to tell you something I've kept to myself for years. None of you knew George Gipp—it was long before your time. But you all know what a tradition he is at Notre Dame. And the last thing he said to me, "Rock," he said, "sometime, when the team is up against it, and the breaks are beating the boys, tell them to go out there with all they got and just win one for the Gipper. I don't know where I'll be then, Rock," he said, "but I'll know about it . . . and I'll be happy."

—Pat O'Brien as Knute Rockne, *Knute Rockne: All-American* (1940)

Ronald Reagan played Gipp. Not only did Gipp never give the dying testimonial, Rockne never gave this speech in the Yankee Stadium dressing room on November 10, 1928. It was based on some scant mention in the *New York Daily News*'s game account by reporter and Irish alum Francis Wallace, apparently incorporated by Hollywood director Lloyd Bacon. Gipp apparently contracted strep throat and pneumonia caused when he, after continually breaking school curfew to go gambling and drinking, was locked out of his dorm by a zealous priest, forcing him to sleep on the freezing steps. Rumors swirled around Gipp's death and gambling debts. On November 20, 1920, he sat out the game at Northwestern. According to the Notre Dame media guide, it was because of a shoulder injury incurred one week earlier versus Indiana. Other stories claim he already was sick and sat shivering in a blanket on a freezing day; that he owed money to gamblers and agreed to sit out the game to keep the spread down in return for forgiving the debt; that he entered the game out of a crisis of conscience, throwing the touchdown pass that put the Irish above the spread, foiling the gamblers; and that the exertion worsened the illness. The official story is that Gipp stayed in Chicago to "give punting instructions to a high school team coached by a former teammate," where he got sick. This makes little sense, since Notre Dame was scheduled to play at Michigan State only five days later (November 25). Between practice, school, and travel there was no extra time to hang around at a high school practice in Chicago. Either way, he was gravely ill, was hospitalized, did not play against the Spartans, and died of complications (pneumonia) from the strep on December 14, 1920, at the age of 25.

The recent rivalry between Charlie Weis and Pete Carroll added a new wrinkle to the rivalry. When Weis took over at Notre Dame after being the offensive coordinator of three New England Patriots Super Bowl winners, he told his team, "I never lost to that [expletive deleted] in the NFL, and I don't intend to lose to him now." When USC visited Notre Dame Stadium in 2005, Weis instructed the groundskeeper to grow the grass as high as the Indiana wheat fields at harvest time. It was a vain attempt to slow down Reggie Bush.

Notre Dame versus the Elite Ten (110–83–9 through 2008)

Alabama (5–1), Miami (15–7–1), Michigan (15–20–1), Nebraska (7–8–1), Ohio State (2–2), Oklahoma (8–1), Penn State (8–9–1), Southern California (42–33–5), Texas (8–2)

Then there are the movies. USC, despite being "Hollywood's school," with numerous alumni making their mark as directors, writers, producers, and actors, has only a TV movie about tragic running back Ricky Bell, who died young of a rare disease, and a low-budget effort about women's basketball called *Love and Basketball. Boyz n the Hood*, directed by USC alum John Singleton, touched on the death of a Trojan football recruit but was not about the school. Many films are shot on location at USC but mention the school in a peripheral manner. Ironically, *The Hunchback of Notre Dame* was filmed at USC.

Notre Dame's *Knute Rockne: All-American* and *Rudy*, however, were blockbusters that remain classics to this day. Ronald Reagan built his image in large measure based upon his portrayal of George Gipp in *Knute Rockne: All-American*. A film based on the book *One Night, Two Teams: Alabama vs. USC and the Game That Changed a Nation* (2007), which details how the 1970 USC-Alabama game helped end segregation, may be USC's Hollywood answer to Irish cinema dominance, but even its proposed pitch line demonstrates adherence to Notre Dame: "Finally, USC's *Rudy*."

Despite an occasional accusation, Notre Dame is the cleanest of all programs. Among big-time athletic programs, only Penn State, Duke, Stanford, and possibly Michigan approach their overall academic/athletic record. Notre Dame has claimed an incredible 98 percent graduation rate. They have never been on NCAA probation. Even their media guide is, unlike many other schools, impeccably honest. With their great record, there are many opportunities for exaggeration or misleading information, but they do not inflate their national championship record, All-American roster, or the like.

They are a Catholic institution and therefore remain devoted to the idea that the Lord Jesus Christ watches them, knows what is in their hearts, and judges them accordingly. They are a school made up of human beings and therefore they have their failings, but Notre Dame's adherence to Christian principles is real. Even their greatest rivals, USC, Michigan, . . . and everybody else, admires them for that.

Notre Dame's awesome image is not all movies, magic, and morals. It is not all dominant seasons and runaway victories, either. They have played an inordinate number of extremely big games; made some incredible comebacks; ended some long winning streaks; overcome incredible odds; and to the consternation of their opponents, whether it be real or not, have at times seemed to have the kind of "luck of the Irish" that gives the impression that, every so often, God favors them.

Their greatest, most legendary games include:

- Notre Dame 11, Michigan 3 (1909)
- Notre Dame 35, Army 13 (1913)
- Notre Dame 27, Army 17 (1920)
- Notre Dame 13, Army 7 (1924)
- Notre Dame 27, Stanford 10 (1925 Rose Bowl)
- Notre Dame 12, Army 6 (1928)
- Notre Dame 7, Carnegie Tech 0 (1929)
- Notre Dame 60, Penn State 20 (1930)
- Notre Dame 18, Ohio State 13 (1935)
- Notre Dame 0, Army 0 (1946)
- Notre Dame 27, Southern Methodist 20 (1949)
- Notre Dame 7, Oklahoma 0 (1957)
- Notre Dame 51, Southern California 0 (1966)

- Notre Dame 24, Texas 11 (1971 Cotton Bowl)
- Notre Dame 23, Southern California 14 (1973)
- Notre Dame 24, Alabama 23 (1973 Sugar Bowl)
- Notre Dame 13, Alabama 11 (1975 Orange Bowl)
- Notre Dame 49, Southern California 14 (1977)
- Notre Dame 38, Texas 10 (1978 Cotton Bowl)
- Notre Dame 35, Houston 34 (1979 Cotton Bowl)
- Notre Dame 38, Southern California 37 (1986)
- Notre Dame 31, Miami 30 (1988)
- Notre Dame 27, Southern California 10 (1988)
- Notre Dame 34, West Virginia 21 (1989 Fiesta Bowl)
- Notre Dame 28, Southern California 24 (1989)
- Notre Dame 31, Florida State 24 (1993)

Crowd shots of two games eleven years apart tell the story of Notre Dame's impact on America. The 1913 "forward pass" win over Army was played before a high school-sized gathering at Notre Dame. The 1924 Four Horsemen win over Army was played before a packed Polo Grounds throng in New York. The 1925 Rose Bowl win over Stanford was played in front of a huge crowd in Pasadena. The 1928 "win one for the Gipper" win over Army occurred before a packed "House That Ruth Built."

In addition to these games, the Irish helped fill the Coliseum for games against USC. At Chicago's Soldier Field, 120,000 (1927) and 112,000 (1929) saw Notre Dame beat the Trojans.

There have been "agonies" too, as listed in *The Fighting Irish: Notre Dame Football Through the Years* by William Gildea and Christopher Jennison. They include:

- Southern California 16, Notre Dame 14 (1931)
- Great Lakes Naval Training Station 19, Notre Dame 14 (1943)
- Army 59, Notre Dame 0 (1944)
- Army 48, Notre Dame 0 (1945)
- Purdue 28, Notre Dame 14 (1950)
- Iowa 14, Notre Dame 14 (1953)
- Southern California 20, Notre Dame 17 (1964)
- Michigan State 10, Notre Dame 10 (1966)
- Texas 21, Notre Dame 17 (1970 Cotton Bowl)
- Southern California 55, Notre Dame 24 (1974)
- Miami 58, Notre Dame 7 (1985)
- Michigan 24, Notre Dame 23 (1986)
- Miami 27, Notre Dame 10 (1989)
- Stanford 33, Notre Dame 16 (1992)
- Boston College 41, Notre Dame 39 (1993)
- Northwestern 17, Notre Dame 15 (1995)
- Oregon State 41, Notre Dame 9 (2001 Fiesta Bowl)
- Southern California 34, Notre Dame 31 (2005)

William Gildea's description of the 1974 loss to Southern Cal is classic: "How could it be possible for a team not equipped with knives or guns to score fifty-five straight points on the Fighting Irish?"

"I still don't know how it happened," USC coach John McKay told reporters. "I can't understand it. I'm going to sit down tonight and have a beer and think about it. Against Notre Dame? Maybe against Kent State. But Notre Dame?"

In the *History of USC Football* DVD, McKay stated, "I have no idea what happened, but I guarantee I was there . . . and I clapped."

Even in defeat, Notre Dame helped shape a nation. The losses to Great Lakes Naval Training Station and Army during the middle of World War II undoubtedly had the Nazis and Japanese scratching their heads, wondering how the American military could field teams good enough to beat our best football squad while simultaneously beating *them* from one corner of the globe to another. Only America.

Prior to Rockne taking over in 1918, Notre Dame had gone unbeaten in 1912 and 1913. Consensus All-Americans included Gus Dorais (1913) and Frank Rydzewski (1917). Rockne's first team featured Curly Lambeau, who would go on to a Pro Football Hall of Fame career as a pioneering NFL player and coach with the Green Bay Packers. Lambeau Field is named after him. In 1919, when the Irish were 9–0 under Rockne, back George Gipp made his mark and followed that up with an All-American campaign in the 9–0 1920 campaign. George Trafton went on to a Hall of Fame career with the Chicago Bears.

Eddie Anderson earned consensus honors in 1921. In 1924 the Irish fielded what still may be their greatest team. The Four Horsemen of Notre Dame were 10–0 with a victory over Stanford in the Rose Bowl. Three of the Four Horsemen, Harry Stuhldreher, Jim Crowley, and Elmer Layden, were consensus All-Americans. Other All-Americans of the 1920s were Bud Boeringer (1926), John Smith (1927), Jack Cannon (1929), Frank Carideo (1929–30), and the great Marchy Schwartz (1929–30).

Rockne, talked into the USC rivalry ostensibly by his wife, led Notre Dame to victory over the Trojans in four of his last five years. A single point in each game (13–12, 7–6, 13–12) achieved the first three victories. These were instant classics. Between 1928 and 1932, the national champion was the winner of this game. USC achieved their true status as a great program only when they upended Notre Dame, 27–14, on the way to their 1928 national title. Their 16–14 fourth-quarter comeback against the Irish in the new Notre Dame Stadium (1931) did everything to elevate their prestige to the greatest of heights. Above all else, it placed them on an equal status with the Irish after having lost to them four of the first five times, albeit by the narrowest of margins.

Notre Dame won 20 straight games between 1929 and 1931. They carried a 26-game unbeaten streak into the 1931 USC game. Rockne's teams were 105–12–5 during his thirteen years. They won national titles in his last two seasons, 1929 and 1930. They were surefire favorites to do it again in 1931.

When USC beat Notre Dame three straight times (1931–1933), it was the end of coach Hunk Anderson's tenure and the beginning of Elmer Layden's. Consensus All-Americans of the 1930s were Tommy Yarr (1931), Joe Kurth (1932), Jack Robinson (1934), Wayne Millner (1935), Chuck Sweeney (1937), and Ed Beinor (1938). When the NFL Draft started in 1936, Notre Dame's Bill Shakespeare was Pittsburgh's first-round choice. Millner is in the Pro Football Hall of Fame, having played for the Boston and Washington Redskins in the NFL.

The Four Horsemen of Notre Dame

Outlined against a blue-gray October sky the Four Horsemen rode again. In dramatic lore they are known as famine, pestilence, destruction and death. These are only aliases. Their real names are Stuhldreher, Miller, Crowley and Layden. They formed the crest of the South Bend cyclone before which another fighting Army football team was swept over the precipice at the Polo Grounds yesterday afternoon as 55,000 peered down on the bewildering panorama spread on the green plain below.

—Grantland Rice, *New York Herald Tribune*, October 19, 1924

The Four Horsemen were quarterback Harry Stuhldreher, halfbacks "Sleepy Jim" Crowley and Don Miller, and fullback Elmer Layden. The name was based of course on the Biblical reference and the 1924 film *The Four Horsemen of the Apocalypse*. Notre Dame press assistant George Strickland made mention of the movie in the Polo Grounds press box, inspiring Rice's lead. A week later Strickland arranged a photo of the four Irish stars on steeds from a local South Bend stable. It was really the victory over Stanford in the Rose Bowl two and a half months later that fixed them in the public's imagination.

Notre Dame's 7–0 victory over Carnegie Tech in 1938 had them thinking that this would be their first national championship without Rock, but USC's 13–0 win over them ended that. They held out hope the polls might favor them if the chips all fell into place in 1939, but again USC dispelled the notion by virtue of a 20–12 victory in South Bend, which served to elevate Troy to the number one position.

Frank Leahy came on the scene in 1940. Nobody did it better: 8–0–1 (1941), 7–2–2 (1942), 9–1 (national champions, 1943), 8–2 (1944), 7–2–1 (1945), 8–0–1 (national champions, 1946), 9–0 (national champions, 1947), 9–0–1 (1948), and 10–0 (national champions, 1949). Three Irish players—Angelo Bertelli (1943), Johnny Lujack (1947), and Leon Hart (1949)—earned Heisman Trophies. The Irish never lost a game in the 1941, 1946, 1947, 1948, and 1949 seasons, compiling a 21-game winning streak (1946–1948) and a 39-game unbeaten streak (1945–1950). Only a stunning 14–14 tie against USC in 1948 prevented what may have been their fifth title of the decade while keeping them from capturing an elusive three-straight AP crowns.

Did You Know . . .
That the 1946–1947 two-time national champion Notre Dame Fighting Irish never trailed in a game (although in 1946 they played Army to a 0–0 tie)?

Not just consensus All-Americans but College Hall of Famers strode the legendary Notre Dame stage: Bob Dove, Pat Filley, Creighton Miller, Jim White, John Yonakor, George Connor, Bill Fischer, Emil Sitko, and Bob Williams. Connor (1946) and Fischer (1948) won Outland Trophies. Many, including Beano Cook to this day, call the 1947 Irish the best team ever assembled. They never trailed in a game and posted three shutouts in a row.

First-round draft choices: Angelo Bertelli (Boston, first overall pick, 1944), Creighton Miller (Brooklyn, 1944), Frank Szymanski (Detroit, 1956), John Yonakor (Philadelphia, 1945), Frank Dancewicz (Boston, first overall pick, 1946), Johnny Lujack (Chicago Bears, 1946), George Connor (New York Giants, 1946), Emil Sitko (Los Angeles Rams, 1946), Frank Tripucka (Philadelphia, 1949), Bill Fischer (Chicago Cardinals, 1949), Leon Hart (Detroit, 1950). George Sullivan was the first pick of the Chicago Rockets of the All-American Football Conference in 1947. Connor played for the Chicago Bears and was elected to the Pro Football Hall of Fame.

The 1946 0–0 tie with Army remains mythical in status. After getting blown out 59–0 (1944) and 48–0 (1945) by Mr. Inside and Mr. Outside (Doc Blanchard and Glenn Davis), the Irish met Red Blaik's juggernaut before 74,121 at Yankee Stadium on November 8, 1946. With the war won, the game had all the trappings of the Greeks holding an Olympics to celebrate the end of the Peloponnesian War, or the Romans holding gladiatorial contests at the Coliseum in celebration of Caesar's triumphs abroad.

Notre Dame was the heavy underdog but somehow held Army scoreless. The play of the game was Lujack's open-field tackle of Blanchard after a 21-yard rumble at the Notre Dame 36. The tie was considered a "moral victory" for the Irish. It turned out to be more than that when the Associated Press voted them number one at season's end.

In the 1950s, two Notre Dame stars won Heisman Trophies: Johnny Lattner (1953) and Paul Hornung (1956). Great Irish stars of the decade were Jerry Groom, Art Hunter, Bob Toneff, Ralph Guglielmi, Al Ecuyer, and Monty Stickles. First-round draft picks were Bob Williams (Chicago Bears, 1952), Jerry Groom (Chicago Cardinals, 1952), Art Hunter (Green Bay, 1954), Johnny Lattner (Green Bay, 1954), Neil Worden (Philadelphia, 1954), Ralph Guglielmi (Washington, 1955), Frank Varrichione (Pittsburgh, 1955), Joe Heap (New York Giants, 1955), Paul Hornung (Green Bay, 1957), Nick Pietrosante (Detroit, 1959), George Izo (Chicago Cardinals, 1960), and Monty Stickles (San Francisco, 1960).

Elite Ten by the Numbers

Most drafted classes (through 2009)

1.	Notre Dame	16 (1946)
2.	Southern California	15 (1953)
2.	Notre Dame	15 (1945)
4.	Southern California	14 (1977)
4.	Southern California	14 (1975)
6.	Southern California	11 (2009)
6.	Miami	11 (2002)

Spoilers

Notre Dame has ended twelve perfect seasons (one tie). They have twelve unbeaten, untied seasons; ten unbeaten (with a tie) seasons; and twenty-eight one-loss years. They have finished in the AP Top 10 thirty-five times.

While national championships escaped their grasp, it was a decade filled with monumental moments. In 1953, Notre Dame opened the season with a 28–21 victory at Oklahoma. It was the last time the Sooners would lose over the next 47 games. The Irish then ended Georgia Tech's 31-game unbeaten streak, 27–14 at South Bend. A 14–14 tie with Iowa ended their national title aspirations.

Terry Brennan took over for Leahy in 1954. He carried the success over with 9–1 and 8–2 seasons. In 1956 Notre Dame was only 2–8, yet the season remains a memorable one thanks to the great Paul Hornung. He captured the school's fifth Heisman Trophy. A colorful personality whose persona was similar to Frank Gifford's, he was one of pro football's all-time greats with Vince Lombardi's Packers. Hornung is a member of both the College and Pro Football Halls of Fame.

Notre Dame Coaches' Winning Percentages

1. Knute Rockne (.881)
2. Frank Leahy (.855)
3. Ara Parseghian (.836)
4. Elmer Layden (.770)
5. Lou Holtz (.765)

The following year (1957), a dejected Irish squad arrived in Norman, Oklahoma, on the heels of successive losses: 20–6 to Navy and 34–6 to Michigan. Bud Wilkinson's Sooners had won 47 straight games and showed no sign of letting up. Just as they had done with Army eleven years earlier, the Irish defense stiffened, producing a shutout. The 7–0 victory was one of their great moments.

There was little to celebrate over the next six seasons, however. The game appeared to have passed them by. USC and Alabama came back with a vengeance. The South began to rise again with Auburn and LSU also winning national championships for the first time. Eastern football re-emerged in the form of an integrated powerhouse at Syracuse.

In 1964 Notre Dame brought in Ara Parseghian. The "Era of Ara" was one of the most successful in school history. In his first year, Parseghian inherited some talented seniors, namely, quarterback John Huarte and tight end Jack Snow. They grew up in Orange County, California, where they developed pass patterns on the beach during summers. Playing great defense and steady, ball-control offense, the Irish marched through their schedule unbeaten.

Notre Dame's Biggest Rivals? Everyone . . .

Notre Dame versus number one-ranked opponents (1936–2005): 8–16–1.

Notre Dame is 62–13–3 when playing as the number one-ranked team.

The Fighting Irish are 141–118–10 versus ranked opponents.

Alabama's heralded quarterback, Joe Namath, was the Heisman favorite in 1964. When he went down with an injury in the seventh game of the season, Huarte was able to win the award. Still operating under a no-bowl policy, all the Irish needed to do was get past Southern California in a packed L.A. Coliseum.

Oh, that's all.

Huarte engineered Notre Dame's 17–0 halftime lead, but Southern Cal quarterback Craig Fertig led Troy all the way back in the second half. Desperately trying to ward off USC, Notre Dame had one last chance to stop the Trojans on a fourth-down play with about a minute left. Fertig hit receiver Rod Sherman over the middle for a touchdown. It was all over.

Two years later, Notre Dame fielded one of their all-time greatest teams. Led by sophomore quarterback Terry Hanratty, they won their first eight. The Irish defense pitched three consecutive shutouts against Army (35–0), North Carolina (32–0), and Oklahoma (38–0); then two more against Pittsburgh (40–0) and Duke (64–0). As great as their defense was, Michigan State's defense was considered even more dominating, led by defensive end Bubba Smith and linebacker/rover George Webster.

On November 19, Notre Dame traveled to East Lansing for the "Game of the Century." It was hard-fought and competitive, an incredible game, and a big part of history, but other games overshadow it. With the score tied 10–10 late in the fourth, Parseghian had a chance to make it the real "Game of the Century." Had he masterminded a final drive, utilizing the passing of talented Coley O'Brien (who replaced the injured Hanratty) plus the running of Rocky Bleier and Nick Eddy, Notre Dame might have driven into field position—the way USC did against them twelve years later—and kicked a game-winning field goal that *would have made it* the "Game of the Century." Instead, it went down as the "tie one for the Gipper" game.

A week later, Parseghian's Irish came to Los Angeles with their minds on the polls. Despite the tie, Notre Dame maintained the number one position in the Associated Press (although they fell to second in the United Press International). Michigan State stayed number two in the AP, but moved to first in the UPI. Alabama, who started the season number one but fell to third as the year moved on, stayed at number three even though they were unbeaten and untied.

In 1966, both the AP and UPI voted their last poll prior to the bowls. Notre Dame had no bowl to play in. Neither did Michigan State, since they were constrained by the Big 10's no-repeat rule and had no more games. Alabama still had Southern Mississippi and Auburn left, then a Sugar Bowl date with Nebraska.

Parseghian reasoned that he held the top spot in the AP. Michigan State would have no further opportunity to impress the voters, but Alabama did. Furthermore, the voters might figure that a 'Bama victory in the Sugar Bowl, even if it did not technically affect the final AP vote, would figure in voters' thinking. He also knew that the voters had been embarrassed by their awarding of the national title to Alabama two years earlier, only to see the Crimson Tide illegitimatized by their Orange Bowl defeat against Texas. This was followed by another embarrassment when the UPI was stuck calling Michigan State their champions despite its losing to UCLA in the 1966 Rose Bowl.

Did You Know . . .

That when Notre Dame football star Rocky Bleier was injured in Vietnam, the military doctor said just before putting him under for surgery, "Rocky, I went to USC and was in the stands the day Notre Dame beat us, 51–0 at the Coliseum"? Thanks in part to the USC man's excellent work, Bleier eventually was able to make a pro football comeback with the Steelers. Much like the doctors who saved Ronald Reagan after he was shot and told them, "I hope you're Republicans"—the reply was, "We're all Republican today, Mr. President"—in this case, the USC doctor and his staff were all Fighting Irishmen. Lucky ones . . . and good.

The calculation, to Parseghian's way of thinking, was that a big win over the Trojans would garner the title for Notre Dame for four reasons. For one, the voters would rather play it safe and give it to a team that had no bowl game they could lose and therefore make everybody look bad; two, another national title for Alabama followed by a potential loss to Nebraska in the Sugar Bowl seemed an intolerable possibility; three, a large majority of the writers were from the East Coast and were of Catholic persuasion; and four, in the heat of the civil rights struggle, all-white 'Bama was not, to use a 1990s term, the "politically correct" team.

Many people found fault with Notre Dame for "running up the score" against USC, 51–0, in front of their home fans on November 26, 1966—all except the Trojans players, fans, and coaches, all of whom agreed that instead of getting mad at the Irish, it was their job to stop them. They failed.

Parseghian's Machiavellian calculations played out just as he foresaw them. The Irish had the first national title in the "Era of Ara." To what extent the 51–0 drubbing inspired USC against Notre Dame over the next decade and a half is debatable. What is not debatable is that, following this game, beating Southern California became a rare accomplishment for the Notre Dame Fighting Irish. Between 1967 and 1982 they did it twice.

Notre Dame fielded some of the best teams in their history during this period, but they were denied glory year after year by USC. The 1970, 1971, 1974, and 1978 teams all had a good or decent shot at the title but for the USC game. The 1973 and 1977 teams were the only ones to accomplish the feat, and they finished number one on each occasion.

In the 1960s, Notre Dame's consensus All-Americans included Jack Snow, John Huarte, Dick Arrington, Nick Rassas, Nick Eddy, Jim Lynch, Alan Page, Tom Regner, Tom Schoen, Terry Hanratty, George Kunz, and Mike McCoy.

First-round draft picks were Jack Snow (Minnesota, 1965), Nick Eddy (Denver, 1966), Paul Seiler (New York Jets, 1967), Alan Page (Minnesota, 1967), Tom Regner (Houston, 1967), Kevin Hardy (New Orleans, 1968), George Kunz (Atlanta, 1969), Jim Seymour (Los Angeles, 1969), and Mike McCoy (Green Bay, 1970). Snow became a star with the great Los Angeles Rams teams coached by George Allen. After retirement, he was a popular sportscaster. His son, J. T. Snow, became a fancy-fielding first baseman for San Francisco, playing in the 2002 World Series. Page spearheaded great Vikings teams to four

Elite Ten by the Numbers

Associated Press national championships (1936–2008), writers' poll

1. Notre Dame   8   *
2. Oklahoma   7   @
3. Alabama   6   #
4. Southern California 5
5. Miami   5
6. Ohio State   4
7. Nebraska   4
8. Texas   3
9. Michigan   2
10. Penn State   2

*5 no bowls

@1 lost bowl, 1 probation

#1 lost bowl

Alabama (6): 1961, *1964 (split/Arkansas – Billingsley, Football Research, Football Writers, Helms, Poling, National Championship Foundation), 1965, 1978 (split/Southern California – UPI), 1979, 1992

  *Lost Orange Bowl

Miami (5): 1983, 1987, 1989, 1991 (split/Washington – UPI), 2001

Michigan (2): 1948, 1997 (split/Nebraska – USA)

Nebraska (4): 1970, 1971, 1994, 1995

Notre Dame (8): *1943, *1946, *1947, *1949, *1966, 1973 (split/Alabama lost bowl – UPI), 1977, 1988

  *No bowl

Ohio State (4): *1942, 1954 (split/UCLA no bowl – UPI), 1968, 2002

  *No bowl

Oklahoma (7): *1950, 1955, @1956, #1974 (split/Southern California – UPI), 1975, 1985, 2000

  *Lost Sugar Bowl

  @No bowl

  #Probation/no bowl

Penn State (2): 1982, 1986

Southern California (5): 1962, 1967, 1972, 2003, 2004

Texas (3): 1963, 1969, 2005

Notre Dame's "Teammate Heismans"	
1943	Angelo Bertelli
1947	John Lujack
1947	John Lujack
1949	Leon Hart
1953	John Lattner
1956	Paul Hornung (freshman/ineligible '53)

Super Bowls (1970, 1974, 1975, 1977). Pro football's Player of the Year in 1971, when Minnesota's defense carried the terrific moniker Purple People Eaters, Page is a member of the Pro Football Hall of Fame. He became an associate justice of Minnesota's state Supreme Court.

From 1968 to 1970, Joe Theismann starred at Notre Dame. He was frustrated, as Brady Quinn would be thirty-six years later, from achieving ultimate glory. In 1968 Notre Dame was 7-2-1. In 1969 they were 8-2-1. The great 1970 squad, which may have been the best team in the country, was 10-1. Each season, something happened to trip up the Irish. Theismann passed for a school record 526 yards against Southern California in a driving rainstorm at the Coliseum in 1970, but USC won 38-28. Theismann closed out his college career with a monumental 24-11 win over Texas in the Cotton Bowl, ending the Longhorns' national championship aspirations.

Theismann, despite all his accomplishments, was not considered a major professional prospect. He took his services to Canada. Eventually, he went to the National Football League, where he starred for the 1982 Washington Redskins' Super Bowl championship team. In January 1984 Theismann, the NFL Player of the Year that season, brought a 14-2 Redskins team into the Super Bowl against the Los Angeles Raiders. Ex-USC star Marcus Allen overshadowed him, winning the game's MVP trophy while leading his team to a 38-9 triumph. Theismann's career eventually ended on *Monday Night Football* when he suffered an excruciating injury. He has been a leading personality on pro football telecasts, including *Monday Night Football*, for years. Theismann has led a celebrity life and may well join Golden Domers Curly Lambeau, George Trafton, Wayne Millner, George Connor, Paul Hornung, Alan Page, Joe Montana, Nick Buoniconti, Dave Casper, and Johnny "Blood" McNally in the Pro Football Hall of Fame at Canton, Ohio, some day. He was inducted into the National Football Foundation College Hall of Fame in 2004.

America's Team

Notre Dame is 178–91–3 on national TV (through 2005).

In 1973, Notre Dame was itching to get back to the promised land. The field looked to be obstacle laden. Defending national champion and preseason number one Southern

California would have to be contended with at Notre Dame Stadium on October 27. In addition, Ohio State, Michigan, and Alabama were juggernauts that year.

The Trojans, who had not lost since midway through the 1971 campaign, came in with a 23-game unbeaten streak. Quarterback Tom Clements, halfback Eric Penick, and cornerback Luther Bradley pulled out all the stops before a more-fired-up-than-usual Notre Dame crowd. The 23–14 victory spurred the Irish to an unbeaten regular season. When Michigan and Ohio State tied in their big game, the Sugar Bowl, played on New Year's Eve, was for the national championship against unbeaten Alabama.

Clements, Penick, and tight end Dave Casper starred in one of the all-time great college football games. Alabama quarterback Richard Todd scored on a pass-catch-and-pass to put the Tide up 23–21 late in the game. Clements hit tight end Robin Weber on a key third-down conversion deep in Irish territory. From there, Notre Dame drove until Bob Thomas kicked a 19-yard field goal. Alabama had time to rally but Notre Dame held on to win a "barnburner," 24–23. Parseghian had his second national championship. It was Alabama's seventh straight bowl loss.

In 1974, Notre Dame's defense allowed an average of only two yards per rush and was ranked first in the nation when the Irish (9–1) traveled to the Coliseum. Up 24–0 just before the half, they were calculating that with Oklahoma on probation, if they could beat Alabama in the Sugar Bowl while USC beat Ohio State in the Rose Bowl, a repeat national championship might just be theirs. They were almost right; the Irish did beat the Crimson Tide in a donnybrook, 13–11 in the Sugar Bowl, while USC squeaked out a thrilling 18–17 win over the Buckeyes in Pasadena. There was only one problem with their plan: Their 24–0 lead was converted, within the span of just seventeen minutes, into probably the greatest USC victory of all time, 55–24. To this day, nobody has ever adequately explained what happened. Not John McKay; not Trojan assistant coach Craig Fertig; not linebacker Richard "Batman" Wood, quarterback Pat Haden, wide receiver J. K. McKay, or rover Charles Phillips.

Some Notre Dame historians have postulated that the only way it could happen would be if USC had been equipped with "guns and knives." Perhaps the star of the day, the ultimate "Notre Dame killer" himself, Anthony Davis, stated it best: "We turned into madmen." A. D., as he is known, has lived off his performances against Notre Dame in 1972 and 1974 to this day, marketing and signing T-shirts, cups, and posters, in person or through websites.

1974–1975 will not go down as great years at Notre Dame. They were 9–2 with a wonderful win over Alabama in the Sugar Bowl in 1974, then 8–3 in 1975. Defeat against USC, whether by big scores or close scores, tugged at their elbows. But years later, those two seasons turned out to be some of the most memorable in the school's history. That was when Rudy Ruettiger, a walk-on practice player, was part of the program. His story is told in the inspiring 1993 film *Rudy*, starring Sean Astin. Rudy played in the final home game of the 1975 season, a 24–3 win over Georgia Tech. There was a freshman quarterback on that team named Joe Montana.

1977 played out in similar manner to the 1973 campaign after Notre Dame lost to Ole Miss in the second game of the season. Montana, a junior from western Pennsylvania, had come to South Bend with great promise but had so far not shown much of it. USC, now coached by John Robinson, maintained their place at the heights of glory. By the fifth game of the season USC was ranked number one in the nation.

On October 22, the Trojans entered Notre Dame Stadium thinking about the national championship. Notre Dame—not coach Dan Devine, who took over from the retired Parseghian in 1975; not their players; nor their fans—was truly willing to think such grandiose thoughts. A loss to Troy, the second of the season, would end such hopes and make it difficult just to play out a semisuccessful—by Notre Dame standards—season.

Montana got the start, but it was a shaky call. He had performed erratically and engendered little confidence from Devine or the Golden Domers. Devine was not quite as taciturn as he was portrayed in *Rudy*, but he was charismatically challenged. He was a football man. His game was *X*s and *O*s; blocking and tackling; fundamental football. He was at Notre Dame, with all that lore, magic, mystique; how to use that?

A few years earlier, Burt Reynolds had starred in a film about a football game between prison convicts and guards called *The Longest Yard*. In that film, the cons surprise everybody by emerging on the field in new uniforms emblazoned "Mean Machine."

Devine, perhaps desperate, trying to conjure up the image of Rockne inspiring his team with some kind of outside influence, took enough time away from practice and game planning to make an inspirational move of his own. It could be a big hit, but if it did not work out he ran the risk of making himself and his team look foolish. He took the risk.

Devine ordered special green jerseys for the game, but kept it a secret. The Irish warmed up in their traditional blues, then went into the dressing room for final preparations before the contest. USC came out, swaggering with the confidence of champions, waiting for their opponents to take the field.

Twenty minutes before making that entrance, Devine pulled out a box and informed his team that it contained their uniform tops for this game. The players were stunned but immediately sensed that the Kelly green, a symbol of Irish luck, was not just a motivational tool for them, but would electrify the crowd. Not to mention, the Trojans would be thinking about it, too.

When the crowd got sight of the "green machine," they went ballistic, which is saying something. Every Notre Dame crowd goes ballistic, but this was over the top. USC was indeed stunned. They tried to laugh it off as a ploy and at first hit hard to force a fumble with a touchdown recovery. Notre Dame started slowly, but Montana, tight end Ken MacAfee, and linebacker Bob Golic made big, smart plays to create separation. The crowd sensed the upset. In the second half they got it in spades when Montana directed his team to a 49–14 rout.

Oh, what a day. Irish eyes were smiling.

With USC knocked off, Notre Dame set their sights on the only unbeaten team, number one Texas, led by the great Earl Campbell. Montana, his confidence finally restored, led the Irish to an excellent second half, but they remained stuck at number five because the teams ahead of them did not lose. The final regular season poll ranked Texas (11–0) number one, followed by Oklahoma (10–1), Alabama (10–1), Michigan (10–1), and

Notre Dame (10–1). Arkansas, Kentucky, and Penn State were all 10–1 also. The polls had the potential of turning the national championship vote into a chess match. Who would play Texas in the Cotton Bowl?

Michigan was aced out of the equation by virtue of being locked into the Rose Bowl against Washington. A Texas-Oklahoma Cotton Bowl seemed possible, but the Sooners, as Big 8 champions, traditionally played in the Orange Bowl. They had already lost to Texas during the season, anyway. Oklahoma went to battle Arkansas in Miami. Alabama could play Texas in the Cotton Bowl; there was precedent, but as Southeastern Conference champions their tradition was to play in the Sugar Bowl. So they did, against Ohio State.

Notre Dame, who had played Texas in two memorable Cotton Bowls in 1970 and 1971, got the invitation to Dallas. It was the first game of the day, as it always is. If Texas would win, they would be the undisputed national champion. They were favored. In pregame calculations, Oklahoma, Alabama, Michigan, Arkansas, even Penn State, rooted for the Irish, thinking that if they won unimpressively each of these teams would have a shot. Maybe there would be a split vote. Many tried to convince themselves that there would be no "leapfrogging" from fifth to first; that a second-ranked Oklahoma, for instance, would automatically move to number one.

Because of pro football Sunday play-offs, the bowls were held on January 2. Notre Dame linebacker Bob Golic (eighteen tackles) teamed with defensive ends Ross Browner and Willie Fry to lay wicked hits on Texas, who coughed up six fumbles. Campbell gained 116 yards but was never a factor. Jerome Heavens and Vagas Ferguson keyed the ground game. Joe Montana displayed the steady hand that would win four Super Bowl championships in the next twelve years. Notre Dame 38, Texas 10. The dominance of the Irish immediately placed them in a favorable poll position, but they needed to wait it out.

Michigan's outside hopes went out the window when Warren Moon and Washington upended them in the Rose Bowl, 27–20. When Alabama destroyed Ohio State 35–6, Notre Dame hearts sank. Bear Bryant was now a beloved figure, not the accused segregationist of 1966. Would the voters cast in favor of 'Bama to "make up" for the 1966 "Catholic vote" and the 1973 Sugar Bowl?

If Oklahoma could beat Arkansas in the Orange Bowl, further confusion would ensue. Instead the Razorbacks, coached by a young Lou Holtz with an even younger assistant named Pete Carroll, blew the Sooners away, 31–6. That left it between Notre Dame and Alabama. Many Alabamians still think the "Catholic vote" cost them when Notre Dame emerged number one in both the Associated Press and United Press International polls. While the Crimson Tide certainly did all they could do, nobody argued against the notion that Notre Dame took the field against the top-ranked team and the nation's best player in front of their de facto home crowd, winning as convincingly as could be asked of them. They deserved it.

Form continued to play out in 1978. Just as USC extracted revenge in 1974 for the 1973 upset in South Bend, so too did they fight their way back into the victory column that year. In 1978, Notre Dame lost their first two games, 3–0 to Missouri and 28–14 to

Michigan. Then they reeled off eight straight wins heading into the Southern Cal game. The Irish were out of the national picture, but USC was in the hunt.

In many ways the nature of the 1974 and 1978 games reversed itself. The reversal occurred in that USC got out to a big lead, as the Irish had in 1974. Then Joe Montana brought Notre Dame back, as USC had done four years earlier. His performance in that game ranks as one of the greatest ever seen. But in the end, a Frank Jordan 37-yard field goal ended Irish hopes for an upset. The 27–25 Trojan victory rates as one of their most memorable moments, propelling them to victory over Michigan in the Rose Bowl and another national title a little over a month later.

Consensus All-Americans in the 1970s were Larry DiNardo, Tom Gatewood, Clarence Ellis, Walt Patulski, Greg Marx, Dave Casper, Mike Townsend, Pete Demmerle, Gerry DiNardo, Steve Niehaus, Ross Browner, Ken MacAfee, Luther Bradley, Bob Golic, Dave Huffman, and Vagas Ferguson. First-round draft picks of the decade included Walt Patulski, the first choice of the 1972 draft (Buffalo), Clarence Ellis (Atlanta, 1972), Mike Kadish (Miami, 1972), Mike Fanning (Los Angeles, 1975), Steve Niehaus (Seattle, 1976), Ken MacAfee (San Francisco, 1978), Ross Browner (Cincinnati, 1978), Luther Bradley (Detroit, 1978), and Vagas Ferguson (New England, 1980). Joe Montana of the San Francisco 49ers of course was the MVP of three Super Bowls and is a member of the Pro Football Hall of Fame. Casper was an All-Pro member of the 1976 Oakland Raiders world champions. He, too, is in the Pro Football Hall of Fame.

In 1980 Notre Dame was 9–0–1 with a strong shot at the national championship when they rolled into the Coliseum against an injury-depleted Trojan team. Backup running back Michael Harper keyed Southern California's 20–3 win. The Irish had one last-gasp try to grab the voters' attention but were beaten by unbeaten Georgia and Herschel Walker in the Sugar Bowl. The Bulldogs took their first national title.

In 1981, the nature of Notre Dame football changed. Gerry Faust, who had built Moeller High School in Cincinnati into the greatest of all prep football powerhouses, was hired. Faust had no previous college coaching experience. A devout Catholic, strict academician, and rule abider, his was most definitely the moral high road. When Faust's Irish beat Louisiana State in the opener 27–9, *Sports Illustrated* touted him as, perhaps not the "second coming," but up there with John the Baptist. When the Irish lost at Michigan

Elite Ten by the Numbers

Associated Press number one poll rankings (1936–2008)

1. Southern California	90		6. Miami	62
2. Notre Dame	89		7. Texas	46
3. Oklahoma	88		8. Alabama	34
4. Ohio State	86		9. Michigan	32
5. Nebraska	65			

25-7 the next week, and in October fell to Marcus Allen and USC 14–7, Irish fans began to look at him the way Herodias, the wife of King Herod's brother Philip, looked at John the Baptist. It would take five years, but eventually Faust would meet the football version of John the Baptist's fate and lose *his* figurative head.

Faust brought in hotshot quarterback Steve Beuerlein from Servite High School in Anaheim, California, but he was no "second coming" of Montana. Faust's teams were a pedestrian 5-6 (1981), 6-4-1 (1982), 7-5 (1983), 7-5 (1984), and 5-6 (1985). Their gravest sin was a 58-7 loss at the hands of the "criminal element" Miami Hurricanes in 1985, which some fans portended to be a sure sign of the Apocalypse. Lost in the consternation over Faust's weak record was the fact that, after losing again to Southern California, 17–13 in 1982, he beat the Trojans three straight years (1983–1985), starting Notre Dame on a thirteen-year unbeaten streak against USC.

Faust was unceremoniously dumped. A man some thought of as his total opposite, Lou Holtz, was brought in. Holtz may have been given a bad rap. He, too, was a Catholic boy and lifelong Notre Dame fan now fulfilling his dream job, so the image of the mercenary coach being drafted from the pro ranks (his stay with the New York Jets was actually a brief one) is not quite accurate. But if Faust was "letter of the law" straight, Holtz was not. To the extent that somebody—alumni, faculty, the Pope?—gave him free reign to restore Notre Dame football luster at all costs has been speculated upon yet not truly deciphered.

What is known is that Holtz did restore Notre Dame football luster. For a couple of years, his teams were as good—as fast, talented, and powerful—as any the school has ever had. In Notre Dame's world, that was not necessarily considered a good thing.

"Notre Dame always fielded country boys from the Midwest," wrote Bill Dwyre, long-time editor of the *Los Angeles Times* and a Notre Dame alum. "They'd come to the big city and win in underdog fashion."

The historical memory conjured up the image of outmanned Irish teams rising up like David to strike down such Goliaths as Army, Georgia Tech, Oklahoma, USC, Alabama, and Texas. Somehow, the fact that *Notre Dame* has more often than not been Goliath has not resonated, at least as far as the mythology goes. "Country boys," in Dwyre's terminology, more often than not meant white kids with Italian-, Irish-, or Polish-sounding names: Bertelli, Szymanski, Dancewicz, Lujack, Siko, Mastrangelo, Connor, Sullivan, O'Connor, Tripucka, Ostrowski, Guglielmi, Varrichione, Pietrosante, Buoniconti, Lamonica, Kelly, Goeddeke, Hanratty, Kuechenberg, Gladieux, McCoy, Patulski, Mahalic, Niehaus, MacAfee, Golic, Montana.

Knute Rockne, the son of Finnish émigrés, had played to the cities and started a tradition of Ellis Island second- and third-generation immigrant kids who sounded like they just *had* to have come from Chicago, Boston, the Bronx; the steel mills of Pennsylvania; factory towns in Ohio and Michigan.

A few came from the South. Paul Hornung was a Kentucky boy. An endless aqueduct of California gold had never flowed into South Bend, absent the occasional trickle: John Huarte, Jack Snow, Daryle Lamonica, Steve Beuerlein. It was hard to convince a California "blue-chipper" that the monastic life of Notre Dame was better than the party scene at USC, where a guy might see more good-looking girls walking from Heritage Hall to Howard Jones Field every day than he would in four years under "touchdown Jesus."

But Holtz reversed form. He got guys that Miami wanted. He stole kids from USC and UCLA. He used his Ohio connections to outrecruit the Buckeyes. Brought 'em in from the South. Holtz inherited a new kind of player Faust had managed to land, Tim Brown from Woodrow Wilson High School in Dallas. Then he went after the sort of guy one expected to see wearing a Hurricane or Seminole uniform, Raghib "Rocket" Ismail.

Notre Dame, in accord with its Christian principles, had always been open to black players, but its location and "smash mouth" big-line reputation had attracted more guys whose names ended with vowels. Holtz recognized that this was part of the past. A new day had arrived.

With the South thoroughly integrated by 1986, the SEC and all teams on that side of the Mason-Dixon Line were scooping up all that African American talent. It was no longer ticketed for USC and Michigan State, where a Clarence Davis or a Bubba Smith landed in the hands of John McKay and Duffy Daugherty like so much manna from Heaven.

It was also an age of steroids, new TV contracts, big money, corruption, and recruiting pressures. It was now an era of bowl games that were no longer New Year's Day festivals but rather enormous paydays for universities otherwise lacking the endowments of Harvard and Yale. Holtz knew it. He knew how to play the game. He had a national reputation, having coached Arkansas to glory. He had NFL imprimatur, the savvy, the contacts. He was like a "rainmaker," a former Senator or winner of a big televised trial who is hired by a law firm to attract wealthy clients who do not pay attention to how many billable hours they are being charged.

Holtz was there for eleven seasons and won one national championship, yet the Irish missed three, maybe even four others by some very thin margins. As a practice coach, game strategist, referee baiter, press manipulator, recruiter, alumni schmoozer, and competitor, he was among the best. He was a winner.

It took two years to weed out Faust's slow players, figure out a way to make use of his one fast one—Tim Brown—and bring in more speed of his own. They were 5-6 in 1986, then 8-4 in 1987 with a 35-10 loss to Texas A&M in the Cotton Bowl. In these two years, however, there were highlights for the ages.

In 1986 the Irish trailed USC 37–20 in the fourth quarter at the Coliseum. The L.A. crowd had mixed emotions. On the one hand, it looked as if they would *finally* beat the Irish after three straight desultory losses. On the other hand, Trojan alums were no happier with coach Ted Tollner than Golden Domers had been with Faust. If Tollner won, then won his bowl game, he would not be fired. Nobody around USC much figured that the program could attain past glories with Tollner.

Tim Brown (252 all-purpose yards) gave them, perhaps in a rude manner, what they were "looking for," leading Notre Dame in a furious 18-point comeback to win 38–37. Coliseum fans were shocked. Even more shocked were TV viewers. John Carney's 19-yard game-winning field goal came during a CBS commercial, so all people saw was an Irish celebration and a replay. Tollner (1–7 versus Notre Dame and UCLA, 0–4 against the

Elite Ten by the Numbers

All-Americans (all services through 2008)

1.	Ohio State	179 first team
2.	Notre Dame	176 first team, 76 second team
3.	Southern California	153
4.	Oklahoma	148
5.	Michigan	125 first team (through 2005)
6.	Texas	124
7.	Nebraska	106 first team
8.	Alabama	104; 92 first team, honored 103 (through 2005)
9.	Penn State	91
10.	Miami	81

Irish) was dumped. Brown's national TV effort against Southern California vaulted him into Heisman contention. In 1987 his spectacular performance won him the award.

1988 was a seminal year in college football, or at least it looked that way most of the season. Notre Dame went to the veer offense, led by athletic quarterback Tony Rice. It was a new wrinkle at Notre Dame, where traditional drop-back quarterbacks engineered ball-control offenses, mixing short passes with a low-risk running game. That was the secret of John Huarte's, Terry Hanratty's, Tom Clements's, and Joe Montana's success. Joe Theismann had been a little more wide open. Nobody, however, had ever mistook the Irish offense for the Sooners, the Longhorns, the Razorbacks . . . until now.

The opener was a humdinger, with Raghib Ismail announcing his presence with authority in the 19–17 squeaker over Michigan. Early on USC, now coached by Larry Smith, faced adversity but managed to withstand challenges from Stanford and Washington to remain unbeaten. The best team in the country in the beginning appeared to be UCLA, where quarterback Troy Aikman led the Bruins to a startling 41–28 victory over Nebraska.

Did You Know . . .

That seventy Notre Dame coaches/alumni have also been pro football coaches (as of 2006)?

On October 15, defending national champion Miami arrived at Notre Dame Stadium. The excitement that hung in the air was reminiscent of Crusaders defending Christendom from the Mohammedan hordes in order to earn eternal salvation. The annual game with USC certainly revived in Notre Dame hearts the sense that they represented Midwestern piety against Hollywood worshipping the "golden calf" in the form of Oscar statues, but in reality USC's reputation as a conservative, patriotic, former Methodist school belied the conundrum of its Beautiful People reputation. But *Miami* . . . ?!

They called it the "Catholics versus the Convicts." Only one year earlier, Miami's Jerome Brown, dressed in full battle fatigues, had orchestrated a walkout of a Fiesta Bowl banquet with Penn State. The Hurricanes were loud and obnoxious. Many had been in trouble with the law or were seemingly always on the verge of so doing. Their image was of a bunch of guys sleepin' in until noon, grabbin' some free grub courtesy of a booster's credit card, getting in a nice ride provided by a friendly car dealer, then driving to a pro-style practice run by coach Jimmy "My Slick Hair Never Moves" Johnson. They were fast, "juiced," and "hip-hopped" to the nth degree. The rap scene was hitting hard, and their guys played the part of "public enemies" and "outlaws."

While Notre Dame was no longer just a bunch of Polish fellas named Patulski and Szymanski—in truth they probably had as many fast, athletic black players as the Hurricanes—nobody could help making mental note of the racial element that was outlined against a blue-gray October sky, under the watchful eyes of "touchdown Jesus." To the Notre Dame faithful, it was good versus evil. It was a chance at redemption after the 58-7 drubbing administered by Miami three years earlier, not to mention the 20-0 loss to the Hurricanes in 1983, the 31-13 loss to them in 1984, the 24-0 shutout at their hands the year before. . . .

How good was this game? In Notre Dame's eyes it may have been the sweetest of them all. The best game ever played? Well, weighing all the factors that go into that consideration—a bowl game, for the national title late in the season, a Heisman battle, traditional rivals—perhaps others rank higher. However, for sheer drama, Notre Dame mystique, and the glory of beating an opponent one considers not merely "illegitimate" in that they took it upon themselves to rewrite the rules, but were somehow "morally inferior"—well, this was one righteous fall Saturday.

A pregame shoving match did little to help Notre Dame gain the moral high ground at first. Miami came out with their smoking offense, led by dynamic quarterback Steve Walsh. The teams were explosive in the first half, battling to a 21-21 tie. Many quietly felt relief that the Irish could hold their own, but the sense that Miami was about to turn the thing into a track meet was palpable. Trailing 21-7, Walsh had led two quick scoring drives to tie it. Irish linebacker Frank Stams saved the day, forcing two fumbles while making eight tackles. Slowly but surely Notre Dame began to gain control in the second half. The partisan crowd no doubt affected Miami. Trailing 31-24, the Hurricanes drove within sight of the Irish goal, but Notre Dame linebacker Michael Stonebreaker recovered running back Cleveland Gary's fumble. It was a controversial call that Jimmy Johnson vociferously argued was an incomplete pass, but what was done was done.

Both teams lost fumbles in their succeeding possessions, setting up a final game-deciding drive by Walsh and Miami. The crowd was on pins and needles, the prospect of a Miami comeback in their house too horrendous to bear. A blasphemy of some kind. To the horror of the South Bend throng, Miami scored on a 7-yard fourth-down touchdown pass by Walsh to Andre Brown.

There was no overtime then. Nobody wanted to see a tie. Both teams could lose their national title chances if they tied. Johnson calculated that the upset of a tie would play like a Miami loss with voters. He went for two. Walsh tried for the corner. Bodies collided in the

Elite Ten by the Numbers
Consensus All-Americans (through 2008)

1. Notre Dame	96	6. Nebraska	52
2. Southern California	86	7. Texas	48
3. Ohio State	84	8. Miami	37 (through 2004)
4. Michigan	73 (through 2005)	9. Penn State	34 (through 2004)
5. Oklahoma	65	10. Alabama	29

air. In football, there is the perilous sense that a pass interference call can be flagged on virtually any close aerial play. A loose hand, bodies brushing together, a defensive back blocking out the receiver too aggressively. It would have taken courage for the referee to make that call in that stadium at that time. Replays show that it was close, but they also do not reveal that it was pass interference. It was football, and the best referees "let 'em play." The ball fell harmlessly on the "green plain" while *this* Miami team was "swept away by the South Bend cyclone," their 36-game regular season winning streak now a thing of the past.

Oh, may Irish eyes be smiling!

With Miami out of the way, UCLA took over as the top-rated team in the nation. A unique triangulation had occurred, with all three teams set for a quasi-play-off in November. It looked like 1988 was a "California year," an event that occurs every so often; 1962 and 1972, in particular. In the spring, Stanford had won the College World Series and the Los Angeles Lakers the NBA championship. The Oakland A's and Los Angeles Dodgers won their respective leagues, meeting in an all-California World Series, with the Dodgers prevailing in five games. The San Francisco 49ers were on their way to Super Bowl victory. Now UCLA and USC looked to be the class of collegiate football. The struggle for the number one ranking and the Heisman Trophy, between UCLA's Troy Aikman and USC's Rodney Peete, was in the offing just as it had been with UCLA's Gary Beban and USC's O. J. Simpson when the teams played for a Rose Bowl and national championship twenty-one years prior.

Then UCLA lost to Timm Rosenbach and Washington State on October 24 to fall to 7–1, but they would still have their shot at unbeaten, number two USC. Notre Dame took over the number one position. Despite their perch, conventional wisdom held that the explosive Peete, playing in front of a home crowd at the Coliseum, would inspire Troy over the Irish. Surely Notre Dame could not extend their winning streak over USC to six games . . . could they?

The teams played it out without further upset, and on November 19 UCLA hosted their crosstown rivals in front of more than 100,000 fans at the venerable Rose Bowl. The Bruins looked to be the favorite, playing as the home team with Aikman considered to be the better quarterback. Their respective professional careers demonstrated that he was, but not on this day. Peete engineered a steady 31–22 win, setting up one of the most ballyhooed regular season epics of all time.

Incredibly, despite all the incredible games played between USC and Notre Dame since 1926, never had the teams met as one-two until now. Accusations that Holtz was a "win at all costs" coach went out the window when he suspended stars Tony Brooks and Ricky Watters for "excessive lateness." Southern Cal was unable to stop Rice on the option and was dominated in first-half play but was within hailing distance at 14–10 when the teams went into the half.

In the second half, however, cornerback Stan Smagala intercepted Peete. With Frank Stams running crushing interference, he returned it 64 yards for the touchdown that broke Trojan hearts. Notre Dame, 27–10. Neither Peete nor Aikman won the Heisman Trophy. The great Barry Sanders of Oklahoma State could not be denied in the end.

This set Notre Dame up for an oddly anticlimactic national championship showdown with 11–0 West Virginia in the Fiesta Bowl. After monumental battles between the Trojans and Bruins and the Trojans and Irish, America had become used to traditional rivals playing each other for the highest stakes. It was a "coming-out party" for the Mountaineers, who were never thought of as much beyond the basketball school producing Jerry West—at least not until January 2, 1989. Rice was his usual effective self, running to set up the pass, while Stams simply dominated. A boring 23–6 Notre Dame blowout got interesting late when Rice was intercepted, but it was never really in doubt, 34–21. Holtz had his national title.

Michigan entered the 1989 campaign with national championship aspirations, which served only to make Notre Dame's 24–19 victory over the Wolverines on September 11 that much more important. Another season played out, with powerhouses angling for the eventual "gunfight at the O-K corral" in the form of top-ranked 11–0 Notre Dame losing to number seven Miami, 27–10 at the Orange Bowl. It was a bitter pill to swallow for Notre Dame. Not only was it defeat at the hands of a hated rival, but it ended (a) their chances at a repeat national championship, (b) their 23-game winning streak, and (c) their 19-week run atop the AP polls (at the time a new record, having eclipsed the old mark of 17 set by USC in 1972–1973).

A 21–6 victory over Colorado in the Orange Bowl game completed the 12–1 season, good for a number two ranking in the AP, third in the UPI. Miami captured their third national championship and thus ended hopes for Notre Dame's mythical "Team of the Decade" status. In the 1980s, Notre Dame started with a national championship contender, slipped into mediocrity, then vaulted back into the highest echelons of collegiate excellence. Consensus Irish All-Americans include John Scully, Bob Crable, Tim Brown, Frank Stams, and Michael Stonebreaker (1988, 1990). Additional star players were Stacey Toran, who went on to an excellent career with the Los Angeles Raiders; Mark Bavaro, a Super Bowl player with the New York Giants; running back Allen Pinkett; and Steve Beuerlein, a starting quarterback for the Raiders. First-round NFL draftees were Crable (New York Jets, 1982), Tony Hunter (Buffalo, 1983), Greg Bell (Buffalo, 1984), Eric Dorsey (New York Giants, 1986), Tim Brown (Los Angeles Raiders, 1988), and Andy Heck (Seattle, 1989). Brown is a surefire Hall of Famer, considered one of the greatest receivers in NFL history with the Raiders.

1990 turned out to be a season of upsets. Notre Dame, Miami, and Florida State were among the powerhouses that fell by the wayside. The Irish certainly were as good as any team in the land, but in the end their chance to "upset the apple cart" against number one Colorado fell one point short, 10–9 in the Orange Bowl. The Buffaloes and Georgia Tech shared the national title, while Notre Dame (9–3) finished a disappointing sixth in both polls.

In 1991 Notre Dame was 10–3, ranked thirteenth, but the season ended on a very upbeat note when they beat Florida 38–29 in the Sugar Bowl. In 1992, a 17–17 tie with Michigan left a bad taste in their mouths, but it was nothing compared to the 33–16 upset administered to them when Bill Walsh's Stanford Cardinal came to Notre Dame Stadium. At 10–1–1, the Irish finished fourth in the Associated Press after beating Texas A&M 28–3 in the Cotton Bowl. 1993 turned out to be one of the most exciting, crazy, "close but no cigar" years in college football history.

Defending national champion Alabama, Florida State, Nebraska, and Notre Dame, plus on-probation Auburn, all battled each other at various points in the season. Even though both Bobby Bowden's Seminoles and Tom Osborne's Cornhuskers were juggernauts—two of the best teams in respective school history—the Irish looked to have made it through one of the most Darwinian "survival of the fittest" seasons ever.

The 1988 USC-Notre Dame game in Los Angeles was huge, but the 1993 Notre Dame-Florida State battle in South Bend was, as they say, "off the hook." This time, action on the field lived up to the pregame hype. ESPN was big by then, with a *GameDay* presence fueling the intense enthusiasm engulfing Notre Dame Stadium on November 13, 1993.

Amazingly, the Irish had never knocked off a top-ranked opponent at home. Florida State's Heisman Trophy-winning quarterback, Charlie Ward, threw a touchdown pass to Kevin Knox, putting number one Florida State in front by 7–0. Notre Dame roared back to take a 21–7 lead. Florida State seemed to lose focus and trailed by 24–7 and 31–17. With 2:26 left, the Seminoles scored on a fourth-and-goal pass by Ward to Kevin McCorvey from 20 yards out. It barely slipped through Irish defender Brian Magee's hands.

Just like the 1988 Miami game, Notre Dame needed to hang on against a determined foe. A partially blocked punt gave Ward one last shot, but Shawn Wooden knocked down his last-gasp pass to give Notre Dame the 31–24 triumph, one of the biggest in their hallowed history. But it did not seem to settle much. There was immediate talk of a Notre Dame-Florida State bowl rematch, which left unbeaten Nebraska and West Virginia wondering where they fit into the picture. Notre Dame was in the driver's seat any way you cut it . . . for a week.

Number seventeen Boston College came to town. Few if any games have seesawed in such wild fashion. Irish fans were exhausted by the previous week's football version of Anzio or Bastogne. BC, the little Catholic school, hardly seemed much of a concern. For years, Notre Dame had not played other Catholic colleges. This disturbed some who felt that had they played the likes of the University of San Francisco, the University of Santa Clara, Loyola, St. Mary's, and other small but once-strong Catholic schools, those programs would have survived instead of withering on the vine . . . thus leaving Notre Dame as the only real major college choice for Catholic players. That is, except for BC, who had stuck it out and were looking to get at the Irish for their perceived slights of the Catholic brethren, not to mention a 54–7 shellacking at the hands of Notre Dame in 1992. That game seemed to have validated the "no Catholics" policy.

The Eagles jumped out to a 28–14 lead. Quarterback Glenn Foley appeared to have iced the upset win with a touchdown pass to Pete Mitchell, making it 38–17. But Notre Dame forged a comeback for the ages. A quick scoring drive was followed by a turnover and another touchdown. It was 38–32 BC, with four minutes remaining. Notre Dame held, setting up a brilliant, tumbling fourth-down catch from 4 yards out by Lake Dawson from quarterback Kevin McDougal with a mere 1:09 to play. The scene was utter bedlam as only Notre Dame Stadium can get.

Notre Dame kicked off. BC got the ball with 15 extra yards tacked on by virtue of a personal foul against Notre Dame. Foley then threw two passes to Mitchell and a screen to Ivan Boyd. Racing upfield against the notorious "prevent defense" (which as every fan has joked seems good only in "preventing victory"), the Eagles were at the Irish 24. A dropped interception, however, was what killed Notre Dame, giving BC one last shot via a 41-yard field goal by David Gordon that was straight and true. 41–39, Boston College. Few teams—perhaps only USC and Michigan on occasion, but not many others—had ever reversed the tables on Notre Dame in this manner. Miracles were the province of the Irish, but "touchdown Jesus" smiled on Gordon and his Catholic-school teammates that memorable November night.

Notre Dame's invite to the Cotton Bowl, which by this time was held in a crummy, dilapidated stadium in a game with little of the old prestige, was a big anticlimax, even with an exciting 24–21 win over Texas A&M. They finished number three in the final rankings.

That night, Florida State beat unbeaten Nebraska 18–16 to give Bobby Bowden his first national championship. It was quite a lackluster defensive struggle. Notre Dame players were forced to watch, feeling that they were better than both of the teams playing.

Irish fans leaving the Cotton Bowl after the win over Texas A&M were happy, as all college football fans are when their team wins a big bowl game, regardless of residual disappointment over having fallen short of the ultimate prize. They still had a great team that dominated the field of play; a genius-level coach bringing in a plethora of national "blue-chippers"; and expectations that they would continue to play "Notre Dame football" as God intended it for years to come. That proverbial "Top 25 poll of the twenty-first century" would have placed the Irish firmly at the very top. Their longtime rivals, Southern Cal, were floundering amid hope that there was still enough of the *Picture of Dorian Gray* hanging on the Heritage Hall wall to keep them in the top five. Notre Dame had kept up with the Joneses, or at least the Miamis, Florida States, and Nebraskas. Alabama had fallen but picked themselves back up. Penn State was still a contender for the throne. USC was almost embarrassed to still call themselves Notre Dame's "rival." Their performance against their other main competitor, UCLA, was no better.

Thus is the nature of hubris and sports. The win over the Aggies turned out to be Notre Dame's last bowl victory. An *NCAA record nine consecutive bowl losses* followed. They lost to:

- Colorado, 41–24
  (1995 Fiesta Bowl)
- Florida State, 31–26
  (1996 Orange Bowl)
- Louisiana State, 27–9
  (1997 Independence Bowl)
- Georgia Tech, 35–28
  (1999 Gator Bowl)
- Oregon State, 41–9
  (2001 Fiesta Bowl)
- North Carolina State, 28–6
  (2003 Gator Bowl)
- Oregon State, 38–21
  (2004 Insight Bowl)
- Ohio State, 34–20
  (2006 Fiesta Bowl)
- Louisiana State, 41–14
  (2007 Sugar Bowl)

Just as disturbing as the defeats is the fact that after the 1996, 1999, 2001, and 2003 seasons, Notre Dame did not even play in a bowl game. In 1994, USC ended the 11-game winning streak with a 17–17 tie. In 1995, the Irish beat a good 6–0 Trojan team 38–10, but the unbeaten skein finally came to an end in the form of a 27–20 loss to John Robinson's Trojans in the 1996 game at the Coliseum.

Don Yaeger's 1993 bombshell book, *Under the Tarnished Dome*, purported to tell "how Notre Dame betrayed its ideals for football glory." After its publication, Notre Dame cut back on the recruiting tactics Holtz had used to assemble his great champions of the 1980s and early 1990s. It had produced 1990s All-Americans like Raghib "Rocket" Ismail, Chris Zorich (Lombardi winner, 1990), Todd Lyght, Mirko Jurkovic, Aaron Taylor (Lombardi winner, 1993), Jeff Burris, and Bobby Taylor.

The pros had come a-callin', too: Lyght (first round to the Rams, 1991), Ricky Watters (San Francisco, 1991), Zorich (Bears, 1991), Ismail (Raiders, 1991), Stonebreaker (Eagles, 1991), Derek Brown (first round to the Giants, 1992), quarterback Rick Mirer (first round to the Seahawks, 1993), Jerome Bettis (first round to the Rams, 1993), Tom Carter (first round to the Redskins, 1993), Irv Carter (first round to the Saints, 1993), Demetrius DuBose (Buccaneers, 1993), Bryant Young (first round to the 49ers, 1994), Aaron Taylor (first round to the Packers, 1994), and Jeff Burris (first round to the Bills, 1994). Watters and Young starred with the 49ers. Bettis helped Pittsburgh win the 2006 Super Bowl. Taylor had an outstanding career on great Green Bay Packers teams before embarking on a television sportscasting career.

But after the 1993 season, there was a sharp decline. No Irish player would earn a consensus All-American selection in the remaining years of the 1990s. The pipeline of first-round picks dried up with the exception of Renaldo Wynn to Jacksonville (1997) and Luke Petitgout to the New York Giants (1999).

Notre Dame's College Hall of Famers (48)

Players				
Jerry Groom	1948–1950	John Huarte	1962–1964
Adam Walsh	1922–1924	Johnny Lujack	1943–1947
Tommy Yarr	1929–1931	Harry Stuhldreher	1922–1924
Hunk Anderson	1918–1921	Joe Theismann	1968–1970
Jack Cannon	1927–1929	Bob Williams	1948–1950
Bill Fischer	1945–1948	James Crowley	1922–1924
Frank Hoffmann	1930–1931	George Gipp	1917–1920
Bert Metzger	1928–1930	Johnny Lattner	1951–1953
John Smith	1925–1927	Creighton Miller	1941–1943
George Connor	1942–1947	Don Miller	1922–1924
Ziggy Czarobski	1942–1947	Marchy Schwartz	1929–1931
Jim Martin	1946–1949	William Shakespeare	1933–1935
Edgar Miller	1922–1924	Red Sitko	1946–1949
Fred Miller	1926–1928	Ray Eichenlaub	1911–1914
Bob Dove	1940–1942	Elmer Layden	1922–1924
Leon Hart	1946–1949	Louis Salmon	1900–1903
Jim Martin	1946–1949	Jim Lynch	1964–1966
Wayne Millner	1933–1935	Chris Zorich	1987–1990
Ross Browner	1973–1977	Tim Brown	1984–1987
Alan Page	1964–1966	*Coaches*	
Ken MacAfee	1974–1977	Dan Devine	1975–1980
Angelo Bertelli	1941–1943	Jesse Harper	1906–1917
Frank Carideo	1928–1930	Frank Leahy	1939–1953
Ralph Guglielmi	1951–1954	Ara Parseghian	1964–1974
Paul Hornung	1954–1956	Knute Rockne	1918–1930
		Lou Holtz	1986–1996

It would not be entirely accurate to blame the demise of Notre Dame between 1994 and 2004 (or the present day, depending upon their standards) on the conscious decision not to recruit a certain "type" of player who might not have lived up to their long-held academic traditions, or been a little more of an off-field problem than was deemed acceptable in South Bend (although quite normal in Miami, Norman, and other places).

In 1994 a new quarterback came on the scene, and he was "cursed." Ron Powlus was the most heralded prep quarterback in the nation, a player who entered college with as many accolades as Todd Marinovich had arrived at USC with in 1988. But the "curse" of Powlus came in the form of longtime college football analyst and notoriously biased

All-Time Notre Dame Team

Selected by *Blue and Gold* magazine

OFFENSE		DEFENSE	
Pos.	*Player*	*Pos.*	*Player*
LG	Hunk Anderson	DE	Leon Hart
G	Bill Fischer	DE	Ross Browner
T	George Connor	DT	Alan Page
T	Jim Martin	DT	Chris Zorich
C	Adam Walsh	LB	Jim Lynch
TE	Dave Casper	LB	Bob Golic
FL	Raghib Ismail	LB	Bob Crable
FL	Jeff Samardzija	DB	Luther Bradley
QB	Joe Montana	DB	Johnny Lattner
TB	George Gipp	DB	Todd Lyght
FB	Jerome Bettis	DB	Johnny Lujack
PK	John Carney	P	Craig Hentrich
UT	Paul Hornung		

Notre Dame fan Beano Cook. He breathlessly informed America that young Mr. Powlus would "win two or three Heismans."

Charles White, who had bragged the same thing about himself when he entered USC in 1976, could have told Powlus how tough such an accomplishment was, not to mention living up to the prediction even if it had been not by him but on his "behalf." White had one of the greatest college careers in history, setting numerous records, yet came away with "only" one himself.

Powlus started four straight years. Notre Dame was 6–5–1 (1994), 9–3 (1995), 8–3 (1996), and 7–6 (1997). He was not terrible; he led the team in passing every season—but won no Heismans, not to mention no bowl games and, in his last two years, no games against USC, or Michigan, or Stanford. Hawaii fell, 23–22 in Honolulu, if there was any consolation to be had.

All reports were that Powlus was a fine young man and a credit to the University of Notre Dame, but he was never even drafted. His name appears on the roster of the 2000–2001 Philadelphia Eagles, yet his contribution to their cause was nil. Unlike Marinovich, Powlus never embarrassed anybody, but his case points out the great mystery of sports; the fallibility of scouting; and the deadly, hypercompetitive nature of greatness. Many are called, few are chosen. When observing the Joe Montanas, Paul Hornungs, and Alan Pages, consider the Ron Powluses and so many others like him. Fans need to understand that in Montana, Hornung, Page, and their like, one is in the presence of greatness rarer than the most exquisite piece of art or fine diamonds.

Between 1997 and 2004, Notre Dame's coaches were Bob Davie and Tyrone Willingham. The 1998 squad entered the USC game 9–1, but losses to the Trojans and to

Elite Ten by the Numbers

All-Star Games (Hula Bowl, East-West Shrine, Senior Bowl,
College All-Star, Japan Bowl, Coaches All-America, Blue-Gray, et al.) (through 2006)

1. Notre Dame: College All-Star (163; 2 MVPs, 6 coaches), Blue-Gray (42), Japan (41), Gridiron Classic (13), Hula (76; 1 coach), East-West Shrine (118; 4 MVPs), Senior (51; 1 MVP); Total: 504
2. Southern California: Hula (130), East-West Shrine (102), Senior (54), College All-Star (72), Japan (40), Coaches All-America (26); Total: 424
3. Ohio State: Hula (77), East-West Shrine (111), Senior (57), Blue-Gray (39), Rotary (15); Total: 299

Georgia Tech in the Gator Bowl ended that season with a thud. Similarly, the 2000 team had the shine of a 9–2 record going into the Fiesta Bowl. When Oregon State made the game look like a track meet in a 41–9 drubbing, it seemed they would have been better off not going at all. Willingham's first team (2002) also started 10–1 but was lambasted by Southern Cal (44–13) and North Carolina State in the Gator Bowl (28–6).

Charlie Weis came in 2005 with a tremendous reputation built as the offensive coordinator of the three-time Super Bowl champion New England Patriots. A former Notre Dame student (but not a player), he represented a unique combination of pro savvy and school loyalty. In his first year, the Irish came *this close* to beating USC at home. In the end, however, the Trojans' 34–31 victory over Notre Dame turned out to be one of the greatest moments in the history of Southern California.

Notre Dame was never a team to consider close losses "moral victories," and neither did Weis when asked if he would characterize the last-second defeat in such a manner. His practical NFL side was plain to see as he said that a loss was a loss, not a "moral victory."

Like Davie's 1998 team and Willingham's 2002 squad, however, the 2005 Irish ended their season in ignominy with a resounding 34–20 loss to Troy Smith and Ohio State in the Fiesta Bowl. Beano Cook and many pundits predicted a national championship for Notre Dame along with a Heisman Trophy for senior quarterback Brady Quinn in 2006. It was a year of incredible comebacks, and indeed Quinn may have been the nation's best player. But Michigan destroyed them in South Bend, and USC destroyed them in Los Angeles. LSU also destroyed them in the Sugar Bowl. Their 10–3 record and number seventeen finish in the AP poll (nineteenth in the *USA Today*/BCS) demonstrated that a good record in late November followed by consecutive crushing losses when the games count is little more than a bluff; a façade; a Potemkin village hiding the shaky reality beyond first glance. Quinn was completely outplayed by LSU's JaMarcus Russell in the Sugar Bowl. Russell was the first pick of the 2007 draft, Quinn number twenty-two (Cleveland).

If these mediocrities did not occur while Pete Carroll and Southern California were simultaneously imitating, if not threatening, to altogether create a better record than Knute Rockne's Irish (1920s), Frank Leahy's Irish (1940s), Bud Wilkinson's Sooners

(1950s), John McKay's Trojans (1960s), and Bear Bryant's Crimson Tide (1970s), then Notre Dame would still have enough polish to hold them off. Their tradition would still be the number one all-time collegiate football dynasty.

Carroll and the Trojans, however, have simply been too dazzling. They have caught them or passed them in too many historical statistics. Their modern record is too great in comparison with the "leather helmet" mystique of the Irish. The Trojans have passed the Irish.

This said, the Irish can take solace. First, USC has been there before, namely in the early 1980s, but like the 101st Airborne Division defending Bastogne, Notre Dame fought them off. The history of Notre Dame football is one in which the program has achieved enormous success with occasional down periods. This describes every collegiate tradition. No program goes forever without slipping up. USC has had its fair share of failures, as have Alabama, Oklahoma, Ohio State, Miami, Nebraska, Texas, Michigan, and Penn State. Many schools were hardly even on the college football map for decades while Notre Dame was defining what the game meant to America.

There is a cyclical nature to success in college sports. The right coach must combine with the right recruiting classes. Luck and geography play a part in it. Notre Dame has advantages and disadvantages. They must get players who meet high academic standards; who often must be willing to attend school far from home, in a small town with cold weather and little nightlife. The average eighteen-year-old is tempted by Hollywood (USC), South Beach (Miami), or coeds who look like *Playboy* Playmates (LSU). All of these realities are more enticing at first glance than the pious opportunity to serve Christ at Notre Dame. However, for this very reason, the players Notre Dame does get tend to have moral fiber, and when that is combined with athletic greatness, they represent high ideals, making them "America's team."

The title "college football's all-time greatest tradition" is a fluid, democratic concept. Like elections, it changes. It is not written in stone. Over the next years and decades, Notre Dame will come back. They will compete for the title with USC, Alabama, Oklahoma, and the other storied programs that make college football the best game there is! Yes, their fans will again "hallow their name."

Chapter 3

Alabama Crimson Tide

NOW WE COME TO the Alabama Crimson Tide. Perhaps no school has more loyal fans and alumni. Alabama supporters jealously guard the school's tradition, legends, and place in history. They are extremely sensitive to Alabama's image: the football program, the state, and the legacy of the legendary Paul "Bear" Bryant.

University of Alabama
Tuscaloosa, Alabama
Founded: 1831
Enrollment: 15,888
Colors: Crimson and white
Stadium: Bryant-Denny Stadium (opened: 1929; capacity: 83,818)
All-time record (1882–2008): 750–307–44
All-time bowl record: 31–22–3 (through 2008)
National championships: 1925, 1926, 1930, 1934, 1961, *1964, 1965, *1973, 1978, 1979, 1992
*Illegitimate; lost bowl game
Southern/Southeastern Conference championships: 21 (through 2008)
Outland Trophies: Chris Samuels (1999), Andre Smith (2008)
First-round NFL draftees: 33 (through 2009 draft)
Website: www.rolltide.com
Notable alumni: Supreme Court Justice Hugo Black; baseball broadcaster Mel Allen; *To Kill a Mockingbird* author Harper Lee; actors Jim Nabors and Sela Ward

The notion that two schools—USC and Notre Dame—might be ranked ahead of Alabama among the all-time most storied traditions is met by argument from a legion of true believers, most armed with a wealth of knowledge to support its theses and rebut detractors.

The average USC fan does not have this kind of historical knowledge. He generally accepts the blessings of victory and moves on his merry way. The average Notre Dame fan has a dogmatic sense of Irish superiority, not wishing any facts to get in the way of this concept. But the average Alabama fan harbors some eighty years of slights, as if any poll not favoring the Tide, any attempt to downgrade its champions, and God forbid the notion that Bryant did not walk on water—yes, he actually did: in a Coca-Cola billboard prominently displayed on the highway outside of Birmingham—is met by the same vociferousness marking Southern sensibilities in the years after the Civil War or during the civil rights movement.

Alabama and the South have now planted themselves on the right side of history, although it took some doing. When they finally came around, the blessings of freedom, prosperity, and righteousness were bestowed upon a place that proudly calls itself the "Bible belt." Many battles have been won here. Air conditioning made it possible for big business to be conducted. Its major cities—Atlanta, Nashville, Charlotte, Orlando, New Orleans—became international marketplaces. Enormous population shifts built many regions of the South into trendsetting metropolises of the twenty-first century. The Republican Party somehow harnessed pride in the old with a sensitive acceptance of the new, thus husbanding the South back into the Union. The region became an electoral juggernaut, a "GOP lock." Once all the "troubles" of integration were resolved, the South "rose again" with a series of franchise shifts and expansion baseball, basketball, football, and hockey teams occupying all its major cities. In 1996, the ultimate multicultural event gave imprimatur and acceptance of the South by the world, and vice versa, in the form of the Olympic Games in Atlanta.

With the Civil War relegated to "battlefield reenactments," Reconstruction just a chapter in history books, and the black heroes of the civil rights movement now honored on steps of city halls and state capitals, the "last argument" left is college football. College football is "religion" in the South, no place more so than the University of Alabama.

It was in college football and at Alabama where the final nails in segregation's coffin were nailed, in the form of the 1970 USC-Alabama game at Birmingham's Legion Field. Black players with the Atlanta Braves, with the Atlanta Hawks, or even at other Southeastern Conference schools, did not really "count" until Bear Bryant and 'Bama made the whole thing "official." According to one story, Bryant met a shirtless Reggie Jackson in the Birmingham Barons' dressing room in 1966. The articulate ex-football player from Arizona State impressed Bryant. He declared that a man like Jackson was just what he needed to "get it done in school real easy." In the aftermath of that 1970 USC-Alabama game, the teams may be "more black" in the South than in the West or the North. There are black coaches, referees, students, cheerleaders, fans, professors, and administrators. The seamlessness of integration after so much angst offers the sense that God's hand was at play, changing hearts and minds.

So it is that Alabamians cling to their Crimson Tide, insisting with religious fervor on its superiority. They have a darn good argument. While USC and Notre Dame claim their legitimate eleven national championships, the Alabama media guide states the Tide has won twelve, plus the "other five." There are websites that say the Tide has won thirteen. The argument over 'Bama's titles both favors and does not favor them. The 1941 team, which was 9–2 and beat Texas A&M 29–21 in the Cotton Bowl, was the number one team, according to the Houlgate System. However, Bernie Bierman's unbeaten Minnesota Golden Gophers are the only truly legitimate champions of that season.

The 1964 and 1973 teams, discussed ad nauseum throughout this book, are officially "national champions" according to the Associated Press (1964) and United Press International (1964, 1973). One of the purposes of this book is to get beyond the mistakes and obvious fallacies of the system, which, beyond a play-off, is subject to human error large and small. Many legitimate national championships can be argued against, but they still stand in the face of logic and reason. The 1964 and 1973 'Bama titles do not. When a team walks off the field in abject disconsolation after their last game of the season, which was by far their most important against the most difficult competition, picked to play them for the express purpose of determining in fact *who is* number one . . . well, that team *IS NOT THE NATIONAL CHAMPION*!

This is evidenced, for example, by the case of the 1972 U.S. Olympic basketball team. They were robbed of the gold medal by Communist officials, who gave the Soviets the ball three times until they finally scored the winning basket. There are books, pamphlets, trophies, and much "evidence" supporting the notion that they were the "silver medalists" in 1972. No player on that team ever accepted the silver. Some have wills forbidding their heirs from ever accepting it. They know, and in the "eyes of God" it is probably known, that they were not the silver medal winners, but the legitimate gold medal winners. The same logic, in a reverse kind of way, applies to the 1964 and 1973 Alabama "national champions."

However, Alabama supporters can be forgiven if they feel the right to include these, because in fact there are other teams denied the title that *were* very worthy. The 1945 unbeaten Tide became the first team ever to beat Southern California in a bowl game after the Trojans had won the first eight Rose Bowls they played in (not to mention the little-known 1924 Christmas Festival). That was the era of Red Blaik's Army juggernauts, legendary teams led by Mr. Inside and Mr. Outside (Doc Blanchard, Glenn Davis). They eschewed a bowl invite, yet nobody was going to get the vote over Army. With World War II now won, they symbolized American dominance and were heroes "almost" on par with Dwight Eisenhower, George Patton, and Douglas MacArthur.

The one that sticks in 'Bama supporters' craws the most is the 1966 number three vote behind Notre Dame and Michigan State. The Tide, led by Ken "Snake" Stabler, was unbeaten, was untied, and beat the heck out of an integrated Nebraska team in the Sugar Bowl. With tension high amid civil rights unrest, Martin Luther King's "agitation," and growing angst over the Vietnam War, it appeared social politics had affected a vote angrily referred to as the "Catholic vote" and the "antisegregation vote."

The 1975 and 1977 teams both had one loss and a bowl victory, but the vote went to Oklahoma and Notre Dame, respectively, for reasons that are basically subjective absent a play-off.

But the 'Bama pendulum swings back and forth on this subject. True, the 1945, 1966, 1975, and 1977 teams had records as good or even better than teams ranked ahead of them, but in each of those four seasons the winner was a legitimate champion. There were no frauds, no teams with bowl losses sneaking in on technicalities, like a lawyer who gets a murderer off because the cops stopped him for speeding only to discover mayhem.

Furthermore, unique changes in the voting rules awarded 'Bama the 1964 and '65 titles in ways that other schools did not benefit from. After the obvious mistake of 1964, in 1965 the AP decided that they would wait until after the bowls. Michigan State was number one prior to the bowls that year. They would have "won" the title the same way 'Bama did the previous year. With the new rules in place, their loss to Michigan State in the Rose Bowl gave 9-1-1 Alabama, Orange Bowl victors over Nebraska, the surprise title.

On top of that, in 1978 Alabama hosted USC at Birmingham's Legion Field. The Trojans won big. Both teams ended the season with one loss and bowl wins. The voters had the unique opportunity to make the obvious, clear choice of picking one team that, all else being equal, had beaten the other team fair and square, on the losing team's home field to boot. Somehow, for mystical reasons, the Associated Press saw fit to give it to Alabama. The United Press International awarded the trophy to the deserving champions from USC. However, this is still a legitimate championship, coming on the heels of a bowl win, which is imperative if a team wishes to claim a righteous national championship.

The argument in favor of Alabama includes other criteria. They have played in the most bowl games of any team (fifty-six), and are tied with USC for the most bowl wins (thirty-one). However, there are factors well worth considering in which the Tide is found lacking. No Alabama player has ever won the Heisman Trophy. A worthy case can be made that this is actually in their favor. It means they do it with teamwork and great coaching, which they most certainly have done. The Heisman, it is said, is a product of marketing, advertising, hype. Who needs such a thing?

That said, the idea that a great Alabama player would not be hyped to the very maximum of hype by the 'Bama sports information department, the regional press, and their fans is preposterous. It would be over the top.

Then there is the elephant in the room, which is impossible not to notice when discussing the historical Alabama: segregation. The Tide was all white until 1971. They played in an all-white conference and mostly against all-white nonleague foes. This means they did not field the best players from the widest talent pool (which helps explain why they have fewer Heisman winners, All-Americans, and NFL stars than other storied programs). It also means their competition was not quite as good as what other schools, presumptively USC, Notre Dame, Michigan, et al., were playing.

This argument makes sense, but like much of the Alabama record deteriorates somewhat upon closer examination. Alabama did not shy away from bowl games. When Minnesota and Michigan were winning national championships without going to bowls in the 1920s and 1930s, the Crimson Tide took on the great challenge of traveling to Pasadena for repeated bouts with the "best of the West." In games with Washington, Stanford, Washington State, California, and USC, they demonstrated something between equal competence and utter dominance.

Their champions of the 1960s played some segregated teams and some integrated teams in bowl games, but there is no evidence that all-white Arkansas, their opponent

Alabama versus . . .

Southeastern Conference	350–160–20 (through 2008)
Mid-American Conference	4–1
Western Athletic Conference	9–12

in the 1962 Sugar Bowl, or all-white Texas, their opponent in the 1965 Orange Bowl (just to name a couple), were not powerhouses of the first order. Perhaps because of external factors—growing Western population shifts, the music of the Beach Boys, California trends—it was generally assumed that in the 1960s and 1970s USC and UCLA represented a new shift in sports dominance, as well. Therefore, it was easy to make the statement that the Pacific-8 (later Pacific-10) Conference was the best in the country. The professional rosters in all sports were dominated by players from the West, from California, and from the Pac-8. Professional sports on the West Coast had made a big impact. UCLA's basketball dynasty created something between the illusion and the reality that the best sports were being played out there. It stood to reason the Pac-8 was "better" than the Southeastern Conference.

A closer examination of the conferences during the roughly equal dynasties of Paul "Bear" Bryant at Alabama (1958–1982) and the combined runs of John McKay/John Robinson at USC (1962–1982) reveals that the SEC was at least as good and, if the polls can be believed over the years, better.

So it is with Alabama that the program is a conundrum of sorts. When arguing over the ultimate merits, they have a case to be made, but must also defend a few weaknesses. Overall, when everything is added up, they are a consistent dynasty, a major power, and a storied tradition of legendary players, coaches, and teams. They are legitimately ranked third on the all-time list.

After the Civil War, the South always had a "chip on its shoulder." The famed Georgia Peach, Ty Cobb, was razzed unmercifully by his Detroit Tigers teammates when he came to the big leagues in 1905. The South was considered backward in all things. There was little respect for Southern sports, despite the fact that Dixie took to athletics in a major way.

The good weather, open spaces, and natural country exuberance of Southern youth made for playful children who wanted to express themselves through physical activity. Huntin' and fishin' have always been popular. The need for physical heroism combined with family loyalty and religious discipline always produced a greater percentage of soldiers from the region.

Alabama versus the Elite Ten (36–38–2 through 2008)

Miami (14–13), Michigan (1–2), Nebraska (3–2), Notre Dame (1–5), Ohio State (3–0), Oklahoma (1–2–1), Penn State (8–5), Southern California (5–2), Texas (0–7–1)

The qualities of good soldiering also produced a mind-set for the game of football, that most militaristic of all sports. It took in the South right from the beginning. But lack of media and a sense that the South was "separated" from the "real America" prior to World War II meant that Southern football was not respected.

Auburn, Texas, and Oklahoma all fielded strong teams that gained some national recognition in the 1910s. Georgia Tech was the biggest powerhouse in Dixie, but the "Wramblin' Wrecks from Georgia Tech" were considered a cut above their Southern brethren. They were upper class, engineers, rare students in an "uneducated" place, or so the outside feeling went.

Alabama was an independent until 1921. They were moderately successful until 1919, but nobody north of the Mason-Dixon Line cared. Football was an Eastern sport. Its kings were Ivy League powers such as Princeton, Yale, and Harvard; coaches like Walter Camp and Percy Haughton. If not the Ivy League, then it was a Midwestern game. In the Big 10 Minnesota, Fielding Yost's "point-a-minute" Michigan teams, and Amos "Alonzo" Stagg's Chicago squads had dominated. Notre Dame was now on the map, as were Pacific Coast teams: Washington, Cal, Stanford. "Unexplored territory" was Arizona, which to most Americans was still the "gunfight at the O-K Corral," the Rocky Mountains . . . and Dixie.

New coach Xen Scott led the Crimson Tide to 8–1 and 10–1 records in 1919 and 1920. The "conference" referred to in history books was simply the *Southern* Conference. Alabama joined in 1921. It was not really a conference, rather a loose confederation of some twenty-one teams. This included teams not in the South*western* Conference (Texas, Texas A&M, Arkansas, Baylor, Oklahoma State, Baylor, Rice, SMU). The teams in the Southern Conference roughly make up what is now the Southeastern Conference and Atlantic Coast Conference.

According to the *ESPN College Football Encyclopedia*, Florida State won the conference title in 1922 with a 7–1 record (10–2) overall. However, this is an error. Florida State was a girls' school until the late 1940s and supposedly did not even play football until 1947. The *ESPN College Football Encyclopedia* does not list the Southern Conference in 1921.

The Alabama media guide has incomplete information. They claim that 'Bama joined the Southern Conference in 1919. If Florida State had a football team, they did not play 'Bama. The Tide played a series of games against local teams, then LSU, Vanderbilt, Florida, Georgia, Mississippi State, and Tulane (no Auburn) in 1921.

In the aftermath of World War I, with trains, roads, and airplanes connecting America, the game nationalized. On January 1, 1926, second-year coach Wallace Wade brought his 10–0 team to the Rose Bowl for the fourth New Year's Day game to be played at the new Pasadena stadium. It was the school's football version of the "debutante ball." Dartmouth, Yale, and Colgate all turned down invites. Then somebody mentioned the unbeaten Tide.

"I've never heard of Alabama as a football team and can't take a chance on mixing a lemon with a Rose," remarked one Rose Bowl committeeman.

Humorist Will Rogers called them "Tusca-*losers.*" The L.A press called them "swamp students." Sociology played a role even more than usual. A Protestant religious revival was sweeping the South. This gave unfortunate rise to the peculiarly un-Christian notion of "white supremacy." This in turn revitalized the KKK (which had been dormant for years). Cross burnings and persecution of blacks and Catholics became a focus of the new Federal Bureau of Investigation. There was more division between the North, the West, and the South than there had been since Reconstruction.

Alabama ventured to California, amid this set of circumstances, to do battle with mighty Washington. The Huskies had been the kings of college football in the 1910s when coach Gil Dobie's dynasty went on an unbelievable 63-game unbeaten streak. When Washington sprinted to a 12-0 lead, it looked like Alabama would be sent home and not be invited back. But halfback Johnny Mack Brown caught a key touchdown pass to spearhead the stirring 20-19 comeback win. When it was all said and done Alabama—not Dartmouth, Yale, or Colgate—is considered the legitimate, sole national champion of 1925. They earned this on the strength of accepting the Rose Bowl challenge those other "elite" teams turned down. The Crimson Tide was on the map, and the Rose Bowl was now seen as the place where a team needed to go in order to win a national title.

In 1926, Wade and his team were invited back. This might have been the first so-called "Game of the Century," the "best of the East,"—at least the South—versus the "best of the West." That was Stanford, led by legendary coach Pop Warner. Both teams were unbeaten and untied after playing a tough conference schedule. The state of California was considered "football central" in 1926. California's Wonder Teams had not lost a single game over a 50-game stretch between 1920 and 1925. Stanford, their biggest rival, had produced the legendary Ernie Nevers. USC, under new coach Howard Jones, was a rising power. Only Notre Dame, who had defeated Warner, Nevers, and Stanford in the Rose Bowl two years earlier (and beaten USC by a single point at the Coliseum in 1926), was considered to be as worthy as the Pacific Coast juggernauts.

Alabama still felt the need to prove themselves, but the game ended in a frustrating 7-7 tie. This resulted in a co-national championship, but playing Warner's Indians to a standstill in their home state was seen as a victory of sorts for Alabama. In 1930, Wade returned to Pasadena with consensus All-American tackle Fred Sington. This time the Tide left no doubt. His team's 24-0 triumph over Washington State capped a perfect 10-0 season, but again the national title was split, this time with Notre Dame. Wade left Alabama and returned to Pasadena a few years later with a Duke team considered one of the best ever, only to lose to USC. A cantankerous sort, Wade feuded with detractors. He was particularly upset about the last-minute loss to USC in the 1939 Rose Bowl. However, he and USC quarterback Doyle Nave later met in the Navy during World War II. Nave reported that Wade was a Southern gentleman whose blood had simply run hot in the glare of competition.

Frank Thomas took over the program between 1931 and 1946. On the surface Wade's three national titles to Thomas's one would seem to overshadow him, but Thomas achieved great things. His teams were 9-1, 8-2, and 7-1-1 in his first three years (1931-1933). In 1934 the Tide fielded one of their most hallowed teams, if not the most hallowed. Bear Bryant certainly would preside over greatness in Tuscaloosa, but the 1934 Crimson Tide is enshrined in their memory.

For one thing, this team did have Bear Bryant on it—as an end. He was a good player to be sure, a scrapper out of Fordyce, Arkansas. But on the other side of the ball one of Alabama's all-time greats lined up opposite Bear. Don Hutson, Alabama's second consensus All-American, was the first great receiver in college and pro football history.

The game had always been ground oriented. Quarterback Gus Dorais and end Knute Rockne used the newfangled "forward pass" to lead Notre Dame over Army in 1913. The pass was an integral part of the game by the 1930s, but the size of the ball made it harder to throw than it is today. The game, however, was changing.

For one thing, diet and exercise increased the arm strength of kids growing up in America. Baseball, America's "national pastime," instituted use of the "lively ball" in 1920. Prior to that, baseball pitchers tended to be "spitball artists" who used guile to get hitters to ground out to infielders. But Babe Ruth ushered in a new era of "power baseball" that effected not just free-swinging hitters but also hard-throwing pitchers. Kids growing up developed their fastballs more. Naturally, most football quarterbacks also played baseball. Most were pitchers. By the 1930s a new breed of strong-armed hurlers and quarterbacks had changed the dynamics of their respective sports. Fireballers such as Dizzy Dean, Lefty Grove, and Bob Feller came on the baseball scene. "Longball" quarterbacks like Sammy Baugh and Davey O'Brien arrived on the football scene.

The speedy, sure-handed Hutson revolutionized Alabama's use of the passing game in a remarkable 10–0 season in 1934. Other consensus All-Americans were tackle Bill Lee and back Dixie Howell. One thing could never be said of the Tide: Nobody could accuse

All-Time Alabama Team

Chosen by fans for their 1992 centennial

OFFENSE		DEFENSE	
Pos.	Player	Pos.	Player
T	Fred Sington	DL	Bob Baumbower
OL	Vaughn Mancha	DL	Marty Lyons
OL	Billy Neighbors	DT	Jon Hand
OL	John Hannah	LB	Lee Roy Jordan
C	Dwight Stephenson	LB	Barry Krauss
TE	Ozzie Newsome	OLB	Cornelius Bennett
WR	Don Hutson	OLB	Derrick Thomas
QB	Joe Namath	DB	Harry Gilmer
QB	Kenny Stabler	DB	Don McNeal
RB	Bobby Marlow	DB	Jeremiah Castille
RB	Johnny Musso	DB	Tommy Wilcox
RB	Bobby Humphrey	P	Johnny Cain
PK	Van Tiffen		

them of turning down a challenge. While many teams refused invites to the Rose Bowl out of fear their unblemished records would be sullied, the Tide came out every chance they got to do battle with Pacific Coast Conference champions in Pasadena. In a way, they were the Florida State of their era, playing "anybody, anyplace, any time"—and winning—in order to earn a "place at the table" in college football's hierarchy. But by 1934 they were no secret. They were going after their fourth national title.

This time it was Stanford in a rematch between the co-national champions of 1926. Led by the Vow Boys, the Indians were no match for Hutson and the Tide and fell 29-13. The national championship was shared between Alabama and Bernie Bierman's first great team at Minnesota, although the Golden Gophers did not play in a bowl. Hutson went on to a fabulous career with the Green Bay Packers and is a member of the College as well as the Pro Football Hall of Fame.

In the late 1930s, the Southeastern Conference was dominated by Bob Neyland's Tennessee Volunteers, but Thomas's Tide was a power almost every year (8-0-1 in 1936, 9-1 in 1937, 7-1-1- in 1938). The 1937 team would have brought the school's fifth national championship back to Tuscaloosa, but they finally met their match in the form of California's Thunder Team.

The unbeaten Tide again came to Pasadena, this time against a school that had dipped under the radar in the wake of USC, Stanford, and Washington dominance in the PCC. Led by Vic Bottari and Sam Chapman, the Golden Bears earned their last national title by defeating Alabama 13-0. It is worth noting that the 1938 Rose Bowl game was not just for that season's championship, but for a historical ranking of sorts, too. Cal's fourth national championship tied them with Alabama for the most of any program since World War I. USC won their fourth two years later. Entering the 1940s, Notre Dame and Minnesota each had three. Other consensus Alabama All-Americans of the 1930s were Riley Smith (1935) and Leroy Monsky (1937).

During the war years, Thomas's teams were competitive as usual, but the conflict took a big toll on the state and school. Southerners tend to be the most patriotic sorts, volunteering for military service in disproportionate numbers. In 1943, when Notre Dame fielded enough stars to win national championship glory, Alabama saw fit to cancel its season in favor of the war effort.

The state and the nation were awash in victory when the 1945 season began. 'Bama came out rolling with an unbeaten season, which included a 34–13 thrashing of Southern Cal at the Rose Bowl. It was USC's first-ever bowl loss of any kind, helping to reestablish the Tide. But in those years Army and Notre Dame received all the attention. Red Blaik's Army Black Knights were one of the legendary teams of all time, at the apex of their powers in 1945 in every way. Alabama was overshadowed and forced to accept the second position in the Associated Press poll. Consensus All-Americans of the 1940s were Holt Rast (1941), Joe Domnanovich (1942), and Vaughn Mancha (1945).

Between 1946 and 1956, Alabama and Southern football seemed to recede. After World War II, integration became an issue. Jackie Robinson's ascendancy to the big leagues in 1947 and President Harry Truman's integration of the Army, then the *Brown v. Board of Education* decision (1954), spotlighted the case. Several small California schools

Elite Ten by the Numbers			
Bowl victories (through 2009)			
1. Southern California	31	6. Nebraska	23
1. Alabama	31	7. Miami	19
3. Penn State	26	7. Michigan	19
4. Texas	25	9. Ohio State	18
5. Oklahoma	24	10. Notre Dame	14

had come to the South for bowl games, emerging victorious. Suddenly the practice of integrated Western or Northern teams traveling to New Orleans (Sugar Bowl) or Miami (Orange Bowl) became political debates. The 1951 University of San Francisco Dons were uninvited to the Sugar Bowl because they refused to leave their black players at home. Those players happened to be stars. One of them, Ollie Matson, is one of the all-time great college and pro running backs.

Southern teams began to draw back from the national exposure of previous years, when they would play in the Rose Bowl. With the PCC-Big 10 deal in place beginning with the 1947 Rose Bowl, this was no longer an option for SEC teams. The Orange, Sugar, and Cotton Bowls increasingly became Southern affairs. Occasional games with integrated teams like Navy, USC, Pitt, and Penn State were fraught with racial controversy.

College football became a Midwestern game, for the most part, in the late 1940s. Notre Dame and Michigan replaced Army (eventually beset by a cheating scandal) as the major powerhouses. Ohio State rose to great heights. Out West, UCLA became a national team on the strength of their integrated policies.

Alabama's College Hall of Famers (18)			
Players		Johnny Mack Brown	1923–1925
Lee Roy Jordan	1960–1962	Dixie Howell	1932–1934
Vaughn Mancha	1944–1947	Johnny Musso	1969–1971
John Hannah	1970–1972	Pooley Hubert	1922–1925
Billy Neighbors	1959–1961	Johnny Maulbetsch	1911–1916
Fred Sington	1928–1930	Cornelius Bennett	1983–1986
Don Whitmire	1941–1944	Woody Lowe	1972–1975
Don Hutson	1932–1934		
Ozzie Newsome	1974–1977	*Coaches*	
John Cain	1930–1932	Paul Bryant	1958–1982
Riley Smith	1933–1935	Wallace Wade	1923–1950

But the South never dipped too far. Georgia Tech again made their presence known nationwide after a down period. The Southwest also developed as never before. Oklahoma, a border-state school playing in a Midwestern conference, became the great team of the 1950s, but unlike in Dixie Bud Wilkinson integrated his program despite much angst. In 1957, the SEC reasserted itself in the form of Auburn's national championship team. In 1958, Louisiana State won the national championship, too. That same season, Alabama hired Paul "Bear" Bryant.

Bryant, the one-time end who starred opposite Don Hutson, served in the Navy before embarking on a coaching career at Maryland, Kentucky, and Texas A&M. 'Bama football had taken beatings in the years before he arrived. Under coach J. B. Whitworth, the Tide was an unmentionable 0–10 in 1955. Nary a single Tide player earned consensus All-American honors in the 1950s. A good quarterback, Bart Starr, emerged from the program, but his great success in Green Bay could never have been predicted by his years in Tuscaloosa.

Before there was Roger Staubach, Terry Bradshaw, Joe Montana, Tom Brady, or any of the other quarterback heroes of Super Bowl lore, there was Starr. In an era of great quarterbacks, he was the most successful and arguably the best. In a game that values winning above all other results, Starr's admirers can argue with great validity that he was, for this reason, superior to Johnny Unitas just as Montana was to Dan Marino, and until the 2007 Super Bowl at least, Tom Brady was to Peyton Manning. Starr was the most valuable player of Super Bowl I (Green Bay's win over the Chiefs at the L.A. Coliseum, 1967) and Super Bowl II (over Oakland in Miami's Orange Bowl, 1968).

Bryant turned a 2–7–1 team into a 5–4–1 team in 1958. His 1959 squad (7–2–2) made it to the Liberty Bowl, where they lost to Penn State 7–0. In 1960 Alabama came on strong (8–1–2), but the 1961 squad is one of the most beloved in school history. Led by

Elite Ten by the Numbers
Super Bowl MVPs (through 2009)

1. Alabama: 3
   Joe Namath, New York Jets (1969); Bart Starr, Green Bay (1967, 1968)
1. Michigan: 3
   Tom Brady, New England (2002, 2004); Desmond Howard, Green Bay (1997)
1. Notre Dame: 3
   Joe Montana, San Francisco (1982, 1985, 1990)
4. Southern California: 2
   Marcus Allen, Los Angeles Raiders (1984); Lynn Swann, Pittsburgh (1975)
4. Miami: 2
   Ray Lewis, Baltimore Ravens, (2001); Otis Anderson, New York Giants (1991)
6. Ohio State: 1
   Santonio Holmes, Pittsburgh (2009)
6. Penn State: 1
   Franco Harris, Pittsburgh (1975)

consensus All-American tackle Billy Neighbors and the great linebacker Lee Roy Jordan (consensus All-American, 1962), the Tide rambled to an 11–0 record, including a hard-fought 10–3 triumph over Arkansas in the Sugar Bowl. They won their first national title in twenty-seven years. The quarterback was Pat Trammell, a utilitarian signal-caller who nobody would ever mistake with the likes of Joe Namath or Ken Stabler. But Trammell was a leader, and Bryant often spoke of him as one of his all-time favorite players. He represented just the kind of man Bear wanted: unselfish, disciplined, smart, adaptable.

Alabama versus Auburn	39–33–1

Trammell never went on to great pro fame. He got married, started a family, and became a successful doctor, but died tragically of cancer. Bryant immortalized his memory through a foundation set up to take care of his children and increase cancer research.

The 1961 Tide may not have been the most physically gifted team in America. They were small and made up of mostly local players, but they obeyed Bryant as if his words emanated from the "burning bush." Bryant's legend was made.

In 1962, sophomore quarterback Joe Willie Namath led the team to a 10–1 record complete with a 17–0 shutout over Oklahoma and the man Bryant considered his coaching model, Bud Wilkinson. After the game Wilkinson entered Alabama's dressing room to personally congratulate Bryant, his staff, and his players. It was a class act that had a big effect on Coach Bryant.

In 1963 Alabama was 9–2 with a 12–7 Sugar Bowl win over Mississippi. Some national pundits scorned the fact that two SEC teams played each other in the Sugar Bowl. In that volatile year, two black students had to be escorted by federal soldiers for a first-ever class registration against the protests of Governor George "segregation now, segregation forever" Wallace. The region was considered backward or, in the football sense, inward.

But it was also around that time Coach Bryant made an acquaintance with a man who together with him would make a profound change on football in the social sense. Bryant enjoyed traveling to California in the off-season. The weather, the golf, friendships with celebrities such as Bob Hope, and the chance to relax a little bit lured him there. He was happy to accept the invitation of California high school coaching clinics to come out and speak. Through this he was able to expand his recruiting horizons.

Bob Troppmann was the football coach at Redwood High School in Marin County, a suburb of San Francisco. Troppmann started a popular clinic called the Diamond B Football Camp. It was through this camp that Troppmann became acquainted with both Bryant and USC football coach John McKay. It was through camps like Troppmann's that McKay and Bryant became friends.

They liked to drink whiskey, do a little duck huntin', and talk football. Over the next years, the possibility of a football game between McKay's USC Trojans and Bryant's Crimson Tide was discussed. The racial implications of such a big game were talked about. Bryant expressed to McKay that he wanted to integrate the program but was dealing with some difficult political problems, namely in the form of Governor Wallace.

According to legend, one of these conversations took place at Troppmann's camp in which a freshman on his team, fourteen-year-old future USC football coach Pete Carroll (one of the "campers") slept in a cabin not too far away. Whether this is legend or pure fact is debatable, but in essence Bryant saw in his friend McKay and the USC program a model of sorts for integrating his own team. This is not in dispute.

But when the Tide won the back-to-back national titles in 1964 and 1965, followed by an unbeaten 1966, many white Alabamians figured the program did not *need* to integrate in order to maintain superiority. Namath developed into the nation's best quarterback. In 1964, he was well on his way to earning the school's first Heisman Trophy. Namath started out as a veer quarterback, and he was "the best athlete I ever saw," said assistant coach Clem Gryska. "I could see right away he was a Cadillac, not a Ford."

Namath, also a top-flight baseball player, was fast and agile enough to handle the veer duties, but by his senior year Bryant was utilizing Namath's strong right arm. In the seventh game of the season he went down with a debilitating knee injury, costing him the Heisman, which went instead to Notre Dame's John Huarte. Namath managed to make a gimpy return in time for the 1965 Orange Bowl. He gamely brought the Tide back from a deficit, but in the end fell just short against Texas, 21–17. It was a game he later described as his most disappointing ever. It did not cost Alabama the AP or UPI national championships, but after unbeaten Arkansas' 10–7 win over Nebraska in the Cotton Bowl, it was obvious that the vote-before-the-bowls system employed by both the AP and the UPI was highly flawed. This fact had been known since the early 1950s, when three of the first four "national champions" of the dual AP/UPI era were illegitimatized by bowl defeat. College football had "dodged a bullet" since then (with the exception of the Minnesota "championship" of 1960), either by national champions winning their bowls too, or by awarding it to schools that did not have to deal with a bowl challenge.

There was some argument still in effect that the bowls were a "reward" for a great regular season but should not count. They were "exhibitions," according to some, like an all-star game. Some coaches said it was impossible to keep a team in fighting trim between the final regular season game, generally played on Thanksgiving weekend or before, and New Year's Day more than a month later. They were off partying, drinking, chasing girls, and not concentrating on practice, it was theorized.

Elite Ten by the Numbers
Bowl games (through 2009)

1. Alabama	56	6. Penn State	41
2. Texas	48	7. Ohio State	40
3. Southern California	47	8. Michigan	39
4. Nebraska	45	9. Miami	34
5. Oklahoma	42	10. Notre Dame	29

None of these arguments carried any validity, of course. Arkansas had to settle for second place in both the Associated Press and United Press International polls. The old "systems," which received little if any publicity and were viewed as relics of a bygone past, were dusted off and used to anoint "true national championship" status upon a Razorback team that, incidentally, included a future Cowboys coach (Jimmy Jones) and owner (Jerry Jones).

Namath was the number one draft choice of that year's class. His entrance into professional football came at a most opportune time for him, financially and in every other way. The American and National Football Leagues were at "war" with each other. The winners of the "war" were prized college draftees like Namath, who found themselves wealthy beyond their imagination when the leagues entered into "bidding contests" for their services. Namath went with the New York Titans, who were about to change their name to the Jets and begin play at the brand spanking new Shea Stadium. Joe Willie was immediately rich by virtue of a then unheard of bonus contract in the $400,000 range. New York's second draft pick, Notre Dame's John Huarte, received almost as much.

Huarte was a bust in pro football. Namath entered that rarest of all pantheons: the iconic New York sports superstar, an elite status reserved only for such all-time greats as Babe Ruth, Joe DiMaggio, Frank Gifford, Mickey Mantle, and Tom Seaver. Namath's place in this pantheon was based first on his leading the underdog Super Jets to a world-shaking 16–7 victory over Baltimore in Super Bowl III (1969). His knee, injured at Alabama, was reinjured many times. It cut his pro career short, but not enough to deny him a career that ended up with his enshrinement in Canton. But Namath's persona is what elevated him above the others, in New York and on the world stage. Known as Broadway Joe, he was a ladies man of legendary status whose autobiography is titled *I Can't Wait until Tomorrow . . . 'Cause I Get Better Looking Every Day*. Namath represented the "swingin' '60s" and was part of a new generation of "playboy athletes" who spoke their minds and lived life for the moment.

Namath was not from Alabama. He was part of the great western Pennsylvania tradition producing such stalwarts as Johnny Unitas, Tony Dorsett, Joe Montana, Jim Kelly, and Dan Marino. Sylvester Croom was a young black kid in Tuscaloosa when Namath first made his mark as a sophomore in 1962. Eventually Croom became an All-American lineman at Alabama, then the first black head football coach in SEC history at Mississippi State

"Namath would come down to the black neighborhoods by himself," recalled Croom. "He'd glad-hand the folks, who were amazed. He was like . . . a cool jazz singer."

In 1965 the Tide finished the regular season with an 8–1–1 record, led by consensus All-American center Paul Crane. The UPI concluded its final vote as follows:

1. Michigan State
2. Arkansas
3. Nebraska
4. Alabama

Duffy Daugherty's Spartans were number one in the AP too, but after the 1964 fiasco the Associated Press decided to wait until after the bowls before conducting their final vote this time around. New Year's Day 1966 was a memorable one. Michigan State was upset by UCLA 14–12 in the Rose Bowl. Arkansas fell to LSU 14–7 in the Cotton Bowl.

Suddenly, Alabama found itself with an unlikely shot at the national title. Michigan State was forced to leave the Rose Bowl with their tails between their legs. Their UPI "national title" plaque was now worthless, but the AP version was up for grabs.

In a memorable game, the Tide beat number three Nebraska 39–28 in the Orange Bowl. It was enough to spur the AP voters into making Alabama the number one team. It was also impeccable timing in terms of the team's ability to benefit from the vagaries of the polling system. No Alabamians complained about their good luck. Plenty complained when the system did not benefit them, as in the 1966 season.

Possibly Bryant's greatest team, they were led by junior quarterback Kenny "Snake" Stabler, who replaced Steve Sloan. Stabler hailed from the so-called Redneck Riviera, a coastal enclave of honky-tonks, pool halls, and gambling houses. He was a product of his environment: a hard-charging partier and skirt chaser. Bryant loved him immediately but saw in him a major challenge.

Bryant had for the most part harnessed the personality of his players into team unity. His guys were "Yes, sir" and "No, sir" types who adhered to his discipline and hard ways. Snake was an individualist, but in him Bryant saw himself. But what Bryant loved most was his competitiveness.

"I've known many athletes over the years," the late Bill King, longtime Oakland Raiders' announcer, once said. King broadcast Stabler's most exhilarating professional moments. "Many were driven by fear, such as [Oakland A's reliever] Dennis Eckersley. Stabler was the polar opposite, utterly devoid of fear no matter the pressure or the situation."

"Coach loved Kenny," said assistant coach Jack Rutledge, "because on game days he was the greatest competitor we ever had."

Stabler had overcome personality clashes with Bear. He had played for the freshman team, then sat behind Steve Sloan in the national championship 1965 season. His drinking and womanizing resulted in team rules being broken. Bryant, for the sake of unity, penalized Snake. At one point he was sent home on suspension, where he seriously considered quitting.

"I drove back to Tuscaloosa," Stabler once recalled, "drinking a six-pack of beer and throwing the empties on the side of the highway. During this drive I thought long and hard about what I wanted to do. I decided I'd play by Coach Bryant's rules, be a part of the team. That's what I did."

Stabler engineered the brilliant unbeaten season of 1966, but things were dicey from the get-go when it came to the pollsters. Alabama had a bye in the season's first week and tried to fill it with a nationally ranked team from out of the region. However, for varying reasons, none was willing or able. USC for instance had their hands full at Austin, Texas. The resulting 34–0 win over Louisiana Tech did not satisfy those who felt they needed to play an integrated Northern or Western team.

"A lot of folks didn't realize Louisiana Tech was real good that year," Bryant remarked later, "but it didn't change anybody's opinions."

Stabler and consensus All-American end Ray Perkins may have gotten the offensive headlines, but the team won with overwhelming defense. Tackle Cecil Dowdy also earned All-American honors. The Tide put up scores that reminded people of the 1932 USC Trojans or 1938 Duke Blue Devils. This included no fewer than six shutouts, including four in a row to close out the season. Auburn fell 31-0. Mississippi State's 14 points were the most scored against them. Tennessee was the only other team to reach double figures in a hotly contested 11-10 Alabama victory. Mississippi scored 7, Vanderbilt 6. Bob Devaney and Nebraska met them in the Sugar Bowl, but unlike the previous year it was not competitive: 34-7, 'Bama. *Sports Illustrated* featured a color photo of Stabler leading his team to victory.

But the AP and the UPI had both gone for Notre Dame. The AP inexplicably reverted back to the prebowl vote. The UPI never veered from theirs. The Irish not only tied Michigan State and did not play in a bowl, they actually *went for* the tie, which galled most observers. 'Bama fans were understandably mad. For sure they fielded a superb, national title-worthy outfit, but in truth Notre Dame was a team for the ages in 1966. The Michigan State game had been a showdown dubbed the "Game of the Century." What probably annoyed the Alabama fans even more was the fact that Michigan State was also ranked ahead of them in both polls, but they were a defensive juggernaut possibly unmatched in history. It was just one of those years, a season in which truly great college football teams roamed the landscape.

Race and religion were considered major side issues in voters' minds in 1966. 'Bama fans unveiled a banner reading, "'BAMA PLAYS FOOTBALL, N. DAME PLAYS POLITICS" and "ARA PLAYS TO TIE—BEAR PLAYS TO WIN." Looking back, segregation was less important than the prebowl voting issue and, just as disturbing, the Catholic influence of Eastern sportswriters.

Three years later, the press had every opportunity to show social pathos when all-white Texas and integrated Penn State both finished unbeaten and untied with bowl wins. First, President Richard Nixon, a Californian who as a Duke law student had argued on behalf of blacks when debating Southerners, "announced" in the Texas dressing room after the Longhorns beat Arkansas 15-14 in another "Game of the Century" that Texas was the true national champion. That statement caused much consternation for Penn State coach Joe Paterno, who despite the slight supported Nixon and later even spoke at the Republican National Convention.

Alabama "deserves to be win number one, and if I had a vote they would be," Bryant said after the victory over Nebraska. But that was about all he said on the issue.

"Coach Bryant was very particular about what he said in 1966," recalled Clem Gryska. "He knew how people felt and didn't want to say anything that would put the program in a bad light. Privately he was disappointed but he always said you needed to win it in such a way so that there would be no question in anybody's mind. He was not the kind who complained."

Stabler went on to professional greatness on par with Namath. Had Stabler done what he did in New York instead of Oakland, he too would already have his deserving plaque in Canton. Stabler was a Pro Bowl quarterback on the greatest of all Oakland Raiders teams, engineering a series of memorable comeback victories, all announced in breathtaking, poetic fashion by Bill King.

"Branch left, Biletnikoff slot right, Stabler calling the signals," King would bark. "Raiders: two yards from the promised land." Stabler got them there on numerous occasions. In 1976 he painted his masterpiece in the form of a 13–1 record, the American Football Conference championship, and a 32–14 triumph over Minnesota in Super Bowl XI.

"Jascha Heifetz never tuned a violin," stated the opera-lover King, "like Kenny Stabler is tuning the Minnesota Vikings' defense on the Rose Bowl field today."

Bryant's class act despite 1966 disappointment would pay dividends down the line. In 1970, his team slipped to 6–5–1 with a Bluebonnet Bowl tie with Oklahoma. It was his second straight subpar year. The Miami Dolphins courted him. Bear reportedly agreed, but a legal problem interfered with that move. Many questioned whether the game had passed him by. He was in his mid-sixties with the face of an older man after years of sunburns, whiskey, and cigarettes.

The team had recruited players from all over the country, but some were "prima donnas," according to Clem Gryska. Dennis Homan and Bobby Johns were consensus All-Americans in 1967, but the program took a slide because "the players we brought in were not Coach Bryant's type of players," said Gryska.

"The athletic director will decide whether I leave as football coach at Alabama," Bryant declared defiantly, "and I'm the athletic director."

But privately there were doubts. When Bryant was considering the Dolphin offer, he approached John McKay to see if he would like to replace him at Alabama.

"Why would I want to leave USC?" asked McKay.

"You wouldn't have to drive those freeways," replied Bryant.

"I don't mind driving the freeways, Paul," said McKay.

On another occasion, McKay was visiting Bryant and his wife, Mary Harmon, at a hunting cabin he owned in rural Alabama. A 'Bama booster was also a guest. Bryant took off by himself to have a walk in solitude. The booster told McKay that Bryant's day had passed. McKay adamantly insisted it had not. He certainly was correct.

Elite Ten by the Numbers

Bowl Hall of Famers (through 2008)

1.	Alabama	21: Orange (11), Sugar (4), Cotton (4), Rose (2)
2.	Southern California	19: Rose (19)
3.	Ohio State	5: Rose (5)

Bryant was a man who capitalized on opportunity. His day had not passed. Early in 1970 he was in Palm Springs for the Bob Hope Desert Classic. He called McKay and told him to meet him at the Los Angeles Airport. McKay was not sure what the meeting was for. His assistant, Craig Fertig, knew nothing. Bryant drove from Palm Springs and after a few drinks in the Western Airlines Horizon Room offered McKay a lucrative package if he would come to Birmingham to open the season in September. It was the first year in which the NCAA allowed an eleventh game. Instead of filling it with Louisiana Tech this time, Bryant wanted the unbeaten Trojans to come play his .500 Crimson Tide.

McKay and Bryant had spoken of this. Many, including McKay's own children, his family friend Pat Haden, and his assistant coaches, were not aware of the plans Bryant and McKay had made over the years to play and, as a result, create a window of opportunity to integrate the program. There are plenty who dispute the game was planned for the purposes of integrating Alabama football, pointing out that had Alabama won it would not have had the effect it did. They are wrong.

Bryant wanted a classy, integrated, national title–contending team like USC—a team 'Bama fans could respect, led by a coach they knew McKay respected—to perform at a high level on their own Legion Field turf. Win or lose, the sight of the USC team would create the impact Bryant wanted. The times were "a-changin'," what with the war turning for the worse, Governor Wallace out of office, and a sense of "new wind" blowing over the country two years after the assassinations of Martin Luther King Jr. and Robert Kennedy.

Many myths surround that game, won by USC 42–21 when the Trojans' black fullback Sam "Bam" Cunningham ran for 135 yards and two touchdowns. First, that it integrated Alabama football. Bryant had already done so. Freshman running back Wilbur Jackson of Ozark, Alabama was in the program, watching the game from the stands (frosh were ineligible in 1970) with mixed emotions. John Mitchell was already being recruited. Sylvester Croom and others were known by Bryant, who was already reaching out to them for the future. The game was scheduled in large part to pave the way for Jackson's smooth entrance into the limelight. An All-American and captain of the 1973 Crimson Tide before a successful pro career, Jackson's entrance and stay *was* smooth indeed.

Second, Bryant is said to have taken a shirtless Cunningham into the Alabama dressing room, announcing, "Gentlemen, this here's what a football player looks like." He did not. Exactly what happened is still a mystery to this day. Most likely, Bryant said something like that once or more than once, heard by reporters, fans, alumni. It was repeated many times, often by USC people. But in the dressing room with Cunningham?

"It never happened," Alabama quarterback Scott Hunter said, "but it should have."

For years people predicted the disastrous results of full integration in the South. It had been occurring incrementally for years, much of it court ordered. A lawsuit against Bryant demanded his recruitment of black players, but to the surprise of many he revealed that for years he *had* been scouting black players in the state. Bryant provided the court details of these star players: their schools, grades, and other criteria.

The fact is that it happened in such a clean, easy way it seemed there never had been anything to worry about in the first place. There are two explanations for this, which apparently go hand in hand. The first speaks to the "miraculous" changing of hearts and minds, at least outwardly, as displayed in 1970–1971 as opposed to the way folks reacted in 1963–1964. In the Christian South, the explanation that this could only have been the work of God is not a hard one to make. Bryant's mother was a lay preacher and he believed in God, "although he was not a Bible-thumpin' man," said assistant coach Jack Rutledge, but he "did use Old Testament language, always talkin' about the players was 'chosen,' they were the 'chosen ones.'"

The second explanation is that Bryant was so respected, organized, meticulous, and careful when it came to the smooth operation of his football program that anything he did was going to be successful. Either way, Bryant would probably not dispute the notion that God's hand played a role in these seminal events in American history, and history judges that he was a winner.

What is not in dispute is that, now armed with an integrated team—which got more integrated year after year—the Crimson Tide, arguably the best team in college football in the 1960s, exploded in their best decade ever in the 1970s. The man who had seen the game "pass him by" truly lived up to those Coca-Cola billboards that showed him walking on water; well, he at least came close.

In 1971, Alabama traveled to Los Angeles with Jackson and John Mitchell. Breaking out the veer that Bryant had put in mothballs, they stunned Troy 17–10. Wearing the infamous "tearaway" jerseys, running back Johnny Musso rushed for 1,137 yards to finish fourth in the Heisman Trophy balloting.

The 11–0 Tide was rolled, however, by the juggernaut Nebraska Cornhuskers, effecting revenge for two bowl losses to 'Bama in the mid-1960s. The score was 38–6. Musso made consensus All-American before moving on to the Chicago Bears. Hunter replaced Bart Starr as the quarterback in Green Bay. Offensive lineman John Hannah made consensus All-American in 1972 before embarking on a Hall of Fame career with the Patriots.

Year after year in the 1970s, however, ultimate victory evaded Alabama. Between 1970 and 1977, Alabama compiled the best record in the nation. They beat USC two of three times, but the Trojans got all the glory in the form of two famous national championships (1972, 1974) to the Tide's zero. In years in which Troy did not win, Alabama generally compiled better records, but the teams play for national titles above all other things. In 1973 Alabama's stunning 24–23 loss to Notre Dame in the Sugar Bowl cost them the final number one ranking. There was no really good reason why USC (1974), Oklahoma (1975), and Notre Dame (1977) finished number one ahead of Alabama, but

Elite Ten by the Numbers

Coach of the Year awards (through 2008)

1. Alabama: Touchdown Club of Atlanta (12), AFCA (4), FWAA (2)
2. Notre Dame: AFCA (2), FWAA (3)
3. Southern California: AFCA (2), FWAA (2)

they did. Consensus All-Americans like Buddy Brown, Woody Lowe, and the great Ozzie Newsome starred for Alabama. Newsome became an All-Pro tight end for the Cleveland Browns and is in the Pro Football Hall of Fame. Lowe is in the College Hall of Fame.

Frustration, however, was the order of the day. The success of integration was found as much in what did not happen as in what did happen, as in there was little if any tension or problem, at least not outwardly. The torch had been passed.

Then in 1978 defeat turned to victory in the kind of way that demonstrates the irony of football and life. For years Alabama had toiled in the shadow of national rivals USC and Notre Dame, whose annual game was always billed as a showdown for number one. Alabama, ofttimes sporting as good if not better records, played strong Auburn teams in games that seemed anonymous in comparison to the USC-Notre Dame slugfests—or so it seemed outside of Dixie.

Alabama had beaten USC 17–10 in 1971, but nobody remembered that. All anybody remembered was the Sam Cunningham blowout game of 1970, the subject of books and a movie, too. In 1978 number seven USC ventured back to Legion Field. This time Bryant's team was not in a rebuilding mode, as they had been in 1970. They were number one. A national TV audience tuned in to one of the biggest games in years. Instead of getting the respect they felt they deserved with a big win over Troy, which would vault the Tide to the national title, all they got was 199 yards from USC's Charlie White in a convincing 24–14 USC victory. The national championship looked to be out of reach. Another year of disappointment seemed their destiny.

But destiny favored Alabama this time. USC lost to Arizona State and Alabama lost to nobody else. Penn State was unbeaten and would have to be knocked off in order for Alabama to reach number one. It was the Tide who got their shot at the Nittany Lions in the Sugar Bowl, which 'Bama won 14-7.

When USC beat Michigan in the Rose Bowl, 17–10, it seemed there would be more frustration. Logically, the Trojans had the edge. Both teams had the same record (in fact USC was one better, 12–1 to 11–1), but USC's win at Birmingham in September seemed to make them the obvious choice.

But Bryant's class in handling the 1966 poll disappointment; sympathy over "close but no cigar" seasons throughout the decade; the reversal of the "Catholic vote" at the expense of Notre Dame's biggest rival; and undoubtedly Bryant's masterful handling of integration had made him more than a sympathetic figure by 1978. Now he was beloved, a legend, a mythological coach of Rushmore status. This factor above all others persuaded a majority of AP voters into making 'Bama their national champions for the first time in thirteen seasons. The coaches, voting in the UPI poll, went for Southern California in a split national championship year.

1979 was another classic collegiate football season. Like 1966, it featured storied traditions having some of their best-ever seasons. Unlike 1966, Alabama came out on top this time. USC started off ranked first but was tripped up by Stanford, who tied them 21–21. Ohio State separated themselves and had the inside track, carrying an unbeaten, untied record and the number one ranking into the Rose Bowl. USC broke their hearts with a last-minute 17–16 victory. The Trojans rooted for Arkansas to beat unbeaten, un-

Crimson Tide on the Run

Year	Record	Run
1924	8–1 F/1–0	8–1 (1924)
		1–0 (1924)
1925	10–0	18–1 (1924–25)
		11–0 (1924–25)
1926	9–0–1 S/9–0	27–1–1 (1924–26)
		20–0 (1924–26) **20 games**
		27–0–1 (1924–26)
1930	10–0	10–0 (1930)
1931	9–1	19–1 (1930–31)
1932	8–2	27–3 (1930–32)
1933	7–1–1 F/4–0	34–4–1 (1930–33)
		4–0 (1933)
1934	10–0	44–4–1 (1930–34)
		14–0 (1933–34)
1935	6–2–1 S/1–0–1	50–8–2 (1930–35) **60 games**
		15–0–1 (1933–36)
1960	8–1–2 F/6–0–1	8–1–2 (1960)
		6–0–1 (1960)
1961	11–0	19–1–2 (1960–61)
		17–0–1 (1960–61)
1962	10–1 S/8–0	29–2–2 (1960–62)
		25–0–1 (1960–62)
1963	10–1	39–3–2 (1960–63)
1964	10–1 S/10–0	49–4–2 (1960–63)
		45–3–2 (1960–63) **50 games**
1965	9–1–1	58–5–3 (1960–65)
		53–5–3 (1960–65) **60 games**
1966	11–0	69–5–3 (1960–66)
		64–5–3 (1960–66) **70 games**
		11–0 (1966)
1967	8–2–1 S/3–0–1	77–7–4 (1960–67)
		67–5–4 (1960–67)
		71–5–4 (1960–67) **80 games**
		19–2–1 (1966–67)
1971	11–1	11–1 (1971)
1972	10–2	21–3 (1971–72)
1973	11–1	32–4 (1971–73)

(continues)

Crimson Tide on the Run (*continued*)

Year	Record	Run
1974	11–1	43–5 (1971–74)
1975	11–1	54–6 (1971–75) **60 games**
		44–6 (1971–75) **50 games**
1976	9–3	63–9 (1971–76)
		61–9 (1971–76) **70 games**
1977	11–1	74–10 (1971–77)
		70–10 (1971–77) **80 games**
1978	11–1	85–11 (1971–78)
		79–11 (1971–79) **90 games**
1979	12–0	97–11 (1971–79)
		89–11 (1977–79) **100 games**
1980	10–2 S/7–0, 8–1	107–13 (1971–80) **120 games**
		99–11 (1971–80) **110 games**
		104–11 (1971–80)
1991		11–1 F/10–0 11–1 (1991)
		10–0 (1991)
1992	13–0	24–1 (1991–92)
		23–0 (1991–92)
		20–0 (1991–92) **20 games**
1993	9–3–1 S/5–0, 7–0–1	33–4–1 (1991–93)
		28–0 (1991–93)
		30–0–1 (1991–93)
		29–0–1 (1991–93) **30 games**
1994	12–1	45–5–1 (1991–94)
		44–5–1 (1991–94) **50 games**
1995	8–3 S/2–0	53–8–1 (1991–95)
		47–5–1 (1991–95)
		52–7–1 (1991–95) **60 games**

S/start season; F/finish season

tied Alabama in the Sugar Bowl, giving them a second straight national championship. The Crimson Tide would have none of it, winning *their* second straight title by virtue of a convincing 24–9 win over the Razorbacks.

The 1978–1979 Tide featured two consensus All-Americans, defensive lineman Marty Lyons and tackle Jim Bunch. Quarterback Jeff Rutledge was a steady, although not spectacular, passer. Running back Tony Nathan, later a mainstay in Miami, keyed a ball-control offense. But the greatest player of that period was center Dwight Stephenson. Recognized as the premier center of his time, if not of all time, Stephenson was an All-Pro and Pro Bowl selection five straight years with the Dolphins before entering the Hall of Fame.

Bryant retired after the 1982 season, the winningest college coach in history. Numbers aside, he is generally viewed as the finest coach ever, which is saying something considering that the likes of Pop Warner, Knute Rockne, Howard Jones, Bob Neyland, Frank Leahy, Bud Wilkinson, John McKay, Joe Paterno, and Bobby Bowden have accomplished the extraordinary things they accomplished.

In the 1980s, Tommy Wilcox, Mike Pitts, Cornelius Bennett, Derrick Thomas, and Keith McCants made consensus All-American. Ray Perkins and Bill Curry maintained standards in Tuscaloosa, but it was Gene Stallings, one of the Junction Boys, who led the 1992 Crimson Tide to a 13-0 record. The Tide finished up with a 17-0 triumph over Auburn; a 28-21 victory over Florida in the SEC championship game; and a surprise 34-13 whipping of Miami in the Sugar Bowl to capture the national title. 1990s consensus All-Americans: Philip Doyle, John Copeland, David Palmer, Antonio Langham, and 1999 Outland Trophy-winner Chris Samuels.

When Alabama beat USC 24-3 in the 1985 Aloha Bowl, it pushed them past the Trojans into the number one spot for all-time bowl wins, a boast the Trojans had been previously able to make going back to their first Rose Bowl victory in 1923. When Alabama won the 1992 national championship, it marked their ninth legitimate, historically recognized title. At that time, USC was "down in the dumps," having fired coach Larry Smith in the aftermath of the disastrous Todd Marinovich fiasco. In 1992 Troy also boasted nine titles, but their last one had been gathering dust for fourteen years in Heritage Hall.

At that point, a strong argument could have been made that, in light of greater success in more recent years, Alabama had passed USC for second place among *College Football's All-Time Top 25 Traditions*. But in the 2000s, Alabama fell on hard times. In January 2009, when 'Bama lost to Utah in the Sugar Bowl while Southern Cal dominated Penn State in the Rose, Pete Carroll's Trojans tied the Crimon Tide for most bowl wins (31). The Trojans have embarked on the kind of run Bryant's teams enjoyed. In light of *USC's* more recent success—two national championships (almost a third) and three Heismans—they have unquestionably moved past Alabama and Oklahoma, if they ever actually trailed them in the first place.

While this historic "poll" is "fluid," subject to change over succeeding years, Alabama has a tough "road to hoe" in a bitterly difficult conference. They also do not boast the Heismans, Outland winners, large numbers of All-Americans, and first-round draft picks that characterize many of the teams in the "elite ten." However, they have always been a *team*. If they are to maintain or even improve on their number three ranking, it will be by virtue of the team concept; when they do, it will be "Roll Tide!"

Chapter 4

Oklahoma Sooners

THIS IS A BOOK that dares to explore and declare what the greatest collegiate foot-ball tradition of all time is. In so doing, certain dates are used as "dividing lines," so to speak. 1960, for instance, is seen as the embarkation of a newer, more "modern" era. This truth remains relatively self-evident through the viewing of photographs, which show for instance a marked difference in uniform quality (facemasks, helmets, padding) and player size and color. It ushered in a new era of offensive innovation, giving us the veer, the wishbone, the "run 'n' shoot," and the like.

Oklahoma University
Norman, Oklahoma
Founded: 1890
Enrollment: 20,966
Colors: Crimson and cream
Stadium: Gaylord Family-Oklahoma Memorial Stadium (opened: 1923; capacity: 82,112)
All-time record (1895–2008): 791–297–53
All-time bowl record: 24–17–1 (through 2009 bowls)
National championships: *1950, 1955, 1956, 1974, 1975, 1985, 2000
*Illegitimate; lost bowl game
Big 6/8/12 Conference championships: 41 (through 2008)
Heisman Trophies: Billy Vessels (1952), Steve Owens (1969), Billy Sims (1978), Jason White (2003), Sam Bradford (2008)
Outland Trophies: Jim Weatherall (1951), J. D. Roberts (1953), Lee Roy Selmon (1975), Greg Roberts (1978), Jammal Brown (2004)
First-round NFL draftees: 37 (through 2009 draft)
Website: www.soonersports.com
Notable alumni: Speaker of the House Carl Albert; Oklahoma Governor David Boren; Chairman of the Joint Chiefs of Staff Admiral William S. Crowe; actors James Garner, Ed Harris, and Tony Hillerman; Olympian Shannon Miller

1998 is more clearly now seen as another dividing line, this being the first year of the Bowl Championship Series. National championships in the decade of BCS competition are harder to come by than they used to be. Teams that win them rightly get a few extra "points" for so doing.

Wars are also viewed as natural periods of great change in all areas of life, including sports. This book places its greatest emphasis on collegiate football accomplishments after World War I (beginning with the 1919 season). If not, then there is little choice but to anoint Princeton as the finest college football program this great nation has ever produced. Common sense does not allow for this.

World War I was of course an era of great disruption. A review of scores in 1918, for instance, reveals that the college game took a backseat to the war effort. In 1919 it all started up again with a vengeance. The "Black Sox" gambling scandal of that year diverted many baseball fans to other sports, namely college football, which was a major part of the Roaring '20s. American sports mania in that decade explains much about this nation.

If World War I is not used as the great dividing line separating the "Ivy League era" from the new nationalization, which manifested itself in the form of radio broadcasts, intersectional play, and the growing popularity of bowl games, then Notre Dame would be forced to eliminate much of its most storied past. We cannot have that.

By placing much emphasis on the 1920s and 1930s, Notre Dame, USC, and Alabama are glorified in ways no other programs can be. However, World War II ushered in enormous change, as well. In terms of world affairs, the period after 1945 is almost the "beginning of history." It is the dawning of the American Empire, for instance. This country, by virtue of the events of this time, became the most powerful nation humankind has ever witnessed. Changes in society have been monumental. If one makes the determination that World War II, not World War I, is the dividing line best used to judge college football, then Oklahoma makes a strong case that they are number one.

> Oklahoma versus the Big 8/12: 425–134–22 (through 2008)

Prior to Bud Wilkinson's first year in Norman (1947), OU was just another school. The state was beset by the "dust bowl" of the Great Depression 1930s. Its citizens were mocked as "Okies" or sympathized with by John Steinbeck's readers. He described their sad migration to California in books like *The Grapes of Wrath*. OU's 1915 team was 10-0 and made some claim on the national championship. The 1938 Sooners were 10-1. All in all, Sooner football was competent but nothing much more than that.

Oklahoma versus the Elite Ten (111–95–10 through 2008)

Alabama (2–1–1), Miami (2–3), Michigan (1–0), Nebraska (44–37–3), Notre Dame (1–8), Penn State (1–0), Southern California (2–6–1), Texas (58–40–5)

Elite Ten by the Numbers			
Top 5 in Associated Press polls (1936–2005)			
1. Oklahoma	342	6. Southern California	256
2. Nebraska	294	7. Texas	246
3. Notre Dame	273	8. Alabama	243
4. Ohio State	272	9. Florida State	204
5. Michigan	262	10. Miami	201

After the war, Wilkinson turned them into an amazing juggernaut. There appear to be no great reasons behind it. There may have been some ancillary economic benefit in being next to the Texas "oil patch," which in the 1940s and 1950s saw boom times, attracting East Coast "old money" like future president George H. W. Bush. But Oklahoma was mostly mocked as "Baja Texas."

The Commerce Comet, Mickey Mantle, did much for the state's image when he took New York by storm, but Wilkinson's ability to harness what talent was available to him, turning it into Sooner dominance, marks him as very possibly the most effective coach of all time. The change in the way America now looked at Oklahoma and Oklahomans was incalculable.

The OU football media guide certainly wishes to convey the notion that college football "started" in 1946, one year prior to Wilkinson's arrival. By doing this they demonstrate that between 1946 and 2005, the Sooners' record of 513–157–13 (.760) is the greatest in the country.

Through 2008 the Sooners have won 41 conference championships, which they claim to be the most of any school (Michigan claims 42). They have had 148 All-Americans (65 consensus). One of their most impressive accomplishments is the fact that five Sooners have won the Outland Trophy, five the Heisman, four the Butkus, three the Lombardi, and three the Jim Thorpe Award. Sooner football has made the cover of twenty-nine *Sports Illustrated* covers. OU has made forty-two bowl appearances (through the 2008 season).

Since World War II, OU has won seven national championships (1950, 1955, 1956, 1974, 1975, 1985, 2000). During this period, USC has also won seven, Notre Dame seven, Alabama seven, Miami five, and Nebraska five. However, these numbers come with a caveat. Two of Alabama's come with bowl defeats (1964, 1973). One of OU's comes with a bowl defeat (1950) and another in a probation year (1974). The 1956 Sooners, perhaps Wilkinson's greatest team, won their second straight national title without playing in a bowl game due to a conference "no-repeat" rule.

All of USC's seven titles come with hard-fought Rose Bowl victories over Big 10 powerhouses, with the exception of its 55–19 2005 BCS Orange Bowl win over . . . Oklahoma. Notre Dame's national championships include only three via bowl victory.

Oklahoma beat Florida State to win the 2000 national championship. They were on the upswing of history while Southern California and, to a lesser extent, Notre Dame and Alabama were on a downswing. In the case of USC, it was less of a down-

Best Win-Loss Records (1946–2005)

1.	Oklahoma	513–157–13 (.760)
2.	Ohio State	472–159–20 (.740)
3.	Penn State	485–172–9 (.734)
4.	Michigan	470–172–15 (.726)
5.	Nebraska	484–194–10 (.718)
6.	Texas	481–190–11 (.713)
7.	Alabama	486–191–20 (.711)
8.	Notre Dame	457–189–14 (.703)
9.	Tennessee	466–197–24 (.695)
10.	Southern California	458–198–23 (.691)
11.	Florida State	436–205–17 (.675)
12.	Miami (Ohio)	411–203–19 (.664)
13.	Miami	433–224–7 (.657)
14.	Arizona State	429–222–10 (.656)
15.	Georgia	437–224–2 (.655)

swing than "rock bottom." The Sooners were making a major bid to pass USC in the historical rankings while taking dead aim at the others. In 2003 and 2004, they had their shot at becoming the "Team of the New Millennium," the best program in the young twenty-first century. In 2003 they fielded one of the finest college powerhouses ever only to falter inexplicably, first to Kansas State in the Big 12 Championship Game, and then in embarrassing circumstances against Louisiana State in a tainted BCS national title contest at the Sugar Bowl.

All would have been forgiven had the 2004 Sooners won the BCS Orange Bowl. It was a battle not just for that year's title but in many ways also for historical bragging rights between OU and USC. The result left the Sooners in disarray. Since then the program has experienced a myriad of problems on and off the field. They are and continue to be a power, but their most recent bids fall into the disappointing "close but no cigar" category.

In 1915, when Oklahoma put itself on the national map, a group of Sooner football players attended an OU basketball game. They were cheering in a loud and raucous manner. A fan sitting nearby yelled, "Sit down and be quiet, you roughnecks." That gave birth to a game-day spirit tradition called the Ruf/Neks, which lives to this day. The term also became applied to "wildcatters" and oil workers in the Southwest.

Oklahoma became a charter member of the Southwest Conference when it was formed in 1915 but moved to the Missouri Valley Conference in 1920. This proved to have a major effect on its image. Oklahoma is in the *South*west as much or more than it is in the *Mid*west. Its citizens speak with a Southern twang and tend to identify with Southern traditions. Its most conspicuous neighbor, Texas, is indisputably Southern, going back to its origins as a destination of Southern rural mountain men who came west at the behest of the Mexican government to fight Indians, then ended up defeating the Mexicans when they tried to say *they* were Mexicans, not Americans.

But Oklahoma was always humble. Its humility did not quite fit in with the sense of pride, even hubris, that marks Southern (i.e., Confederate) military tradition. The Great Depression made it an underdog. In turn, when it came to integrating the program, Bud Wilkinson was able to get it done much earlier than other teams in the same general geographical region.

By joining the Missouri Valley Conference instead of staying in the mostly Texan SWC, OU became a quasi-Midwestern school and state. When it came to social progress, this made them part of a more tolerant group than they would otherwise have been. In 1928, OU and five other schools (Iowa State, Kansas, Kansas State, Missouri, and Nebraska) withdrew from the MVC to form the Big 6 Conference. The league became the Big 7 in 1948 with the addition of Colorado. In 1960 Oklahoma State (the university, not the prison; see Burt Reynolds's *The Longest Yard*) made it into the Big 8.

However, Oklahoma has always straddled the cultural differences of the Big 8 and the Southwest Conference. Their oldest rivalry is with Texas, who they first played in 1900. The series shifted to "neutral" Dallas (halfway between Norman and Austin on the Red River) beginning in 1911. When the Cotton Bowl was built, the game was shifted to that location. Played as part of the Texas State Fair, it became known as the Red River Shoot-out, partly as homage to the 1948 John Wayne Western *Red River*.

Over the years, sheer competitiveness overcame any geographical disparities, making the Oklahoma-Nebraska game one of the great rivalries in the college game.

"Forget about Bosnia, forget about Iraq," legendary announcer Keith Jackson once said. "It's Oklahoma-Nebraska!"

The entrance of Colorado helped make the Big 8 a more cosmopolitan conference, too. Its reputation as the home of upscale ski resorts and Western Rocky Mountain social *mores* contrasted with the hardscrabble of Oklahoma or the Midwestern prairie. Then, in 1996, it all became one great big happy family. The SWC joined the Big 8, forming the Big 12, turning it into a "super conference," at least at first.

The SWC got rid of dead weight in the form of Houston and SMU, who had been hit with the infamous NCAA "death penalty" in the 1980s. North and South Divisions were created with a moneymaking conference-title game usually played at Kansas City's Arrowhead Stadium.

Since 1996, the Big 12 has produced three national champions (Nebraska, 1997; Oklahoma, 2000; Texas, 2005) while sending six teams to the BCS title game (Oklahoma, 2000; Nebraska, 2001; Oklahoma, 2003–2004; Texas, 2005; Oklahoma, 2008). Advocates of the Southeastern Conference say their league is better but so competitive they knock each other out of contention, while individual teams tend to dominate the Big 12. Their argument has some limited validity. Certainly the Big 12 has had overrated teams. Nebraska (2001) and Oklahoma (2003–2004, 2008) made poor showings, but the 2000 Sooners did the Big 12 proud, as did Texas in 2005.

Oklahoma more than any other team is associated with the Orange Bowl, which over the years has maintained a loose affiliation with the Big 8 (now Big 12). OU's first

Orange Bowl came on January 2, 1938, when the Sooners came in unbeaten against Tennessee. It was a "donnybrook" for the national championship that would not be decided until the end of the day. Texas Christian had won the AP national title prior to New Year's, but the systems rightly wanted to consider the bowl picture. On that fateful day, unbeaten Duke was upset by Southern California in the Rose Bowl, 7–3; Texas Christian beat . . . Carnegie Tech, 15–7; and the Vols shut out Oklahoma, 17–0. That ended it for the Sooners. TCU had the imprimatur of the AP vote, although victory over Carnegie Tech hardly improved their position in comparison with Tennessee shutting out Oklahoma. Some of the systems went for Tennessee, but history accords a consensus national title—their last—on TCU.

Coach Jim Tatum came to Norman for one year (1946), leading the Sooners to their first bowl win, a 34–13 triumph over North Carolina State in the Gator Bowl. On Tatum's staff was a young man who had entered his family's mortgage-trading business (depicted as heartless land-grabbers in John Steinbeck's novels).

Charles Burnham "Bud" Wilkinson grew up in Minnesota, an unlikely place for an Oklahoma icon. After leading Bernie Bierman's 1936 Golden Gophers to their third straight national championship, he served as an aircraft carrier deck officer. Not content with mortgage trading, Wilkinson went back into football as an assistant on Tatum's staff. In 1947 the thirty-one-year-old Wilkinson was elevated to head coach. No single individual—including Mickey Mantle, Johnny Bench, or Oral Roberts, for that matter—did more to discredit the Steinbeck myths than Wilkinson.

Wilkinson was clean-cut, articulate with no twang, and nattily dressed. He did not fit the image of the old whiskey-drinkin' Southern football coach, craggy-faced guys like Bear Bryant. Wilkinson was more like a matinee idol, a movie star type, a Pete Carroll image long before Carroll came along.

"His teams dispelled the 'dust bowl' *Grapes of Wrath* image of the Depression years," said former Oklahoma president George L. Cross. Aside from Steinbeck's novels and the movie version starring Henry Fonda as Tom Joad, *Life* magazine had printed searing photos of forsaken cabins outlined against the blood-red sunset of the drought-stricken plain; beaten-down-by-life farmers next to barren crop fields; tired-as-the-day-is-long mothers with hungry children hugging their dirty dresses. These were real-life depictions of Charles Dickens's image of *want* from *A Christmas Carol*. The Socialist-Communist Steinbeck desperately wanted to convey the lie that these images represented the *norm* in America, from "sea to shining sea."

Wilkinson's natural instincts for offensive innovation, honed as Bierman's quarterback, resulted in his developing the modified split-T, an advance on Clark Shaughnessy's new schemes, which he used successfully at Stanford and in the NFL. Wilkinson was 145–29–4 in seventeen seasons at Norman. That record pales in comparison to his initial run, in particular his record between November 29, 1947, and November 16, 1957. It was the most dominant decade since World War I (only Gil Dobie's ten-year unbeaten reign at Washington stands above it).

There was a 31-game winning streak (1948–51), a 47-game winning streak (1953–57), and a 48-game unbeaten streak over that same stretch of years. Prior to Wilkinson, the

Sooners boasted one consensus All-American (Waddy Young in 1938). Under him they produced the likes of Buddy Burris (1948), Leon Heath (1950), Jim Weatherall (1950–1951), Billy Vessels (1952), J. D. Roberts (1953), Max Boydston (1954), Kurt Burris (1954), Bo Bolinger (1955), Jerry Tubbs (1956), Tommy McDonald (1956), Bill Krisher (1957), Bob Harrison (1958), and Jim Grisham (1963). Wilkinson, a Republican, left to run for Oklahoma's U.S. Senate seat in 1964. Despite Oklahoma's staunchly Democrat reputation (today they are a thoroughly "red state"), Wilkinson's defeat was almost as shocking as Winston Churchill's rejection at Great Britain's 1946 polls one year after World War II. As if to further refute all that Wilkinson stood for, Oklahoma actually hired a man named *Gomer* Jones, who lasted two years and was fired after going 3–7 in 1965.

It all began in 1947 when the Sooners were a creditable 7–2–1. After losing to Santa Clara 20–17 in the 1948 opener, they embarked on Wilkinson's first streak, the 31-game skein, including a 10–1 record with a 14–6 win over North Carolina in the 1949 Sugar Bowl. The 1949 Sooners, like the 1929 USC Trojans, 1938 Tennessee Vols, 1945 Alabama Crimson Tide, 1947 Michigan Wolverines, or the 1948 Notre Dame Fighting Irish, very easily could have won the national championship but did not. After killing LSU 35–0 in the Sugar Bowl, the AP vote favored bowl-less Michigan (9–0).

In 1950 OU started an unusual player named Claude Arnold at quarterback. He arrived at Norman eight years earlier but left to serve in the military. When he came back, Darrell Royal started ahead of him. He finally got his opportunity in 1950. Against Texas A&M the Sooners looked to him to lead them back from a 28–21 fourth-quarter deficit. Arnold engineered a 69-yard scoring drive, but the 2-point conversion failed, leaving OU still trailing by a point. The Sooner defense held. Arnold got the ball back with 1:09 left to play. Oklahoma pushed into the end zone, escaping with a 34–28 win.

Elite Ten by the Numbers

Winning streaks—modern era (1919–2008; includes bowls, no ties)

1.	Oklahoma	47 (1953–57)
2.	Southern California	34 (2003–06)
2.	Miami	34 (2000–03)
4.	Oklahoma	31 (1948–51)
5.	Texas	30 (1968–71)
6.	Miami	29 (1990–93)
7.	Alabama	28 (1991–93)
7.	Alabama	28 (1978–80)
7.	Oklahoma	28 (1973–75)
10.	Nebraska	26 (1994–96)
11.	Southern California	25 (1931–33)
12.	Michigan	25 (1946–49)

Wilkinson's team was awarded the national championship in prebowl voting by both the AP and the new United Press International rankings in 1950. That was marred by an enormous upset, 13–7 at the hands of Bear Bryant's Kentucky Wildcats. It was the only blip on Wilkinson's "radar screen" between 1948 and 1960, when the program dropped to 3–6–1.

In 1951 and 1952 Wilkinson's teams were a combined 16–3–1. On September 26, 1952, in the opener at Norman, Notre Dame came in and won by a score of 28–21. The loss to the Irish did not actually open the door to a winning streak, since they tied Pitt 7–7 the following week. But on October 14 OU beat Texas 19–14 in the Red River Shoot-out. They were on their way. Their 7–0 Orange Bowl win over Maryland illegitimatized the Terrapins' 1953 AP and UPI national championships. Had the polls closed after the game, the national title would have gone to Oklahoma or Notre Dame.

The 1954 Sooners (10–0), like the 1949 team, could feel only frustration at the pollsters' vote for AP choice Ohio State (winners of the Rose) and UPI pick UCLA (like OU, denied a bowl repeat by conference rules). There was some talk that their conference was weaker than the Big 10 and the PCC, but in 1955 the Sooners left no question. They posted four shutouts to close the regular season then beat up on Maryland 20–6 in the Orange Bowl, claiming the school's first truly unfettered national championship

In 1956 the team was even better, returning all their star players including halfback/defensive back Tommy McDonald (Maxwell Trophy winner) and center/linebacker Jerry Tubbs (Walter Camp Trophy). A 54–6 conquest of Nebraska and 53–0 thrashing of Oklahoma State closed out the regular season. The conference still did not allow a return to a bowl game. The national title was theirs again.

In 1957 Oklahoma was number one until the October 28 poll. They carried a 7–0 record with a 47-game winning streak and a 48-game unbeaten streak into the November 16 game against number twenty Notre Dame (4–2) in Norman. On that day, the Irish beat them 7–0.

"I worked that game," recalled Ross Porter, a native Oklahoman who later became Vin Scully's sidekick as the Dodgers' baseball announcer. "After Notre Dame had won somebody came into their dressing room and announced, 'This is for all the Catholics in Oklahoma.' Somebody then said, 'Yeah, all seven of 'em.'"

The game cost the Sooners a third straight national title, but they managed to beat Duke 48–21 in the Orange Bowl. The "beatings went on" in 1958 with a 10–1 team that knocked off Syracuse 21–6 in the Orange Bowl. That was an integrated Sooner team, a great credit to Wilkinson. From 1959 to 1963, the Sooners declined and Wilkinson became burned out by coaching. How he figured life in between the "beltway" of Washington would be less stressful does not make much sense, though.

Since World War II, OU football has been streaky with doldrums in between. So it was in the 1960s. Gomer Jones (1964–1965) was about as successful as *Gomer Pyle*. Jim Mackenzie was there one year (1966) before Chuck Fairbanks took over and went 10–1 in 1967. Fairbanks does not cut a swath in Oklahoma football lore like the ones fashioned by Wilkinson, Barry Switzer, or even Bob Stoops, but he was a great coach and a good example of why those who leave really good college jobs for NFL money

Sooners on the Run

Year	Record	Run
1947	7–2–1 F/5–0	7–2–1 (1947)
		5–0 (1947)
1948	10–1	15–1 (1947–48)
1949	11–0	26–1 (1947–49)
		20–0 (1948–49) **20 games**
1950	10–1	36–2 (1947–50)
1951	8–2	46–4 (1947–51) **50 games**
1952	8–1–1	54–5–1 (1947–52) **60 games**
1953	9–1–1 S/0–1, F/9–0	65–6–2 (1947–53)
		62–6–2 (1947–53) **70 games**
1954	10–0	75–6–2 (1947–54)
		72–6–2 (1947–54) **80 games**
1955	11–0 S/10–0	83–6–2 (1947–55)
		82–6–2 (1947–55) **90 games**
1956	10–0	93–6–3 (1947–56)
		91–6–3 (1947–56) **100 games**
1957	10–1 S/7–0, F/7–1	103–7–3 (1947–57)
		100–7–3 (1947–57) **110 games**
1958	10–1 S/6–1, F/4–0	113–8–3 (1947–58)
		109–8–3 (1947–58) **120 games**
		113–8–3 (1947–58)
1959	7–3 S/3–3	120–11–3 (1947–59)
		116–11–3 (1947–59) **130 games**
		93–10–4 **(decade: 1950s)**
1970	7–4–1 F/1–0–1	7–4–1 (1970)
		1–0–1 (1970)
1971	11–1	12–1–1 (1970–71)
1972	11–1	23–2–1 (1970–72)
1973	10–0–1	33–2–2 (1970–72)
1974	11–0	45–2–2 (1970–74)
1975	11–1	46–2–2 (1970–75) **50 games**
		55–3–2 (1970–75) **60 games**
		56–4–2 (1970–75)

1976	9–2–1 S/4–0	62–6–2 (1970–76) **70 games**
		65–6–3 (1970–76)
		60–4–2 (1970–76)
1977	10–2	70–7–3 (1970–77) **80 games**
		75–8–3 (1970–77)
1978	11–1	79–8–3 (1970–78) **100 games**
		86–9–3 (1970–77)
1979	11–1	97–10–3 (1970–79) **110 games**
1980	10–2 S/1–0	98–10–3 (1970–79)
		107–12–3 (1970–79)
		113–16–3 **(decade: 1970s)**

S/Start season; F/Finish season

often make a mistake. Had Fairbanks stayed on at Norman he would have been a legend instead of an afterthought.

Like Wilkinson he was not an "old school" type, with his stylish hair and corporate looks. His 1967 team beat Tennessee in a memorable Orange Bowl, 26–24. In 1968 the Sooners lost to SMU in a Bluebonnet Bowl donnybrook, 28–27. His 1969 and 1970 teams posted fair records and, in 1970, a tie with Alabama in the Bluebonnet Bowl.

That game portended 1970s dominance by both programs. Fairbanks's teams in 1969 and 1970 may have had less-than-stellar records, but they were highly entertaining and extremely talented. In 1969 they featured Heisman Trophy-winning running back Steve Owens. Quarterback Jack Mildren came on the scene and ran a "wishbone" offense that was revolutionizing college football.

Nebraska was the dominant Big 8 team of the 1960s. Outside of somehow letting Gale Sayers from Omaha "escape" to Kansas, they got the best Midwestern talent that previously went for Norman. Darrell Royal seemingly put up a border fence at the Oklahoma line preventing any Texas blue-chippers from "defecting."

In the 1960s, Ralph Neely, Carl McAdams, Granville Liggins, and Steve Owens were consensus All-Americans. Wide receiver Lance Rentzel went on to play for Minnesota and Dallas. But the most honored player was Bob Kalsu, the number one pick of the Buffalo Bills in 1968. Kalsu played one year in pro football, then went to Vietnam where he became the only pro athlete to die in that war.

But Fairbanks fought back and by 1971 had a great team in place—one of the greatest teams *never* to win a national title. Senior quarterback Jack Mildren hardly ever put the ball in the air, but he could run and pitch out with the best of 'em. Running back Greg Pruitt ran for 1,665 yards, with Mildren adding more than 1,000. A 33–20 victory over Southern California demonstrated that OU was for real.

All eyes were on Thanksgiving weekend when number one defending national champion Nebraska came to town. Few regular season games have ever had such a buildup, and fewer still have lived up to the advance notice in such a way. The Sooners received great national attention in 1971 after years of ceding the spotlight to the likes of Southern Cal and Notre Dame. This was a Big 8 year. *Sports Illustrated* did much for OU's image (not to mention recruiting) with a color photo of a model-quality majorette above the caption, "Everything's OK at OU." Miracle of miracles, capitalism had worked and the days of Depression-era mothers with starving kids were over. SI also previewed the Sooner-Cornhusker match with a memorable cover depicting the two team's squared off against each other with the headline "THE UNSTOPPABLE FORCE MEETS THE IMMOVABLE OBJECT."

It was cold and blustery on November 25. Nebraska's Johnny Rodgers set OU back immediately with a daring punt return for a touchdown. It is still considered one of the most exciting plays of all time. Running backs Pruitt and Joe Wylie were held in check by Nebraska defensive ends Willie Harper and John Adkins. They were employed wide, where the Sooners preferred to run. Forced to the middle, they ran into Nebraska's all-everything Rich Glover, who made no fewer than twenty-two tackles.

The Cornhuskers went up by 14-3, but Mildren took control. He produced 267 yards in total offense. Unable to penetrate Nebraska via conventional means, the Sooners went to trick plays, which years later still make Husker eyes roll. Mildren, who nobody ever mistook for Joe Namath or Johnny Unitas, threw for two touchdown passes. The game tightened to the delight of the Sooner faithful.

Every time OU crawled back in, Nebraska quarterback Jerry Tagge, running back Jeff Kinney, and Rodgers responded in kind. They went back up, 28-17. Then OU came back. Mildren ran for one score then threw to Jon Harrison in the end zone. With Oklahoma up 31-28, the nation held its breath. Could the Big Red juggernaut be stopped?

On third-and-8, Rodgers made a game-saving catch to keep the drive going. Kinney finally ran it in from the 6. Nebraska had won the "Game of the Century" (1971 version), 35-31. After dismantling Auburn 40-22 in the Sugar Bowl, Oklahoma finished number two.

Up until the early 1970s, Oklahoma certainly had their share of great players. Billy Vessels and Steve Owens had won the Heisman Trophy, Jim Weatherall the Outland. Jack Mildren and Greg Pruitt were great college stars, but perhaps their first true superstar was Lee Roy Selmon. Selmon was the youngest of nine children from Eufala, Oklahoma. Three played at OU. All were stars.

"God bless Mrs. Selmon," was a common refrain.

Lee Roy's older brother Lucious made his recruiting trip to Norman in the winter of 1969-1970. Lee Roy and brother Dewey, already giant kids, tagged along and were spotted piling food on their plates by assistant coach Barry Switzer.

"Who's that?" asked Switzer.

The recruiting of the younger Selmons began then and there. After beating Penn State 14-0 in the 1973 Sugar Bowl, Fairbanks left to take over the New England Patriots. It seemed like a good idea at the time. The Pats had young talent in the form of ex-Stanford Heisman Trophy winner Jim Plunkett, former Alabama All-American offensive lineman John Hannah, and one-time USC All-American fullback Sam "Bam" Cunningham. In reality, the Patriots did have some play-off worthy teams in the mid-1970s, but Plunkett never panned out. There are no Hall of Fames with plaques of Fairbanks.

There is one, however—the College Football Hall of Fame—that has one for Fairbanks's successor, Switzer. Had Fairbanks stayed he would be in there, but alas he went for the bucks instead. In the end Switzer made more money than Fairbanks coaching football anyway.

In 1973 Lee Roy and Dewey Selmon teamed up on one of Oklahoma's all-time greatest defensive teams. Mighty defending champion Southern California, ranked number one and riding a 19-game unbeaten streak, hosted the Sooners in Los Angeles. Anthony Davis, Pat Haden, and company were unable to do anything against the Selmons. The 7-7 tie was the only blemish on Oklahoma's 10-0-1 record, but probation kept them out of a bowl.

The 1974 Sooners were even better. Running back Joe Washington (1,321 yards), quarterback Steve Davis, and defensive lineman Jimbo Elrod teamed with the Selmons to lead the Sooners to an 11-0 record, including three shutouts and a 44–13 wipeout of Nebraska. Probation cost them the UPI national championship, won by USC, but the AP was willing to look the other way when it came to their probationary status.

In 1975 the NCAA got off their backs and Selmon won the Outland Trophy. Elvis Peacock joined forces with Washington. A stunning 23-3 loss to Kansas temporarily derailed the train, but defending national champion USC, after starting 7-0, fell to California, leaving the title chase wide open. It was not quite as impressive as the 1974 squad, but in a year with no unbeatens, Oklahoma's 35-10 beatdown of Nebraska followed by a defensive 14-6 throttling of Michigan in the Orange Bowl gave them a rare repeat AP national championship. It was a feat previously accomplished only by Minnesota (1935-1936, 1940-1941), Army (1944-1945), Notre Dame (1946-1947), Oklahoma (1955-1956), (in theory at least) Alabama (1964-1965), and Nebraska (1970-1971). Selmon became the number one pick in the entire NFL Draft (Tampa Bay).

Switzer was somehow perfect for Oklahoma in the disco 1970s. He was young, hip, a wisecracker who liked to joke that his team would "hang a half a hun'" (a hundred points) on some poor opponent. He played for the 1964 (revised) national-champion Arkansas team, anointed by the long-mothballed systems to wear that crown when they went unbeaten after "number one" Alabama lost to Texas in the Orange Bowl. Switzer's teammate at Arkansas was Jerry Jones, later the owner—and his boss for a Super Bowl-winning 1995 season—in Dallas. Switzer liked to drink and party. He did not fit the modern image of the workaholic football coach and was known to take liberties with coeds, which he considered a perk of the job.

Despite playing in barren Norman, OU was straight out of Hollywood. Their players were flashy, often sporting white shoes and knee-high socks. Their black players were the "new breed"—confident, freewheeling—not the old-style "colored" players afraid to make waves. The team mirrored the coach, living in a fancy football dorm that became "party central": hot girls, alcohol, drugs, boosters with cash.

Elite Ten by the Numbers

Vince Lombardi, Jim Thorpe, Dick Butkus, Walter Camp, Johnny Unitas, Doak Walker, Lou Groza, John Mackey, Chuck Bednarik, Bronco Nagurski, Davey O'Brien, Fred Biletnikoff, Ray Guy, Mosi Tatupu, Ronnie Lott, Pop Warner, Dave Rimington, and Maxwell award winners (through 2005)

1. Oklahoma   23
2. Southern California 19 (through 2008)
3. Miami   15
3. Notre Dame   15 (through 2006)
5. Nebraska   13
6. Ohio State   12
7. Michigan   10
8. Alabama   5

Alabama (5): Lombardi (Cornelius Bennett, 1986), Butkus (Derrick Thomas, 1988), Unitas (Jay Barker, 1994), Thorpe (Antonio Langham, 1993), Lott (DeMeco Ryans, 2005)

Miami (15): Mackey (Kellen Winslow, 2003), Rimington (Brett Romberg, 2002), Maxwell (Vinny Testaverde, 1986; Gino Torretta, 1992; Ken Dorsey, 2001), Butkus (Dan Morgan, 2000), Lombardi (Warren Sapp, 1994), Thorpe (Bennie Blades, 1987), Bednarik (Dan Morgan, 2000), Nagurski (Warren Sapp, 1994; Dan Morgan, 2000), O'Brien (Vinny Testaverde, 1986; Gino Torretta, 1992), Unitas (Craig Erickson, 1990; Gino Torretta, 1992)

Michigan (10): Maxwell (Tom Harmon, 1940; Desmond Howard, 1991), Thorpe (Charles Woodson, 1991), Bednarik (Charles Woodson, 1997), Nagurski (Charles Woodson, 1997), Butkus (Erick Anderson, 1991; Jarrett Irons, 1995), Biletnikoff (Braylon Edwards, 2004), Rimington (David Baas, 2004), Walker (Chris Perry, 2003)

Nebraska (13): Lombardi (Rich Glover, 1972; Dave Rimington, 1982–83; Grant Winstrom, 1997), Maxwell (Mike Rozier, 1983), Walter Camp (Johnny Rodgers, 1972; Mike Rozier, 1983; Eric Crouch, 2001), Johnny Unitas (Tommie Frazier, 1995), Davey O'Brien (Eric Crouch, 2001), Butkus (Broderick Thomas, 1988; Ed Stewart, 1994), Rimington (Dominic Raiola, 2000)

Notre Dame (14 through 2006): Lombardi (Walt Patulski, 1971; Ross Browner, 1977; Chris Zorich, 1990; Aaron Taylor, 1993), Walter Camp (Ken MacAfee, 1977; Tim Brown, 1987; Raghib Ismail, 1990), Maxwell (Leon Hart, 1949; John Lattner, 1952–53; Jim Lynch, 1966; Ross Browner, 1977; Brady Quinn, 2006), Unitas (Tony Rice, 1989, Brady Quinn, 2006)

Ohio State (12): Lombardi (Jim Stillwagon, 1970; John Hicks, 1973; Chris Spielman, 1987; Orlando Pace, 1995–96; A. J. Hawk, 2005), Butkus (Andy Katzenmoyer, 1997), Thorpe (Antoine Winfield, 1998), Biletnikoff (Terry Glenn, 1995), Rimington (LeCharles Bentley, 2001), Guy (B. J. Sanders, 2003), Groza (Mike Nugent, 2004)

Oklahoma (23): Butkus (Brian Bosworth, 1985–86; Rocky Calmus, 2001; Teddy Lehman, 2003), Lombardi (Lee Roy Selmon, 1975; Tony Casillas, 1985; Tommie Harris, 2003), Thorpe (Rickey

Dixon, 1987; Roy Williams, 2001; Derrick Strait, 2003), Nagurski (Roy Williams, 2001; Derrick Strait, 2003), Bednarik (Teddy Lehman, 2003), O'Brien (Jason White, 2003–04), Unitas (Jason White, 2004), Maxwell (Tommy McDonald, 1956; Jason White, 2004), Walter Camp (Jerry Tubbs, 1956; Steve Owens, 1969; Billy Sims, 1978; Josh Heupel, 2000), Tatupu (J. T. Thatcher, 2000), Heisman (Sam Bradford, 2008)

Southern California (12): Lombardi (Brad Budde, 1979), Thorpe (Mark Carrier, 1989), Butkus (Chris Claiborne, 1998), Walter Camp (O. J. Simpson, 1967–68), Maxwell (O. J. Simpson, 1968; Charles White, 1979; Marcus Allen, 1981), Unitas (Rodney Peete, 1988; Carson Palmer, 2002; Matt Leinart, 2005), Walker (Reggie Bush, 2005), Mackey (Fred Davis, 2007), Bednarik (Rey Maualuga, 2008)

In 1976 it was starting to get bad. Switzer's first two years had been probationary, and even though he had been in it up to his eyeballs as an assistant, the feeling was that he inherited it from Fairbanks, who escaped to the NFL. But it was Switzer. Darrell Royal of Texas, a former Oklahoma quarterback, supposedly tried to play by the rules. In 1976 he offered Switzer and assistant coach Larry Lacewell $10,000 if they would take a lie detector test to swear they had not planted a spy in Austin. They declined. The question of whether "the eyes of Texas" upon the Longhorns were really the "eyes of Oklahoma" was never fully resolved.

But by Oklahoma standards, which were to "build a university the football team could be proud of," according to OU president George Cross (1943–1968), Switzer was "OK." The first order of business was to beat Nebraska. Switzer accomplished that task, and then some. Revenge for the 1971 loss was achieved via six straight wins between 1972 and 1977. Those games took on a life of their own in that Oklahoma's "cult of

Elite Ten by the Numbers

Unbeaten streaks—modern era (1919–2008; includes bowls and ties)

1.	Oklahoma	48 (1953–57)	12.	Southern California	28 (1978–80)
2.	Notre Dame	39 (1945–50)	13.	Oklahoma	28 (1973–75)
3.	Oklahoma	38 (1972–75)	14.	Southern California	27 (1931–33)
4.	Southern California	34 (2003–06)	15.	Nebraska	26 (1994–96)
5.	Miami	34 (2000–03)	16.	Alabama	26 (1960–62)
6.	Nebraska	32 (1969–72)	17.	Southern California	25 (1931–33)
7.	Alabama	31 (1991–93)	18.	Michigan	25 (1946–49)
8.	Penn State	31 (1967–70)	19.	Alabama	24 (1924–27)
9.	Oklahoma	31 (1948–51)	20.	Southern California	23 (1971–73)
10.	Texas	30 (1968–71)	21.	Notre Dame	23 (1988–89)
11.	Alabama	29 (1978–80)	22.	Ohio State	22 (1967–69)

Oklahoma's All-Century Team
Chosen by the Tulsa World, 1999

OFFENSE		DEFENSE	
Pos.	Player	Pos.	Player
OL	Stan West	DL	Max Boydston
OL	Tom Catlin	DL	Lee Roy Selmon
OL	Tom Brahaney	DL	Ricky Bryan
OL	Mike Vaughan	DL	Tony Casillas
OL	Greg Roberts	LB	Jerry Tubbs
TE	Keith Jackson	LB	Rod Shoate
WR	Eddie Hinton	LB	Brian Bosworth
QB	Jack Mildren	DB	Clendon Thomas
QB	Jason White	DB	Randy Hughes
QB	Sam Bradford	DB	Rickey Dixon
RB	Billy Vessels		
RB	Steve Owens		
RB	Billy Sims		
PK	Uwe von Schamann		

personality" revolved around the flamboyant Switzer. Nebraska resembled their strait-laced new coach, Tom Osborne. Cornhusker fans hated Switzer for beating their guys like "red-headed stepchildren." Sometimes he won big. Other times he resorted to trick plays. The result was always the same.

In 1977 and 1978, however, Switzer's teams was deprived of entrance to the promised land. The 1977 Sooners won game three of the season in one of the wildest finishes in school history. Leading 20–0 over Ohio State, they relinquished 28 straight points. The Buckeyes forged a 28–20 lead. OU came back to score but the 2-point conversion failed, leaving them down a point. Then kicker Uwe Von Schamann squibbed an on-sider that was recovered by Oklahoma. They drove to the 24. Ohio State coach Woody Hayes called a time-out to try to "ice" von Schamann, who stood facing the giant Columbus throng imploring their team to "Block that kick!" Defiantly, von Schamann raised his hands like an orchestra conductor leading the chants. Then he drilled a 41-yarder and was mobbed by his teammates—and one might guess a coed or two upon the team's triumphant return to Norman.

Years later von Schamann said he had no idea why he did that, since if he had missed it he would have looked "pretty stupid." Switzer coined the phrase "Sooner magic" after that game.

But Texas, led by the great Heisman Trophy-winning running back Earl Campbell, held Oklahoma 13–6. It was "revenge" for the "espionage," although Royal was no longer the Longhorns coach. Fred Akers was. Nebraska fell, 38–7. On January 2 Oklahoma decided to forget all about 1957, becoming for a day the biggest Notre Dame fans in the world.

When the Irish knocked off Texas, the "Red Sea" was opened, revealing a path to the national championship. This time "Pharaoh's army," in the form of feisty coach Lou Holtz and Arkansas, caught the Sooner-Israelites before they could reach destiny. The score was 31–6, and it assured Notre Dame of Heaven in the form of a final number one ranking in both polls.

Led by Outland Trophy winner Greg Roberts, the 1978 Sooners dominated the competition. The season began with a stirring 35–29 win over the best Stanford team Bill Walsh ever coached. Kansas, a thorn in the Sooner side throughout the decade, was overcome by a 17–16 score. Nebraska, despite losing to almost nobody else in the 1970s, was by then considered almost an afterthought. This time they rose up like David to strike down Goliath, 17–14. That left the national championship to be decided between Penn State, USC, and Alabama. The Trojans and Crimson Tide captured the elusive prize. In an odd twist of fate that rarely happens, a rematch was held between Oklahoma and Nebraska at the Orange Bowl. The Sooners won this time around, 31–24. Billy Sims outpolled USC's Charles White, among others, for the Heisman Trophy.

In 1979, quarterback J. C. Watts led Oklahoma to a glistening 11–1 record that included a return-the-favor 17–14 win over Nebraska, but also a 16–7 upset at the hands of Texas. They beat Florida State 24–7 in the Orange Bowl, but another three-way race for number one, this time between USC, Ohio State, and Alabama, was won by the Tide. OU finished third. The Republican Watts later represented Oklahoma, by then a GOP stronghold, in Congress. For a brief time his name was bandied about as a potential vice presidential contender.

The 1970s came to an end, but not the glory days. Consensus Sooner All-Americans included Greg Pruitt, Tom Brahaney, Lucious Selmon, Rod Shoate, John Roush, Joe Washington, Lee Roy Selmon, Dewey Selmon, Jimbo Elrod, Mike Vaughan, Zac Henderson, Greg Roberts, Billy Sims, and George Cumbry. Other notable players were Horace Ivory, Kenny King, and Reggie Kinlaw.

In a decade that saw such "drug, alcohol, and sex" book and movie exposés as *Ball Four*, *Semi-Tough*, and *North Dallas Forty*, Switzer's crew lived up to it. When the Dallas Cowboys, coached for a few years by Switzer, became as well known for their wild parties as their on-field success in the 1990s, it was as if they were an Oklahoma alumni team.

The Sooners represented the swingin' ways of the '70s, but unlike the sobering events curtailing the previously-never-ending porn party in *Boogie Nights*, Switzer's Sooners continued that swashbuckling reputation into the 1980s. There were bumps in the road. In 1980 Stanford came to town for the ultimate culture clash. OU barely took the "academics" seriously, but sophomore John Elway turned out to be one of the greatest quarterbacks of all time. The 31–14 walloping he helped the Cardinal administer to Oklahoma on their home field was his "coming-out party."

Texas again beat the Sooners—in contrast to domination over Nebraska, the Texas rivalry was not in Switzer's favor of late—but they beat the Cornhuskers 21–17 and Florida State 18–17 in a doozy of an Orange Bowl.

Flying high, Oklahoma entered the Los Angeles Coliseum on September 26, 1981, ranked number two against number one Southern Cal. It was one of those rare one versus two matchups. In one of the most exciting games ever played, Oklahoma saw Marcus Allen and the Trojans drive down the field in the closing seconds. Eschewing the tying field goal, USC went for the winning touchdown and made it for a 28–24 win. The next year USC went into Norman and ended Oklahoma's all-time record 181 straight games in which they scored points. Not since a 38–0 shutout at the hands of Notre Dame in 1966 had the Sooners been shut out. On September 25 the Trojans beat them 12–0. It had taken the two greatest college dynasties of all time to stop them cold in the years (1966, 1982) that in many ways bookmarked an era dominated by the Trojans and Irish. But Oklahoma, whether or not they got the national attention Notre Dame and USC received, had never strayed far behind. In the mid-1980s they forged ahead of those programs.

At first, however, there was a period of relative mediocrity, at least by Oklahoma's unreal standards. Nebraska briefly reasserted itself as a national powerhouse. A sense of parity reached college football in the 1980s. Some of the old powers were down a bit. New dynasties emerged at Miami and Florida State. Recruiting, now an entirely national and integrated affair, spread the wealth. The days in which great talent might be centered within rivals of a single conference—think of USC-UCLA (1967), Texas-Arkansas (1969), and Nebraska-Oklahoma (1971)—were no longer as prevalent.

But Switzer was not one to let the moss grow under his shoes. He hit the recruiting trail and landed two blue-chippers. Quarterback Troy Aikman was from rural Oklahoma by way of suburban Los Angeles. Linebacker Brian Bosworth was from a Marvel comic strip. Actually, he was from Texas. After the Longhorns shamefully went for the "sister-kissing" tying field goal in the 15–15 1984 game with OU, Bos announced that UT "burnt orange" made him "puke."

A 28–17 loss to number two Washington in the 1985 Orange Bowl seemed to provide incentive to his team the next season. Stacked with the spike-haired Bosworth, tight end Keith Jackson, and all-everything defensive lineman Tony Casillas, the 1985 Sooners rolled to an 11–1 record and the national championship.

The key was the quarterback position. Hotshot Aikman had been brought in to "modernize" the Sooner offense from its old "wishbone" gain-7-yards-and-fumble ways to a standard pro-style set, complete with Troy's golden arm completing aerial spirals to the likes of Jackson.

But Switzer was like a guy sitting in church thinking about strip clubs. There was always something else enticing him. In this case it was the "wishbone," an old "sin" he could not stop loving despite its tendency to cause "fumble-itis." He replaced Aikman with wishbone master Jamelle Holieway. Nobody in his right mind would ever suggest that Holieway could hold Troy Aikman's dirty jockstrap. Aikman transferred and almost won the Heisman at UCLA before enshrinement in the Pro Football Hall of Fame courtesy of three Super Bowl victories in Dallas. But at Norman in 1985, Holieway was the right guy in the right place at the right time.

Oklahoma's College Hall of Famers (25 through 2009 inductions)

Players			
Kurt Burris	1951–1954	Forest Geyer	1913–1915
J. D. Roberts	1951–1953	Claude Reeds	1910–1913
Tony Casillas	1982–1985	Tom Brahaney	1970–1972
Jim Weatherall	1948–1951	Troy Aikman	1984–1985
Lee Roy Selmon	1972–1975	Tom Brahaney	1971–1972
Jim Owens	1946–1949	Keith Jackson	1984–1987
Waddy Young	1936–1938	Jerry Tubbs	1954–1956
Tommy McDonald	1954–1956		
Steve Owens	1967–1969	*Coaches*	
Greg Pruitt	1970–1972	Lawrence Jones	1926–1941
Billy Sims	1975–1979	Barry Switzer	1973–1988
Billy Vessels	1950–1952	Bud Wilkinson	1947–1963
Joe Washington	1972–1975	Bennie Owen	1905–1926
		Jim Tatum	1946

Texas was overcome in a difficult manner 14–7, but Miami was making life miserable for everybody in the 1980s. They knocked the Sooners out of the unbeaten ranks, 27–14. But it was not a year for unbeatens in the end. The Sooners beat Colorado 31–0 and Nebraska 27–7. Penn State was no match in the Orange Bowl, 25–10. The national title was Oklahoma's in all the polls. Casillas won the Lombardi Trophy.

In 1986, Bosworth was larger than life, winning the Butkus Award for the second straight season. Whether or not he is the greatest individual defensive player in college football history is subjective. Certainly the man Bosworth's trophy was named after, Dick Butkus of Illinois, deserves consideration. George Webster of Michigan State is credited with creating the "rover" position. Ronnie Lott of USC and Kenny Easley of UCLA were monsters of the defensive backfield in the late 1970s and early 1980s. Later, "Neon Deion" Sanders of Florida State revolutionized the way the position can be played. Linebacker Lawrence Taylor of North Carolina is credited with doing the same thing at his position. Following him, Junior Seau of USC was a monster.

But those players are best known for their great NFL careers. Bosworth's career in Seattle was not a failure, but he never lived up to the hype. Hollywood came calling, but despite screen presence, for some reason he was one of those guys who became a comic caricature of himself, which was deadly to his career as an actor.

As pure college stars, Lee Roy Selmon gets his share of votes, as does Orlando Pace of Ohio State, Tommy Nobis of Texas, and Lee Roy Jordan of Alabama. The list is long and distinguished, but when it comes purely to collegiate achievement, Bos was "the man."

In 1986 he, Jackson, and Holieway anchored a team that also included running back Spencer Tillman. Again, it was Miami who crashed the party, 28–16, but this time one loss was not good enough. Penn State beat the Hurricanes in the Fiesta Bowl to capture the crown while OU settled for a 42–8 Orange Bowl thrashing of Arkansas and the third spot in the AP.

Without Bosworth, the 1987 Sooners reloaded with Holieway, alternate quarterback Charles Thompson, and Jackson again. A huge win over Texas (44–9) and a 17–7 victory over Nebraska put them into the Orange Bowl against nemesis Miami. Switzer hated those guys after they won the national title, 20–14. The Hurricanes, considered thugs barely above the law, were now making Oklahoma's "outlaws" look like choirboys.

As if to "catch up" with Miami's criminal ways, Oklahoma went on a rampage of sorts. One Sooner shot another, and three others were charged with rape. Thompson was arrested for dealing cocaine. His orange prison jumpsuit photo made *Sports Illustrated*'s cover, which no doubt made his mother mighty proud. As if to "emulate" miscreant Sooner behavior once out of school, former Oklahoma running back Stanley Wilson was banned from the National Football League for snorting cocaine, making himself unable to perform for the Cincinnati Bengals in San Francisco's narrow 20–16 victory in the 1989 Super Bowl. Bosworth pleaded from the pro ranks for Switzer to quit, and that was that. Gary Gibbs took over in 1989.

Consensus All-Americans of the decade include Louis Oubre, Terry Crouch, Rick Bryan, Casillas, Bosworth, Jackson, Mark Hutson, Dante Jones, Rickey Dixon, and Anthony Phillips. After Sims had been drafted in the first round by Detroit in 1980, David Overstreet was chosen first by Miami in 1981. In the 1984 draft, Rick Bryan (Falcons), Jackie Shipp (Dolphins), and Dwight Drane (Bills) all went in the first round. The Rams chose Marcus Dupree. Steve Sewell was a first-round pick by the Rams in 1985, and Casillas was Atlanta's first choice in 1986. Bosworth was the first selection of the entire 1987 draft by Seattle. In 1988, Rickey Dixon (Bengals) and Keith Jackson (Eagles) were both first round selections.

Not *one single Sooner* earned consensus All-American honors in the 1990s. Only Cedric Jones (Giants, 1996) and Stockar McDougle (2000) were first-round selections. The shocking events of 1989 not only ended Switzer's tenure but ushered in the increasingly mediocre-to-bad tenures of Gibbs, Howard Schnellenberger, and John Blake. It was like the football version of the AIDS virus, which had America in hysterics at that time. After years of "unprotected sex," it seemed the lifestyle Switzer and the Sooners embodied had finally caught up with the program. The Sooners were respectable for a few years but could not break the .500 mark between 1994 and 1998. It was the decade of Nebraska. This was the "unkindest cut of all," as Shakespeare wrote.

Gibbs beat the Cornhuskers 45–10 in 1990, but from 1991 to 1997 they never won over the Cornhuskers. That was just the half of it. The 1995 Cornhuskers, considered perhaps the finest team in history, annihilated Oklahoma 37–0. In 1996 it was even worse: 73–21. 1997: 69–7. But that was *still* not the whole story. When the Big 12 was formed in 1996, the Oklahoma-Nebraska game was deemphasized. Usually played around Thanksgiving or thereabouts as part of the traditional rivalry weeks, it was now pushed up and represented just another game . . . at least to Nebraska, now facing more serious competition from Colorado, Oklahoma State, Texas A&M, Missouri, and Texas.

In 1998 and 1999 *there was no Oklahoma-Nebraska game.* The reason for this, it was explained, was to conform with the new requirements of the Big 12 scheduling rotation, but it looked more as if OU was avoiding embarrassing Cornhusker beatings.

Enter Bob Stoops, a young assistant. It was not unlike when Ara Parseghian took over a moribund Notre Dame program, turning them around in 1964. Parseghian inherited a journeyman quarterback, John Huarte, turning him into the Heisman Trophy winner. In Stoops's case it was a utilitarian signal-caller named Josh Heupel. Heupel lost a close Heisman vote to Florida State's Chris Weinke but got the last laugh when he led the 13–0 Sooners over Weinke's Seminoles in the BCS Orange Bowl, 13–2, for a surprise national title. Heupel was a consensus All-American, as were linebackers J. T. Thatcher and Rocky Calmus.

It was one of the greatest seasons by a first-year coach ever, matched the next year by Miami's Larry Coker. Nebraska found its way back on the 2000 schedule, albeit on the pedestrian date of October 28. OU prevailed, 31–14. Kansas State gave them all they could handle in the Big 12 title game, and Florida State was a substantial favorite in Miami, but OU's defense simply shut them down.

Seasons of 11–2 and 12–2 with wins over Arkansas (Cotton Bowl) and Washington State (Rose Bowl) followed in 2001 and 2002. Roy Williams was Dallas's first choice in 2002, Andre Woolfolk Tennessee's number one pick in 2003. Roy Williams, Tommie Harris, and Teddy Lehman were consensus All-Americans.

In 2003, Oklahoma came out firing on all cylinders. Led by Heisman Trophy-winning quarterback Jason White, the 2003 Sooners may well have been the greatest offensive juggernaut of all time. Army (1945) and USC (2005) are among the very few teams that might measure up. A 77–0 thrashing of Texas A&M goes down as one of the single greatest games any team has ever played. They looked to be as close to unbeatable as a team can be.

USC and LSU survived a competitive field and on the final weekend of the season were the last teams standing in what still looked to be a consolation prize. But USC had dominated the second half of the season after an upset at California. When the Trojans destroyed Arizona on WTBS, Brian Bosworth, doing analysis for the station, declared them to be the best team in the nation. He was reminded that his alma mater was still unbeaten. Bos looked like a deer caught in the headlights trying to correct himself, but his first instincts were right. USC *was* better. That fact was demonstrated, first when Oklahoma lost a shocker, 35–7, to Kansas State in the Big 12 title game at Arrowhead Stadium; second when USC beat Michigan 28–14 in the Rose Bowl to win the national championship; and third when OU lost a nobody-looks-like-they-want-to-win Sugar Bowl 21–14 to LSU. Rarely had the mighty fallen so thoroughly.

Antonio Perkins and Derrick Straight were consensus All-Americans. Tommie Harris won the Lombardi Award and was Chicago's first pick in the draft. Lehman won the Butkus Award before being selected by Detroit. Mark Clayton was an All-American wide receiver. Jammal Brown was an All-American at offensive tackle.

Incredibly, much of the 2003 juggernaut was back in 2004. OU and USC dominated from the first preseason poll to the final one in January, with the Trojans holding the top spot every week, the Sooners at number two. When the BCS rankings came out there was no variation on the theme, no surprises. The two storied programs dominated week after week until they met in a "Game of the Twenty-first Century."

White, the returning Heisman winner, was not the favorite this time. USC's Leinart was after leading Troy to the promised land for the first time since 1978 the previous year. Oklahoma was no less devastating in 2004 than they had been in 2003, only this time they did not stumble. They beat Colorado 32-3 at Arrowhead Stadium, and it was on to the BCS Orange Bowl to face Southern Cal.

First there was the Heisman presentation at New York's Downtown Athletic Club. White, who threw thirty-five touchdown passes, and sensational Sooner freshman running back Adrian Peterson (1,925 yards) hobnobbed with USC's Leinart and Reggie Bush. Leinart won the Heisman in a runaway, a portent of things to come.

Southern Cal maintained a slight edge in the pregame line, but by game time it was almost even. Then they started to play. It was "embarrassing," according to White. Details are too painful to examine in a chapter on Sooner football history. If any team was ever better than the University of Southern California on January 4, 2005, it is not readily known of. Trojans 55, Oklahoma 19.

Jammal Brown won the Outland Trophy, and Peterson was a consensus All-American pick. Brown went in the first round to New Orleans, Clayton to Baltimore with their first pick. White, remarkably, was not drafted and is out of football.

In 2005 the Sooners returned to Earth. Davin Joseph was Tampa Bay's first pick. In 2006 the Sooners wanted the world to believe that they should have been in the BCS title game. Instead, an unbelievable 43–42 overtime loss to Boise State in the Fiesta Bowl left Stoops with a look of frustration for the ages on his face. Peterson left early for Minnesota, who picked him with their first draft choice in 2007. In 2008 and 2009, OU's supporters were left with massive egg on their faces. The Sooners competed in competitive, season-long battles for BCS supremacy with the usual suspects and a few surprise teams. Fan punditry continued to espouse the notion that Oklahoma was the best this and the best that. Then they played the bowl games, and the result was . . . too dismal to detail in a chapter extolling the program's virtues. Sam Bradford was the Heisman winner in 2008, as Jason White had been in 2003, and like White (in 2003–04), Bradford's performance in the BCS title game (versus Florida in Miami) had most folks thinking about Federal Express—not because they sponsor BCS games, but because Bradford should have had them return his trophy to the Downtown Athletic Club.

Ups and downs, streaks and defeats . . . Oklahoma football has seen it all. Mostly, it has seen victory, and the future promises more of the same for "Boomer Sooner, OK U!"

Chapter 5

Ohio State Buckeyes

MICHIGAN CONSIDERS ITSELF the be-all and end-all of college football. They were the first non–Ivy League team to emerge as a national powerhouse. Before Notre Dame established itself in the American conscience, Michigan *was* Midwestern football. The Wolverines were winning national championships in the early part of the twentieth century. Their all-time record is the best, going back almost to Reconstruction.

Ohio State University
Columbus, Ohio
Founded: 1870
Enrollment: 37,509
Colors: Scarlet and gray
Stadium: Ohio Stadium (opened: 1922: capacity: 101,568)
All-time record (1890–2008): 808-305-53
All-time bowl record: 18–22 (through 2009 bowls)
National championships: 1942, 1954, 1957, 1968, 2002
Big 10 championships: 32 (through 2008)
Heisman Trophies: Les Horvath (1944), Vic Janowicz (1950), Howard Cassady (1955), Archie Griffin (1974–75), Eddie George (1995), Troy Smith (2006)
Outland Trophies: Jim Parker (1956), Jim Stillwagon (1970), John Hicks (1973), Orlando Pace (1996)
First-round NFL draftees: 67 (through 2009 draft)
Website: www.ohiostatebuckeyes.com
Notable alumni: Olympians Jesse Owens and Max Whitfield; golfer Jack Nicklaus; basketball coach Bobby Knight; Hall of Fame basketball player John Havlicek; basketball players Jerry Lucas, Larry Siegfried, Jim Jackson, and Greg Oden; baseball announcer Jack Buck; comedian Richard Lewis; author R. L. Stine; Limited, Inc., founder Leslie H. Wexner

Michigan had a tremendous rivalry with Notre Dame almost from the beginning. When the Big 10 formed itself, their stiffest competition came from Minnesota and Chicago. Ohio State was an afterthought.

Michigan thinks of itself as the upscale school. Better academics, wealthier students. Ohio *State* carries with it the unfortunate moniker of just that, a state institution. Even though Michigan is, too, they take on the airs of a private school. They most definitely look down on Ohio State's team. Its alumni are considered yokels.

A funny thing happened along the way, however. Ohio State, Michigan's lapdog, built a great football program. After many years, Michigan had to admit that their biggest rivalry was not with old powerhouse Minnesota, and certainly not with Chicago (who eventually gave up football), but with the Buckeyes.

There are no other Big 10 teams in Ohio. The rivalry based itself on intense, great football matchups. Like other fantastic rivalries, Ohio State-Michigan elevated both programs to higher status, which is the mark of the best rivals. But to Michigan's great chagrin, the Buckeyes passed them. The Wolverines have plenty of gaudy numbers to throw out there, much of them built in the "leather helmet and rugby" era. It may not be a cut 'n' dried case, but all things considered, Ohio State is today the greater tradition by a narrow margin. Had the Buckeyes not collapsed against Florida and LSU in the 2007 and 2008 BCS title games, respectively, there would be little question. In addition, the Buckeyes would have asserted a strong argument that they had replaced USC as the "Team of the Decade" for the 2000s.

Alas for them they did not, but Buckeye football is nevertheless steeped in great lore. There is something extra special about these guys: the decals on their helmets, their great nickname—*Buckeyes*—and the sense that they are the embodiment of rough, tough, cold, raw Midwestern football. Ohio is a state that has seen its share of tough times. It is a blue-collar state, a factory state. Michigan's factories are seen as cutting-edge auto shops. Ohio is coal mines and textile mills.

There are two major cities in Ohio, Cleveland and Cincinnati. Cleveland tends to be liberal, has more minorities, and lacks glamour. Cincinnati tends to be conservative, is primarily white, and lacks glamour. There is passion for professional sports in both cities: the Browns, Indians, Cavaliers, Bengals, Reds. Then there is Columbus. Passion for Buckeye football in Columbus supersedes all other consideration. Whether you are a fan of the Browns, Indians, Cavaliers, Bengals, or Reds, you *better* root for the Bucks.

Ohio State versus Michigan: 42–57–6 (through 2008)

The Buckeye is the state tree. The decals on Ohio State helmets are those of the tree. However, the term *Buckeye* elicits the image of something more powerful than a tree (which Stanford, for instance, receives endless heat over since that seems to be their mascot, sort of). A Buckeye sounds more like a tough, Medieval warrior—some guy who warded off the invading Romans or Moors, maybe using a battle-ax called a "buckeye."

On November 24, 1900, mighty Michigan deigned to allow Ohio State to travel to Ann Arbor for a football match. The Wolverines were just beginning the greatest run in school history and thought little of lightly regarded Ohio State. The game ended in a 0–0 tie, a decided "victory" for Ohio State.

Fielding Yost's "point-a-minute" teams did not forgive the intruders from Columbus. Between 1901 and 1909, Michigan destroyed Ohio State by mostly embarrassing scores: 21–0, 86–0, 36–0, 31–6, 40–0, 6–0, 22–0, 10–6, and 33–6. To Ohio State's credit, they kept coming back for more. Then, in 1910, they tied Michigan again, 3–3. Two more shutout losses followed. In 1913 Ohio State called it quits. Despite being a member of the so-called Western Conference, which was given the popular appellation "Big 10," they did not play Michigan for years.

Then something really crazy happened. Under coach John W. Wilce, Ohio State went unbeaten in 1916 and 1917. In 1918 Michigan found itself back on their schedule. Same result: 14–0, Wolverines. In 1919, it was the Fourth of July, the Emancipation Proclamation, and the fall of the Berlin Wall all in one: Buckeyes 13, Wolverines 3. The timing could not have been better. With World War I over, America turned its attention to college football from coast to coast, mountain to prairie. The Rose Bowl invited the unbeaten Buckeyes to Pasadena on January 1, 1921, to play the greatest power in the land, California's Wonder Team. It was a game for the national championship, for renewed Midwestern respect after a down period, and the chance to put Ohio State football on the map. The 28–0 pounding they took at the hands of Brick Muller and the Golden Bears set the program back two decades.

Michigan regained their place, winning national titles in 1923 and 1933. Ohio State under Wilce, then coaches Sam Willaman (1929–1933) and Francis Schmidt (1934–1940), fielded an array of winning and near .500 teams, none of which made anybody forget that Michigan and Minnesota ruled the Big 10. There were no bowl invites anywhere. There were some great players, to be sure. Chic Harley was a three-time consensus All-American. Other consensus choices included Charles Bolen, Iolas Huffman, Gaylord Stinchcomb, Ed Hess, Wes Fesler, Gomer Jones, and Esco Sarkinnen.

High school football was almost as big in Ohio as Ohio State. It fit in perfectly with the small-town values of its rural citizenry. One school rose above the rest, the very first of the great prep dynasties. Before there was Cincinnati Moeller, Long Beach Poly, Santa Ana Mater Dei, or Concord De La Salle, there was Massillon of Ohio. The name alone connotes something substantial. Massillon *of Ohio*! Its coach: Paul W. Brown.

The argument over who is the greatest football coach ever creates a lengthy discussion worthy of many beers and maybe a few shots for good measure. Amos "Alonzo" Stagg, Knute Rockne, Vince Lombardi, Bud Wilkinson, Bear Bryant, Bill Walsh . . . just to get warmed up.

But if somebody chooses to make the case that Paul Brown is the greatest of all football coaches, it is as worthy a choice as any. When it comes to men who forged dynasties at the high school, college, and pro levels, he did it better than anybody. As an innovator, he ranks with Pop Warner, Clark Shaughnessy, and Sid Gillman. From the halls of Massillon did Brown emerge, and within one year ultimate victory was achieved in Columbus. In 1942 Ohio State went 9–1, beat Michigan 21–7, and was voted number one in the final Associated Press poll. Michigan was forced to take them seriously now.

Unfortunately, the only thing anybody really took seriously over the next couple years were the German and Japanese armies. Brown left after the 1943 season. The fact that Iowa Pre-Flight had a better team than Ohio State that season indicated where the best talent was in the war years. After World War II, Brown took over the Cleveland *Browns*, and turned them into the greatest professional juggernaut heretofore seen.

Ohio State was 9–0 under coach Carroll Widdoes in 1944, but nobody was going to get the votes that went for Army's national title. The Big 10's Rose Bowl arrangement was not yet in place, so there were no New Year's Day games to give the program any added luster. There was not much luster of any kind until 1949. The Buckeyes salvaged a season that included a frustrating 7–7 tie against Michigan (then at the height of the program's glory) by gaining revenge for the 1921 shutout loss to California.

The Golden Bears were unbeaten and finished third in the final Associated Press rankings behind Notre Dame and Oklahoma. However, a Rose Bowl win would give imprimatur to the Pacific Coast Conference, which had lost prestige since the death of USC's Howard Jones a decade earlier. Cal fans still argue that a bad call cost them the 17–14 loss to Ohio State.

On November 25, 1950, Ohio State, led by coach Wes Fesler, lost 9–3 to Fritz Crisler and Michigan in brutal snow, ten-degree temperatures, and forty-mile-per-hour winds. Fesler was fired after the season. That game, contrasted with eighty-degree New Year's Day Rose Bowl games, is credited with much of the enormous migration of Midwesterners to California over the next decade.

By the end of the 1940s, Ohio State was a competent college football program, but far below the standards of Michigan (established as their primary rival when their game was scheduled at the end of the season beginning in 1935). Consensus All-Americans of the 1940s include Jack Dugger, Bill Hackett, and Warren Amling. Les Horvath won the 1944 Heisman Trophy. In 1950, Vic Janowicz won the school's second Heisman. In 1951, everything changed for Ohio State football fortunes. Woodrow "Woody" Hayes made his arrival.

"He's the stompin', snortin', fire-breathin' bully who ran a caveman 'three yards and a cloud of dust' offense, tormented game officials, tore up yard markers, smashed his wrist watches and went down swinging," according to the *ESPN College Football Encyclopedia*.

A lieutenant commander in the Navy, Hayes modeled football strategy and discipline after military strategy and discipline. General George Patton, above all others, was the man he wanted to emulate. In his mind, a football team moved downfield on the ground, via the "infantry." A pass could result in one of only three things "and two of them are bad."

In 1954, Hayes returned Ohio State to the promised land. A 21–7 triumph over archrival Michigan capped a perfect regular reason and the Associated Press national championship. But the game everybody wanted to see, a matchup against the United Press International's number one team, Red Sanders's UCLA Bruins, did not happen because for a few years the Pacific Coast Conference instituted the notorious "no-repeat" rule. UCLA was prevented from a trip to Pasadena. Southern California went in their stead after getting hammered by the Bruins 34–0 in front of 102,548 fans.

A rare rainstorm hit Pasadena, meaning that Ohio State played in Ohio State weather. A crowd of 89,191 observed quarterback Dave Leggett lead his team to a resounding 20–7 victory, preserving the integrity of the national championship following three disastrous years in which the 1950, 1951, and 1953 "champions" all fell in ignominious manner after the votes were in.

All-Time Ohio State Team

Chosen by the Columbus Touchdown Club, 2002

OFFENSE		DEFENSE	
Pos.	*Player*	*Pos.*	*Player*
OL	Jim Parker	DL	Bill Willis
OL	John Hicks	DL	Jim Stillwagon
OL	Orlando Pace	LB	Chris Spielman
E	Wes Fesler	LB	Andy Katzenmoyer
WR	Cris Carter	LB	James Laurinaitis
WR	David Boston	DB	Jack Tatum
QB	Rex Kern	DB	Neal Colzie
QB	Art Schlichter	DB	Antoine Winfield
QB	Joe Germaine	P	Tom Skladany
QB	Troy Smith		
RB	Chick Harley		
RB	Les Horvath		
RB	Howard "Hopalong" Cassady		
RB	Archie Griffin		
RB	Eddie George		
PL	Vlade Janakievski		

Hayes began his long-standing feud with the Tournament of Roses Committee. Even though the muddy conditions probably played to the Buckeyes' strength, he criticized a decision not to cover the field with a tarpaulin and to allow the bands to play on the field. Up until that time, the 1952 Trojans were the only PCC team to beat a Big 10 team in the Rose Bowl arrangement that began on January 1, 1947. Hayes had little praise for USC, Pasadena, Los Angeles, the film industry, Southern California, the state of California, the Pacific Coast, the West Coast, the "left coast," the West, or liberalism, which in his mind was a cancer on society manifesting itself in the immoral ways of Hollywood and environs. The contrast to this was that one of Hayes's favorite politicians, then vice president Richard Nixon, was a Southern Californian Republican.

The following season, Howard Cassady won Ohio State's third Heisman Trophy. He was given the nickname "Hopalong" because his last name sounded the same as a famous cowboy figure in the movies known as Hopalong Cassidy. In 1956, Bob White made consensus All-American and big Jim Parker won the Outland Trophy. In 1957 the Buckeyes won Hayes's second national championship.

After beating Michigan 31–14, Woody again led his team to Pasadena. Oregon was a strong foe, but with the game tied 7–7 with five minutes remaining in the game, the Bucks drove for the winning field goal in a 10–7 victory. Hayes and his program were on top of the world. Parker was made the first-round choice of the Baltimore Colts, where he and Johnny Unitas teamed up to create a great NFL powerhouse.

The 1950s seemed to be a decade tailor-made for Ohio State and its conference. The conservative tenor of those times fit perfectly well with Woody's strict personality. The PCC continued to flounder amid a recruiting and payola scandal.

The 1961 Buckeyes were 8-0-1, with a 50–20 pasting of Michigan. Led by running back Bob Ferguson, they were named national champions by the football writers, who awarded them the MacArthur Bowl. However, Alabama was unbeaten, was untied, and won their bowl game after being voted number one in both the AP and UPI prebowl polls. Ohio State, for unfathomable reasons, actually voted not to accept a Rose Bowl invitation. Victory in Pasadena would have at least strengthened their argument that the MacArthur Bowl carried some prestige. When they stayed home instead, the MacArthur trophy became just a piece of hardware. Woody and the Buckeyes were known to accept challenges, but the decision not to travel to Pasadena looks very much like avoidance of a possible loss in a lame effort at preserving an unbeaten record. Historical legitimacy, as well as both polls, accords Alabama the undisputed consensus national championship of 1961.

In the 1960s, USC and UCLA established themselves as the glamour rivalry of college football, raising the prestige of their conference from its lowest depths in the 1950s to a position arguably as the best in college football. Power shifted to the Trojans, who in 1967 and 1969 won death struggles with the Bruins, their most significant threat. The USC-Notre Dame rivalry was revived in a big way too, and Alabama reasserted themselves under Bear Bryant.

After 1961, Woody's Buckeyes and the Big 10 in general were competent but not dominant. Then, in 1968 Ohio State emerged with a team that probably stands out above all others as the greatest of the decade. It was the beginning of a bittersweet period.

Hayes was a firm believer in people earning their "place at the table." He preferred seniors and upperclassmen to inexperienced youngsters because they had put the time in and deserved to be rewarded for it, and also because they were generally better through maturity and experience. But talent trumps all other considerations.

The Massillon High School program had continued to thrive long after Paul Brown left. They provided the nucleus of Hayes's greatest team. Five "super sophomores" started for the Buckeyes, including quarterback Rex Kern, defensive back Jack Tatum, and defensive end Jim Stillwagon. After an early-season upset of number one Purdue, they averaged 32 points and 442 yards a game, mostly on the ground. It was more than "three yards and a cloud of dust," however. The Buckeyes were likely to knock off 5 or 6 yards before the dust cloud formed.

Defensively they allowed 15 points per game and annihilated Michigan, 50–14. *Finally*, the AP had come to their senses once and for all. Their decision to vote the final

Ohio State versus the Elite Ten (71–89–7)

Alabama (0–3), Miami (2–1), Michigan (42–57–6), Nebraska (2–0), Notre Dame (2–2), Oklahoma (1–1), Penn State (12–11), Southern California (9–12–1), Texas (1–1)

rankings after the bowls meant that the 1969 Rose Bowl game between Ohio State and defending national champion Southern California was one for the ages. The Trojans featured the unstoppable O. J. Simpson. The challenge of beating Troy in what amounted to a "home game" for USC was monumental.

1968 was the epoch of America's cultural divide. The Vietnam War raged, assassinations and war protests roiled the land, and sides were taken: hippies and "fellow travelers" on one side, the "Silent Majority" on the other. Hayes was the "Silent Majority," although not so silent. He campaigned for Republican nominee Richard Nixon, who beat Hubert Humphrey to attain the White House that year.

The University of Southern California is a conservative, private institution. Los Angeles was still relatively Republican and Christian in 1968. Its origins were Southern and Midwestern, so much so that *L.A. Times* sports columnist Jim Murray dubbed nearby Long Beach "Iowa West." But Hayes characterized the trip to Pasadena as Daniel venturing into the "lion's den" of Hollywood, immorality, and values run amok. He and John McKay had more in common than not, but for purposes of motivating his team, he wanted them to feel as if they were facing not just enemies of Buckeye football, but tacit enemies of the state.

The Trojans got out to a 10–0 lead on the strength of an 80-yard touchdown run by Heisman Trophy winner Simpson, one of the most remarkable of his collegiate and pro career. But five USC turnovers allowed Ohio State back into the game. They ground Southern Cal down in the second half to give Hayes vindication and another national championship, 27–16.

With a sophomore-laden team, predictions of a first-ever three straight national-title dynasty in Columbus were made. The 1969 Buckeyes were immediately installed as the greatest team in college football history. *Sports Illustrated*'s headline after their opening game was simply "62–0," the score of their demolition of Texas Christian. The Buckeyes rolled through the season ranked number one. They never trailed in a game and did not veer one bit from the concept that they were indeed the best college team ever.

With the ridiculous no-repeat rule still in place, the Buckeyes needed only a victory over Michigan to capture the national title even without a trip to the Rose Bowl. On November 22 Ohio State traveled to Michigan, led by new coach Bo Schembechler, a one-time Hayes assistant. Ohio State scored two touchdowns but missed extra points on both. It did not seem to matter much, but Michigan came roaring back. They stopped the Buckeyes cold, winning one of the greatest upsets in history, 24–12. Schembechler's legend was made.

In 1970, Hayes's team were all seniors. They were again a dominant group, but like other great college sports teams that returned superstars—think of the 1974 UCLA Bruins basketball team, the 1991 UNLV basketball team, or the 2005 USC Trojans football team—they had a slight case of "senioritis." They were certainly a great team, some think Woody's best ever, but there were small chinks in the armor.

By 1970, the culture Hayes came to despise had crept closer and closer to Columbus. The war was not going well. Shootings at nearby Kent State University brought it home even further. Woody liked to show a movie to his team the night before a game. His favorite fare, not surprisingly, were John Wayne movies like *The Sands of Iwo Jima*. In 1970, *Patton* was released. Woody thought it was not just the greatest war movie ever made but also perfect pregame inspiration. Woody himself could not deliver a more fiery speech than George C. Scott's opening oration outlined by an oversized American flag.

His players enjoyed the film, so much so that Woody began to count on them to go see it on their own instead of the usual team gatherings. Prior to one game, Woody encountered two of his players returning from the movie theater. He inquired what they had seen.

"*Easy Rider*," was the answer.

"*EASY RIDER?*" Hayes responded in disgust. "You can't play football after seeing that crap."

Buckeyes on the Run

Year	Record	Run
1967	6–3 F/4–0	6–3 (1967)
		4–0 (1967)
1968	10–0	16–3 (1967–68)
		14–0 (1967–68)
1969	8–1 S/8–0	24–3 (1967–68)
		22–0 (1967–68)
		22–1 (1967–68)
		20–0 (1967–68) **20 games**
1970	9–1	33–4 (1967–70)
		31–2 (1967–70)
1972	9–2	9–2 (1972)
1973	10–0–1	19–2–1 (1972)
		10–0–1 (1972)
1974	10–2	29–4–1 (1972–74)
		20–2–1 (1973–74)
1975	11–1	40–5–1 (1972–75)
		31–2–1 (1973–75)
1976	9–2–1 S/2–0	49–7–2 (1972–76)
		42–6–2 (1972–76) **50 games**
2002	14–0	14–0
2003	11–2	25–2 (2002-03)
2004	8–4	33–6 (2002-04)
2005	10–2	43–8 (2002-05)
2006	12–1	55–9 (2002-06)
2007	11–2	66–11 (2002-07)
2008	10–3	76–14 (2002-08)

S/Start season; F/Finish season

Woody Hayes and Earle Bruce—A Sustained Run

1951	4–3–2 Woody Hayes	1970	9–1
1952	6–3	1971	6–4
1953	6–3	1972	9–2
1954	10–0	1973	10–0–1
1955	7–2	1974	10–2
1956	6–3	1975	11–1
1957	9–1	1976	9–2–1
1958	6–1–2	1977	9–3
1959	3–5–1	1978	7–4–1
1960	7–2	1979	11–1 Earle Bruce
1961	8–0–1	1979	9–3
1962	6–3	1980	9–3
1963	5–3–1	1981	9–3
1964	7–2	1982	9–3
1965	7–2	1983	9–3
1966	4–5	1984	9–3
1967	6–3	1985	10–3
1968	10–0	1986	6–4–1
1969	8–1		

On January 1, 1970, the Buckeyes came out to play the ultimate *Easy Rider* team, Stanford. Earlier in the day, the defending national champions, number one-ranked Texas, fell to Notre Dame 24–11. All Ohio State needed to do was beat outgunned Stanford and they would have their second national title in three years. It would cap the greatest class in history, a three-year run not approached before or since. The game started and Ohio State took the lead, but Heisman Trophy-winning Stanford quarterback Jim Plunkett led the Indians all the way back to a resounding 27–17 victory. It was a California earthquake felt across the country. That night, Nebraska squeaked past LSU 17–12 to win a surprise national championship.

Consensus All-Americans in the 1960s included the likes of Bob Ferguson, Dave Foley, Jim Otis, Jack Tatum, and Jim Stillwagon. Tatum is considered one of the finest defensive backs in college football history. He starred for great Oakland Raiders teams where he was given the unfortunate moniker "Assassin" after his hit of New England's Darryl Stingley resulted in Stingley's paralysis. Stingley died in 2007.

The loss to Stanford in the 1971 Rose Bowl was the symbolic end of one era and the beginning of another. From 1972 to 1975, Ohio State went to four straight Rose Bowls, but it was a period of terrific frustration for Woody. His greatest player, Archie Griffin, won two Heisman Trophies (1974–1975). Incredible success—but ultimate glory, again enticingly close, was not attained.

Woody's feud with the state of California intensified. Losses to USC and UCLA, sometimes by blowout, sometimes by the barest of margins, enraged him. He told his team to "be polite to everybody, but don't say anything. No son of a b---h out here wants you to win." When a *Los Angeles Times* photographer got too close at an inopportune time, Woody punched him. A lawsuit ensued.

Hayes was incensed by what he considered the insouciance of Trojan coach John McKay. McKay was a wisecracker who seemingly joked his way to victory over the Buckeyes. One year McKay sent his assistant, Dave Levy, to a series of pregame functions in his place. Hayes was nonplussed.

"He should be here," he snapped to Levy, expressing the attitude that McKay showed disrespect via nonattendance. What Woody did not know was that both McKay and his son, Trojan wide receiver J. K. McKay, had received death threats—from a Buckeye fan?—and were advised by the FBI to stay out of public view as much as possible.

When USC's Sam Cunningham kept going over the top of the Ohio State line to score four touchdowns against the Buckeyes in the 1973 Rose Bowl, McKay motioned to Woody from across the field that Cunningham was going "over the top," implying that even though they knew it was coming the Bucks could not stop him. Cunningham did precisely that. Woody seethed.

The Trojans destroyed Ohio State that day 42–17 to take the national title and gain revenge for O. J.'s 1969 loss. In 1973 the Buckeyes were back with one of the best teams in their history. They were a juggernaut on offense and produced three straight shutouts on defense.

All season long, America waited for the battle with Michigan. Both teams were unbeaten and untied coming into the game at Ann Arbor. It was for the Big 10 title and a trip to the Rose Bowl. For the first time, the no-repeat rule was done away with, meaning that Ohio State could return with a win. Ranked number one for eight weeks, it would also give the Buckeyes—or the Wolverines—the "poll position" going into the bowls, although a "national-title game" between unbeaten Alabama and Notre Dame promised to upset the apple cart.

Ohio State jumped out to a 10–0 lead but stayed on the ground for forty-nine straight plays. Woody's lack of inventiveness on offense cost him. Michigan bottled the Buckeyes up, especially Griffin, who hurt his leg after having gained most of his 163 yards. Michigan rallied. The game settled into "trench warfare," the gridiron version of the Germans and English at Verdun.

Woody's admonition that the forward pass could result in "three things and two of them are bad" seemed to justify itself when he went to the air late in an effort to drive into field goal position. The resulting Wolverine interception gave Michigan their shot, but a field goal try failed. The 10–10 tie was totally unsatisfying. It also killed national championship hopes for either team. Notre Dame beat Alabama in an extraordinary Sugar Bowl to win it.

With a repeat to Pasadena now available, Ohio State lobbied hard to go. Gone were the days of 1961, when they turned down the invite. Big bucks had come to college football. Television money was exorbitant. The Rose Bowl was the most lucrative of all TV deals.

Big 10 officials gathered for the vote. A 5–5 tie would send Michigan, since Ohio had gone the year before. But it came in 6–4 for Woody's team. Bo Schembechler was livid. Hard words and accusations were thrown about. Michigan State's representative voted against their in-state rival, reportedly as reprisal against Michigan's decades-old attempt to keep the Spartans out of the Big 10 Conference. The fact that Michigan suffered debilitating injuries, potentially weakening them against USC—the Pac-8 champion— played into the decision, too. In the end, however, Ohio State deserved to go. They had tied Michigan at Ann Arbor and were considered the better team all season.

Retribution was Woody's when his team came out *throwing* in a 42–21 win over the Trojans. Notre Dame coach Ara Parseghian advised Woody to do just that against USC. Hayes called it the "greatest victory" in Ohio State history, which probably says as much about USC as it does about Ohio State. Beating the Trojans in those days was like knocking off Napoleon's *Grand Armée* or the . . . Trojans when the Mycenaean Greeks burned Troy after the "stealing" of Helen, the "face that launched a thousand ships."

The January 1, 1975, "Trojan War" involved no bloodshed, but USC was out to avenge their loss just as Agamemnon had set out to avenge, on behalf of Menelaus, Helen's "capture" by a lovestruck Paris. The stakes were not nearly so complicated at the Rose Bowl: just the national championship, up for grabs again. Oklahoma was on probation. The UPI finally joined the postbowl party. Southern California beat Notre Dame in one of the wildest games ever played, 55–24 in Los Angeles. Woody's 10–1 team had hopes that victory over USC would give them the national title. Sitting in the Coliseum press box, where he was an analyst on the national TV broadcast, he saw USC dismantle the Irish on the green plains below. He must have felt like a German military commander with a binocular view of Patton's tanks marching through the low countries, knowing the only thing he had was Hitler's order to "stop the Americans at the Saar."

Fat chance, that.

The USC fans, knowing Woody was in the house, began to chant, "Woody, you're next." It was a surreal day. One month later, the Buckeyes were back in Pasadena. USC supporters, having also observed the football version of the American Army rumbling through the *Wehrmacht* in the late winter of 1945, probably thought Ohio State would fall in like manner. Not so quick there, Johnson.

USC came out looking for a little payback after what it considered a bad Heisman vote. The junior Griffin indeed outplayed USC senior tailback Anthony Davis most of the season, although the differential was not enormous. In the days before the Internet and fax machines, votes had to be mailed in and received. The tradition was to vote prior to the weekend's last games. In 1974, USC played Notre Dame on November 30, a fairly late date. Most ballots were already in the "snail mail" when Davis had what many historians consider one of the finest games any player has ever had against the Irish, or anybody else. The prevailing view is that A. D.'s game against Notre Dame would have pushed him ahead of the underclassman Griffin had the votes been cast after the game, as they should have been. That said, A. D. was hurt early in the Rose Bowl and was not a big factor. Griffin went on to a repeat Heisman in 1975 and a better pro career and is seen as the greater of the two players.

The Buckeyes played USC straight up and down. All-American defensive back Neal Colzie kept breaking up Trojan quarterback Pat Haden's passes to J. K. McKay and Shelton Diggs, then taunting the Trojans. In the end the last laugh was on him.

Haden led Troy on a two-minute drive and a touchdown pass to McKay in the corner of the end zone . . . over Colzie. Then Haden's 2-point conversion pass to Diggs, a desperation move when a wall of Buckeyes prevented him from running it in, broke Woody's heart. The national title belonged not to Ohio State but to USC.

The game was heartbreaking, but on New Year's Day, 1976, came the straw that broke the Buckeyes' backs. Oklahoma had a loss. Unbeaten, second-ranked Texas A&M lost 20–0 to Southern California in the Liberty Bowl. Undefeated Arizona State, not yet in the Pacific-10 Conference, was not considered national championship material.

The Buckeyes faced 8–2–1 UCLA, who had survived a down, competitive Pac-8 schedule to emerge as champions. The Bruins survived seven fumbles in their 25–22 win over the Trojans in a game in which nobody looked as if they wanted to win. Ohio State, led by the two-time Heisman winner Griffin, was heavily favored. Was it *possible* that this team could lose to such a mediocre team as UCLA?

The score was 23–10, Bruins. UCLA's All-American quarterback, John Sciarra, was masterful. The Bruins dominated Ohio State; it was never really close. Just like the 1969, 1970, and 1974 seasons, a national title eluded Woody Hayes in the final game—for the third time versus a team he was heavily favored to beat. Only against a team considered even or favored to beat them—USC in the 1974 and 1975 Rose Bowls—had Ohio State won and then really made it close.

The frustration built into a crescendo for Woody. Here was a genuinely good man who asked his players to "pay it forward" by doing good deeds for the community. Hayes was a groundbreaker when it came to recruiting black players. He turned boys into men who graduated, and God did he love them. They loved him, too, because he truly cared about them, their families, and their lives. He was utterly sentimental, emotional, and real. He was not a mercenary; he *was* Ohio State football.

But his autocratic ways were made fun of. West Coast fans and writers took to belittling him. In the days of long hair and loose morals, Woody's style was looked upon as old school, yesterday, by the lesser lights and unimpressives who criticized him but could not carry his dirty jockstrap. But on the field, Woody was so fiery and competitive that it got the best of him. Finally, on December 29, 1978, it *did* get the best of him. With Ohio State trailing Clemson 17–15 in the Gator Bowl, the Buckeyes were driving when Clemson's Charlie Bauman intercepted Art Schlichter's pass, sealing a Buckeye loss. Hayes lost control. In the heat of the moment he grabbed Bauman and tried to punch him. By Monday morning he was out of his office. That said, Woody is the best thing that ever happened to Ohio State football, and one of the finest people in the history of this great game. His human faults were just that, oh so human like the rest of us,

Ohio College Hall of Famers (25)

Players			
Gomer Jones	1933–1935	Archie Griffin	1972–1975
Jim Parker	1954–1956	Chic Harley	1916–1919
Aurealius Thomas	1955–1957	Vic Janowicz	1949–1951
Gust Zarnas	1935–1937	Gaylord Stinchcomb	1917–1920
Jim Stillwagon	1968–1970	Bob Ferguson	1959–1961
Warren Amling	1944–1946	Randy Gradishar	1971–1973
Jim Daniell	1939–1941	Jack Tatum	1968–1970
John Hicks	1970–1973	Rex Kern	1968–1970
Bill Willis	1942–1944	Chris Spielman	1984–1987
Wes Fesler	1928–1930		
Jim Houston	1957–1959	*Coaches*	
Les Horvath	1940–1944	Woody Hayes	1946–1978
Hopalong Cassady	1952–1955	Francis Schmidt	1919–1942
		John Wilce	1913–1928

whose best approach to his memory is to "forgive us our trespasses, as we forgive those who trespass against us."

Woody won 205 games and thirteen Big 10 championships. He passed in 1987 a larger-than-life figure. No successor has approached his record or persona. But he was an old man in 1978, and it was time for a change anyway. Earle Bruce led Ohio State to another one of those brutally disappointing seasons; disappointing because so much success preceded ultimate failure; disappointing because it became, and continues to this day to be, the mark of Buckeye football over the past forty years.

Led by the sophomore Schlichter, Ohio State surprised many by rolling to an 11–0 record. They kept getting better every week, capping the regular season with an 18–15 triumph over Michigan. Ranked number one heading into the Rose Bowl, all they needed to do was beat a team that many considered the greatest of all time!

Defending national champion Southern California was the preseason number one, but a 21–21 tie with Stanford was the single bump in their road. It opened the door for Ohio State and Alabama, both unbeaten and untied. Early talk about the Trojans being the best team ever assembled did not quite hold up, but they were so that good blind people came to the Coliseum to hear them hit opponents.

Schlichter kept the Trojans off-balance all afternoon. Ohio State managed a spare 16–10 lead in the defensive struggle, but Southern California got the ball with minutes left to play. Eschewing the pass, USC coach John Robinson used Heisman Trophy-winning tailback Charlie White to pound out yardage until Troy was in the end zone;

the point after was good, 17–16; and Ohio State was forced to walk off the Rose Bowl field in abject disappointment once again. The Big 10 had lost ten of the last eleven Rose Bowl games.

USC rooted for Arkansas to beat Alabama in the Sugar Bowl, which would have given them back-to-back national championships, but the Crimson Tide was victorious. Despite so many "close but no cigar" seasons, it was one of the greatest decades in Buckeye football history. It had produced consensus All-Americans Jim Stillwagon, John Hicks, Randy Gradishar, Steve Meyers, Kurt Schumacher, Archie Griffin, Ted Smith, Tim Fox, Bob Brudzinski, Chris Ward, Tom Cousineau, and Ken Fritz. Stillwagon was the 1970 Lombardi Award and Outland Trophy recipient. Griffin is to this day the only two-time Heisman Trophy winner. Hicks also earned 1973 Outland and Lombardi honors.

Led by running back Keith Byars, Bruce's Buckeyes returned to Pasadena on January 1, 1985. Their opponent: Southern California again. This may have been the weakest Trojan team ever to make it to the Rose Bowl, but the result was a familiar one: 20–17, Troy. The Buckeyes finished 9–3. Consensus All-Americans in the 1980s include Marcus Marek, Byars, Jim Lachey, talented receiver Cris Carter, and Tom Tupa. Chris Spielman was a dominant two-time All-American linebacker (1986–1987) and winner of the Lombardi Award his senior year.

In 1995, running back Eddie George earned Ohio State's sixth Heisman Trophy when he rushed for 1,927 yards and twenty-four touchdowns. His other honors included Doak Walker, Maxwell, Walter Camp, and Big 10 Player of the Year awards. George was Houston's first pick of the 1996 draft. He was named the NFL's Rookie of the Year and earned All-Pro in a highly successful career with the Tennessee Titans (after Houston's franchise moved to Nashville).

Under coach John Cooper, Ohio State was 11–1 with a 20–17 Rose Bowl win over Arizona State in the 1996 season. They were led by two-time consensus All-American offensive lineman Orlando Pace. Pace won the Outland Trophy and twice the Lombardi Award. Chosen by the St. Louis Rams with the first pick of the 1997 NFL Draft, Pace is considered one of the finest linemen in collegiate football history, if not the finest.

Wide receiver Terry Glenn, winner of the 1995 Biletnikoff Award, is considered one of the best college pass-catchers of all time. Certainly his career represented a paradigm shift at Ohio State from the old "three yards and a cloud of dust" offense to a more wide-open approach.

In 1997, linebacker Andy Katzenmoyer won the Dick Butkus Award. In 1998, Antoine Winfield was named winner of the Jim Thorpe Award. Other consensus All-Americans of the decade include Dan Wilkinson, Korey Stringer, Mike Vrabel, Shawn Springs, and Rob Murphy.

Jim Tressel took over at Columbus in 2001. The 2002 Buckeyes rival the 1968 champions as the greatest team in the school's hallowed history. They played stifling defense and were led by a utilitarian, ball-control quarterback, Craig Krenzel. Ohio State survived all challenges to take on the mighty Miami Hurricanes in the BCS Fiesta Bowl in Tempe, Arizona, for the national championship. Despite carrying a 13–0 record into the contest,

Tressel's team was a decided underdog. But Miami had suffered some key injuries and were tense trying to defend the weight of history: a repeat national title; a then all-time record of twenty straight weeks ranked number one in the nation; and a 34-game winning streak that, with victory against the Bucks, would put them within one undefeated regular season of Oklahoma's all-time record 47 straight (1953–1957).

The game has been described as one of the greatest in collegiate history. In terms of pressure, unbeaten teams, stakes, and the fact it was a close contest that went into two overtimes, it was. But it was also marked by mistakes, questionable officiating, and decided tentativeness, especially by the Hurricanes. But Ohio State refused to buckle down against one of the fastest, strongest, talented teams ever assembled.

Roscoe Parrish made a clutch 50-yard punt return. This set up Todd Sievers's 40-yard field goal for Ohio State on the final play of regulation, forcing overtime, 17–17. Miami scored to take the lead, but Krenzel converted a fourth-and-14 pass. Later, his fourth-down end zone pass resulted in a controversial interference call against Miami's Glenn Sharpe. Given a second life, Ohio State pushed it in to keep the dream alive.

In the second overtime freshman running back Maurice Clarett ran for a 5-yard touchdown to put Ohio State up 31–24. Miami drove to the Buckeye 2, but Ohio held on four plays to capture its sixth national championship.

Four years later, the Buckeyes were the dominant team in college football. They entered the season full of momentum, following up a decisive 34–20 Fiesta Bowl win over Notre Dame to end the 2005 campaign. In 2006, Ohio State was not "utilitarian." Heisman Trophy-winning quarterback Troy Smith may not have had great size or a strong arm. He was not considered a major NFL prospect, but under his leadership the Buckeyes were an explosive offensive force.

Ohio was ranked number one from the preseason through the entire regular campaign. Michigan, after beating the Irish early, settled in at number two. The game between the two teams at Ohio Stadium ("the Horseshoe") had the greatest buildup in the history of the rivalry. The old "Game of the Century," or at least "Game of the Twenty-first Century," maxim was applied. Troy Smith earned the Heisman Trophy, and the game lived up to its billing with the Buckeyes prevailing by a 42–39 score.

Unbeaten Ohio State moved on to the Bowl Championship Series national-title contest, played at the brand new University of Phoenix Stadium in suburban Glendale, Arizona. Their opponents, after much angst, were the once-beaten Florida Gators, survivors of a regular season BCS battle with Michigan and USC to earn the trip.

What the Gators did that night to Ohio State might not be legal. After the 41–14 pounding, Ohio State looked to be the seventh or eighth best team in the nation, not the first. In the history of the Heisman Trophy, many winners had failed in subsequent bowl losses, but none ever looked as terrible as Smith. Details are just too dreary to recount herein. It was just bad.

Tressel's team entered the game looking for their second national championship of the young century. Had they won, it would have matched Southern California's two, and this could have effectuated a strong argument on behalf of the Buckeyes that they were the new "Team of the Century." It did not happen.

In 2007, Ohio State made a return trip to the BCS title game, this time against LSU. For the sake of Ohio's confidence in themselves, details are omitted. Again, it was dreary beyond any value in recounting (unless you are a Tiger fan).

Consensus All-Americans in the new century include LeCharles Bentley, Mike Nugent, Matt Wilhelm, Mike Doss, Will Allen, A. J. Hawk, Donte Whitner, Nick Mangold, Antonio Pittman, Anthony Gonzalez, Ted Ginn Jr., Smith, and James Laurinaitis (who also won the Bronco Nagurski and Butkus awards before being drafted by St. Louis). Bentley was the 2001 Rimington Award winner. B. J. Sanders won the 2003 Ray Guy Award. Kicker Mike Nugent earned the Lou Groza Award in 2004. Two-time All-American linebacker A. J. Hawk, one of Ohio State's all-time greats, was the 2005 Lombardi Award honoree. In 2007, Ted Ginn Jr. went in the first round to Miami; Anthony Gonzalez, also a first rounder, went to the Colts.

Victory in Glendale (2007) or New Orleans (2008) would have replaced the 1950s, when Woody Hayes's team won two national titles, as the best in school history. Nevertheless, the 2000s were shaping up to be even better than the 1970s. By winning their sixth national title and their seventh Heisman Trophy (tying Southern California and Notre Dame), Ohio State moved past Nebraska into the fifth spot among college football's all-time top 25 traditions. In so doing, and also by beating Michigan in 2006, the Buckeyes established themselves as the greater of the two rivals going back more than 100 years. Michigan fans can argue the point, and they come to the debate well-armed with many facts on their side. However, Hayes began a period in Buckeye history that overshadowed Michigan.

His rivalry with Bo Schembechler was fairly even but favored Woody. Michigan had many opportunities over the decades to assert themselves in the national picture, but with some exceptions fell short too often. Ohio State is the greater team in modern times, having won five national championships since the 1950s compared to Michigan's one.

However, the situation is fluid. With a 2006 national championship, which would have been their seventh, Ohio State may well have moved past Oklahoma into the fourth position in the "all-time poll." They will be battling the Wolverines, the Sooners, the Trojans, and the rest of collegiate football's powerhouses for ultimate supremacy well into the new century. What a grand game it is, and Buckeye fans will "fight to the end for O-hi-o."

Chapter 6

Nebraska Cornhuskers

T HE HISTORY OF Nebraska Cornhusker football is so much a part of the American experience that it seems they should be ranked higher than sixth on the all-time list. On the one hand, that history is so relatively recent that it is remarkable they are ranked above Texas, Michigan, and other programs.

University of Nebraska
Lincoln, Nebraska
Founded: 1869
Enrollment: 15,742
Colors: Scarlet and cream
Nickname: Cornhuskers
Stadium: Memorial Stadium/Tom Osborne Field (opened: 1923; capacity: 73,918)
All-time record (1890–2008): 817–337–41
All-time bowl record: 23–22 (through 2009 bowls)
National championships: 1970, 1971, 1994, 1995, 1997
MVC-Big 7/8/12 Conference championships: 42
Heisman Trophies: Johnny Rodgers (1972), Mike Rozier (1983), Eric Crouch (2001)
Outland Trophies: Larry Jacobson (1971), Rich Glover (1972), Dave Rimington (1981–1982), Dean Steinkuhler (1983), Will Shields (1992), Zach Wiegert (1994), Aaron Taylor (1994)
First-round NFL draftees: 59 (through 2009 draft)
Website: www.huskers.com
Notable alumni: General John "Black Jack" Pershing; U.S. Senator Bob Kerrey; comedian Johnny Carson; financier Warren Buffett; Nobel Prize-winning geneticist George W. Beadle; Pulitzer Prize-winning author Willa Cather; Olympian Merlene Ottey; rock star Tommy Lee

They have played football in Lincoln since 1890, but until 1970 the Cornhuskers were just another program. Their great claim to fame was the 1925 game with Notre Dame, but perhaps the correct word is *infamous*. Led by the theologian–political orator

William Jennings Bryan, Nebraska had over the years become increasingly evangelical. This movement reached a fever pitch in the mid-1920s.

Unfortunately, the Christian revivalist movement of the 1920s had dark overtones. In the South it morphed with the "white supremacy" of the Ku Klux Klan. In the Midwest it took on strongly anti-Papal aspects. The Notre Dame players Knute Rockne brought to Lincoln on November 26, 1925, were treated harshly because of their Catholicism. The game was played in bitter cold, and the Irish lost 17–0. Afterward, Rockne felt he had enough of both freezing late-November temperatures and religious intolerance.

He determined he would shift from road trips to rural towns to cosmopolitan cities. This was a major reason why he accepted the offer from the University of Southern California to come out to sunny Los Angeles, beginning that rivalry.

Nebraska played good football but was a second-tier program. On January 1, 1941, they made their first bowl appearance, a 21–13 defeat at the hands of national-champion Stanford in the Rose Bowl. They never played in another bowl game until a 34–7 loss to Duke in the 1955 Orange Bowl. Consensus Cornhusker All-Americans prior to 1960 include Guy Chamberlin, Ed Weir, George Sauer, and Sam Francis. When Bob Devaney arrived in 1962, however, they upgraded in a major way. Despite losing Omaha native Gale Sayers to Kansas, the Cornhuskers built their program in much the same way USC and UCLA did—by integrating with quality black stars when some of the country was not.

In the 1960s, Nebraska was a foil for the best teams. Devaney's 'Huskers were 9–2 and 10–1 in his first two years, both with bowl wins. The 1964 squad was 9–1 when the ill-fated bowl season rolled around. Alabama was beaten by Texas in the Orange Bowl, creating a big black asterisk on their "*AP national title." Unbeaten Arkansas held off Nebraska in the Cotton Bowl 10–7 to claim the (revised) national championship even if the two wire-service polls did not award it to them.

The Cornhuskers brought an unbeaten integrated team to the 1966 Orange Bowl, losing a thriller 38–29 to all-white Alabama. With the AP switching its national championship award to a postbowl vote, the game was for the ultimate prize since Michigan State lost that day to UCLA.

In a rematch against Alabama on January 2, 1967, 9–1 Nebraska fell to unbeaten Alabama 34–7 in the Sugar Bowl. Segregationists in 'Bama seized on this as proof that they did not need to recruit black players to win. 1960s consensus All-Americans include Bob Brown (who went on to a Hall of Fame career with the Raiders), Larry Kramer, Freeman White, Walt Barnes, LaVerne Allers, and Wayne Meylan.

In 1969 the Cornhuskers lost their opener to USC, 31–21 at Lincoln, and three weeks later to Missouri. After that they reeled off a 32-game unbeaten streak. The only flaw was a 21–21 tie at Southern Cal in 1970.

In 1970, Nebraska laid low throughout an exciting regular season in which Texas, Notre Dame, Ohio State, and Michigan competed for the number one position. One after another teams were knocked out. When Notre Dame beat Texas in the Cotton Bowl and Stanford upset Ohio State in the Rose Bowl, Nebraska seized their chance with a 17–12 win over LSU in the Sugar Bowl. This secured for them the AP national championship.

Nebraska's All-Century Team

Chosen by 10,000 Cornhusker fans, 2000

OFFENSE		DEFENSE	
Pos.	*Player*	*Pos.*	*Player*
OT	Bob Newton	DT	Neil Smith
OT	Zach Wiegert	DT	Jason Peter
OG	Dean Steinkuhler	NT	Rich Glover
OG	Will Shields	DE/OLB	Broderick Thomas
C	Dave Rimington	DE/OLB	Trev Alberts
TE	Junior Miller	DE	Grant Wistrom
WR	Johnny Rodgers	LB	Tom Novak
WR	Irving Fryar	LN	Mark Munford
QB	Tommie Frazier	LB	Ed Stewart
IB	Roger Craig	CB	Michael Booker
IB	Mike Rozier	S	Mike Minter
FB	Tom Rathman	S	Mike Brown
FB	Joel Mackovicka	P	Jesse Kosch
PK	Kris Brown	PR	Johnny Rodgers
KR	Tyrone Hughes		

The next season there was no question. The 'Huskers were ranked number one in every poll from beginning to end, compiling a 13–0 record. Junior receiver/kick returner Johnny Rodgers was spectacular. Defensive tackle Larry Jacobson won the Outland Trophy. On November 25 Nebraska traveled to Oklahoma for the "Game of the Century." *Sports Illustrated* called it the "IRRESISTIBLE FORCE MEETS THE IMMOVABLE OBJECT." Oklahoma was the "irresistible force." They were at times irresistible, but they were resisted. Nebraska was the "immovable object." OU indeed did move them, but in the end the teams and the game lived up to the moniker.

The Cornhuskers outplayed OU but almost let it slip away thanks to some trick plays by the Sooners, catching them off guard. Their 35–31 victory steered them to an Orange Bowl date with Bear Bryant's unbeaten Crimson Tide.

There was an entirely new dynamic from the 1966–1967 bowl games with Alabama, when the all-white nature of the Tide played such a large role in the proceedings. This Alabama team was integrated and fast, but no match for Nebraska. The 38–6 win remains one of the most impressive bowl performances ever. It capped a season that at that point in time was believed to have produced the very best college football team ever assembled.

Los Angeles, California, turned out to be a city Nebraska fans had no love for in 1972, however. First, they traveled to UCLA only to have their 32-game unbeaten streak

Cornhuskers on the Run

Year	Record	Run
1969	9–2 F/7–0	9–2 (1969)
		7–0 (1969)
1970	11–0–1	20–2–1 (1969–70)
		18–0–1 (1969–70)
1971	13–0	33–2–1 (1969–70)
		31–0–1 (1969–70)
		29–0–1 (1969–71) **30 games**
1972	9–2–1 F/0–1	41–4–2 (1969–72)
1981	9–3	9–3 (1981)
1982	12–1	21–4 (1981–82)
1983	12–1	32–5 (1981–83)
1984	10–2	42–7 (1981–84)
1993	11–1	11–1 (1993)
1994	13–0	24–1 (1993–94)
1995	12–0	36–1 (1993–95)
		29–1 (1993–95) **30 games**
1996	11–2 S/1–0, 2–1, F/1–0	38–2 (1993–96) **40 games**
		47–3 (1993–96) **50 games**
1997	13–0	60–3 (1993–97)
		57–3 (1993–97) **60 games**
		14–0 (1996–97)
1998	9–4 S/5–0, 6–1	69–7 (1993–98)
		66–4 (1993–98) **70 games**
		19–0 (1996–98)

S/Start season; F/Finish season

Elite Ten by the Numbers

Outland Trophy winners (through 2008)

1. Nebraska	8		6. Alabama	2	
2. Oklahoma	5		6. Miami	2	
3. Ohio State	4		8. Southern California	1	
4. Notre Dame	3		9. Penn State	1	
5. Texas	3		10. Michigan	0	

ended by Mark Harmon and UCLA at the Coliseum, 20–17. Then USC compiled a season that in the minds of many erased Nebraska's 1971 team as the best in history. At 9-2-1 with a 40-6 Orange Bowl win over Notre Dame, it might have been considered a great year, but in the Devaney era the standards had changed. A 17-14 loss to Oklahoma was hard to swallow, but unfortunately portended a strange future.

Tom Osborne was Devaney's handpicked successor in 1973, but he did not beat Oklahoma until 1978. Nebraska teams after 1971 were winners; they won bowl games; they were excellent; yet they could not beat the Sooners or capture the national title. 1970s consensus All-Americans were Bob Newton, Larry Jacobson, Johnny Rodgers, Willie Harper, Rich Glover, John Dutton, Marvin Crenshaw, Rick Bonness, Dave Butterfield, Kelvin Clark, and Junior Miller.

In 1983, led by Irving Fryar, Mike Rozier, and legendary offensive guard Dean Steinkuhler, Nebraska looked better even than in 1971. They rolled through all opposition like Nebraska alum "Black Jack" Pershing's forces during the Argonne Offensive. Their opponent in the Orange Bowl was almost a joke. Led by coach Howard Schnellenberger and quarterback Bernie Kosar, Miami was 10-1, but their appearance in the Orange Bowl seemed unlikely.

Few people really thought of Miami as a big-time college football program prior to 1983. They were seen as a commuter school (albeit a private one) serving a growing metropolitan area in the wake of recent heavy Cuban immigration in the Castro/post-revolution era. Florida, where Steve Spurrier had won the 1966 Heisman Trophy, was *the* football school in the state. Florida State was a recent invitee among the "elites." But Miami was just a team on the schedule. The great Ted Hendricks had starred at Miami in the 1960s. A game with O. J. Simpson and USC had garnered attention in *Sports Illustrated*, but when it came to national championship contenders, fans thought of Nebraska, Oklahoma, USC, Notre Dame, Penn State.

But things were changing. The Trojans and the Irish were in down periods. In the 1980s Georgia won their first undisputed national title, followed by a highly unlikely Clemson team. In 1984, Brigham Young would capture it all.

The Orange Bowl may have appeared to be an easy Nebraska triumph, but there were a few *uneasy* signs. First, Miami would be the "home" team playing in their stadium. Second, the weather in Nebraska, always bad in December, was even worse that year. The Cornhuskers hardly got outside. Until they got to sunny Florida they had to practice indoors while their counterparts were honing their skills under God's blue sky.

When the game started, all bets were off. Nebraska was tentative, slow off the ball, and mistake-prone. Miami came out guns blazing, taking chances that paid off, and raced to a 17-0 lead. But Nebraska made a terrific comeback to narrow it to 17-14, going to trick plays as Oklahoma had done in coming back against them in 1971.

But the 'Canes stormed back to a 31–14 advantage. Nebraska quarterback Turner Gill engineered a furious second-half rally to narrow it to 31–30 after Jeff Smith scored with forty-eight seconds on the clock. Next came the decision that may have irritated some but in retrospect made Tom Osborne's legend. With no overtime, he chose to go for a 2-point conversion rather than kick the point-after for a tie. The tie would have given Nebraska an un-disputed national championship. It was a sure thing, but unlike Ara Parseghian in 1966, Osborne went for immor-tality. If this was to be considered the "greatest team of all times," then they would have to earn it with a victory. Miami stopped them, however, and finished number one.

Mike Rozier won the Heisman in 1983. A tough kid from the mean streets of Cam-den, New Jersey, he overcame a difficult upbringing to star at Nebraska after transferring from Coffeyville J.C. in Kansas. He became a 1,000-yard rusher with the Oilers and Fal-cons, eventually finding his niche speaking to kids about the troubles of street life.

The remainder of the 1980s looked like more of the 1970s: winning teams, mostly bowl defeats, and Oklahoma dominance. The fans saw Osborne as a coach incapable of taking his team to the promised land. Consensus All-Americans include Randy Schle-usener, Jarvis Redwine, Dave Rimington, Mike Rozier, Irving Fryar, Dean Steinkuhler, Mark Traynowicz, Danny Noonan, Jake Young, and Broderick Thomas.

The 1990s started like the 1980s finished off. The Cornhuskers were a powerhouse and had finally broken past Oklahoma in the Big 8 Conference. But the game's dominant teams were Florida State, Miami, Notre Dame, and others. In 1993, Osborne almost seemed to have burned his last bridge when he brought an un-beaten squad to the Orange Bowl against once-beaten Florida State.

The 1993 Cornhuskers were considered to be a juggernaut on par with the 1971 and 1983 teams. They were favored over Bobby Bowden's Seminoles. The game was a pure dud, with neither group apparently willing to put themselves on the line for victory. It was like one of those old-time Harvard-Yale games: trench warfare, despite the speed and athleticism both teams possessed.

Florida State's 18–16 win was a bitter pill; victory at least for Bowden, who like Os-borne had never won it despite coming close many times. Osborne looked like a loser, but in 1994 he and his team erased all doubt. Victory over the vaunted Miami Hurricanes gave them a 13–0 record and an unquestioned national championship. The 1995 team was selected by computer analyst Jeff Sagarin to be the best ever (with the 1971 Corn-huskers second). Behind quarterback Tommie Frazier Nebraska scored 52.4 points per game and won by an average of 38.7. Their 62–24 rout of Florida in the Fiesta Bowl is undoubtedly one of the best bowl performances (and single-game efforts) ever, if not the

Nebraska's College Hall of Famers (14)

Players		Bobby Reynolds	1950–1952
Dave Rimington	1979–1982	Sam Francis	1934–1936
Bob Brown	1961–1963	George Sauer	1931–1933
Rich Glover	1970–1972	Grant Wistrom	1994–1997
Wayne Meylan	1966–1967		
Ed Weir	1923–1925	Coaches	
Guy Chamberlin	1911–1915	Tom Osborne	1973–1997
Clarence Swanson	1918–1921	Edward Robinson	1898–1925
Johnny Rodgers	1970–1972		

best. The back-to-back national champions of 1994–1995 may well be the finest two-year run of all time.

The 1993–1995 period marks a three-year reign that has few if any equals. In 1997 the Cornhuskers again won the national championship. Overall they beat out Florida State to be "Team of the Decade" for the 1990s. Consensus All-Americans include Will Shields, Trev Alberts, Zach Wiegert, Brenden Stai, Ed Stewart, Tommie Frazier, Aaron Taylor, Grant Wistrom, Jason Peter, and Ralph Brown.

In the 2000s Nebraska slipped, although it was not obvious at first. In 2001, the Cornhuskers were destroyed by Colorado 62–32 in the final regular season game. Oregon was the obvious choice to face unbeaten Miami in the BCS Rose Bowl, but the computer system, in place since 1998, failed the Ducks. Nebraska was selected and they were destroyed again, this time by one of the greatest teams ever. Miami ran over them by a 37–14 score. Quarterback Eric Crouch won the 2001 Heisman Trophy.

Osborne left to go into politics. His conservatism served him better at the polls than Bud Wilkinson's Republican views in Oklahoma back in 1964. Osborne's successors, however, have not upheld Nebraska tradition. In 2005 the Cornhuskers had one of the top recruiting classes according to *USA Today*, but under coach Bill Callahan's NFL mind-set (the so-called West Coast offense), it never materialized, at least not in the manner to which Nebraska fans have become accustomed. Consensus All-Americans in this decade include Dominic Raiola and Toniu Fonoti.

Nebraska ranked fourth in all-time victories with 803 entering the 2007 season. They appeared in an NCAA-record thirty-five straight bowl games between 1969 and 2003. In the modern post-World War I era, the only teams to win back-to-back national championships with perfect records have been Nebraska (1994–1995), Minnesota (1934–1935),

Nebraska versus the Elite Ten (59–72–2)

Alabama (2–3), Miami (5–4), Michigan (1–3), Notre Dame (7–7–1), Ohio State (0–2), Oklahoma (36–40), Penn State (5–6), Southern California (0–3–1), Texas (4–4)

Elite Ten by the Numbers
Conference (co)championships

1.	Nebraska	42 (MVC/Big 8/12)
1.	Michigan	42 (Big 10)
3.	Oklahoma	41 (Big 6/8/12)
4.	Southern California	38 (PCC-AAWU-Pacific-8/10)
5.	Ohio State	32 (Big 10)
6.	Texas	27 (Southwestern/Big 12)
7.	Alabama	21 (Southern/Southeastern)
8.	Miami	8 (Big East, 0 Atlantic Coast)
9.	Penn State	3 (Big 10)
10.	Notre Dame	0 (independent)

Army (1944–1945), and Oklahoma (1955–1956). The only programs ever to capture three national titles in a four-year span are Nebraska (1994, 1995, 1997), California (1920, 1921, 1922), Minnesota (1934, 1935, 1936), and Notre Dame (1946, 1947, 1949).

They lost only three home games in the 1990s and were ranked in the polls thirty-five of thirty-seven seasons prior to 2006. They are approaching 300 straight sellouts at Memorial Stadium/Tom Osborne Field and boast thirty-two first-round NFL draft choices. Bob Devaney and Tom Osborne were a combined 356–69–5.

Three Huskers are in the Pro Football Hall of Fame (Bob Brown, Guy Chamberlin, Link Lyman). Forty-five of their players have made fifty-eight Super Bowl appearances through the 2007 Super Bowl. Great pros include Roger Craig, Vince Ferragamo, Pat Fischer, and Irving Fryar.

Chapter 7

Miami Hurricanes

IN ASSEMBLING THIS BOOK, particularly the "elite ten," there was little surprise at the "usual suspects": USC, Notre Dame, Alabama, Oklahoma, Ohio State, Nebraska, Texas, Michigan, and Penn State. Each has long football histories. Penn State and Nebraska are relative newcomers but feature legendary coaches Joe Paterno, Bob Devaney, and Tom Osborne. There may be some disagreement over the order—certainly Michigan fans consider their "point-a-minute" national championships should count as much as Ohio State's "three yards and a cloud of dust" title teams, just to name one.

University of Miami
Coral Gables, Florida
Founded: 1925
Enrollment: 9,794
Colors: Orange, green, and white
Nickname: Hurricanes
Stadium: Orange Bowl (opened: 1937; capacity: 72,319)
All-time record (1926–2008): 544–310–19
All-time bowl record: 19–15 (through 2009 bowls)
National championships: 1983, 1987, 1989, 1991, 2001
Big East/Atlantic Coast Conference championships: 8
Heisman Trophies: Vinny Testaverde (1986), Gino Torretta (1992)
Outland Trophies: Russell Maryland (1990), Bryant McKinnie (2001)
First-round NFL draftees: 59 (through 2009 draft)
Website: www.hurricanesports.com
Notable alumni: Actors Sylvester Stallone and Charles Grodin; singers Gloria Estefan, Enrique Iglesias, and Jon Secada; Tampa mayor Sandy Freedman; National Organization for Women president Patricia Ireland; basketball Hall of Famer Rick Barry; baseball player Al Rosen

But one team always gets a raised eyebrow, for more than one reason. That school is the University of Miami. One eyebrow is raised at the concept that just since 1983, the Hurricanes could have amassed so much success that they can be rated among the very highest echelon of historical collegiate powerhouses. The second raised eyebrow concerns the fact that a supposedly "outlaw" program, a school that allegedly does not graduate its players, allows and condones criminals within its ranks, and stands for all that is wrong with Division I-A football should be given such a lofty perch.

No, Miami is not great academically, at least not as far as their football players are concerned. They have a spotty coaching record. They have produced numerous players with drug, alcohol, and violence problems both while in school and in their pro careers. They are as well known for their "bling" as anything else. They are not always a clean program. They have broken the rules.

But in the 2000s, the sad fact is that many athletes, coaches, and programs break the rules. The recent steroid scandals in professional sports are emblematic of this. As long as we keep score and play to win, the fact that Miami wins cannot be ignored. It is somehow fitting that one of their most famous alums, football player Dwayne Johnson (actually a real good guy with a law 'n' order side to him), became known as WWF (now WWE) celebrity The Rock. The Rock made his reputation with a combination of dazzle, attitude, and intimidating ability, just like Miami football.

Miami plays its football games in the Orange Bowl, which opened in 1937. The NFL's Dolphins moved into the Orange Bowl in the mid-1960s. The stadium and its New Year's Day bowl extravaganzas—then its Super Bowls—were more famous than its oldest occupant. Miami was bigger on the college football scale than Pasadena City College, who played some of their games at the Rose Bowl for years, but nobody was mistaking the Hurricanes for the Thundering Herd or the Seven Blocks of Granite.

Prior to 1983, Ed Cameron, William Levitt, Bill Miller (who played for the Packer Super Bowl teams), Tom Beir, Ted Hendricks, Tony Cristiani, Rubin Carter, and Fred Marion were the school's only consensus All-Americans. Hendricks was the only legitimate superstar, although quarterback George Mira (1961–1963) was a top player. Running back Pete Banaszak became a journeyman on great Oakland Raider outfits. The well-traveled Lou Saban coached at Miami from 1977 to 1978. The team was often mediocre. Attendance was down. As the neighborhood around the Orange Bowl got worse, the crowds continued to thin.

The team's nickname, Hurricanes, stems from the devastating 1926 pounder that apparently was not willing to wait until so-called global warming to demonstrate the wrath of God. It canceled the season opener, killed 130, and ruined the yet-to-be-completed on-campus stadium then under way.

The 'Canes were a solid midlevel program under Hall of Fame coach Andy Gustafson (93–65–3 between 1946 and 1963). They played in one Orange Bowl, one Gator Bowl, one Liberty Bowl, and the 1962 *Gotham Bowl* (?), where they lost to Nebraska 36–34. It was a matchup between two programs that had little previously to cheer about but would share national prominence a few decades later. The Cornhuskers got off the ground sooner with the win, which served notice in Bob Devaney's first season that things were different in Lincoln. Miami was still little noticed.

In fact, Miami *of Ohio* was considered to be at least as strong a program. When commentators and score-givers talked about college football, they felt the need to make the differentiation. The Hurricanes were usually Miami (of Florida). Only in

Miami's College Hall of Famers (6 through 2009 induction)			
Players		*Coaches*	
Bennie Blades	1984–1987	Andy Gustafson	1926–1963
Ted "The Mad Stork" Hendricks	1966–1968	Jack Harding	1926–1947 (assistant)
Don "Bull" Bosseler	1953–1956		
Arnold Tucker	1943–1946		

later years did they reach the point where nobody felt they needed to let folks know where they were from.

From 1967 to 1968, linebacker Ted Hendricks was a devastating superstar, perhaps the finest collegiate player at his position ever. Coach Charlie Tate's squad was 2–0 and ranked thirteenth when it entered the L.A. Coliseum in 1968. *Sports Illustrated* ballyhooed it as a match between two beach powers, but USC left no doubt that the 'Canes were a long way from prime time with a 28–3 whuppin'.

The history of Miami football is somewhat curious. Geographically, they are the most Southern of all colleges, but of course they have never really been a Southern town. Rural Florida always has been, but Miami always was cosmopolitan, more Caribbean than Confederate, mixed with retired Jews from New York and not-so-retired gangsters. They were not in a conference and lacked traditional rivals. Their unique demographics might have made it a groundbreaking place for black athletes in the South, which, given the courage and the vision to accomplish such a thing, may have given Miami a big advantage as early as the 1940s or 1950s. But black professional baseball players were not treated well even in southern Florida. The school never became a vanguard of integration.

The talent level of black athletes in the South, particularly in Florida, is astounding. So is the talent level of Florida athletes in general. Coach Ron Fraser developed Miami's baseball team into a national juggernaut years before the football team turned heads. The basketball program produced the likes of scoring champion Rick Barry. Even without blacks, Miami's failure to develop is incongruous. The school is located in a pleasant suburb called Coral Gables. It benefits from warm weather, great beaches, tanned bathing beauties, and terrific nightlife. But Miami football never became a factor until after the Mariel boatlift of 1980. Whether this has anything to do with it is not clear. It would not seem that it would.

The boatlift brought thousands of Cuban criminals to Miami and turned a conservative, white/Jewish enclave into a schizophrenic hybrid of rabid conservatives, Christian anti-Communist Cuban Castro haters, and drug dealers. Over the years, a fair number of Hurricane stars have been Hispanic, but it really does not seem that the talent pool of Miami football benefited in a huge way from Cuban immigration. But the anti-Castro Republicanism of the "new Miami" in the 1980s spotlighted the city and made it important to the Reagan Administration. Perhaps it was through this confluence of economic and political clout that Miami was able to make itself a world-class city, capable of attracting world-class athletes who otherwise might have been ticketed for Florida, Florida State, Alabama, Georgia, and points north and west.

Whatever the cause, it all came together beginning with the 1979 debut of coach Howard Schnellenberger. Schnellenberger was perfect for Miami in terms of his amorphous name, which sounded slightly Jewish and therefore went over well with those retirees from New York. But Schnellenberger was a good ol' boy who earned his spurs under the coaching tutelage of the great Paul "Bear" Bryant when he served on the University of Alabama staff. While he had gone on to become an assistant under Don Shula with the Miami Dolphins by 1970, he was well aware of the circumstances surrounding the 1970 USC-Alabama game. 'Bama had their hats handed to them by integrated Southern Cal. Schnellenberger knew that the future of Southern football lay in the recruitment of great, fast black athletes.

Schnellenberger was a mercenary, not one of Bryant's longtime loyalists who stayed on his 'Bama staff seemingly from "cradle to grave." He stayed at the University of Miami just long enough to convert them from a .500 team to a national champion, but no sooner did he accomplish this seeming miracle than he was off to the USFL, later to Louisville.

He never came close at another school, but in 1983 he brought the Hurricanes all the way. The season started in rotten manner with a 28-3 pasting at the hands of Florida, but freshman quarterback Bernie Kosar steered the team to ten wins and an Orange Bowl berth. The key was a 17–16 squeaker over Bobby Bowden and Florida State. It would not be the first of its kind. Despite Kosar's passing theatrics, Miami did it with defense, but for a team that got past East Carolina 12-7, the Orange Bowl match with seemingly unbeatable Nebraska appeared to make the 'Canes look like the Washington Generals to the Cornhuskers' Harlem Globetrotters. In one of the greatest games ever played, Miami prevailed 31–30, and the first national title in state history had come to Florida.

The next year under new coach Jimmy Johnson, Miami was unnerved by Doug Flutie's famed "Hail Mary," which beat them 47-45. After losing to UCLA 39-37 in the Fiesta Bowl, it looked as if the Hurricanes of 1983 had been a one-shot wonder. Then

Elite Ten by the Numbers
Associated Press Defensive Player of the Year

1. Miami: 5
   Cortez Kennedy, Seattle DT (1992); Warren Sapp, Tampa Bay DT (1999); Ray Lewis, Baltimore LB (2000, 2003); Ed Reed, Baltimore S (2004)
2. Notre Dame: 1
   Alan Page, Minnesota DT (1971)
3. Ohio State: 1
   Randy Gradishar, Denver LB (1978)
4. Oklahoma: 1
   Lee Roy Selmon, Tampa Bay DE (1979)

sophomore Kosar left school early to enter the draft, where he was chosen by his home-town Cleveland Browns.

Kosar was a mystery. The Miami Jewish community claimed him based on his Jewish-sounding name, his curly hair, his "Jewish features," and the fact he was a top student, another supposed "Jewish trait." Kosar had to disappoint many when he revealed that he was in fact Catholic. But he was a great quarterback and an excellent student. His early departure for pro football came about only because he had taken such a big academic load that he was able to graduate—not merely leave—early.

In 1985, a major moment was reached. Miami demolished Notre Dame, 58–7. It was considered by many in and out of South Bend, Indiana, to be a sure sign of the Apocalypse. In 1986, quarterback Vinny Testaverde won the Heisman in a runaway, but this time the circumstances of 1983 were reversed. Miami was 11–0 and favored over Penn State in the Fiesta Bowl. It was the first of the supposedly arranged "national championship games" twelve years prior to the BCS.

It featured two independent teams not locked into a particular bowl. The Fiesta Bowl was now considered a major game on an equal basis with the Rose, Orange, and other New Year's bowls, only this was arranged the night after New Year's. Competing all by itself, the ratings were through the roof.

In pro football, the Oakland Raiders were considered the "Hells Angels" of the NFL. For the first time a college team took on a similar identity. Defensive lineman Jerome Brown and many teammates showed up at a pre-Fiesta Bowl banquet with Penn State wearing fatigues. Prior to dinner being served, Brown stood up and said, "Did the Japanee siddown ta dinna wit Pearl Harba before dey bombed him? No! Fellas, let's go." With that, two things became known: (a) Miami was an "outlaw" program, and (b) the question as to whether Brown was a "dumbbellionite" was no longer a question.

Immediately, America's rooting interests turned to the classy Joe Paterno and his Nittany Lions, a team that got it done on the field and in the classroom. Testaverde was completely off but still had Miami driving for the game-winning score when he was intercepted deep in Penn State territory. The 14–10 Lion win gave Paterno his second national title.

The 1987 Hurricanes are considered one of the greatest teams of all time. They went 12–0 with a win over Oklahoma in the Orange Bowl. This included a 31–4 whomping of Florida, a 26–25 squeaker over Florida State (causing the Christian Bowden to look to the Heavens), and a 24–0 triumph over the Irish.

In 1988 the Hurricanes lost one of the wildest, and some still contend most controversial, games ever played. It was the "Convicts vs. the Catholics" epic, won by Notre

---

Miami versus the Elite Ten (29–49–1 through 2008)

Alabama (3–14), Michigan (1–1), Nebraska (5–5), Notre Dame (7–15–1), Ohio State (1–2), Oklahoma (3–2), Penn State (6–7), Southern California (1–1), Texas (2–2)

Miami versus Conferences (through 2006)

Atlantic Coast (37–19–1), Big East (72–11), Big 10 (22–9), Big 12 (19–12), Big West (6–0), Mid--American (4–1), Pacific-10 (9–8), Southeastern (55–76–1), Western Athletic (9–2), Sun Belt (2–2), Independents (15–17–1)

Dame at South Bend by a 31–30 score. It was likely the only thing keeping Miami from an unprecedented three straight national titles.

New coach Dennis Erickson took over when Johnson was enticed by his former Arkansas teammate, Jerry Jones, to right the listing ship of the Dallas Cowboys. Florida State beat the Hurricanes 24–10, but that was it. A 33–25 victory over Alabama in the Sugar Bowl gave them an 11–1 mark and another title.

When the decade of the 1980s began, Miami was little more than a few lines in the "Southeast roundup" of most Sunday newspapers in the fall. The game's giants all stood tall: Southern Cal, Notre Dame, Alabama, Oklahoma. There had been a shake-up. Some of those giants were not standing so tall; others held their ground. But one team had risen above all of them, the "Team of the Decade": the Miami Hurricanes.

Consensus All-Americans from 1983 to 1989 were Eddie Brown, Willie Smith, Vinny Testaverde, Jerome Brown (despite his bad acts he was a great star and a terrific pro with the Eagles, who made him their first draft pick), Benny Blades, Daniel Stubbs, quarterback Steve Walsh, Bill Hawkins, and Greg Mark.

Miami versus Florida State 30–23 (through 2008)

In 1990, BYU's Heisman Trophy-winning quarterback, Ty Detmer, engineered a 28–21 opening-game win over Miami. Notre Dame also toppled the Hurricanes, 29–20. The 'Canes beat Marshall Faulk and San Diego State 30–28 in a wild affair, then demolished outmanned Texas 46–3 in the Cotton Bowl to finish 10–2.

1991 was a year of greatness in college football. Miami, led by California-bred quarterback Gino Torretta, won another one-pointer over Florida State for all the marbles on a missed Seminole field goal, 17–16. A 22–0 stomping of Nebraska in the Orange Bowl gave them a 12–0 record and the AP national title. But Washington, also unbeaten and untied, was a juggernaut team in 1991, one of the best ever. They took the UPI and *USA Today* national titles.

A shot at a repeat was lost when Alabama ran all over Miami (11–1), 34–13 in the 1993 Sugar Bowl. Between 1985 and 1993, Miami's 81–9 record was, up until that time, the best 90-game mark ever. Butch Davis took over in 1995, and the program took a turn for the worse. The team went on probation, and so did many players—as in court-ordered probation, or worse—and in 1997 *Sports Illustrated* called for Miami to abolish their program. SMU had been given the so-called death penalty a few years earlier. The once-famed USF basketball program had dropped the sport for a few years in the 1980s, too.

Elite Ten by the Numbers
First-round draftees, season (through 2009 draft)

1. Miami	6 (2004)	4. Miami	4 (2003)
2. Southern California	5 (1968)	4. Notre Dame	4 (1946)
2. Miami	5 (2002)	4. Notre Dame	4 (1993)

But Miami made their entrance back into the realm of college football powerhouses on December 5, 1998. A September game with UCLA had been postponed due to a . . . *hurricane*. The unbeaten number three Bruins needed only to win this game against 7-3 Miami at the Orange Bowl to advance to the first BCS title game with Tennessee.

In one of the wildest contests ever played, the Hurricanes prevailed 49-45, breaking UCLA's hearts. Consensus All-Americans of the 1990s were Maurice Crum, Russell Maryland, Carlos Huerta, Darryl Williams, Gino Torretta, Michael Barrow, Ryan McNeil, and Warren Sapp. However, there were none after Sapp in 1994.

Davis's 2000 team went 11-1. After a 39-24 loss at Washington, the Hurricanes won ten straight, including a 37-20 pounding of Florida in the Sugar Bowl. With the return of Miami in the wake of national titles at Florida State (1993, 1999) and Florida (1996), the Sunshine State was now the epicenter of college football. A well-worn path of great players from *California*, including several excellent quarterbacks, chose to attend college in Florida during this period, leading to the general conclusion that the likes of USC and UCLA were now relegated to the archives.

In 2001, the Hurricanes lent further credence to this notion while making it clear that in a three-way battle for Florida supremacy, they were the alpha males of the bunch. Davis took off for professional football. This had become a habit for Miami coaches. The school did not seem to engender the kind of loyalty or love that a Notre Dame garners, or that a Pete Carroll feels for USC. The professional nature of its players while still in school seemed to extend to its coaches, who viewed winning records at Miami as stepping stones to the NFL. The unspoken truth is that Miami coaches often felt the need to depart before the next disaster struck, whether that be probation, scandal, criminality run amok, or even the natural kind, as in recent hurricanes blowing in from the Atlantic Ocean.

Either way, Larry Coker inherited a juggernaut in 2001. It is to his credit that he took that team and ran with them. Ken Dorsey was another one of those California quarterbacks. He hailed from Orinda, near Oakland. Dorsey played his high school ball not far from where a previous California quarterback, Gino Torretta of Pinole, had played. Torretta won the Heisman Trophy, leading Miami to the national championship. Dorsey finished third in a close Heisman vote, but like Torretta engineered another Miami title.

The only close call was a 26-24 win over Virginia Tech. Nebraska was like a lamb brought to slaughter against Miami in the BCS Rose Bowl. Oregon cried foul. The

Hurricanes on the Run

Year	Record	Run
1985	10–2	10–2 (1985)
1986	11–1	21–3 (1985–86)
1987	12–0	33–3 (1985–97)
1988	11–1	43–4 (1985–88)
		37–3 (1985–88) **40 games**
1989	11–1	54–5 (1985–89)
1990	10–2	64–7 (1985–90)
		54–6 (1985–90) **60 games**
		63–7 (1985–90) **70 games**
1991	12–0	76–7 (1985–91)
		73–7 (1985–91) **80 games**
1992	11–1	77–8 (1985–92)
1993	9–3	86–11 (1985–93)
		81–9 (1985–93) **90 games**
1994	10–2	96–12 (1985–94)
		88–12 (1985–94) **100 games**
2000	11–1 F/10–0	11–1 (2000)
		10–0 (2000)
2001	12–0	23–1 (2000–01)
		22–0 (2000–01)
		20–0 (2000–01) **20 games**
2002	12–1 S/12–0	35–1 (2000–02)
		34–0 (2000–02)
		34–1 (2000–02)
		30–0 (2000–02) **30 games**
		35–2 (2000–02)
2003	11–2 S/7–0	46–4 (2000–03) **50 games**
		38–2 (2000–03) **40 games**
		45–3 (2002–03)
		39–1 (2002–03) **40 games**

S/Start season; F/Finish season

Pacific-10 champions naturally wanted an invite to Pasadena, but a computer glitch gave Nebraska the BCS bid. That said, the Ducks were probably better off going to the Fiesta Bowl, where they polished off Colorado (the team that annihilated Nebraska).

Miami's 37–14 victory over Nebraska was never in question. This group ranks as one of the greatest in college history. They were the epitome of team speed, athleticism, and strength. The issue of steroids was less prevalent in 2001 than it is today. If the Hurricanes were "juiced," they were no more so than most college football teams. They just had the talent.

Bryant McKinnie, Jeremy Shockey, Phillip Buchanon, Edward Reed, and Mike Rumph all went in the first round of the 2002 draft, equaling USC's 1968 draft class for most first-round picks. The 2003 team did them one better: six first-round picks (Sean Taylor, Kellen Winslow, Jonathan Vilma, D. J. Williams, Vernon Carey, Vince Wilfork).

The 2002 Hurricanes went 12–0, increasing the winning streak that started under Butch Davis in 2000 to 34 straight games. Led by the senior Dorsey, they were odds-on favorites against Ohio State in the BCS Fiesta Bowl, but injuries slowed the Hurricanes down. It was a relatively lackluster game, certainly from an offensive standpoint, but despite tentativeness it was close and therefore a masterpiece of sorts. In two overtimes, Ohio State held off Miami for the national championship, 31–24. Miami appeared to have it won, but Buckeye quarterback Craig Krenzel's desperate fourth-down pass in the fourth quarter was flagged for interference against the 'Canes. Given another chance, Ohio State scored to force the extra period. Trailing by a touchdown, Dorsey's fourth-down pass on the Buckeye 1 was batted down. Ohio State had the title with the 31–24 double-overtime victory.

The Miami run appeared to be something nobody would see again. They won the first seven games of the 2003 campaign and finished 11–2. But slowly the program fell back as they had in the mid-1990s. Then came USC, doing it even more impressively than Miami had done. The success of Miami and USC in the 2000s made experts rethink what can be accomplished in college football. Despite the BCS system and strived-for parity, a great coach, great players from a seemingly limitless talent pool (Florida and California both offer that), and the right system can create dynasties.

In the 2000s, consensus All-Americans have included Santana Moss, Dan Morgan, Bryant McKinnie, Edward Reed, Willis McGahee, Brett Romberg, Kellen Winslow, Sean Taylor, and Antrel Rolle.

Since 1983, Miami has played in all the major bowl games. They are a consistent draw, a team people want to see in person or on television. They were ranked for 104 straight weeks in the Associated Press polls, the longest streak of any team. They had at least one player drafted in the first round for twelve straight drafts, another record. Miami's 58-game home winning streak between 1985 and 1994 ranks among one of the greatest records in sports.

Tales of academic fraud at Miami may have been true at one point, but in 2005 they graduated all twenty-one seniors (the "highest total in college football") according to their media guide. Still, HBO Sports and Bob Costas centered on Miami in a 2007 exposé of academic misconduct within the NCAA. The high historical ranking of Miami—an "outlaw" program with little history prior to 1983—will outrage the purists. The Michigan supporters will compare their long list of College Hall of Famers to Miami's paltry six (four players, two coaches); Michigan's all-time wins record going back

Elite Ten by the Numbers

USA Today national championships (1982–2008)

Previously USA Today/ESPN/Cable News Network poll

1. Miami (4): 1983, 1987, 1989, 2001
2. Nebraska (3): 1994, 1995, 1997 (split/Michigan – AP)
3. Oklahoma (2): 1985, 2000
4. Penn State (2): 1982, 1986
5. Southern California (1): 2004
6. Texas (1): 2005
7. Ohio State (1): 2002
8. Alabama (1): 1992
9. Notre Dame (1): 1988
10. Michigan (0)

to the Rutherford B. Hayes Administration; and their high-falutin' academic reputation. They will say—and maybe they are right—that it should count for more, that a program like Miami has no "right" to join this "elite ten" fraternity.

But in twenty-five short years, Miami has won five absolutely legitimate national championships, all earned via major bowl victories over the best the nation had to offer. This is the same number of national titles Michigan has won in all the years of the post-World War I modern era (1919–2008), and four of those came without the challenge of any bowl game whatsoever. Since 1983, the figures are more startling: Miami five, Michigan one (and that 1997 title was split with Nebraska).

In their short run, Miami compiled an all-time total of fifty-nine first-round NFL draftees as of the 2009 draft. With the advantage of all their great history, Michigan managed only forty in the same time period. The Wolverines have only a 3–2 edge in Heisman Trophy winners.

America is a competitive country that values excellence, greatness personified. They know it when they see it. Miami has had their run-ins with the law and the NCAA, but Oklahoma and USC, just to name two "elites," have as well. *Nobody* is entirely clean.

Let him who is without sin cast the first stone.

So it is that Miami, who is not without sin, nevertheless has earned their place among the most elite of all traditions. "Hail to the spirit of Miami U."

Did You Know . . .

That in 2006, Miami led all collegiate programs with forty-two players on NFL rosters, according to *Sports Illustrated*?

Chapter 8

Texas Longhorns

TEXAS FOOTBALL IS an anomaly of sorts. On the one hand, it is everything it is cracked up to be: fabulous traditions, winning history, and rightfully placed among the greatest college programs in the nation. The Longhorns are, like their state, larger than life. Everything in Texas is *big*, and the Longhorns have always represented that.

University of Texas
Austin, Texas
Founded: 1883
Colors: Burnt orange and white
Nickname: Longhorns
Stadium: Darrell K. Royal-Texas Memorial Stadium (opened: 1924; capacity: 80,082)
All-time record (1893–2008): 832–316–33
All-time bowl record: 25–21–2 (through 2009 bowls)
National championships: 1963, 1969, 2005
Southwestern/Big 12 Conference championships: 27 (through 2008)
Heisman Trophies: Earl Campbell (1977), Ricky Williams (1998)
Outland Trophies: Scott Appleton (1963), Tommy Nobis (1965), Brad Shearer (1977)
First-round NFL draftees: 41 (through 2009 draft)
Website: www.texassports.com
Notable alumni: Secretary of State James Baker; network anchor Walter Cronkite; political commentator Bill Moyers; actors Matthew McConaughey, Renee Zellweger, and Marcia Gay Harden; baseball players Roger Clemens, Burt Hooton, and Huston Street; University of Texas baseball coach Cliff Gustafson

On the other hand, they have disappointed their fans as often as not. Start with Texas high school football, which is the stuff of legends. In terms of actually *producing* the best teams and players, California ranks far and away as number one in football, as they do in all other sports (except ice hockey). But the Golden State does not come close to the enthusiasm, small-town fervor, and utter *mythology* of Lone Star State prep football. As they say in Texas, the two favorite sports are "football and spring football."

It would stand to reason, then, that the University of Texas would dominate in a manner similar to the way USC, Notre Dame, and Alabama have dominated, but they have not. They played for years in the Southwest Conference, which never produced truly great rivals. Texas A&M, Arkansas, and other SWC teams were often strong, sometimes very strong. The *intensity of emotion* was always there, but these teams usually did not pose the kind of obstacle to greatness that Ohio State and Michigan posed to each other.

Recruiting enticements at Texas are legendary. Austin is a college town, unencumbered by professional sports detracting from interest in the Longhorns. Their facilities are A-1, its alumni, student, and fan support rabid. Night life in Austin is second to none. Then there are the Texas women. Stories of UT "hostesses" seeing to the needs of recruits have been told in awestruck detail for decades.

Texas has always been *the* school in a state with a large population filled with prospects. The state has played an important role in shaping American history. The Alamo became the impetus for Western expansion and the war with Mexico, which was the epitome of Manifest Destiny. Texas politics shaped the modern South, producing two presidents and an electorate that needed to be courted assiduously. It has been the scene of triumph and tragedy on the American landscape.

The Dallas Cowboys became "America's Team," led by the stoic former Texas and New York Giants' football star Tom Landry. The Longhorns owned Saturdays, just as the preps outdrew the Astros and Rangers on Friday nights, the Cowboys getting all the Sunday attention. But when it comes to national prestige, UT football has had to take a secondary position to a hated out-of-state rival that until 1996 played in another conference. Texans always downgraded Oklahoma. They called it *Baja Texas*, its citizens were "Okies from Muskogee." Texans owned the oil rigs that Oklahomans slaved on. But Bud Wilkinson turned the whole "dust bowl," *Grapes of Wrath* image around. He was integrating Sooner football when it was unthinkable in Texas.

Oklahoma became Texas's biggest rival, and to their consternation the greater historical power. They did this, most irritatingly, by recruiting blue-chippers right from under Texas noses. Billy Sims and Brian Bosworth are just two superstar Sooners who hailed from Texas.

Football always fit the Texas mind-set. Officially a member of the Confederacy, Texas looked at itself differently. The way they forged independence from Mexico gave them the imprimatur of victory the Deep South states lacked after the Civil War. The manly aspects of football fit in perfectly with Texas machismo.

They started playing football at UT in 1893. The Ivy League played the sport best. Then in the 1900s the Big 10 Conference established itself. In the late part of the decade and the beginning of the 1910s, the Pacific Coast equaled the others. But the South was on the rise. In 1913, Auburn's unbeaten team served notice. Georgia Tech developed into a powerhouse. In the Southwest Conference, Texas and Oklahoma (they later left the SWC) made claims on the 1914 and 1915 national championships, respectively (Washington State and Oregon, Rose Bowl winners in those years, are the legitimate champs).

Texas All-Century Team

Voted by Longhorns fans via the Internet, 1999

OFFENSE		DEFENSE	
Pos.	*Player*	*Pos.*	*Player*
OL	Scott Appleton	DL	Doug English
OL	Jerry Sizemore	DL	Steve McMichael
OL	Doug Dawson	DL	Kenneth Sims
OL	Blake Brockermeyer	DL	Tony Brackens
OL	Dan Neil	LB	Tommy Nobis
TE	Pat Fitzgerald	LB	Britt Hager
WR	Johnny "Lam" Jones	LB	Winfred Tubbs
WR	Anthony Carter	DB	Raymond Clayborn
WR	Wayne McGarity	DB	Johnnie Johnson
QB	Bobby Layne	DB	Jerry Gray
QB	Vince Young	DB	Bryant Westbrook
RB	Earl Campbell	P	Russell Erxleben
RB	Ricky Williams		
K	Phil Dawson		

Just as USC benefited from its natural identification with the Rose Bowl, so too did Texas grow in prestige with the Cotton Bowl in Dallas. Unlike Notre Dame (who did not play bowl games between 1925 and 1969), Nebraska, Oklahoma, Ohio State, Michigan, Alabama, and Penn State (none of whom had major bowl games in their states) and Texas and USC (then Miami, LSU, and Florida in recent years) had the "home field advantage" in January bowls.

Coach D. X. Bible led the Longhorns to a 1943 Cotton Bowl win over Georgia Tech, 14–7. It was Texas's bid to separate themselves from Texas A&M and Texas Christian, which along with Tennessee, Alabama, and Duke had been seen as the preeminent Southern programs of the 1930s. In the mid-1940s came the man who defined Texas football: Bobby Layne.

Layne was everything Texans could want in a football hero. On the field he was as good as it gets. Off the field he was a notorious rascal, whiskey drinker, and skirt chaser—all activities that Texans have great fondness for. Layne also was an All-American baseball pitcher but went for pro football after college. He starred for the Detroit Lions.

Texas versus Oklahoma (40–58–5), Alabama (7–0–1), Michigan (1–0), Miami (2–2), Southern California (1–4), Notre Dame (2–8)

The duel between Layne and Southern Methodist's legendary running back Doak Walker is storied. In 1947, Walker and SMU beat Texas 14–13. It was their only defeat in a season that otherwise may have resulted in their first legitimate national championship. Under first-year coach Blair Cherry, the 'Horns beat Alabama 27–7 in the Sugar Bowl to finish 10–1.

Darrell Royal, a former Oklahoma quarterback under Bud Wilkinson, arrived on the scene in 1957. That was one year after the blockbuster George Stevens film *Giant*. Starring Elizabeth Taylor, Rock Hudson, and James Dean, it depicted Texas in all its glory and ugliness. Royal would become a "giant" of football fortunes. Prior to Royal's arrival in Austin, UT had produced only four consensus All-Americans: Hub Bechtol, Layne, Bud McFadin, and Carlton Massey.

In 1961 the Longhorns, led by Jimmy Sexton, went 10–1 with a stirring 12–7 win over Ole Miss in the Cotton Bowl. Johnny Treadwell was a consensus All-American in 1962. 1963 was the year everything came together, finally.

Featuring a smothering defense and ball-control offense right out of the old Oklahoma playbooks, Texas ran an 11–0 table that included a stirring 28–6 Cotton Bowl triumph over Roger Staubach and Navy. They had their first legitimate national title, certainly the first of the modern (post–World War I) era.

In 1968, Texas was 9–1–1. After opening with a 20–20 tie against Houston and a 31–21 defeat at the hands of Texas Tech, the Longhorns ran off nine consecutive victories including a 36–13 pounding of Tennessee in the Cotton Bowl. Royal's "wishbone" running attack was in full sync in 1969. Fans in the stands often could not tell who had the ball. Defenders on the field fared little better. A typical "wishbone" play featured quarterback James Street angling to the side, then optioning a pitch to running back Steve "Woo Woo" Worster. Confusion would then reign, followed by a tackle . . . about 8 yards upfield.

1969 was the one hundredth anniversary of college football. Teams all wore a special insignia indicating "100." The action on the field matched the anticipation, but it was almost a turning point in the business, or entertainment, of college football. The AP had finally came around to voting for the national champion only after the bowl games were settled. Notre Dame lifted their no-bowl policy after forty-four years. It was also a year of great traditions having great seasons.

Ohio State and Woody Hayes were the defending national champions. They held the number one spot until losing to Michigan in the last game of the regular season. USC, along with Alabama, the dominant team of the decade, was at the height of their glory

Did You Know . . .

That when the University of Texas opened the 1961 season at Berkeley's Memorial Stadium versus California, the school did not bring their cheerleaders? Enterprising UT alumni instead hired "dancers" from a San Francisco strip joint to perform for the Texas contingent. The Longhorns won, 28–3.

days under coach John McKay. Joe Paterno had Penn State on the rise. Ara Parseghian and Notre Dame were still football's glamour boys.

Texas's traditional rival was Texas A&M, but since losing coach Paul "Bear" Bryant to his alma mater, Alabama, the Aggies had been also-rans. The other dominant team in the Southwest Conference was Arkansas, the de facto national champions of 1964. Despite being a small school in a small state they were a big powerhouse under coach Frank Broyles. Both Texas and Arkansas entered the 1969 campaign expecting to challenge for national supremacy. With Ohio State barred from a Rose Bowl repeat, and the AP voting after the bowls, this increased the chances they could get it in the end.

ABC was looking to capitalize on the one hundredth anniversary concept. Beano Cook looked at Texas's schedule and came up with the bright idea of rescheduling the Texas-Arkansas game from October 18 to December 6 in Fayetteville. Both teams ran the table unbeaten. USC and Notre Dame tied each other, and after Ohio State lost to Michigan it became a true number one versus number two battle for the national title, or at least the right to play for one in the Cotton Bowl.

"It makes them look wiser than a tree full of owls," Royal said of ABC's decision to televise the game at season's end. He then called it "the Big Shoot-out," meaning it was even larger than the Red River Shoot-out with Oklahoma. Few games before or since have had such buildup. President Richard Nixon, a football fanatic, showed up with Christian evangelist Billy Graham. Vietnam War protesters, a rarity in Dixie, showed up outside the stadium but were drowned out by American hubris and football mania.

It was a classic of classics, with the Razorbacks taking a 14–0 lead into the fourth quarter. Then Street broke a 42-yard touchdown run. The 2-point conversion was successful, setting up a wild finish with the score 14–8, Arkansas. Street rarely passed, even though he was a star baseball pitcher (his son, Huston, was an ace reliever of the Oakland A's). On a fourth-and-3 situation on their own 43 with 4:47 to go, Royal went for broke. Street hit wide receiver Randy Peschel, who despite double coverage gathered it in for a 44-yard gain. Two plays later halfback Jim Bertelsen ran it in for the winning touchdown, 15–14.

After the game, Nixon stirred up a "hornet's nest" by announcing that Texas—before the bowls, and seemingly regardless of the AP poll results—was the national champion. Joe Paterno and Penn State, standing tall at 10–0, were nonplussed (Paterno voted Republican anyway).

Despite Nixon's admonition, the bowl games needed to be played. Penn State took care of Missouri in an Orange Bowl yawner, 10–3, but the Cotton Bowl was the most exciting in that game's history.

Dallas, New Year's Day: Enter the gold helmets of Notre Dame, led by quarterback Joe Theismann. Just like the Arkansas game, Texas fell behind and had to rally. Down 17–14, the Longhorns used running backs Worster and Ted Koy in a relentless ground attack that Notre Dame could not stop. A key fourth-down conversion was made at the Irish 20. Faced with another fourth down on the subsequent set of downs, Royal again went to the rare air as he had against Arkansas. This time Street's pass to Cotton Speyrer was caught in brilliant shoestring fashion. Notre Dame stiffened, but on the third try

Elite Ten by the Numbers

Associated Press NFL Offensive Player of the Year (through 2008)

1. <u>Texas</u>: 4

   Earl Campbell, Houston RB (1978, 1979, 1980); Priest Holmes, Kansas City RB (2002)

2. <u>Southern California</u>: 2

   O. J. Simpson, Buffalo RB (1973); Marcus Allen, Raiders RB (1985)

3. <u>Notre Dame</u>: 2

   Joe Theismann, Washington QB (1983); Joe Montana, San Francisco QB (1989)

4. <u>Alabama</u>: 2

   Ken Stabler, Oakland QB (1974); Shaun Alexander, Seattle RB (2005)

5. <u>Nebraska</u>: 1

   Roger Craig, San Francisco RB (1988)

halfback Billy Dale scored with a little over a minute left to give the Longhorns a 21–17 victory. It was Royal's second national title. The names—Street, Worster, Koy, Dale, Speyrer—go down with names like Sam Houston and Davey Crockett in Texas lore.

But another name stands out. Freddie Steinmark was an undersized, big-hearted defensive back from Colorado. Steinmark played in pain throughout the season, including the win over Arkansas. When the game was over, he figured it was more than an ordinary football injury. Hoping to play as long as he could, he had not seen a doctor, but three days after beating the Razorbacks he was diagnosed with cancer. His leg was amputated, and he had appeared at the Cotton Bowl on crutches.

At first he appeared to be a triumphant hero, accepting the crowd's plaudits and writing an inspirational book, *I Play to Win*. But then the cancer spread. When his hair fell out he took to wearing an earring, pretending he was a one-legged pirate, which got laughs. In the end he was a tragic hero, dying at the age of twenty-two in 1971.

In 1970, Texas returned with many of the same cast of characters. It was another monster year in college football. Preseason number one Ohio State held that spot until October 26, when the AP switched to Texas. On November 9 Notre Dame ascended to the top spot, but their chances were lost when USC upset them, 38–28 in Los Angeles. The Longhorns held off Ohio State and accepted a rematch with Notre Dame in Dallas.

Ohio State lost to Stanford in the Rose Bowl, but it did not matter to Texas. This time, Theismann and the Irish manhandled them, ending their 30-game winning streak with a 24–11 victory that denied UT the title, handing it to Nebraska (winners over LSU in the Orange Bowl).

It was the end of an era, of sorts, although Royal did not leave. Texas integrated after that. Unlike Alabama, integration did not turn them into champions. Their win-loss record in the 1970s was among the best in the country, but they did not attain ultimate glory despite great players and teams. Consensus All-Americans under Royal between

Longhorns on the Run

Year	Record	Run
1968	9–1–1 F/ 9–0	9–1–1 (1968)
	9–0 (1968)	
1969	11–0	20–1–1 (1968–69)
	20–0 (1968–69) **20 games**	
1970	10–1 S/10–0	30–2–1 (1968–69)
	30–1–1 (1968–69)	
	30–0 (1968–69) **30 games**	
	30–1 (1968–69)	
1971	8–3 S/3–0	38–5–1 (1968–69)
	35–4–1 (1968–69) **40 games**	
	33–1 (1968–69)	
	38–4 (1969–70)	
	37–3 (1969–70) **40 games**	

S/Start season; F/Finish season

1963 and 1970 include Scott Appleton, the legendary linebacker Tommy Nobis, Chris Gilbert, Bob McKay, Bobby Wuensch, Steve Worster, and Bill Atessis.

Between 1971 and 1976, Texas football was very strong. This included a 10–1 year in 1972 featuring a 17–13 Cotton Bowl triumph over Alabama. But national attention was focused on the Pac-8, the Big 10, the Big 8, and Notre Dame. Arkansas dropped a notch from their 1960s glory. Fans who saw the 1969 "Game of the Century" were confused. Who was Texas's biggest rival, Arkansas or Texas A&M (whom they played most seasons in the final game)?

In 1974, a big old country boy from Tyler, Texas, showed up in Austin. He would become the greatest of all Longhorns, at least until 2005. Earl Campbell was built like a Mack truck and ran like Jesse Owens. In 1977 under new coach Fred Akers, his pounding runs paved the way to an 11–0 start. The Longhorns rolled over all opposition with the exception of Oklahoma (13–6) and Arkansas (13–9), both of whom were overcome on the strength of defense. Ranked first in the nation, with Campbell capturing the Heisman Trophy, the Longhorns were odds-on favorites to win the national title. Fifth-ranked Notre Dame again entered the Cotton Bowl. Texas, Oklahoma, Alabama, and Michigan all looked stronger than the Irish, but in the pre-BCS days they were locked into bowl commitments.

Notre Dame had lost early. Junior quarterback Joe Montana featured pedestrian numbers while fending off competition for his job. A green-jersey win over USC had the appearance more of mysticism than true gridiron greatness. Washington beat Michigan (Rose), Arkansas beat Oklahoma (Orange), and Alabama beat Ohio State (Sugar). But Notre Dame rose up and beat Texas with aplomb, 38–10, before a mostly disappointed crowd in Dallas. The Irish beat out Alabama for number one.

Texas College Hall of Famers (10)			
Players		Johnnie Johnson	1976–1979
Bud McFadin	1948–1950	Chris Gilbert	1966–1968
Tommy Nobis	1963–1965	Malcolm "Mal" Kutner	1939–1941
Jerry Sisemore	1970–1972	Bud McFadin	1948–1950
Bobby Layne	1944–1947	Harley Sewell	1950–1952
Roosevelt Leaks	1972–1974		
Earl Campbell	1974–1977	*Coaches*	
James Everett Saxton	1959–1961	Dana Bible	1913–1946
Harrison Stafford	1930–1932	Darrell Royal	1954–1976

Texas then entered a long, strange period in which they were almost always good, but always fell short. Consensus All-Americans between 1971 and 2004 were Jerry Sisemore, Bill Wyman, Roosevelt Leaks (who helped break the Texas "color barrier"), Bob Simmons, Brad Shearer, Johnnie Johnson, Steve McMichael, Kenneth Sims, Terry Tausch, Doug Dawson, Jeff Leiding, Jerry Gray, Tony Degrate, Tony Brackens, Dan Neil, Ricky Williams, Leonard Davis, Casey Hampton, Mike Williams, Quentin Jammer, Derrick Dockery, and Derrick Johnson.

Akers was 86–31–2 (.731) between 1977 and 1986. His successor, David McWilliams, ran into difficult times. Their old Cotton Bowl "stomping grounds" was the scene of a brutal 46–3 trouncing at the hands of highly superior Miami on January 1, 1991. Coach John Mackovic had several teams rated highly in preseason polls. None rated as high at the end of the season (when it counts).

The Southwest Conference began to fold, too. Southern Methodist endured the "death penalty" after a series of scandals. Houston, once a powerhouse, fell by the wayside. The Cotton Bowl lost its panache, its early New Year's Day start little-watched by hungover West Coast fans. The stadium itself was considered a "dump." Games such as the Fiesta Bowl surpassed it in importance.

The SWC disbanded, becoming part of the Big 12 South beginning in 1996. Under coach Mack Brown, the move to the Big 12 seemed to have been of little benefit to the Longhorns. Nebraska dominated the league, so if national-title aspirations were to be met, then the road led through Lincoln. It was more perilous than the one Dorothy traveled to deliver the Wicked Witch of the West's broom to the Wizard of Oz.

The great Ricky Williams was snagged from San Diego, of all places, at a time when USC, the school that normally would have had the best shot at such a prospect, was down. Williams ran for 6,279 yards in his career, winning the 1998 Heisman Trophy. But two games with UCLA demonstrated the realities of Longhorn football in the late 1990s. In 1997, Texas smothered the Bruins 66–3. The following year UCLA turned it around, beating them 49–31. By the "Darrel Royal standards," UT was an also-ran.

Between 2000 and 2003, a funny thing happened. Brown's teams were winners. However, they were not ultimate winners. Many times over the course of a number of seasons, preseason polls had declared that "this is Texas's year." Each time they were wrong. It started to resemble the "little boy who cries wolf" syndrome. Highly rated Texas would fall. Some true champion would rise above all others.

Then came Vince Young. Now, Earl Campbell is a Texas legend, and Williams holds records. Young never did win the Heisman Trophy. No matter. He is the greatest player in Longhorn history, and one of the best the college game has ever seen.

Young was something entirely new in football. The size, speed, and athleticism of its athletes increased markedly in the 2000s. Young was built like a linebacker: tall, bulky yet chiseled, with an accurate throwing arm and the ability to run over, around, and through defenders, just like Williams.

Only a loss to Oklahoma in 2004 denied Texas an unbeaten season. With USC heading off to Miami, where they dismantled the Sooners in the BCS Orange Bowl for the national championship, Texas filled their slot in a wild Rose Bowl. Young turned it on, rallying the Longhorns in a stirring 38–37 comeback over Michigan. This set the stage for 2005, a year of memory like none other.

Every preseason publication beginning in the late spring predicted USC number one and Texas number two. For months on end all expectations centered on a meeting between Young's Longhorns and the vaunted Trojans, led by the Heisman duo of Matt Leinart and Reggie Bush. It would be a "game to end all games," and for Texas a return trip to the Rose Bowl.

Nobody was disappointed. Simply put, in the 2005 regular season the Longhorns may have been the greatest college football team of all time, and Young among the greatest players ever. They scored more than 50 points per game, annihilating opponent after opponent in the manner of Sherman marching to the sea. There was only one drawback: USC was better.

If the Longhorns were the second, third, or fourth best team in history, USC was *the* best anybody had ever seen. If Young was better even than Campbell or Williams, he still took a backseat to Bush (who won the Heisman), although by season's end he seemed to have caught up with the heralded Leinart, a feat in and of itself. Young was genuinely disappointed that the Heisman did not come his way. Some saw petulance in his attitude, but in truth he was proud, knew he belonged, and wanted it for the program. He was bound and determined to prove his worth in Pasadena.

The month leading up to the Rose Bowl was surreal. USC fans somehow looked past Texas. Their 66–19 pounding of UCLA resembled Caesar parading the prisoners from Gaul through the streets of Rome. Lost in the banners of glory was the fact that on that very day, Texas beat Colorado in the Big 12 title game by an even larger score, 70–3.

The media descended on Los Angeles, but attention was paid mostly to the Trojans. There was Bush, a whirling dervish running back/kick returner compared to Gale Sayers and Tony Dorsett. Leinart was closing in on a four-year career that pundits said was the best of any college player, ever. That was only half of it. USC owned the town. Leinart was hanging out with celebrities, attending hot parties at the trendiest Hollywood nightclubs.

He, Bush, coach Pete "the prince of the city" Carroll, and several other Trojans ascended to a place on the "glitz meter" above multimillionaire actors and directors; above the professional Lakers and Dodgers. In a town devoid of an NFL franchise, they were considered "L.A.'s pro football team."

ESPN did computer analysis, then announced *prior to the game* that USC was the "greatest college football team of all time." Carroll did his best to keep his team's heads out of the clouds. The reminders of Duke (1938), Tennessee (1939), Ohio State (1969, 1970), Nebraska (1983), and other teams thought to be the "best ever" before getting upset, if they permeated the USC consciousness, they did so fleetingly.

Young, Coach Brown, and Texas observed the whole circus surrounding the hometown Trojans and determined that when the time came they would prove their worth. On game day, Texas fans came out in large numbers—loud, draped in burnt orange, their beautiful women clad in chaps and boots. It was a spectacle. The comparison between the Texas and USC women was a world-class contest in and of itself. But Texas fans were wary. They respected USC and its traditions and demonstrated little in the way of great confidence that victory would be theirs. The Trojans were riding a 34-game winning streak. With victory would come a laundry list of firsts and glorification unlike anything college football has ever seen.

All of this flowery applause for the Trojans serves not to demonstrate their superiority, but rather to highlight just what an incredible accomplishment it was when Texas somehow managed to win the game, 41–38. Only one of the greatest teams in history could have beaten the Trojans, and that is what the Longhorns were. There have been many incredible games over the years, but the 2006 Rose Bowl, considering all of its elements, must be considered the best college game ever played.

The Trojans got out to an early lead and had several opportunities to put it away as they had done against Oklahoma in the previous year's BCS title game. A combination of USC errors—mental and physical—and a tenacious Longhorn team refusing to be intimidated turned things around to the point where Texas led at the half, 16–10.

In the second half, Leinart lived up to all of his billing. USC moved at will against Texas. They held Young on some key possessions to move out to a commanding 38–26 lead with slightly more than six and a half minutes remaining. It looked to be over. Then Young took over, driving his team for a quick touchdown to narrow things to 38–33. USC got the ball back, but on a key fourth-and-1.5 around midfield, Trojan coach Pete Carroll decided to go for it rather than punt deep into Texas territory.

Trojan running back LenDale White, who had bulled through Texas consistently all night, was stopped *inches* short of a first down. It was the first time he had been held, but Texas had their best moment when it counted the most.

"We did it because we did not feel we could stop Young," Carroll explained when asked why they did not punt it away. He was right. Carroll's lack of faith in his defense highlighted something that few really talked about amid the hubris. Despite all the talk about being the "greatest college football team of all time," their "chink in the armor" was his defense, beset by early NFL defections, a few key injuries, and the loss of star defensive back Eric Wright due to a run-in with the law. Young drove his team to the

USC 9. On fourth-and-5 with nineteen seconds to play, he dropped back, saw his receivers covered, then ran for the corner just ahead of Trojan tacklers. Texas had reached the promised land.

In the 2006 NFL Draft, four of the top ten players chosen performed in this game. Bush and Leinart went to New Orleans and Arizona, respectively. Young was passed up by his hometown Houston Texans, a move then seen as one of the dumbest of all time. Tennessee picked him, and he showed flashes of brilliance. Consensus All-American defensive back Michael Huff, winner of the Jim Thorpe Award, went to Oakland. In 2007, Michael Griffin went in the first round to Tennessee. The New York Giants made Aaron Ross their number one pick.

In 2008 quarterback Colt McCoy led Texas to a glorious 12–1 record with victory over Ohio State in the Fiesta Bowl (good for fourth in the polls). The Longhorns were heavy national title contenders and McCoy a Heisman finalist. They entered 2009 with number one aspirations and McCoy a leading Heisman candidate.

After "knocking on the door" for decades, Texas under Mack Brown reestablished themselves as one of the elite collegiate football traditions. In so doing, they highlighted their glorious past. When a college program has been great but falls short of those standards—the faded clippings of Bobby Layne and Tommy Nobis; the grainy footage of James Street and Earl Campbell—it becomes easy to mock as "ancient history." But when the program lives up to its heritage, as the Longhorns finally did in 2005, then the "sharper image" of Vince Young becomes part of a beautiful panorama, a montage of Texas football past and present.

Hook 'em, 'Horns.

Chapter 9

Michigan Wolverines

THEN THERE WAS MICHIGAN. In reading Michigan T-shirts, perusing Michigan media guides, and listening to Michigan fans, one hears a strong argument that the Wolverines are not number nine, but number *one*! They have a good case, which includes the most Division I-A victories (872 through 2008), the best winning record (872–295–36), the most Big 10 championships in the oldest conference (forty-two), and the nation's largest stadium (107,501, sold out every game). They have won seven legitimate national championships but, according to some systems, can be credited with between nine and eleven. Eleven, by the way, is the most of any program (a tie between USC and Notre Dame).

University of Michigan
Ann Arbor, Michigan
Founded: 1817
Enrollment: 23,312
Colors: Maize and blue
Stadium: Michigan Stadium (opened: 1927; capacity: 107,501)
All-time record (1879–2008): 872–295–36
All-time bowl record: 19–20 (through 2009 bowls)
National championships: 1901, 1902, 1918, 1923, 1933, 1948, 1997
Big 10 Conference championships: 42 (through 2008)
Heisman Trophies: Tom Harmon (1940), Desmond Howard (1991), Charles Woodson (1997)
First-round NFL Draftees: 40 (through 2009 draft)
Website: www.mgoblue.com
Notable alumni: Hall of Fame baseball executive Branch Rickey; Hall of Fame baseball player George Sisler; baseball player Jim Abbott; basketball player Chris Webber; U.S. Senator Nancy Kassebaum; attorney Clarence Darrow; playwright Arthur Miller; singer Madonna; actors James Earl Jones and Lucy Liu; network commentator Mike Wallace

While the overall numbers demonstrate Michigan greatness, it is something of a misnomer. The Wolverines started playing, and winning, football games in 1879. Rutherford B. Hayes was the president of the United States. The Civil War ended fourteen years before that, Reconstruction only two years prior. Most non-Ivy League teams did not get around to it until the 1890s. That gives the Wolverines ten-, fifteen-, twenty-year head starts over most of their competitors in the "most wins" race. They are still a great power, to be sure. However, compelling modern sensibilities tell us that they are not the greatest overall program. Their records in the 1880s, 1890s, 1900s, and 1910s simply do not carry the weight of records after World War II, and especially not after 1960 (the unofficial "embarkation point" when the game truly changed into what it is today).

To use an imperfect empire metaphor, Babylon, Persia, Athens, and Rome once ruled the known world. That does not mean Iraq, Iran, Greece, and Italy are the "greatest

National Champions—Pre-World War I Era (1869–1918)

1. Princeton   19 legitimate
   1869, 1870, 1872, 1873, 1874, 1875, 1877, 1878, 1879, 1881,1884, 1885, 1886, 1889, 1893, 1896, 1899, 1903, 1911

2. Yale   12 legitimate
   1876, 1880, 1882, 1883, 1887, 1888, 1891, 1892, 1894, 1900, 1906, 1907

3. Harvard   5 legitimate
   1890, 1898, 1908, 1910, 1912

4. Michigan   3 legitimate
   1901, 1902, 1918

5. Washington   2 legitimate
   1909, 1913

6. Pennsylvania   2 legitimate
   1895, 1897

7. Oregon   1 legitimate
   1916

8. Washington State   1 legitimate
   1915

9. Georgia Tech   1 legitimate
   1917

10. Army   1 legitimate
    1914

11. Chicago   1 legitimate
    1905

12. Stanford   1 legitimate
    1905

13. Minnesota   1 legitimate
    1904

countries of all time." We place more importance on World War II than the Peloponnesian War; more importance on the BCS era than the days of the "Yale wedge."

In many ways, Michigan is the story of America. The Midwest became populated in large part by German and Swedish immigrants of the nineteenth century. A look at Michigan football lists shows the offspring of these sturdy settlers starring on the gridiron for the Wolverines: Adolph Schulz, John Maulbetsch, Harry Kipke, Jack Blott, Benny Friedman, Otto Pommerening, Ralph Heikkinen, Dick Riffenburg, Dan Dierdorf, Ed Muransky, Mike Hammerstein, Mark Messner, Greg Skrepenak. The ethnic makeup of Michigan football over the years is indicative of more than a few laughs over steins of beer at the Ann Arbor German-American *Bund*. It is a sociopolitical statement with profound implications.

In the late 1920s, when Adolf Hitler was rising to power in Germany with plans to take the world to war, he assessed his chances and found, for him at least, a disturbing fact. The loss of the "flower of German manhood" in World War I was bad enough, but Hitler further theorized that the very "best" Germans—the strongest, most able of mind, body, and spirit—had left Germany and taken up allegiance in and with America. These "supermen" were in the 1920s asserting their presence on the sporting fields of the good ol' U.S. of A. Little more than a decade later, men with names like Eisenhower would lead us to victory over their grandfathers' *Fatherland*.

Many of these able young men played football for the University of Michigan. Officially, Michigan was a member of the Western Athletic Conference, but it was dubbed the Big 10. It held that moniker even when teams came and went, but it would not become the official name of the league for decades (1987).

Their first consensus All-American was William Cunningham in 1898, but Michigan football hit the big time with the arrival of coach Fielding H. Yost in 1901. His teams immediately went 11–0 (1901), 11–0 (1902), 11–0–1 (1903), 10–0 (1904), and 12–1 (1905). Yost's teams were known as the "point-a-minute" Wolverines, particularly his 1901 powerhouse that beat Stanford 49–0 in the first Rose Bowl. In many ways the Wolverines "ruined" it for everybody else.

Several schools were invited but declined the invite to Pasadena. Yost's team was willing to take on the challenge of travel (no easy task in 1901–1902) and a big game against a mysterious Western opponent. The whole country would pay attention to its outcome. If the Wolverines lost, their success would be forgotten. But the lopsided score dissuaded the Tournament of Roses from continuing with the game, which held no fan interest past its early moments. The Rose Bowl was discontinued in favor of various lackluster activities until January 1, 1916.

Michigan's success under Yost put the Ivy League on immediate notice that great football was being played "out west." Minnesota and Chicago, seemingly spurred on by Big 10 rival Michigan, joined the party. Consensus Wolverine All-Americans of the 1900s include Neil Snow, Willie Heston, Adolph Schulz, and Albert Benrook.

When World War I broke out, there was concern in the United States that the large German American population in the Midwest would not "choose" America over Germany, but these doubts proved unfounded. Despite prejudice, German Americans fought bravely. Many from the University of Michigan served honorably.

National Champions by Conference—Pre-World War I Era (1869–1918)

INDEPENDENTS (PRE-IVY LEAGUE): 38 LEGITIMATE

Princeton	19 legitimate, 19 consensus, no bowls
Yale	12 legitimate, 12 consensus, no bowls
Harvard	5 legitimate, 5 consensus, no bowls
Pennsylvania	2 legitimate, 2 consensus, no bowls

Princeton: 19 legitimate (1869, 1870, 1872, 1873, 1874, 1875, 1877, 1878, 1879, 1881,1884, 1885, 1886, 1889, 1893, 1896, 1899, 1903, 1911)
Yale: 12 legitimate (1876, 1880, 1882, 1883, 1887, 1888, 1891, 1892, 1894, 1900, 1906, 1907)
Harvard: 5 legitimate (1890, 1898, 1908, 1910, 1912)
Pennsylvania: 2 legitimate (1895, 1897)

INDEPENDENTS: 2 LEGITIMATE

Army	1 legitimate, 1 consensus, no bowls
Georgia Tech	1 legitimate, 1 consensus, no bowls

Army: 1 legitimate (1914)
Georgia Tech: 1 legitimate (1917)

PACIFIC COAST: 5 LEGITIMATE
Pacific Coast Conference formed, 1916

Washington	2 legitimate, 2 consensus, no bowls
Washington State	1 legitimate, 1 consensus, 1 bowl win
Oregon	1 legitimate, 1 consensus, 1 bowl win
Stanford	1 legitimate, no bowls

Washington: 2 legitimate (1909/independent, 1913/independent)
Washington State: 1 legitimate (1915/independent)
Oregon: 1 legitimate (1916)
Stanford: 1 legitimate (1905)

BIG 10: 5 LEGITIMATE

Michigan	3 legitimate, 3 consensus, 1 bowl win
Minnesota	1 legitimate, 1 consensus, no bowls
Chicago	1 legitimate, no bowls

Michigan: 3 legitimate (1901, 1902, 1918)
Minnesota: 1 legitimate (1904)
Chicago: 1 legitimate (1905)

National Champions, Chronological Order—Pre-World War I Era (1869–1918)

No bowl games: 1869–1901, 1903–1915

1869	Princeton 1–1	1886	Princeton 7–0–1
1870	Princeton 1–0	1887	Yale 9–0
1872	Princeton 1–0	1888	Yale 13–0
1873	Princeton 1–0	1889	Princeton 10–0
1874	Princeton 2–0	1890	Harvard 11–0
1875	Princeton 2–0	1891	Yale 13–0
1876	Yale 3–0	1892	Yale 13–0
1877	Princeton 2–0–1	1893	Princeton 11–0
1878	Princeton 6–0	1894	Yale 16–0
1879	Princeton 4–0–1	1895	Pennsylvania 14–0
1880	Yale 4–0–1	1896	Princeton 10–0–1
1881	Princeton 5–0–1	1897	Pennsylvania 15–0
1882	Yale 8–0	1898	Harvard 11–0
1883	Yale 8–0	1899	Princeton 12–1
1884	Princeton 9–0–1	1900	Yale 2–0
1885	Princeton 9–0		

First Rose Bowl played January 1, 1902

1901   Michigan 11–0

    Beat Stanford, 49–0/Rose Bowl

      Other: Harvard 12–0

Rose Bowl discontinued, 1903–15

1902   Michigan 11–0

1903   Princeton 11–0

    Other: Minnesota 14–0–1

1904   Minnesota 13–0

1905   Chicago 10–0, Stanford 8–0 (co-national champions)

1906   Yale 9–0–1

1907   Yale 9–0–1

1908   Harvard 9–0–1

1909   Washington 7–0

    Other: Yale 10–0

1910   Harvard 8–0–1

1911   Princeton 8–0–2

1912   Harvard 9–0

1913   Washington 7–0

      Other: Auburn 8–0

1914   Army 9–0

      Other: Texas 9–0

Rose Bowl resumed January 1, 1916

1915   Washington State 7–0

      Beat Brown, 14–0/Rose Bowl

        Other: Oklahoma 10–0

1916   Oregon 7–0–1

      Beat Pennsylvania, 14–0/Rose Bowl

        Other: *Pittsburgh 8–0

1917   *Georgia Tech 9–0

1918   *Michigan 5–0

*No bowl

Consensus Michigan All-Americans of the 1910s include Stanfield Wells, Miller Pontius, Jim Craig, and John Maulbetsch. In 1918, Michigan (5-0) was credited with the national championship in a season abbreviated by America's total (and victorious) involvement in the Great War, which it was known as until the second World War a little over two decades later.

It was after this season, when the boys came home, that America truly took to its sports, namely big-league baseball and college football. Thus was created the dividing line between the "ancient" and "modern" eras determining how collegiate football is judged. Yost stayed on as Michigan's coach through the unbeaten national championship (8–0) 1923 season. George Little coached in 1924, but Yost returned in 1925 and 1926 before retiring. In 1927, Michigan Stadium, now known as "the Big House," was erected on campus. It was a monument to a sport that America, particularly Midwestern America, had by now gone crazy over.

Fans in all regions fell in love with football, but Midwestern football had a special affinity. It was rugged and manly, a perfect complement to the elements of fall weather. It was a game against Michigan in which Harold "Red" Grange of Illinois compiled more than 400 total yards, thus engendering the classic nickname the Galloping Ghost. Grange made pro football popular when he moved on to Green Bay.

Michigan All-Century Team
Chosen by fans via website

COACH   Bo Schembechler

OFFENSE		DEFENSE	
Pos.	Player	Pos.	Player
OL	Dan Dierdorf	ML	Mark Messner
OL	Reggie McKenzie	DL	Glen Steele
OL	John "Jumbo" Elliott	DL	Chris Hutchinson
OL	Greg Skrepenak	LB	Erick Anderson
OL	Jon Jansen	LB	Jarrett Irons
WR	Bennie Oosterbaan	LB	Ron Simpkins
WR	Anthony Carter	LB	Sam Sword
WR	Desmond Howard	DB	Charles Woodson
QB	Rick Leach	DB	Ty Law
RB	Tom Harmon	DB	Tripp Welborne
RB	Tyrone Wheatley	DB	Tom Curtis
PK	Remy Hamilton	P	Monte Robbins

Consensus All-Americans of the 1920s were Harry Kipke, Jack Blott, Bennie Oosterbaan, Benny Friedman, and Otto Pommerening. Kipke took over the program in 1929. In 1930 they were 8–0–1, followed by records of 8–1–1 (1931), 8–0 (1932), and 7–0–1 (1933). Some services rated the 1932 squad as national champions, although USC is easily the consensus champs of that season. But in 1933, the Wolverines won the title in an undisputed manner. The program took some bad years while Minnesota (under Bernie Bierman) dominated Big 10 play the rest of the decade. Consensus All-Americans in the 1930s were Harry Newman, Francis Wistert, Chuck Bernard, Ralph Heikkinen, and the great Tom Harmon. The most famous of all, however, was an All-American but not a consensus one. Gerald R. Ford starred on the 1932 and 1933 teams. He later served as Speaker of the House, vice president, and then president of the United States from 1974 to 1977.

Michigan also deserves kudos for integrating its program early. The famed Branch Rickey broke baseball's "color barrier" when, as general manager of the Brooklyn Dodgers, he brought Jackie Robinson into the Major Leagues. Rickey was a Michigan graduate. He coached the baseball team when the great George Sisler played there.

Michigan's Record versus Biggest Rivals

Versus Ohio State	57–42–6
Versus Notre Dame	20–15–1

Michigan versus the Elite Ten (95–71–8 through 2008)

Alabama (2–1), Nebraska (3–2–1), Notre Dame (20–15–1), Ohio State (57–42–6), Oklahoma (0–1), Penn State (9–3), Southern California (4–6), Texas (0–1)

Gerald Ford played with a black player named Willis Ward. Georgia Tech refused to play against Ward, so he was forced to listen to the game by radio from the fraternity house. When a Tech player made an intemperate remark, Ford reportedly hit him so hard on the next play that the Tech player was forced out of the game. When Ford next saw Ward, he told him, "We got one of 'em for ya, Willie."

Fritz Crisler took over in 1938. He coached at Michigan from 1938 to 1947, during which time he compiled a 71–16–3 (.806) record. Crisler's greatest player was the 1940 Heisman winner, Tom Harmon. Known as Ol' 98, he remains the ultimate Michigan football legend. *Life* magazine put him on its cover with the headline "Michigan's Great Harmon." On September 28, 1940, at Berkeley's Memorial Stadium, the six-foot, one-inch, 195-pounder ran the opening kickoff back for a touchdown, returned a punt 72 yards for a TD, and scored two other times on runs of 86 and 8 yards. On the 86-yard run, a drunken Cal fan named Bud Brennan ran out of the stands to try to tackle Harmon.

In World War II, Harmon's plane was shot down twice. Both times he was listed as missing in the Pacific jungles. He survived and was rescued, earning the Silver Star, the Purple Heart, and a position in the pantheon of well-deserved American hero worship. He was the first pick in the NFL Draft and played for the Los Angeles Rams. In L.A. he took to the Hollywood scene.

Harmon married a beautiful actress, Elyse Knox. He became a popular Southern California sportscaster. His son, Mark Harmon, quarterbacked UCLA to a 1972 upset of Nebraska in the Coliseum, ending the Cornhuskers' 32-game unbeaten streak. Tom announced the game. Mark, a gifted, handsome actor, has had a long, successful career in the movies.

Harmon's time was a fateful period in the history of Michigan, the Big 10, college football, and America, not necessarily in that order. A shift was seen in the conference, with Ohio State under coach Paul Brown briefly assuming dominance in the wake of great years under Bernie Bierman at Minnesota.

Elite Ten by the Numbers

Top 20/25 Associated Press—final poll rankings (1936–2006)

1.	Michigan	54	5.	Southern California	43
2.	Notre Dame	48	6.	Nebraska	40
2.	Ohio State	48	7.	Miami	28
4.	Alabama	46			

Michigan State was not yet in the Big 10. Michigan refused to play them, since to do so would elevate the Spartans closer to their level. Later, they would fight against Michigan State's entrance into the conference. The natural rivalry between the states of Michigan and Ohio manifested itself on the football field. For years the Wolverines denied that Ohio State was their main rival, as if to do so was to admit that the Buckeyes were in their "league" athletically, academically, and socially. A sense of class envy developed between the two schools, which still exists today. But by the time Crisler took over in Ann Arbor, there was no more denying it. In 1942 the Buckeyes won their first national championship under Brown.

While Michigan had won national championships in various systems, they had also been denied. They had won their first on the strength of beating Stanford in the 1902 Rose Bowl. Ohio State had lost to California in the 1921 Rose Bowl. After that, Big 10 teams had eschewed the Rose Bowl. In 1932, the Wolverines might have earned a legitimate national title, which went instead to USC on the strength of their Rose Bowl victory. Michigan sat at home on New Year's Day, 1933.

Minnesota managed to win three straight without the benefit of bowl victories. Some also noted that their titles may have occurred because they chanced no bowl *defeats*. In 1934 Minnesota was cochampion along with Alabama, winners of the Rose Bowl. The "no bowl" Golden Gophers were forced to share the 1940 title when Stanford beat Nebraska in Pasadena. The Big 10 saw some of its prestige waning. Southern schools caught up to the rest of the college football world because they played in Rose Bowls. With the creation of the Cotton, Orange, and Sugar Bowls they had ample opportunity to further show their wares.

A natural arrangement was entered into whereby the champions of the Big 10 would meet the champions of the Pacific Coast Conference in the Rose Bowl. This would have the effect of first glorifying the Big 10 as the most prestigious conference in the country. Over time it would serve to shed light on its overrated position in the hierarchy.

Michigan made their first appearance in Pasadena since 1902 on January 1, 1948. Probably the greatest Michigan team of all time brought a 9–0 mark into a game against Southern California. Great expectations were heaped upon this contest, considered a battle not just for a football game played in 1948 but also for national prestige representing the first half of the twenty-first century. Here were two of the most storied programs in the nation. The nature of "East versus West," or at least "Midwest versus West," meant this was for bragging rights and regional supremacy.

There was a third team in the Rose Bowl that day, although they were not there in physical presence. Notre Dame was Southern California's all-time great rival, and teams—like Michigan—wanted to discredit the Trojans (and by some kind of proxy, Notre Dame) by asserting themselves as USC's betters. In 1947 this premise was made even more obvious by virtue of the fact that Michigan and Notre Dame were locked in a head-to-head struggle for the national championship. Because of the AP's prebowl vote, Notre Dame—and this may have been the best team in Irish history—had been declared number one with no bowl game to besmirch them. Michigan had been denied the title, but if they could beat USC then they could establish at least a sense of equality with Notre Dame.

Washington coach Gil Dobie led the Huskies to a 63-game unbeaten streak.

Notre Dame's John Lattner won the 1953 Heisman Trophy.

TENNESSEE

1987 UNIVERSITY OF TENNESSEE FOOTBALL GUIDE

VOLS' JOHNNY MAJORS ELECTED TO COLLEGE HALL OF FAME

Tennessee head football coach Johnny Majors was elected into the College Hall of Fame

Washington coaching legend Don James

Former Pitt All-American Mike "Iron Mike" Ditka as head coach of the New Orleans Saints

Action shot of former USC Heisman trophy recipient running back Charles White

Herschel Walker played running back for the University of Georgia, where he was an All-American and won the 1982 Heisman Trophy

They did not merely *beat* the Trojans, they *destroyed* them by a score of 49–0. It was the identical score they had defeated Stanford by forty-six years earlier. It had the effect of establishing Big 10 dominance over the PCC that would take years to overcome.

"The Big 10 looked at the Rose Bowl as a chance to hang out at the beach and meet pretty girls," recalled legendary USC football announcer Tom Kelly. "The football game was just an after-thought, it was so automatic they'd win in those years."

In 1948, the Trojans provided a slight favor to Michigan when they tied Notre Dame. It was just enough of a tarnish to drop the Irish to number two. Former All-American Bennie Oosterbaan took over from Crisler that season. This time unable to go to Pasadena because they had been there the previous year, the unbeaten, untied Wolverines finished with the national championship. Consensus All-Americans of the 1940s include Bob Westfall, Albert Wistert, Julie Franks, Bill Daley, Bob Chappuis, and Dick Rifenburg.

On January 1, 1951, Michigan upset favored California in the Rose Bowl, 14–6. After that, aside from a 34–7 Rose Bowl victory over Oregon State in 1965, Michigan football entered its longest period of decline under Oosterbaan and Bump Elliott. They would not truly begin to regain lost stature again until 1969. What made it even more frustrating were two facts. Ohio State under Woody Hayes established themselves as the cream of the Big 10 and a national powerhouse. That was bad enough, but in 1952 *Michigan State*, playing as an independent, won the national championship. In 1953, against the vote of Michigan's representative, the Spartans were admitted into the Big 10 Conference. As if to deny Michigan State their just due, Michigan continued to play Ohio State in the last game of the season, refusing to view the Spartans as equal rivals.

Michigan disdained everything about Michigan State—their green jerseys; their factory town surroundings (East Lansing); and their academic inferiority, at least in Michigan's view when compared to their own student-athlete reputation.

Michigan State did not care. They simply exuded excellence on the field. Duffy Daugherty took over in East Lansing in 1954. For the next thirteen years he and Woody Hayes at Ohio State had the best program in the Big 10. Only one Michigan player made consensus All-American in the 1950s (Ron Kramer). Four earned the honor in the 1960s (Bill Yearby, Jack Clancy, Jim Mandich, and Tom Curtis).

But in 1969 Michigan hired a former Ohio State assistant coach named Glenn "Bo" Schembechler. He immediately improved the Wolverines, but Ohio State had beaten them 50–14 the previous year and were considered to be *better* than the 1968 national championship team.

The week of the game, Schembechler had the Michigan scout team wear jerseys that all read number 50, to remind the Wolverines of the half-century score the Buckeyes had pasted on them in 1968. Ohio State got off to a 12–0 lead at Michigan Stadium, but the Wolverine defense stiffened. Quarterback Don Moorhead engineered a glorious comeback win, 24–12.

Fritz Crisler watched it on television. Afterward he wrote Schembechler a letter telling how he shed tears of joy over "the greatest upset I have ever seen." In 1970,

Wolverines on the Run

Year	Record	Run
1900	7–2–1	
1901	11–0	
1902	11–0	
1903	11–0–1 S/6–0, 6–0–1, F/5–0	33–0–1 (1901–03)
		28–0 (1901–03)
		28–0–1 (1901–03)
		29–0–1 (1901–03) **30 games**
1904	11–0	
1905	12–1	
1906	4–1	
1907	5–1	
1908	5–2–1	
1909	6–1	83–8–3 (1900–09) **decade: 1900s**
1929	5–3–1 F/3–0–1	5–3–1 (1929)
		3–0–1 (1929)
1930	8–0–1	13–3–2 (1929–30)
		11–0–2 (1929–30)
1931	8–1–1 F/5–0–1, 2–0	21–4–3 (1929–31)
		19–1–3 (1929–31)
		5–0–1 (1931)
		2–0 (1931)
1932	8–0	29–4–3 (1929–32)
		27–1–3 (1929–32)
		26–1–3 (1929–32) **30 games**
		13–0–1 (1931–32)
		10–0 (1931–32)
1933	7–0–1	36–4–3 (1929–33)
		34–1–4 (1929–32)
		20–0–1 (1931–33)
		17–0–1 (1931–33)
1946	6–2–1 F/4–0	6–2–1 (1946)
		4–0 (1946)
1947	10–0	16–2–1 (1946–47)
		14–0 (1946–47)
1948	9–0	25–2–1 (1946–47)
		23–0 (1946–47)

1949	6–2–1 S/2–0	31–4–2 (1946–47)
		25–0 (1946–47)
1970	9–1	9–1 (1970)
1971	11–1	20–1 (1970–71)
1972	10–1	30–3 (1970–72)
1973	10–0–1	40–3–1 (1970–71)
1974	10–1	50–4–1 (1970–74)
1975	8–2–2	58–6–3 (1970–75)
1976	10–2 S/2–1	68–8–3 (1970–76)
		60–7–3 **70 games**
1977	10–2	78–10–3 (1970–77)
		78–9–3 (1970–77) **90 games**
1978	10–2	88–12–3 (1970–78)
		88–11–3 (1970–78) **100 games**
1979	8–4 S/1–0	96–16–3 **(decade: 1970s)**
		79–9–3 (1970–77)
		94–13–5 (1970–79) **110 games**

S/Start season; F/Finish season

the Michigan-Ohio State game was more like George Patton and Erwin Rommel, or maybe Wellington and Napoleon. Both Hayes and Schembechler were viewed as football "generals," not just because of their disciplinarian demeanors but because they preferred ground-oriented offensive styles, reminding pundits of an infantry assault. Both teams were unbeaten and untied when they played in Columbus. The national title was up in the air, with the AP waiting to vote until after the bowls. Ohio State gained revenge, 20–9.

But it was the 1972 Rose Bowl that somehow, frustratingly, epitomized the Bo Schembechler era at Michigan. While it is true that Nebraska held the number one spot all year and was not about to relinquish it, nevertheless Michigan woke up on New Year's Day with hopes that a national title could be theirs if they beat Stanford. It was a long shot (the national title, not beating Stanford), but crazier things have happened.

A look at Michigan's 1971 football scores leaves the reader in awe, asking the question, "Could it be possible *anybody* was ever better?" Only one team scored more than 10 points against them in the regular season. In retrospect the Big 10 was slow and far too ground-oriented by 1971, but when a pretty good UCLA team visited Ann Arbor in September, they were sent home with their tails between their legs, 38–0.

Then there was Stanford. In 1971, Stanford represented something more than just a pretty good football team trying to revive memories of thirty-year-old glories. They had become a center of revolutionary political activity during the Vietnam War. In the

Michigan's College Hall of Famers (30)

Players			
		Bob Chappuis	1942–1947
Germany Schulz	1904–1908	Bump Elliott	1943–1947
Ernie Vick	1918–1921	Tom Harmon	1938–1940
Albert Benbrook	1908–1910	Willie Heston	1898–1904
Reggie McKenzie	1969–1971	Crazylegs Hirsch	1943
Dan Dierdorf	1968–1970	Ron Johnson	1966–1968
Merv Pregulman	1941–1943	Harry Kipke	1921–1923
Albert Wistert	1940–1942	Neil Snow	1898–1901
Alvin Wistert	1946–1949	Bob Westfall	1939–1941
Francis Wistert	1931–1933	Tom Curtis	1967–1969
Ron Kramer	1954–1956	Dave Brown	1972–1974
Bennie Oosterbaan	1925–1927		
Neil Snow	1898–1901	Coaches	
Jim Mandich	1967–69	Bo Schembechler	1969–1989
Anthony Carter	1979–1982	Tad Wieman	1927–1942
Benny Friedman	1924–1926	Fielding Yost	1897–1926
Harry Newman	1930–1932		

view of people like Bo Schembechler and Woody Hayes, the "Jane Fonda" wing of the protest movement deserved nothing less than a treason sentence. Schools like Stanford and California had, in their view, allowed their campuses to become rallying grounds for Communism. They could stomach losing to USC, but Stanford? This *was* war!

In 1970, Ohio State needed only to beat a good, but not great, Stanford squad to capture the national championship. They led early but folded in a 27–17 loss. However, Stanford had been led by the great Jim Plunkett, the Heisman Trophy winner, number one pick in the NFL Draft, and eventually a two-time Super Bowl champion. That made them a worthy conqueror.

But in 1971 nobody gave Stanford half a chance. Traditional powers USC and UCLA were expected to dominate the Pac-8. The Trojans, however, were beset by racial animosities in 1971. A red-shirt senior quarterback named Don Bunce led Stanford, whose defense was given the uniquely northern California appellation Thunder Chickens. Bunce was smart; he was just starting medical school and would be Stanford's team doctor for years. But as a college quarterback he was no Jim Plunkett. He might have been able to handle the chores at Michigan, where the signal-caller did little but hand it off to a ball carrier in what was now more like a "nine yards and a cloud of dust" offense.

Bunce certainly did not light up the sky against Michigan, but the Thunder Chickens had no trouble containing the predictable Wolverine ground attack. Stanford held a slim lead late in the game when Michigan tied it up, 10–10. It looked as if it would end in stalemate, like Flanders or the Somme with fewer casualties. When Michigan's kickoff was mishandled into a costly safety, Wolverine fans whooped it up, sort of. Later that night Alabama would play Nebraska. The Wolverines had been so mediocre that a 12–10 win over Stanford courtesy of a "gimme" safety had no chance of impressing voters regardless of who won in the Orange Bowl. That said, it was still better than a *loss*. To the *Thunder Chickens*!

Stanford had just enough time, though. Bunce suddenly looked like Johnny Unitas in 1958, revealing another inconvenient truth, which was that Michigan's—and by proxy the Big 10's—defense could not stop a passing team. Bunce got the Indians (they dropped Indians and went to Cardinal a year later, in solidarity with the Indian takeover of Alcatraz Island in San Francisco Bay) within field goal range. On came Rod Garcia. Against world-beating San Jose State earlier in the season, all Garcia had done was miss two extra points and several chip field goals, including one with no time left, to give the Spartans a 13–12 win over Stanford. This time he was as straight and true as William Tell. The Stanford fans went wild in the wake of the 13–12 win. Michigan's people looked for a rock to crawl under and hide.

Between 1972 and 1974 Michigan was 30–2–1. In 1973, after a 10–10 tie with Ohio State, the Big 10 athletic directors voted for Ohio State to go to the Rose Bowl, the first-ever repeat team from the conference. First-year Michigan State athletic director Burt Smith voted for Ohio State. Some said it was revenge for Michigan trying to keep the Spartans out of the Big 10 in 1953. Others said it was because Michigan quarterback Dennis Franklin was hurt, meaning Ohio would have the better chance in Pasadena (where they in fact won big over Southern Cal). In truth, Michigan kicker Mike Lantry missed tries of 58 and 48 yards, both in the last 1:08. The Wolves had their chances.

"This is the lowest day of my career as a player and coach," Schembechler said after the vote.

The Wolverines went to the Rose Bowl following the 1976, 1977, and 1978 seasons. Each time they were sent home in defeat, always because their ground-oriented offense

Elite Ten by the Numbers

Win-loss records (through 2008)

1.	Michigan (1879–2008)	872–295–36
2.	Notre Dame (1887–2008)	831–284–42
3.	Texas (1893–2008)	832–316–33
4.	Ohio State (1890–2008)	808–305–53
5.	Oklahoma (1895–2008)	791–297–53
6.	Southern California (1888–2008)	766–303–54
7.	Nebraska (1890–2008)	817–337–41
8.	Alabama (1892–2008)	750–307–44
9.	Penn State (1887–2008)	800–349–42
10.	Miami (1926–2008)	544–310–19

was predictable and too easy to stop when faced with a quality opponent. When Michigan was not going to Pasadena, Ohio State was. After the 1974 defeat of USC, Woody and then coach Earle Bruce fared no better. It was a complete turnaround. The Pac-8, now the Pac-10 beginning in 1978, was thoroughly dominant.

Consensus All-Americans in the 1970s were Dan Dierdorf, Reggie McKenzie, Mike Taylor, Paul Seymour, Randy Logan, Dave Gallagher, Dave Brown, Rob Lytle, Mark Donahue, and Ron Simpkins.

In 1978, Michigan revived the Notre Dame rivalry. It had begun when Michigan was a power, the Irish an unknown Catholic school on the prairies, but it had not been maintained. Eventually after 1978, the game became a home-and-home fixture every September, its outcome promising to foretell national championship fortunes. When Notre Dame went on a long run of dominance over USC, Michigan continued to play them tough every season. It indicated a swing back to the Big 10.

On January 1, 1981, Bo finally got a win in the Rose Bowl, 23–6 over Washington. In the 1980s, with bowl opportunities expanding, Michigan had mixed success in postseason contests but lost in two Rose Bowl games against UCLA (1983) and Arizona State (1987). On January 2, 1989, Michigan was out of the national championship picture when they returned to the Rose Bowl. USC, their opponent, had been in the hunt all year until losing a disastrous season-ending game to Notre Dame. This was a new, lesser version of the once great Trojans. Under coach Larry Smith, Southern California seemed to have lost pride in themselves, mailing in an uninspired performance against the Wolverines. Michigan running back Leroy Hoard could not be stopped. Bo had his "most satisfying" victory ever, 22–14.

(Both Woody Hayes and Bo Schembechler have referred to Rose Bowl wins over Southern California as their respective "biggest" and "most satisfying" wins ever.)

The next year, it was the same old story: USC 17, Michigan 10. Consensus All-Americans in the 1980s were the great receiver Anthony Carter, Ed Muransky, Kurt Becker,

Elite Ten by the Numbers

Top 20/25 Associated Press—all poll rankings (1936–2008)

1. Michigan	747	
2. Ohio State	746	
3. Notre Dame	703	
4. Oklahoma	672	
5. Southern California	666	
6. Nebraska	637 (through 2007)	
7. Texas	651	
8. Alabama	625	
9. Penn State	556	

Mike Hammerstein, Brad Cochran, Jumbo Elliott, John Vitale, Mark Messner, and Tripp Welborne.

Gary Moeller took over the program in 1990. In 1991, Desmond Howard won the Heisman Trophy. His famous "pose" in the end zone after scoring a touchdown seemed apropos. Moeller's teams were 44–13–3 between 1990 and 1994, with one blowout loss to Washington (34–14, 1992) and one hard-fought win over the Huskies (38–31, 1993) in two Rose Bowls.

Lloyd Carr became their coach in 1997, returning Michigan to glory. Led by Heisman Trophy winner Charles Woodson and quarterback Brian Griese, the Wolverines went 12–0 and beat Ohio State (20–14) and Washington State (21–16) in the Rose Bowl to finish number one.

Tom Brady came out of the Michigan program, where he was a fair quarterback considered less than a major NFL prospect. In New England he developed into the greatest signal-caller since Joe Montana. Brady is a surefire Hall of Famer. Consensus All-Americans in the 1990s and 2000s have included Greg Skrepenak, Desmond Howard, Jarrett Irons, Charles Woodson, Steve Hutchinson, Chris Perry, Braylon Edwards, David Baas, Marlin Jackson, Ernest Shazor, and Jake Long. Leon Hall was Cincinnati's number one draft pick in 2007. Long was the number one overall pick (Miami, 2008).

But the Carr years have proven to be frustrating. After the national championship glory of 1997, the Wolverines were always strong but beginning with the 2003 season could not win bowl games.

This included a thrilling 38–37 loss to Vince Young and Texas in the 2005 Rose Bowl and two semiblowouts at the hands of obviously superior Southern California teams in the 2004 and 2007 Rose Bowls. In 2006, Michigan and Ohio State ran the table, leading to another "Game of the Century" with the Buckeyes' Heisman Trophy-winning quarterback Troy Smith in Columbus. The game lived up to its billing, but in the end Michigan came out on the losing side of a 42–39 score. What happened after that was an embarrassment.

USC moved ahead of Michigan in the polls to the number two spot, setting up a BCS title game with Ohio State, which did not bother anybody. When the Trojans lost to UCLA, however, Florida jumped ahead of Michigan, causing many to cry foul.

Then they played the bowls.

Elite Ten by the Numbers
Victories (through 2008)

1.	Michigan	872	6.	Penn State	800
2.	Texas	832	7.	Oklahoma	791
3.	Notre Dame	831	8.	Southern California	766
4.	Nebraska	817	9.	Alabama	750
5.	Ohio State	808	10.	Miami	544

Did You Know . . .
That Michigan has produced thirty-one All-Pro selections (through 2005)?

Both Ohio State and Michigan would have been better off staying at home, as they had often done in the old days. Forced to actually compete on the field, Smith and Ohio State were beaten up and down the field by Florida. The Wolverines were at least competitive for a little more than half a game before the Trojans established their dominance in the Rose Bowl. All arguments on behalf of Ohio State, Michigan, and the Big 10 became mere synapses in the air. It was obvious that Florida was the best team in the nation, and further obvious that had USC played Ohio State, while they likely would not have beaten the Bucks as thoroughly as the Gators had, they too were clearly better.

The 2007 bowl games are a microcosm of Big 10 frustration in the modern era. The first and at one point the most prestigious conference was an also-ran in comparison with the historically superior records of the Pacific-10 and Southeastern Conferences. Ohio State and Michigan, longtime stalwarts of the college game who no doubt will remain so for years, decades, could not make the argument that they were still *the* dominant college powers. Michigan has a long list of gaudy accomplishments, but when giving greater credence to glory achieved lately as opposed to glory achieved long ago, they lose points in the harsh sunshine of modern football history. No matter where they rank among college football's all-time top 25 traditions, Michigan represents the kind of passion that makes the college game a cut above the mercenary pros. "Hail to Michigan."

Winningest Tradition

Through the 2006 season the University of Michigan:

- Is the winningest school in college football history (860 wins)
- Has a .746 all-time winning percentage
- Has the highest all-time strength of schedule rating in college football
- Has been named national champions by at least some source eleven times (1901, 1902, 1903, 1904, 1918, 1923, 1932, 1933, 1947, 1948, 1997)
- Has won forty-two conference championships (more than any school in any single conference)
- Has 113 winning seasons (most in college football)
- Has twenty-five undefeated seasons (more than any other Division 1-A school)
- Is one of only three schools with a winning record versus every Division 1-A conference including independents
- Has a 56-game unbeaten streak (second longest in college football history)
- Went thirty-nine straight years without a losing season (longest ongoing streak in the nation)

Chapter 10

Penn State Nittany Lions

PENN STATE FOOTBALL IS a study in duality. Do the Nittany Lions benefit from "East Coast bias," or suffer a bias *against* East Coast football? Certainly, East Coast football was the kingpin in the early days of the collegiate game. The Ivy League dominated. Army, and to a lesser extent Navy, were powerhouses in one way or another until the early 1960s. Over the years, however, the Ivy League fell by the wayside; Army and Navy dropped precipitously. When Notre Dame (with a few exceptions) refused to play them, the Catholic schools fell in prestige. Boston College remains competitive. Pittsburgh has a long and storied history. Syracuse's all-time record would surprise a few people, and lately Rutgers has started to make some noise. Penn State, however, is the kingpin of East Coast football. They have won the Lambert Trophy, signifying "Eastern football supremacy," twenty-seven times. The term "Eastern football" was a common expression, especially when applied to Army's great teams, which was meant as a catch-phrase for "American supremacy."

Penn State University
University Park, Pennsylvania
Founded: 1855
Enrollment: 35,000
Colors: Blue and white
Stadium: Beaver Stadium (opened: 1960; capacity: 107,282)
All-time record (1887–2008): 800-349-42
All time bowl record: 26-13-2 (through 2009 bowls)
National championships: 1982, 1986
Big 10 Conference championships: 3 (through 2008)
Heisman Trophies: John Cappelletti (1973)
Outland Trophies: Mike Reid (1969)
First-round NFL Draftees: 35 (through 2009 draft)
Website: www.gopsusports.com
Notable alumni: Pennsylvania governor Tom Ridge; U.S. Senator Rick Santorum; astronaut Guion Buford; political commentator Margaret Carlson; Olympian Mary Ellen Clark

The rise of Southern, Midwestern, and West Coast college football was inexorable. By the late 1960s there was little doubt that the best, most competitive football was played in these three regions, over and above that played on the East Coast. Still, the so-called East Coast bias remains, at least in the minds of some. Population shifts and demographics may mean that more great athletes and teams rise from the "Sunbelt," but that has not stopped New York City from being a media center. This is still where the influence, the writers, the networks, and of course many of the votes for such things as most valuable player awards, Heisman Trophies, and national championships emanate from.

Penn State earns its way into the Elite Ten by virtue of tradition, but above and beyond its accomplishments between the 1920s and the 1950s, it established itself as a national—not simply an Eastern—powerhouse in the modern era, which is also "the Joe Paterno era."

Pennsylvania is and always has been football crazy. It is a lunch-pail state, a blue-collar region of coal miners and steelworkers. The people are rough and coarse, "shot 'n' a beer" types. But Pennsylvania struggled to find sports Nirvana.

The Pittsburgh Pirates were a baseball power in the early twentieth century but too often an also-ran in the succeeding decades. The Philadelphia A's had two major dynasties but sold them off to pay the bills. The Pittsburgh Steelers were just plain bad.

There was Pitt and Penn State football. Pitt was better. Then came Joe Pa. This ushered in a new era in Pennsylvania sports greatness. The Pirates became champions in the 1970s. The Steelers established the best decade in pro football history up until that time. Penn State passed Pitt and turned Happy Valley into a college football Mecca.

More than 100,000 fans show up for games. Penn State is known as "Linebacker U.," having produced such stalwarts as LaVar Arrington and Jack Ham. They are on the "right side of history" when it came to integration. Under Paterno, Penn State managed to be a winner on the field and in the classroom. Five Nittany Lions players (Lenny Moore, Jack Ham, Franco Harris, Mike Munchak, August Michalske) have been inducted into the Pro Football Hall of Fame.

But Penn State had winning teams every single season from 1939 to 1964. The annual grudge match with Pitt (both teams were independents until Penn State joined the Big 10 in 1993) was one of the best rivalries in the nation.

Hugo Bezdek coached at Penn State from 1918 to 1929. In 1922, Penn State accepted an invitation to play one of the most historical football games of all time. The Rose Bowl stadium was completed that year. The Nittany Lions traveled to Pasadena to take on Southern California. What happened on January 1, 1923, was a portent of things to come.

Los Angeles and environs were already a car-crazy culture. The Penn State team got *caught in traffic* on their way to the stadium. USC's players and coach Elmer "Gloomy Gus" Henderson sat around wondering if their opponents would make an appearance. The fans wanted to know if there would be a game.

Finally, Penn State showed up. Henderson inquired of Bezdek what happened. An argument ensued. Bezdek somehow figured the traffic was a USC plot to throw his team off. Henderson thought it was meant to take the edge off his charges. Punches were almost thrown. The game, a 14–3 Trojan victory, featured bad blood. The traffic delay caused a late start. The early-setting winter sun hid behind the San Gabriel Mountains by game's end, which was played in the dusk. Fans could barely see what was going on. Afterward Bezdek, a former pugilist of some note, wanted to fight Henderson. This catastrophe was avoided, ostensibly because Henderson wore glasses.

Penn State football was solid but not spectacular in the succeeding decades. Pitt won the 1937 national championship and made several Rose Bowl appearances, but Penn State did not play in a bowl game again until a 1948 13–13 Cotton Bowl tie with Doak Walker and Southern Methodist.

The integration of the Penn State program proved problematic, as it did with a number of Northern schools, in the 1950s. Alabamians complained long and loud about having to play them in the 1959 Liberty Bowl, a 7–0 Lion victory. Consensus All-Americans between 1906 and 1964 include Mother Dunn, Bob Higgins, Charles Way, Glenn Killinger, Harry Wilson, Rich Lucas, and Glenn Ressler.

In 1966, the school hired Joe Paterno. He was a graduate of Brown University, where he had been an English major. His family wanted him to go to law school, but he became an assistant football coach at Penn State. Later he said that he "never wanted to coach

Penn State All-Century Team

Chosen by Lou Prato, *Penn State Football Encyclopedia* and director of the Penn State All-Sports Museum

OFFENSE		DEFENSE	
Pos.	Player	Pos.	Player
G	Joe Bedenk	DE	Sam Tamburo
G	Glenn Ressler	DE	Dave Robinson
G	Sean Farrell	DT	Bruce Clark
G	Mike Munchak	DT	Mike Reid
TE	Bob Higgins	LB	Mother Dunn
TE	Ted Kwalick	LB	Dennis Onkotz
QB	Glenn Killinger	DB	Neal Smith
QB	Kerry Collins	LB	Jack Ham
WR	Kenny Jackson	LB	LaVar Arrington
WR	Bobby Engram	DB	Harry Wilson
RB	Harry Wilson	DB	Lenny Moore
RB/KR	Lenny Moore	DB	Rich Lucas
RB/KR	Curt Warner	DB	Mark Robinson
FB	Matt Suhey	P	Joe Colone
PK/FB	Pete Mauthe		

football," but it got into him and stuck. He was an assistant in Happy Valley for sixteen years before taking over.

Entering the 2005 season, Paterno coached sixty-nine first-team All-Americans and twenty-three Academic All-Americans. In 2000, the NCAA reported that his graduation rate was seventy-five percent. The *library* at Penn State was named after him. He also had 383 career victories entering the 2009 season. He passed Bear Bryant for the most victories among all Division I-A coaches, and, in an ongoing "battle" with Florida State's Bobby Bowden, is one victory ahead.

Penn State was 5–5 in Paterno's first year (1966). But after that they separated themselves from the pack. Paterno still says his 1968 team was the best ever. They put Penn State on the map; certainly it elevated them above the moniker "Eastern power" to a national one. Junior tackles Mike Reid and Steve Smear set the tone. Linebacker Jack Ham led the Rover Boys. Quarterback Chuck Burkhart "can't run and he can't pass," said Paterno. "All he does is think and win." Penn State went 10–0, then beat Kansas 15–14 in the Orange Bowl, one of the greatest games ever played. But everybody was watching the Rose Bowl. Unbeaten Ohio State's victory over USC in that year's "Game of the Century" made the Buckeyes' national title a fait accompli.

But in 1969 Paterno and Penn State's supporters started to get mad. They were 11–0 with a 10–3 win over Missouri in the Orange Bowl, but Texas captured the national championship. If the pollsters had voted with social pathos in 1966, when they awarded integrated, once-tied Notre Dame with the national championship over segregated, un-beaten, untied Alabama, there was no such sentiment favoring Paterno's racially diverse 1969 team in comparison with the now archaic all-white Longhorns.

No less an "authority" than President Richard Nixon "awarded" the national championship to Texas coach Darrell Royal in the winning dressing room following their 15–14 win over Arkansas.

"How could Nixon know so little about Watergate and so much about football?" Paterno, a lifelong Republican who even spoke at the GOP national convention, quipped years later.

Penn State had a 30-game unbeaten streak after beating Missouri and would extend that by one more game in 1970. From 1967 to 1974, his teams were 80–10–1. They were unbeaten in 1968, 1969, and 1973 but were not awarded with any national titles (which went to Ohio State '68, Texas '69, and Notre Dame '73).

In 1968, Ted Kwalick made consensus All-American. He later starred at tight end for the San Francisco 49ers. Dennis Onkotz, Mike Reid, Jack Ham (who starred in Pittsburgh with Franco Harris on Super Bowl champions), Dave Joyner, Bruce Bannon, John Skorupan, and John Cappelletti were also consensus All-Americans.

Cappelletti is Penn State's version of the Gipper, only his story—or really the story of his younger brother Joey—is real inspiration, not manufactured. Cappelletti won the 1973 Heisman Trophy, then announced at his acceptance speech that the award was for his little brother, battling leukemia. The story was made into an inspirational movie, *Something for Joey*, after he died in 1976. Consensus All-Americans between 1974 and

Nittany Lions on the Run

Year	Record	Run
1967	8–2–1 F/7–0–1	8–2–1 (1967)
		7–0–1 (1967)
1968	11–0	19–2–1 (1967–68)
		18–0–1 (1967–68)
1969	11–0	30–2–1 (1967–69)
		29–0–1 (1967–69) **30 games**
1970	7–3 S/1–0 F/5–0	37–5–1 (1967–70)
		30–0–1 (1967–70)
		5–0 (1970)
1971	11–1	38–6–1 (1967–71)
		16–1 (1970–71)
1972	10–2	48–8–1 (1967–72)
		26–3 (1970–72)
1973	12–0	60–8–1 (1967–73)
		38–3 (1970–73)
		38–2 (1970–73) **40 games**
1974	10–2	70–10–1 (1967–73)
		69–10–1 (1967–73) **80 games**
		61–8–1 (1967–74) **70 games**
		48–5 (1970–74)
		45–5 (1970–73) **50 games**
1975	9–3	79–13–1 (1967–75)
		78–11–1 (1967–75) **90 games**
		57–8 (1970–75)
		54–6 (1970–75) **60 games**

S/Start season; F/Finish season

1979 were Mike Hartenstine, Greg Buttle, Keith Dorney, quarterback Chuck Fusina, and Bruce Clark.

Paterno's next best shot at a national championship came in 1978, when his team was unbeaten and ranked number one. Given the opportunity to finally win it on the field, the Nittany Lions fell to Alabama in the Sugar Bowl, 14-7, giving a co-title to the Crimson Tide and USC. In four tries, Paterno never beat Bear Bryant.

From 1980 to 1987 Penn State was 76-19-1, including a 23-1 mark between 1985 and 1986. On January 1, 1982, Penn State, led by running back Curt Warner (later a star in Seattle), beat Marcus Allen and Southern California in the Fiesta Bowl, 26-10. Paterno finally won the national title in 1982. Only a 42-21 loss to Alabama marred an 11-1 season that included a 27-23 Sugar Bowl triumph over Herschel Walker and Georgia.

Penn State versus the Elite Ten (44–52–1 through 2008)

Alabama (5–8), Miami (7–6), Michigan (4–10), Nebraska (0–0), Notre Dame (9–8–1), Ohio State (12–12), Oklahoma (0–2), Southern California (4–5), Texas (3–2)

The 1987 Fiesta Bowl was billed as "good versus evil," with Joe Pa's clean-cut Lions representing "good," the fatigue-clad Miami Hurricanes "evil." A college-football-record seventy million TV viewers watched Penn State bottle up Heisman-winning quarterback Vinny Testaverde. They intercepted five Testaverde passes, two by linebacker Shane Conlan, and sacked him five times. Despite being outgained 445–161 in total offense and twenty-two first downs to eight, Penn State stopped Miami's fourth-quarter drive when Testaverde threw his fifth interception to capture Paterno's second national championship (12–0). Consensus All-Americans in the 1980s include Sean Farrell, D. J. Dozier, and Shane Conlan.

In 1993, Penn State joined the Big 10. The move looked to be a good one in the early years. In 1994 the Lions were 12–0 with a 38–20 victory over Oregon in the Rose Bowl, their first return to Pasadena since the 1923 "traffic delay" game. However, Paterno was again denied a national championship, which was awarded by consensus to Nebraska. It was this event that helped to propel what later became the Bowl Championship Series. Consensus All-Americans in the 1990s were O. J. McDuffie, Ki-Jana Carter, Kerry Collins (later a Super Bowl quarterback with the Giants), Jeff Hartings, Curtis Envy, LaVar Arrington, Brandon Short, and Courtney Brown. Brown and Arrington were the first two picks of the 2000 draft, making Penn State the first team since Nebraska in 1984 to have two players selected one-two. In 2007, the Arizona Cardinals made Levi Brown their first draft pick.

In the 2000s, Penn State slipped. Larry Johnson made consensus All-American in 2002. In 2005 the Lions won the Big 10 Conference but did not go to the Rose Bowl, which was reserved for USC and Texas in the BCS national championship game. In 2008, Penn State defeated Ohio State in a Big 10 classic, 13–6 at Columbus, and had the inside track at the BCS title game until barely losing, 24–23 at Iowa. They made a return trip to Pasadena, featuring the ultimate "old versus new" match-up of Joe Pa and USC coach Pete Carroll in the Rose Bowl. Paterno, hampered by ailments, had to sit in the press box and watch his team get dismantled, 38–24, but it not daunt him. He returned in 2009 (as did Bowden at Florida State). The on-going competition for most career wins continues.

PART II

Saturday Spectacle

Chapter 11

The Sweep of History

JUST AS SPORTS in the 1920s reflected American hubris and self-celebration, in the 1930s a social edge played itself out in the athletic world. The 1932 L.A. Olympic Games, coming on the heels of USC's 1931 national championship and preceding their repeat of the same in 1932, was replete with a host of Trojan trackmen and swimmers winning gold medals. It galvanized Los Angeles and California as the "new Greece," where feats of physical greatness reached their zenith in the L.A. Coliseum.

Twice in the 1930s, black American boxer Joe Louis fought the symbol of Aryan "superiority," Germany's Max Schmeling. When Louis beat Schmeling in 1938, he was viewed as the first black hero by a white America concerned with Nazi military preparations and Jewish persecution. In 1936, Adolf Hitler used the Olympics as a propagandistic springboard for his racial theories, but Jesse Owens, a black sprinter/long jumper from Ohio State, won four golds to dismantle the Hitler concept.

California had always been a land of cutting-edge societal trends. Blacks and whites were classmates, teammates, and worthy opponents, years and decades before it was acceptable in other regions of the country. USC and UCLA were leaders in the area of progress for minorities on the field and in the classroom. The integrated USC-UCLA football games of the 1930s had a major impact on social progress. The star of those games, Bruin halfback Jackie Robinson, was chosen to break baseball's "color barrier," which he ultimately did in 1947 largely on the strength of his gridiron exploits.

By the end of 1939, collegiate football had been played for seventy years. Historians of the sport now had an abundance of knowledge with which to formulate the concept of tradition. In viewing the sweep of the game, it was by 1940 obvious that major changes had occurred. Up until the turn of the century, Princeton was the undisputed king of the hill, with Yale their closest competitors. Most colleges started playing football in the 1890s, but Ivy League schools were the only ones considered truly worthy.

In the 1900s, Michigan, Minnesota, Chicago, Stanford, and Washington joined Princeton, Yale, and Harvard. The "Team of the Decade" was Michigan. It all turned around in the 1910s. Washington's 63-game unbeaten streak made them the best of the best. Army, Notre Dame, Pittsburgh, and Georgia Tech were worthy competitors.

In the 1920s, Notre Dame put some distance between themselves and the rest of the pack, although Cal's dominance in the first four years of the decade was extraordinary.

Win-Loss Records (through 2008)

#	Team	Record
1.	Michigan (1879–2008)	872–295–36
2.	Notre Dame (1887–2008)	831–284–42
3.	Texas (1893–2008)	832–316–33
4.	Ohio State (1890–2008)	808–305–53
5.	Oklahoma (1895–2008)	791–297–53
6.	Southern California (1888–2008)	766–303–54
7.	Nebraska (1890–2008)	817–337–41
8.	Alabama (1892–2008)	750–307–44
9.	Tennessee (1891–2006)	760–312–53
10.	Penn State (1887–2008)	800–349–42
11.	Florida State (1947–2006)	442–201–30
12.	Georgia (1892–2006)	702–379–54
13.	Miami (1926–2008)	544–310–19
14.	Louisiana State (1893–2006)	680–376–47
15.	Auburn (1892–2006)	667–384–47
16.	Washington (1889–2006)	646–379–54
17.	Florida (1906–2006)	619–368–40
18.	Miami (Ohio) (1888–2005)	639–352–44
19.	Arizona State (1897–2005)	523–318–24
20.	Colorado (1890–2005)	650–402–36
21.	Central Michigan (1896–2005)	532–338–36
22.	UCLA (1919–2006)	528–346–37
23.	Texas A&M (1894–2005)	639–415–48
24.	Syracuse (1889–2004)	664–435–49
25.	Army (1890–2004)	631–427–51
26.	Michigan State (1896–2006)	599–403–44
27.	Georgia Tech (1892–2006)	646–436–43
28.	Arkansas (1894–2004)	621–422–40
29.	Clemson (1896–2004)	600–413–45
30.	Minnesota (1882–2006)	626–439–44
31.	Pittsburgh (1890–2004)	639–464–42
32.	Stanford (1891–2006)	543–412–49
33.	Mississippi (1893–2004)	583–439–35
34.	California (1882–2006)	602–459–51
35.	Brigham Young (1922–2004)	456–359–26
36.	Maryland (1892–2004)	573–498–43
37.	Illinois (1890–2004)	542–485–50
38.	Texas Christian (1896–2004)	515–502–57

Heisman Trophies, by School

1. Southern California	7	*One each*	
1. Ohio State	7	Colorado	
1. Notre Dame	7	Brigham Young	
4. Oklahoma	4	Houston	
5. Florida	3	UCLA	
5. Nebraska	3	Oklahoma State	
5. Michigan	3	Boston College	
5. Texas	3	South Carolina	
5. Army	3	Pittsburgh	
10. Florida State	2	Penn State	
10. Wisconsin	2	Stanford	
10. Miami	2	Oregon State	
10. Auburn	2	Syracuse	
10. Navy	2	Louisiana State	
10. Georgia	2	Texas A&M	
10. Yale	2	Princeton	
		Southern Methodist	
		Minnesota	
		Iowa	
		Texas Christian	
		Chicago	

UCLA built themselves into a powerhouse largely on the strength of the great black high school stars they recruited from in and around Los Angeles. The Bruin basketball team under John Wooden, in particular, can attribute much of their dominant success to this practice.

USC did not quite match UCLA in the area of social progress but was still ahead of the rest of the country. In 1956 the Trojans brought a black running back named C. R. Roberts back to Austin. Roberts responded with one of the greatest—albeit little

USC and UCLA: Hollywood's Schools

Marion Morrison (John "Duke" Wayne), Southern California (*True Grit, The Sands of Iwo Jima, The Quiet Man, Red River,* etc.); Marv Goux, Southern California (*Spartacus*); O. J. Simpson, Southern California (*Naked Gun,* etc.); Woody Strode, UCLA (*Spartacus*); Mark Harmon, UCLA (*The Presidio, The Deliberate Stranger,* etc.); . . . also check out Ed Marinaro, Cornell (*Hill Street Blues*); and Carl Weathers, San Diego State (*Rocky, Rocky II, Rocky III, Action Jackson*).

The War Effort

On December 2, 1944, Army coach Earl "Red" Blaik received a telegram after his Black Knights defeated Navy to complete a perfect season: "THE GREATEST OF ALL ARMY TEAMS. WE HAVE STOPPED THE WAR TO CELEBRATE YOUR MAGNIFICENT SUCCESS. MacARTHUR." This is perhaps as telling a statement about the greatness of America as any single fact. Consider the following information about the United States entering World War II on December 7, 1941:

- We were unprepared for the war.
- America was still recovering from the Great Depression.
- We were swept by pacifism.
- American Communism was on the rise.
- President Franklin Roosevelt's administration was dotted with actual Soviet agents.
- Our stated, popular policy was isolationism.
- Ambassador to Great Britain Joseph P. Kennedy (father of JFK) stated, "Let's do business with Hitler, we can't beat him."
- The Japanese sneak attack at Pearl Harbor left half the U.S. Pacific fleet destroyed.
- The U.S. was immediately beaten in a series of battles with Germany's "Desert Fox," Erwin Rommel.

Despite this, America utterly, totally, and without question conquered the greatest military power ever assembled up until that time (Hitler's *Wehrmacht*), which was in league with totalitarian Japan in a two-front war continually shifting from North Africa, Sicily, Italy, the skies of Europe, France, Belgium, and Germany in the West, and Hawaii, the Philippines, the Pacific-Asian Islands, Australia, and Japan in the Pacific Theatre, all the while . . .

. . . continuing the Hollywood film industry, Broadway, Wall Street, and all education from grammar school to high school to colleges, postgraduate, public, and private; maintaining police departments, civil engineering, city, county, state, and federal governments in normal operation . . .

. . . *all while playing a full Major League baseball schedule that never missed a game or canceled the World Series; an uninterrupted National Football League complete with the annual draft; all NCAA sports, including a full slate of collegiate football.* There were sports concessions to the war, but probably less in collegiate football than any other. Secretary of War Henry L. Stimson plainly advised college students to graduate first so they could enter the military as officers. The 1942 Rose Bowl was moved from Pasadena to Durham, North Carolina, where Oregon State beat Duke, 20–16. There was a reduction of intersectional games, resulting in the temporary cancellation of the USC-Notre Dame rivalry. As if to thumb their noses at the Japanese threat, in 1942 USC and UCLA played a full schedule to large crowds in the L.A. Coliseum, with UCLA capturing the conference title before losing to Georgia in the Rose Bowl's return to Pasadena. In January 1944, USC played Washington in the Rose Bowl. Three of the best "college teams" in the nation were Great Lakes Naval Air Station, Iowa Pre-Flight, and Randolph Field. In January 1945, Tennessee traveled to the Rose Bowl and lost to USC. In 1944 Army fielded one of the greatest college football teams of all time, which thrilled cheering throngs. In 1945 the war was over when the college football season started. Army again dominated, while Alabama beat USC in the Rose Bowl.

There seems to be little doubt that, while the continuation of major sports in America was a morale booster, its greatest contribution was in the *demoralization* of our enemies. Jimmie Doolittle's "Raiders" were bombing Japan. Chester Nimitz's Navy was dealing blow after blow to their Imperial Navy. George Patton, Omar Bradley, and Mark Clark's forces were blowing through the Germans from one continent to another in the manner of Red Blaik's offense. Typical "buddy" talk revolved around personal allegiance to Ohio State or Michigan, Stanford or Cal, Notre Dame or. . . . Everybody felt as if they were part of West Point or Navy, with a lifetime of kindred spirit for those schools long after the fighting ended. The German and Japanese leadership, living in bunkers, dealing with bomb alerts, their respective countries' societies 100 percent mobilized to support the war, had to observe the fact that America was winning the war while continuing to "play games," concluding therefore that we were unstoppable.

We were.

known—games in history: 251 yards in *the first half* to lead Troy to a 44–20 smashing of all-white Texas. Roberts's presence forced coach Jess Hill's team to find separate hotel digs the night before, at great expense and disruption to plans. It galvanized the Trojans into a fighting force. According to reports, the Texas fans were unmerciful in their treatment of Roberts right until the end, although the Longhorn players—venomous at first but pacified by the athlete's respect of an opponent's performance—reached out to extend handshakes and compliments when it was over. Fourteen years before Sam "Bam" Cunningham's game at Birmingham in 1970, however, the time was not right for a football game to change America. Other games had an impact: Pittsburgh, Navy, and Penn State, among others, venturing South for bowl games with integrated teams.

Auburn and LSU helped return the Southeastern Conference to prominence in 1957 and 1958, but it was the hiring of Paul "Bear" Bryant that changed everything in every way. By the end of the 1950s, Notre Dame—which had fallen on some hard times, at least by their standards—still hung on to the mythical number one position in history.

The 1960s totally and completely changed the face of college football. It started inauspiciously, however. Minnesota won the AP and UPI championship but failed to defend it with a 17-7 loss to Washington in the Rose Bowl. 10-0-1 Mississippi, a 14-6 winner over Rice in the Sugar Bowl, should have been the champion.

Alabama, USC, and Texas won impressive national championships in the next three years. Each represented the glorious, glamorous new wave overtaking the game. 'Bama of course was now coached by Bryant, who stamped his greatness on the program.

His good friend, John McKay, did the same at USC. Each took a great tradition that had not become mediocre but surely was less than it had been. Each restored it to levels of glory greater than any it had known before. These schools would usher in enormous changes to the game. To some extent, so too did Darrell Royal at Texas. His 1963 Long-horns helped to turn them into a storied program.

The well-chronicled 1964 and 1965 fiascoes (Alabama's and Michigan State's bowl losses after wire-service national titles had already been awarded) could not completely overshadow exciting new developments. Television ratings were sky high as by now each home had a set. Color TV became the norm. Further integration gave America a whole new cast of stars to root for. Equipment changed drastically. Recruiting, money, national exposure, coaching techniques, training methods—all served to modernize the game in the 1960s. Three old names—USC, Alabama, Notre Dame—would take the reins of the modern era and make history.

Until 1964, the only thing lacking in the new decade was greatness at Notre Dame. That situation was alleviated when Ara Parseghian took over. He immediately led the Irish to a 9-0 record. The Fighting Irish arrived at the Los Angeles Coliseum one win away from the school's eighth national championship. Alabama fans became Trojan fans. They were jumping for joy when Southern California rallied from a 17-0 halftime deficit to defeat the Irish, 20-17. Notre Dame was out, Alabama was in. The wire services went for the Tide over unbeaten Arkansas. 'Bama lost their bowl game, Arkansas won theirs: chaos ensued.

The 1965 Michigan State/UPI imbroglio further clouded the situation. The AP's one-year reversal gave Alabama that year's championship but may have denied them in 1966. Their Ken Stabler-led victory over Nebraska in the Orange Bowl was impressive enough that it might have swayed some voters over the "no-bowl" Irish. When the AP finally went to a postbowl vote in 1968 for good, it meant the USC-Ohio State Rose Bowl game took on "Game of the Century" overtones. The Buckeyes won in convincing manner. It did not match other earth-shaking games (1931 USC-Notre Dame, 1946 Notre Dame-Army, 1963 USC-Wisconsin Rose Bowl, 1966 Notre Dame-Michigan State, 1969 Texas-Arkansas, 1971 Nebraska-Oklahoma, 1973 Notre Dame-Alabama Sugar Bowl, 1988 Notre Dame-Miami, 2006 USC-Texas Rose Bowl).

Texas (1970) and Alabama (1973) were the last two illegitimate UPI "national champions." The subsequent decision to change the vote to after the bowls certainly did not end controversy or co-national championships, but there have been no illegitimate champs since then.

In 1974, USC rallied from a 24-0 deficit, scoring *55 points in seventeen minutes* to beat Notre Dame, 55-24. The game represented the height of the rivalry. In 1964 USC knocked Notre Dame out. In 1965 USC was 4-0-1 and Notre Dame was 4-0. In 1966 Notre Dame's shutout win over USC won it for them. In 1967 O. J. Simpson's Trojan win at South Bend made them the frontrunner, and they held from there. In 1968 USC's tie with Notre Dame kept them in the hunt. In 1969 their tie with the Irish probably cost them the national championship. In 1970 USC's 38-28 win over Joe Theismann in a driving rainstorm at the Coliseum knocked the Irish out. In 1971 a 2-4 Trojan squad held an Athlete's in Action Christian "demonstration" the week of the South Bend trip.

"A lot of guys accepted Christ that day," recalled lineman Dave Brown, who organized it.

They beat Notre Dame 28–14, ending Notre Dame's unbeaten season and bid for number one. 1972: Anthony Davis's six touchdowns and USC's 45–23 whipping propelled USC to the title. 1973: Notre Dame ended USC's 23-game unbeaten streak and went on to win it. 1974: USC's beyond-belief blowout gave them the championship after they won an almost-as-exciting Rose Bowl 18–17 on a last-minute 2-point conversion over Ohio State.

In 1975 USC's 24–17 win at Notre Dame left them 7–0 and in the driver's seat. In 1976 USC beat Notre Dame and finished second; had Pitt lost their bowl game the Trojans would have won. In 1977 Joe Montana and the green-jersey Irish rode their upset of Troy to the championship. In 1978, a two-seconds-left field goal by Frank Jordan gave USC victory and, after their Rose Bowl win over Michigan, the national championship. In 1979 USC beat Notre Dame and knocked number one, unbeaten Ohio State out of the number one slot in the Rose Bowl. Had Alabama not beaten Arkansas in the Sugar Bowl, Troy would have been a champion again. In 1980, USC's 20–3 victory over Notre Dame ended Irish hopes in the last regular season game. In 1981 USC's defeat of Notre Dame at South Bend left them at 6–1, in the driver's seat for the national championship in a year of upsets. Subsequent Trojan losses ended their dream, but Marcus Allen's performance at South Bend led him to the Heisman Trophy.

Finally, in 1982 (when USC rallied to win, 17–13), the game had no national title implications before or after. After drubbing the Trojans 51–0 in 1966, Notre Dame beat their biggest rivals only twice in the succeeding sixteen seasons. Both times they won the national championship. USC won four titles in that time frame. It could be argued that if these two storied programs did not schedule the annual bloodletting with each other, USC and Notre Dame could have won several more.

The 1978 co-national championship was split between the two dominant powers of Bear Bryant's career: his Tide and McKay's Trojans. It all came to a head in 1978. Ranked number one, Alabama met USC at Birmingham's Legion Field. Trojan tailback Charlie White ran for 199 yards. USC ran away from 'Bama, 24–14. USC's subsequent loss to Arizona State set them back. Penn State looked to be the champions, but once-beaten Alabama defeated Joe Paterno's Nittany Lions in the Sugar Bowl. USC beat Michigan 17–10 in the Rose Bowl.

Now, the same voters who denied Alabama in 1966 for "political" reasons had the Tide's fate in their hands again. Common sense dictated who the rightful champion was. In that rare pre-BCS year in which the two teams in question played, and one had defeated the other on the losing team's home turf, the obvious pick was Southern California. But Bryant had rightfully been credited with skillfully integrating his, and by proxy the entire SEC's, football rosters. The AP showered him with love and their vote. The UPI stuck with Troy.

The next year it looked to be a repeat. It was an incredible season in which the 1979 Crimson Tide, Trojans, and Ohio State Buckeyes all rank among the finest teams in history. But USC tied Stanford, then beat the Buckeyes in the Rose Bowl. Alabama, the last unbeaten, untied team standing, was the AP's sixth repeat champion.

Chapter 12

The West, the Game,
and Societal Evolution

A S THE SUN WENT DOWN on New Year's Day 1980, the landscape of college football had shifted. The pretenders were gone. The Ivy League was no longer a factor. California, Georgia Tech, Army, and Minnesota, traditional powers of yesteryear, were mediocre programs.

Michigan and Ohio State made strong bids but had fallen short. Three champions of the 1920s returned to glory and stood at or near the top: Notre Dame, USC, and Alabama. A fourth program, Oklahoma, which had risen in the 1950s, reemerged as a serious contender for the position with an almost-as-fabulous run in the 1970s. Pittsburgh, after years of poor showings, was a contender once again.

In the previous two decades, Alabama had the better overall record. In the 1960s they were 89–16; in the 1970s 103–16–1 for a total mark of 192–32–5, the height of Bear Bryant's glory. USC was 76–25–4 in the 1960s, then 93–22–1 in the 1970s (169–47–5).

They were titans of the game during a golden age. Determining who was better is not an easy task. By pure win-loss records, it would appear that Alabama was, but many other factors detract from that view. In the 1960s, Alabama was segregated and played a 90 percent segregated schedule. They hardly traveled outside Dixie and appeared to have turned inward in light of Alabama governor George Wallace's "stand in the schoolhouse door" speech of 1963. That speech had been delivered just below the office window of Bear Bryant, who observed it in the company of school president Frank Rose.

USC traveled far and wide, including trips to Waco (Baylor), Dallas (SMU), Austin (Texas), and Miami in the 1960s. The Pac-8 Conference was arguably the toughest in the nation. Included on their schedule were yearly bloodbaths with Notre Dame, during "the Era of Ara," and UCLA in their best decade.

In the 1970s, Sam "Bam" Cunningham and USC traveled to Legion Field, defeating Alabama 42–21. The doors were opened thereafter for black players in the South. Bryant may or may not have said of Cunningham, "This here's what a football player looks like."

In fact, the game was carefully planned by Bryant and McKay with the hopes that it would pave the way for two blacks already recruited by Bryant, freshman Wilbur Jackson and junior college transfer John Mitchell. Furthermore, if Bryant said that Cunningham was "what a football player looks like," he said it in a crowded hallway, not in front of his beaten team in the dressing room. Apocryphal or not, Bryant's reaction to the defeat was gracious, his speedy acceptance of black players and coaches in succeeding years more so. A man considered an enemy of integration, a man whose only legacy may have been wins and losses (much like Kentucky basketball coach Adolph Rupp), now became a legend for all the right reasons. The schedule Bryant's Tide faced in the 1970s was national and integrated. He led the way for others, to the great relief of many white coaches who long wanted to do it but felt they were restrained.

The two teams played each other four times, splitting two each (both on the road). USC's five national titles were all legitimate, coming with impressive Rose Bowl victories over Big 10 juggernauts Wisconsin ('63), Ohio State ('73, '75), and Michigan ('79). 'Bama, as has been chronicled, claims six championships under Bryant, but of course this is a misnomer. Two came with bowl defeats. Four were the real deal. Alabama argues this would be like USC saying they really were the 1968 national champions, not Ohio State (who beat them in the Rose Bowl). The Crimson Tide could argue persuasively they deserved the 1966 and 1977 titles, but it can be more persuasively argued that they did not deserve the shared 1978 title with the Trojans. USC could easily have been the national champions of 1969 and 1979, and some services called them champions of 1976.

USC boasted Heisman Trophy winners Mike Garrett (1965), O. J. Simpson (1968), and Charles White (1979), with a fourth, Marcus Allen, playing on the 1978 national champions before winning the award in 1981. Alabama's Heisman winners: zero. USC far outnumbered the Tide in All-Americans, first-round draft picks (a record five in 1968), number one overall picks (Ron Yary '68, Simpson '69, Ricky Bell '77), and overall draft choices (eleven in 1969, fourteen apiece in 1975 and 1977).

The Trojans dominated the Rose Bowl. It could be said that, if not for the obstacle posed by USC, both Ohio State and Michigan might have been the best teams in the 1970s, a decade in which these schools very possibly fielded the greatest juggernauts in their respective histories. Alabama was winless in bowl appearances between the 1967 and 1973 seasons. For these reasons, USC was the "Team of the Decade" in both the 1960s and 1970s, while their two-decade run between 1962 and 1982 is considered the greatest of all time. The Tide still has a legitimate argument. Notre Dame has less of one since they were dominated by USC for most of these two decades. Oklahoma (two national titles, one Heisman winner) can cite some very compelling statistics favoring themselves in the 1970s. Penn State also went on a run of amazing proportions, but when all the factors are carefully weighed the Trojans reign supreme. This has been their way of doing things for decades.

There have been periods where other teams boasted better win-loss records or had gaudier runs, but Troy has been steady, spectacular when it counted (big games, bowl games), while offering just a little more Hollywood excitement and Heisman star power. When USC defeated Notre Dame for the fifth straight time in 1982, they had for all practical purposes "caught up" with Notre Dame as the greatest of all traditions. Perhaps the Irish still held the slightest of edges, but USC was certainly on the verge of making a breakthrough.

So close, and yet so far. Over the following thirteen seasons, USC never beat Notre Dame. Troy had some very good teams. In 1988 they entered the Notre Dame game at the Coliseum one win away from playing for the national title only to lose. In 1989 promising freshman quarterback Todd Marinovich, reputed to be the most heralded prep player who ever lived, led them to a Rose Bowl triumph. But overall, once head coach John Robinson and his legendary Trojan assistant, Marv Goux, left in the wake of NCAA penalties in 1983, USC experienced down times by their lofty standards.

The rise of Southern California in the John McKay era, like so many other periods, mirrored American society. After World War II, an enormous population boom occurred. The growth of California suburbs resulted in the state producing a "mother lode" of great athletic talent in all sports.

The Big 10 dominated the Rose Bowl, which became a contractual affair with the Pacific Coast Conference beginning with the 1946 season. Between January 1947 and January 1952, the Big 10 won every time—sometimes in routs, sometimes in close games. It was a tremendous setback for Pacific Coast prestige. The conventional wisdom held

Bowl Victories

Teams that have won national championships since World War I (1919–2006)

1. Southern California	31		19. Notre Dame	14
1. Alabama	31		19. Washington	14
3. Penn State	26		21. UCLA	13
4. Texas	25		21. Texas A&M	13
4. Tennessee	25		23. Syracuse	12
4. Georgia	25		23. Colorado	12
7. Oklahoma	24		25. Arkansas	11
8. Nebraska	23		25. Texas Christian	11
9. Georgia Tech	22		27. Pittsburgh	10
10. Florida State	21		27. California	10
11. Miami	19		27. Maryland	10
11. Michigan	19		30. Stanford	9
11. Louisiana State	19		30. Brigham Young	9
11. Mississippi	19		32. Michigan State	7
11. Auburn	19		33. Illinois	6
16. Ohio State	18		34. Minnesota	5
16. Florida	18		35. Army	2
18. Clemson	15		36. Harvard	1

that Big 10 and Midwestern teams were "tough" and "physical," while California kids were "soft," had "gone Hollywood," and were made lazy by the hot sun, inviting beaches, temptation of girls, night life, and "La-La land."

Then the kids in all those West Coast Baby Boomer families started to graduate from high school, entering USC, UCLA, California, Stanford, and Washington. In January 1953 Southern Cal finally ended the Big 10's dominance with a 7–0 shutout of Wisconsin in Pasadena.

But the conference stubbed its own toes, first by instituting a short-lived "no-repeat" policy on its champions (depriving the country of a "national championship" Rose Bowl game between unbeaten Ohio State and unbeaten UCLA in January 1955). Then, a recruiting scandal blew the lid off of the PCC and college football. Stanford, as guilty as the rest of the conference, essentially became the "star witness" for the NCAA, turning in Washington, California, USC, and UCLA. Players were suspended, coaches fired, games forfeited, reputations lost.

It was the proverbial "end" for California. Under legendary coach Pappy Waldorf, the Golden Bears were among the nation's elite in the late 1940s and early 1950s. Their failure to win any of their three straight Rose Bowl games badly hurt the conference, however. Perhaps out of a sense of desperation, Cal began to pay its players in the form of subsidies, supposedly to cover higher rents in Berkeley (the excuse UCLA made for doing the same thing in Westwood). When caught in the vortex of NCAA sanctions in the mid-1950s, Cal made the conscious decision to downgrade the importance placed on intercollegiate athletics. It was part of a growing political climate manifesting itself in California. Sides would be taken.

A great athletic department became mediocre. California had won the 1947 and 1957 College World Series in baseball, and the 1959 NCAA basketball championship under coach Pete Newell. Their track program under (Olympic coach) Brutus Hamilton had been second only to USC.

In the wake of Cal's self-imposed "mediocrity campaign," USC and UCLA built not just great football programs but all-around athletic departments, dominating every aspect of NCAA sports competition over the next two decades. Much of their success came about because of the "vacuum" created by Berkeley. Certainly great Bay Area athletes no longer considered Cal a worthy choice. UCLA's 1967 Heisman winner, Gary Beban, and USC's 1968 recipient, O. J. Simpson, were both from the San Francisco Bay area.

Opportunities for black athletes, embodied by two "modern Moseses of progressivism," John Wooden at UCLA and John McKay at USC, typified the two schools, explaining much of their dominance. The University of San Francisco won two straight NCAA

Did You Know . . .

That the Pac-10 has captured 394 national titles (280 men's, 115 women's), far outdistancing the runner-up Big Ten Conference's 233 titles?

Tackled by Segregation

The 1951 University of San Francisco Dons were 9–0, considered one of the best teams in the nation. In those days, USF was a sports powerhouse. Their basketball team, led by Bill Russell and K. C. Jones, would win 60 straight games and consecutive NCAA championships in 1955–1956. A number of small colleges on the West Coast had stellar football teams until the 1950s, among them Santa Clara, St. Mary's, and Loyola. They were known to play competitively against California, Stanford, and USC. Schools such as Montana and Nevada were early members of the Pacific Coast Conference. Santa Clara had won the 1937 Sugar Bowl, St. Mary's the 1946 Sugar Bowl. The 1951 Dons were led by the great Ollie Matson and featured future 49er Hall of Famer Bob St. Clair. Their SID was Pete Rozelle. The team was invited to a bowl game but asked not to bring their black players, of which Matson was one. They refused and stayed home. A few years later, Pitt's black fullback, Bobby Grier, played against Georgia Tech in the 1956 Sugar Bowl. For USF, however, the loss of revenue from the bowl disinvite, combined with decreased ticket sales to the new NFL franchise, the 49ers, forced them to give up football.

basketball championships on the strength of the liberal recruiting of black players like Bill Russell and K. C. Jones.

But another major factor was the social dynamic caused by the Vietnam War. California became a hotbed of radicalism. Athletes, coaches, and sports were viewed as tools of "bourgeois capitalism," pseudomilitary endeavors to be despised. The downgrading of sports, started in the 1950s in the wake of NCAA sanctions, was furthered by a "dirty play" incident with USC that made *Sports Illustrated* headlines and led Berkeley to view USC as a tyrant of Caesarian proportions. The antiwar protest movement enveloping the campus all but destroyed the school's competitiveness in sports, especially football, for years.

The fact that USC and to a lesser extent UCLA continued to emphasize their sports programs was viewed as a political act. A curious sense of class envy, built on years of

Black Pioneers

Brice Taylor, C. R. Roberts, Willie Wood, and Sam "Bam" Cunningham (Southern California); Jackie Robinson, Kenny Washington, and Woody Strode (UCLA); George Jewett and Willis Ward (Michigan); Frederick Douglass "Fritz" Pollard (Brown); Paul Robeson (Rutgers); Oze Simmons and Jack Trice (Iowa); Fred Moore (Northwestern); Wilmeth Sadat-Singh and Jim Brown (Syracuse); Ed Williams (New York); Johnny Bright (Drake); Buddy Young (Illinois); Prentice Gautt (Oklahoma); Sidney Williams (Wisconsin); Sandy Stephens (Minnesota); Bobby Grier (Pittsburgh); Jerry LeVias (Southern Methodist); Julius Whittier and Roosevelt Leaks (Texas); Lester McClain (Tennessee); Wilbur Jackson, John Mitchell, and Sylvester Croom (Alabama) jealousy resulting from second-class sports status, fueled the northern California versus southern California divide of the 1960s. A conservative Republican from Los Angeles, Ronald Reagan, was elected governor, achieving popularity largely on the strength of his hard-line approach to the protests at Berkeley. Later, it was revealed that he cooperated with the FBI in their investigation of Cal's chancellor and faculty regarding suspected Communist activity. The school, long regarded as just plain "Cal," now found itself more often referred to by the moniker "Berkeley," with attendant social meaning.

Stanford briefly filled the vacuum left by Berkeley. They won the Rose Bowl following the 1970 and 1971 seasons, with quarterback Jim Plunkett capturing the 1970 Heisman Trophy. However, the politics of the era brought them down, too. Their band chose to become radicalized, going so far as to pay a "Tribute to Chairman Mao" at the height of China's Cultural Revolution, when an estimated thirty to fifty million Chinese were murdered by Mao.

The suburban Sun Belt demographic shifts of the post-World War II era were still occurring in the 1970s. The same power that propelled Californians Richard Nixon and Reagan to four successful elections to the White House manifested itself on the fields of play. It was a golden age in the Golden State, at least in the Southland. The Trojans and/or Bruins dominated in football, basketball, baseball, track, swimming, tennis, volleyball, and just about everything. Had either school been a country at the 1976 Montreal Olympics, they would have been among the medal leaders.

The state produced professional champions, too: A's, Dodgers, Raiders, Lakers. With attendance down throughout the country, Los Angeles filled the Coliseum and its marvelous new arenas, Dodger Stadium and the Forum.

College football grew much more in the 1980s. There was an expansion of bowl games. The Fiesta Bowl became a major New Year's Day game. Network and cable TV expanded the game's reach. The state of Florida entered the picture in a big way. Some traditional powers faded, new traditions began.

With home prices rising to out-of-control levels, the family-friendly growth rates of suburban California began to trend backwards in the decade. The South saw a major rise in every aspect of the region. Once considered backward, the South initially made strides after the invention of air conditioning, which made it possible to do business in the summertime.

Did You Know . . .

That the Pac-10 has won the most football national championships with 19 (and 10 Heismans) compared to the SEC with 18 (and 8 Heismans)?

Chapter 13

The South Rises Again

BEAR BRYANT'S INTEGRATION of his program created a tidal wave of minority athletes. Alabama initially dominated until the rest of Dixie caught up. In the 1980s and beyond, Auburn, Tennessee, LSU, Florida, Florida State, and the Southwest Conference integrated fully. They were better off for it, on and off the field. The result was a downgrading of Western collegiate sports success. It was the Western schools that had traditionally benefited the most from segregation. They had great black athletes in their own regions. Western and Northern schools "cherry picked" black superstars like Clarence Davis from Alabama and Bubba Smith from Texas. *Now*, not only were they less likely to get Southern blacks, they were actually *losing* some. A blue-chip African American high school kid in California, in Arizona, in Michigan might just as easily decide to play at Miami, LSU, or Tennessee.

The South had most definitely "risen again." Between 1964 and 1996, a Southern man was elected to the presidency four times. Cities like Tampa, Charlotte, Nashville, Atlanta became economic success stories. Professional sports teams moved in to all the major cities in Dixie. The 1996 Olympics were successfully staged in Atlanta.

There were no co-national championships in the 1980s. The AP, UPI, and newly installed *USA Today*/ESPN polls all were on the same page. The college game had a decidedly Southern or Southwestern flavor to it, with variations. Georgia (1980), Clemson (1981), Miami (1983, 1987, 1989), and Oklahoma (1985) were all champions, as were Penn State (1982, 1986), Brigham Young (1984), and Notre Dame (1988).

In 1984 BYU captured the title with a Holiday Bowl win, which started everybody down a fourteen-year path to the Bowl Championship Series (1998). In 1986, a precursor of the BCS occurred when Miami played Penn State in what was billed as the "national championship game," not on New Year's Day but the next night at the Fiesta Bowl. The game's TV ratings alone (the Lions won, 14–10) were as big a reason for creating a BCS championship game as any other factor.

The 1990s started with a co-national championship: a disappointing Colorado (AP/ *USA Today*) and Georgia Tech (UPI) split. It was a year in which traditional power Notre Dame was excellent, as was king of the hill Miami and relative newcomer Florida State. USC, after a few down years, came into the 1990 season with national championship

Bowl Games

Teams that have won national championships since World War I (1919–2006)

#	Team	Count	#	Team	Count
1.	Alabama	56	20.	Washington	30
2.	Texas	48	21.	Notre Dame	29
3.	Southern California	47	21.	UCLA	29
4.	Tennessee	46	23.	Clemson	28 (through 2004)
5.	Nebraska	45	23.	Texas A&M	28 (through 2004)
6.	Georgia	44	24.	Colorado	26 (through 2004)
7.	Oklahoma	42	25.	Pittsburgh	25
8.	Penn State	41	26.	Brigham Young	23 (through 2004)
9.	Ohio State	40	27.	Syracuse	22 (through 2004)
9.	Louisiana State	40	28.	Texas Christian	21 (through 2004)
11.	Michigan	39	29.	Stanford	20
12.	Florida State	38	29.	Maryland	20 (through 2004)
13.	Arkansas	36	31.	Michigan State	19
13.	Florida	36	31.	California	19
17.	Georgia Tech	35	33.	Illinois	14 (through 2004)
18.	Miami	34	34.	Minnesota	13
18.	Auburn	34	35.	Army	4
19.	Mississippi	31 (through 2004)	36.	Harvard	1

aspirations. Their troubled quarterback, Todd Marinovich, created a morass that would not be cleared up until Pete Carroll's arrival eleven years later.

Colorado, a school with a more impressive history than most people realize, snuck in after winning a controversial "fifth-down game" with Missouri. Georgia Tech's fleeting reemergence in glory's light had people thinking about "Wrong Way" Roy Riegels's infamous "run" that helped the Yellow Jackets beat Cal 8–7 in the 1929 Rose Bowl.

Over the years, due to inequities, strange rules and policies, various polls, many systems, and no play-offs, the game produced a plethora of co-national championships. For many different reasons, the split share of a title, while frustrating and less than 100 percent satisfying, did not usually detract from that team's place in history. Co-championships were dutifully counted and for good reason.

Never has the co-title been more impressively won than in 1991. Miami captured the AP version, but Washington (Rose Bowl winners, UPI/*USA* champions) is considered one of the greatest teams in the game's history. A battle between the Huskies and the Hurricanes would have looked like USC and Texas in the 2006 Rose Bowl, or Oklahoma and Nebraska in 1971. It would have been a war.

The first half of the decade was a "shake-up" period. Notre Dame under Lou Holtz regained its form and enjoyed a "mini-dynasty," but revelations from Don Yaeger's *Under the Tarnished Dome* spelled the end for Holtz and brought down times to South Bend. They have never really recovered from them.

Miami ran its course, at least for a while. Washington was unable to completely repeat their 1991 success. Penn State maintained the same high level that Joe Paterno set beginning in 1968, but then slipped. Oklahoma completely fell apart. The Southwest Conference curiously folded and joined the Big 8, making it the too-bulky Big 12 North and South. Some conferences went for a play-off, creating tricky new poll scenarios. Winning the conference championship game could increase the power rating of an unbeaten champion, but it could also end their national championship run. The concept of a team winning a national title absent a conference title created a disturbing dynamic. New stars in the constellation were born: Virginia Tech, Kansas State.

Two programs fought their way through the incredibly competitive minefield of collegiate football greatness. Tom Osborne's Nebraska Cornhuskers and Bobby Bowden's Florida State Seminoles were major powers. Many argue with much validity that the 1994–1995 Cornhuskers were the greatest back-to-back champions ever assembled; their 1993–1995 or 1995–1997 runs the best over three seasons. Bowden's Seminoles were 109–13–1 in the 1990s; won the national title in 1993 and 1999; and made the BCS championship games in the 1998, 1999, and 2000 seasons. Between 1987 and 2000, Florida State finished in the AP Top 5 fourteen straight seasons. Their toughest competition, as often as not, came within their state: Miami and, to an increasing extent, Florida (the 1996 national champions).

The rise of the South, symbolic and real as it was in so many ways, manifested itself in other sports in the 1990s. In the wake of John Wooden's retirement at UCLA, the Bruins became just another good basketball program. The Atlantic Coast Conference assumed the role of the nation's best. The Southeastern Conference, unquestionably the best in football beginning in the 1990s, also produced champions in baseball (LSU with four). Champions in track, tennis, and women's sports increasingly came not from USC, UCLA, and Stanford, but just as frequently from Georgia, Tennessee, and other Southern programs.

Chapter 14

The New Centurions

THE 1990s WERE the worst decade in the history of USC and the state, at least since World War II. California lost or saw symbolic shifts in political, economic, and athletic prestige. It started off on a bad foot months before the decade began when a major earthquake disrupted the 1989 World Series between Oakland and San Francisco.

The Cold War ended in the 1989–1991 period; good news for the world, not so good for the California economy. Much of the "military industrial complex" was centered in a narrow corridor, roughly "created" by Howard Hughes, along the 405 Freeway in Los Angeles between Santa Monica and Long Beach. The immediate aftereffect of Russian "surrender" was the closing and deescalation of weapons building, with the layoff of thousands of skilled workers.

Republican president George H. W. Bush lost his 1992 reelection bid largely because of this fallout, an ironic case of the Republicans—largely considered the party most responsible for winning the Cold War—being "victims of their own success."

In 1992's "Year of the Woman" election, Southern California lost its traditional power base when two liberal Jewish Democrat women from San Francisco, Dianne Feinstein and Barbara Boxer, ascended to the U.S. Senate.

The state, particularly the Southland, took further hits. A major earthquake caused havoc in L.A. Gang violence escalated. A stray bullet grazed a Trojan player at practice. Orange County declared bankruptcy.

Los Angeles lost the Raiders back to Oakland and the Rams to St. Louis. The Dodgers were mediocre, the Angels disappointing, the Lakers in the dumps. USC managed to win the 1998 College World Series and the 1996 Rose Bowl but little else of consequence. UCLA was competitive in football, beating USC eight straight times, but the Pacific-10 saw a shift to the Arizona schools and the Pacific Northwest, none of which increased their prestige when weighed against the rest of America. The lone "major sports" championship by a California school was UCLA's 1995 NCAA basketball crown, which was short-lived glory when coach Jim Harrick was fired over an accounting scandal, of all things.

In 1997, it was the "last straw." Michigan, long a disappointment, took "advantage" of the Pac-10's down times, managing to beat Washington State in the Rose Bowl, thus capturing the AP national championship. But Nebraska, unbeaten and 42–17 winners over Tennessee in the Orange Bowl, took the *USA Today* crown. The UPI had disbanded their poll after the 1995 season.

In 1998, the Bowl Championship Series was instituted. The Rose Bowl resisted at first but eventually came into the fold. Ironically, the BCS worked against Florida State. Without it, they might have captured poll titles in 1998 and 2000. With it, they found themselves losing to Tennessee in the January 1999 Fiesta Bowl and Oklahoma in the January 2001 Orange Bowl. In between, they captured the 1999 national championship on the strength of a wild Sugar Bowl triumph over Michael Vick and Virginia Tech.

The dawning of the New Millennium revealed a shake-up in collegiate football. A host of awards, lists, and "best ofs" dotted the period as people wanted to know who the greatest teams, athletes, and political figures of the twentieth century had been.

ESPN came up with their "Top 100" athletes. Michael Jordan came in ahead of the likes of Babe Ruth and Muhammad Ali. *Time* magazine apparently felt that Dwight Eisenhower defeating Adolf Hitler, Winston Churchill saving democracy, or Ronald Reagan ending Soviet Communism (which had spawned 100 million murders roughly between 1917 and 1989) were not as inspiring as "Person of the Century" Alfred Einstein's "theory of relativity."

USC got its share of props. They were declared the "Collegiate Athletic Program of the Twentieth Century," while their legendary Rod Dedeaux was named "Collegiate Baseball Coach of the Century" by *Collegiate Baseball* magazine. However, their football program had slipped.

The great traditions were in disarray. Notre Dame, Oklahoma, Alabama, Penn State, and Texas ranged from floundering to semidisappointing. Southern and Florida schools seemed to have won the nationwide recruiting wars. An alarming number of top players from California, including some first-rate prep quarterbacks from the L.A. area, decided the Everglades were more enticing than the "endless strand."

But nobody fell quite as precipitously as the University of Southern California. At the end of the 1982 campaign they were on the verge of overtaking Notre Dame as the "Team of the Century." Over the next eighteen years this dream seemed to have gone up in smoke.

New priorities took over at USC. In the 1990s, the school made a major push toward academic excellence, with great results. A Nobel Prize-winning professor (George Olah) was hired. University president Steven Sample oversaw the building of the business, dental, gerontology, film, communication, and other departments to world-class status. As all of this happened in confluence with below-standard Trojan football, it became an article of faith among the USC alumni that a great educational university could not be maintained alongside athletic domination.

At the dawn of the New Millennium, if USC still held the second spot on the "all-time list," then it was a tenuous hold at best; the plaques and trophies adorning Heritage Hall were fading and tarnished. Notre Dame still held the top slot, but they were slipping, too. Alabama, the old standby, may have passed USC, first in the 1985 Aloha Bowl when they beat the Trojans to pass them as the winningest bowl team, then in 1992 when they completed a national championship season. But the Tide had not built on that 1992 season.

Then there was Oklahoma, the master of streaks. They had taken an enormous plunge in the 1990s, but new coach Bob Stoops led the Sooners to a 13–0 record, victory over Florida State in the Orange Bowl, and the 2000 national championship. A strong argument could be made that OU also passed USC in the all-time pantheon.

It seemed at the beginning of the century, at least to Trojan fans, to be "anybody but USC." Nebraska was still near the top. Miami came back better than ever. In the Pac-10 Conference, the best teams were Washington, Oregon, and Oregon State.

USC's fall seemed to have resembled the "dot-bomb" disaster roiling the Golden State in the early 2000s. When 9/11 hit, the country was at low ebb. However, America fought back. They took the War on Terror, which was being fought in planes, skyscrapers, subways, and the crowded cityscapes of Western democracies, picked it up, placed it in Afghanistan and Iraq, roped it off, and made the terrorists die in *their* neighborhoods. Crowded American sports arenas, once fearful of anthrax, "dirty bombs," and explosions, got back to the freedom of their tailgate parties and alumni cocktail gatherings.

While America fought back abroad, the economy fought back at home. All of those laid-off high-tech workers from the "military industrial complex" had at first fueled the Internet "superhighway." They had survived the false stock market economy of the 1990s. In the 2000s they rode steady growth to unprecedented heights. As 9/11 faded and terrorist acts were quelled, sports rebounded like never before.

The Yankee-Red Sox rivalry, Barry Bonds's 73-home runs in 2001, the NFL's best run, successful Olympics in Utah, a new golden age of college football—America took to sports as they had in the Roaring '20s. In Los Angeles, this rebound was felt in the pocketbook, symbolized by sports renaissance.

Staples Center was built in downtown L.A. Mayor Richard Riordan led a revitalization effort. USC began a gentrification campaign, cleaning up its mean streets, restoring old Victorians to their once stately grace, giving life to neighborhood schools, building professor housing, and creating new business. The two-to-three mile corridor between Staples Center and the USC campus was restored. The building of the Galen Center, a sparkling new basketball arena at USC, helped to create new life—restaurants, nightclubs, trendy boutiques—that had been missing in South Central L.A. since the silent film era.

The economic comeback of Los Angeles was matched by a sports comeback. The Lakers captured three straight NBA titles (2000, 2001, 2002). Down the street at the refurbished, sold-out Coliseum, new coach Pete Carroll built the Trojans—brick by brick by brick—back into the best collegiate football power in the nation.

Had there been a play-off in 2002, USC likely was the best team in the nation at the end of the season. Quarterback Carson Palmer won the Heisman Trophy and was the first pick in the 2003 NFL Draft. Ohio State won a relatively lackluster BCS Fiesta Bowl over injury-depleted Miami, ending the Hurricanes' 34-game winning streak and bid for a second straight national championship.

In 2003, USC captured the AP title in the manner their fans were accustomed to: victory over Michigan in the Rose Bowl. LSU won the BCS version with an uninspiring 21–14 victory over Oklahoma. There are few teams in history that looked better than the 2003 Sooners did in late December, yet fell farther in December and January. The co-national championship of 2003 riled many, not the least of which were USC supporters, since Troy finished the regular season a consensus number one in the AP and *USA Today* polls, only to be denied a trip to New Orleans due to a computer glitch. It made the value of a play-off glaringly obvious but also had a satisfying effect.

As the bowls and the BCS Sugar Bowl played out, with the AP overwhelmingly voting for USC and the *USA Today* coaches poll voting only for Louisiana State because they were contractually bound to do so, the glitz of the so-called national championship game was tarnished in favor of the majesty of the "granddaddy of 'em all," the Rose Bowl. It was as if the football gods were anointing tradition over modernity.

Tiger fans satisfied themselves with their BCS version, happy that they had that, since LSU most likely would have been smoked by the red-hot Trojans if they had been subjected to the experience. The BCS had the effect of eliminating Oklahoma without complaint and letting USC win it at "home," since the Rose Bowl, while rented out by UCLA in the fall, is their winter residence. It also gave much-needed imprimatur to the Associated Press, again viewed as "history's poll," the one that, at least since the afterbowl vote switch of 1968, was the most legitimate of all.

In 2004 USC left no doubt, capturing their second straight national championship in a 13–0 run that included a 55–19 whipping of overwhelmed Oklahoma in a game ESPN analyst Lee Corso called "the best performance I've ever seen." It had LSU fans saying, "Thank *God* we didn't have to play these guys last year!"

In assessing history, the 2004 Trojans may very well have enjoyed the most "perfect" season in history. Quarterback Matt Leinart won the Heisman Trophy. Running back Reggie Bush was a New York finalist. When considering all the factors, only two teams— the 1972 Trojans and the 1995 Nebraska Cornhuskers—remain above them.

The 2005 USC juggernaut was accorded "greatest team in history" status before the season even started. Matt Leinart eschewed pro football, an assured number one overall draft pick, and a multimillion dollar contract to return amid talk that he was the "greatest college football player ever." The tall, handsome superstar was a Hollywood celebrity, hanging out with beautiful starlets and models. USC was bigger than any professional team had ever been in the "city of angels." Selling out the mammoth Coliseum for every

Leaving No Doubt

The 2004 Trojans were the tenth AP repeat national champion (Minnesota 1935–1936, Army 1944–1945, Notre Dame 1946–1947, Oklahoma 1955–1956, Alabama *1964–1965, Nebraska 1970–1971, Oklahoma @1974–1975, Alabama 1978–1979, Nebraska 1994–1995); the second team ever to hold the number one poll position from the preseason until after the bowls (Florida State 1999; Notre Dame 1943, Army 1945, Nebraska 1971, USC 1972 each held the number one spot from the first regular season poll to the postbowl poll).

*Lost bowl game
@Probation

game, they were now said to be "L.A.'s NFL team." No team, no coach, no players in collegiate athletic history were ever as hyped as the 2005 Trojans.

The 2005 regular season played itself out according to what literally seemed to be a Hollywood script. After all, the Trojans dominated the film industry, too. Running back Reggie Bush beat out the other two New York finalists, Leinart and Texas quarterback Vince Young, to capture USC's third Heisman in four years. He and Leinart joined Army's Mr. Inside and Mr. Outside, Doc Blanchard and Glenn Davis, as the only two back-to-back Heisman winners, although not the school's first "Heisman teammates." USC's Charles White (1979) and Marcus Allen (1981) were Heisman teammates between 1978 and 1979. USC's Palmer and Leinart were Heisman teammates between 2001 and 2002. This was *still* not all. Mike Williams, a sophomore All-American wide receiver on the 2003 national champions, had declared for the 2004 draft instead of playing his junior year. Had he come back, he would have been a junior on the 2004 repeat champions and, improbable as it may have been, a senior on the 2005 team.

The Trojans averaged 50 points a game. Second running back LenDale White may well have won the Heisman Trophy if not for teammates Leinart and Bush. They entered the 2006 BCS national championship Rose Bowl game against Texas with a 34-game winning streak and a 45–1 record going back to 2002. Carroll's team was trying for a first-ever three-peat AP national championship. Only California (1920–1922) and Minnesota (1934–1936) had won three straight in the post–World War I, pre-AP era. They billed it as the "Game of the Century," which of course is what they had said of the previous year's Orange Bowl versus Oklahoma until the Trojans turned it into a track meet instead of a football game.

This time, the game matched the hype. It was a duel between USC and Texas's fabulous quarterback, Vince Young, and it was for the ages. The Longhorns' 41–38 victory will rank as the best college football game ever played.

Troy lost much when Young crossed the goal line from 9 yards out with nineteen seconds left. Aside from their third straight title, it would have been USC's twelfth national championship, tying their baseball team, passing UCLA's eleven in basketball . . . and passing Notre Dame for undisputed collegiate football supremacy.

Also lost was a clear regular season run at Oklahoma's all-time 47-game winning streak, which theoretically could have been matched in the 2006 UCLA game at the Rose Bowl, then broken in the BCS title game. The mind boggles.

Aside from that, it would have meant USC would have had a chance at four straight national championships, meaning seniors would have won it every year. It ended Troy's all-time record thirty-three straight weeks ranked number one in the AP poll. Had they won in 2005, they might have been ranked number one entering 2006. As it was they were ranked third.

That third-place preseason ranking in 2006 came despite the loss of juniors Reggie Bush (second overall pick, New Orleans) and White (Tennessee) in the draft. Leinart went in the first round to Arizona. Had White returned, he would have been a Heisman favorite, and USC may well have won the national championship again. The return of Bush *and* White is almost too overwhelming a concept when combined with the entire run between 2002 and 2006, which ultimately produced 34–0, 45–1, and 51–2 records for Carroll's team.

As it was, USC finished 11–2 in 2006, beat Michigan in the Rose Bowl, and finished ranked fourth. An unbelievable-to-believe fluke upset at the hands of UCLA in the last game of the regular season cost them a shot at Ohio State in the BCS title game in Glendale, Arizona. The Buckeyes' humiliating 41–14 demolition at the hands of national champion Florida left little doubt that if USC had their shot, the Trojans may well have won a third national championship in four years. That said, Florida was so impressive that even the most ardent USC fan had to admit they wanted nothing to do with the Gators, at least not the version that showed up on January 8, 2007.

Sports are filled with "what ifs . . . what could have beens . . . almost but not quites." The 2005 USC team, had they beaten Texas, would probably rate as the finest collegiate team ever assembled. They were legends of the green plains worthy of the greatest hype, the most poetic of descriptions, a team for the ages like the 1927 Yankees, the 1973 Bruins basketball team, the 1995 Bulls. . . .

Instead, they go on that short list of truly great college football teams that just missed, like the 1969 Ohio State Buckeyes, the 1973 Alabama Crimson Tide, the 1983 Nebraska Cornhuskers, and the 2002 Miami Hurricanes. Even after eliminating the possibilities and the missed opportunities, Pete Carroll's actual accomplishments in the 2000s rank right up there with what, in similar time frames, Knute Rockne and Frank Leahy did at Notre Dame, Howard Jones and John McKay did at USC, Bud Wilkinson at Oklahoma, Bear Bryant at Alabama, the Miami Hurricanes in the 1980s.

Carroll's greatest strength is in recruiting: consecutive national number one classes in 2003, 2004, 2005, 2006, and 2007. Furthermore, he has done it in a more impressive manner than all previous dynasties. His has been the BCS era. There are no national championships to be won anymore with votes prior to losing bowl games, or even unsatisfactory bowl matchups that leave the best two teams winning against separate opponents, then leaving it to the pollsters.

If the old system were in place, USC would have been the consensus 2003 national champions beyond question, not cochampions with LSU. In 2004 USC would have won the Rose Bowl, Oklahoma would probably have won the Orange Bowl, and the Sooners would have complained all summer about the number one vote going to the "Hollywood Trojans." Instead, they played it out and the Sooners were left with nothing to say. In 2005, the same scenario would have existed. USC would have won the Rose Bowl over a Big 10 foe, Texas would have beaten somebody in the Orange or Fiesta Bowls, most likely, then complained about those number one-ranked . . . "Hollywood Trojans" again. But Vince Young & Co. had their chance. There may have been only two or three teams in history that could have beaten the 2005 Trojans. One of them was the 2005 Longhorns!

USC has done it in an era in which the best juniors leave early, and they always have the best juniors. In the case of Mike Williams, he was the best sophomore. They have done it in the age of major television money, cable, and national recruiting that is more competitive than ever (spurred by up-to-the-minute websites). They have done it in an era in which high school football is bigger than ever; coaching and equipment more so-phisticated; the players faster, stronger, bigger because of better diet and more scientific training methods. In this era, a totally egalitarian landscape gives more schools a better chance. Every ethnic group now plays the game. There is no sense of advantage, which the West and the North once held. Today, blacks, Samoans, Latinos, and international players dot the rosters of teams in every conference. There is more money, more at stake, more fanaticism and interest than ever before. In this übercompetition, USC has emerged as the "new centurions" of the twenty-first century.

In so doing, USC now has edged out Notre Dame as college football's all-time great-est tradition. Had they won the 2005 national title, their twelfth, breaking the historical tie with the Irish, it would have been easier to make this pronouncement. Had the likes of Reggie Bush or LenDale White returned in 2006 to win the school's eighth Heisman Trophy (breaking the seven-all tie now held by USC, Notre Dame, and Ohio State), that would have made it a clearer picture, too. If USC, led by Bush or White, led the team to the title, then the argument would have begun to fade away, replaced by self-evident truth. The same can be said, only more so, had the Trojans beaten Oklahoma's 47-game winning streak, won four straight . . . this all leads back to the "what ifs" that dot poli-tics, history, and the like. By the same token, had Notre Dame's Brady Quinn won the 2006 Heisman Trophy, pushing the Irish back out in front of USC, then it would have diluted the USC argument.

In 2007 and 2008, national champions were not clear-cut. LSU (with two losses) almost won in 2007 by default. Florida was as worthy as anybody in 2008, but nobody could confidently claim they would have won a play-off. Amid an egalitarian landscape, however, emerged true excellence for the ages in the form of Gators quarterback Tim Tebow, who enters the 2009 campaign with a shot at his second Heisman, his third na-tional championship, and, if he pulls this off, the title of "greatest college football player of all time."

Chapter 15

Ranking Tradition

ENTERING THIS CENTURY, USC trailed Notre Dame eleven to nine in national championships and seven to four in Heisman Trophies. Now they are tied with eleven and seven, respectively. USC has for seven straight years beaten Notre Dame, been in the top four, won 11 games or more (an NCAA record), and gone to a BCS game (with another NCAA record six victories). They have played in two straight BCS title games and five Rose Bowls. Their 82–8 record (2002–2008) is the best 90-game mark of the modern era. If they win their first 10 in 2009 they will eclipse Oklahoma (89–8–3, 1947–56) for the best all-time 100-game record.

The historical "tie" with Notre Dame creates the desire to find criteria giving the advantage to one or the other of the two traditions. Alabama has nine legitimate national championships, but like USC and Notre Dame, there are other seasons in which the Crimson Tide can claim some form of the title. They are followed by Oklahoma (six); Ohio State, Nebraska, Miami, and Minnesota (five each); Michigan and California (four); Texas, LSU, and Florida (three); then Army, Florida State, Penn State, Pittsburgh, and Stanford (two each since World War I).

There is much more to study beyond national championships and Heisman Trophies. The "Heisman factor" is nebulous, so much a part of bias and media hype. Many would dismiss it as a major selling point when rating college programs. Far too many Heisman winners have flopped in the NFL or, for that matter, in bowl games played a month later, to truly state with certainty that the winner is the "best college football player" in the land.

That said, USC's Heismans *have done better*! Mike Garrett (1965) played in two Super Bowls, helped Kansas City win one (1970), and was a fine pro running back. O. J. Simpson, if one can compartmentalize the events of June 14, 1994, was at one time considered on par with Jim Brown (whose single-season rushing record he broke wholesale) as the greatest NFL running back ever. Charles White (1979) led the league in rushing one year with the Rams. Marcus Allen (1981) was a Super Bowl MVP and Hall of Famer with the Raiders. Carson Palmer (2002) is a superstar in Cincinnati. The jury is still out on Arizona's Matt Leinart (2004). Reggie Bush (2005) immediately helped turn the New Orleans Saints into a contender.

Furthermore, there is little doubt that had the voters not voted early, USC's Anthony Davis would have won the 1974 Heisman. The vote for UCLA's Gary Beban over Simpson in 1967 is inexplicable. The only explanation is that they could not come to grips with giving it to a junior college transfer, which O. J. was. Rodney Peete seemed to have the 1988 Heisman sewn up as late as Thanksgiving weekend, but losing to Notre Dame combined with *astronomical* numbers by Oklahoma State's Barry Sanders swung the vote, correctly, to Sanders.

Notre Dame's Heisman winners? Angelo Bertelli (1943), John Lujack (1947), and John Lattner (1953) were, uh . . . without research one does not know what they did in the NFL, which answers the question about them. Paul Hornung (1956) was a superstar in Green Bay, a Hall of Famer, and a legend. John Huarte (1964) signed a big bonus with the New York Titans/Jets, was quickly overshadowed by Joe Willie Namath, and today is mostly known for being the *other* Heisman winner from Mater Dei High School in Santa Ana, California. The other? Matt Leinart of USC. There are only two high schools in the nation with a couple of Heisman winners. Woodrow Wilson High in Dallas, Texas, is the other, with Davey O'Brien (1938) and another Golden Domer, the great Tim Brown (1987), a surefire Hall of Famer with the Raiders.

Alabama has no Heisman Trophy winners. Their supporters argue that this is a good thing, emblematic of their team concept over the years. Ohio State's seven had fair success beyond college. Archie Griffin (1974–1975) was a good running back in Cincinnati. Eddie George was a star in Tennessee. Troy Smith's performance in the 2007 BCS title game was abysmal.

Oklahoma's four winners include Steve Owens (1969), a creditable pro in Detroit; Billy Sims (1978); Jason White (2003), a washout; and Sam Bradford (2008), who followed in the long tradition of Heisman winners who failed in January. Nebraska's three are Johnny Rodgers (1972), who went to Canada; Mike Rozier (1983); and Eric Crouch (2001), who went nowhere.

Furthermore, if the Heisman Trophy is not so important to the prestige of a college football program, why do those programs *move Heaven and Earth* in order to promote their contenders? USC and Notre Dame are as good at it as anybody.

The national championship is what the fellows play for, and it makes for the ultimate statistic in search of the greatest tradition, but there is more. Nebraska, for instance, has an impressive eight Outland Trophy winners. Oklahoma has five; Ohio State, Notre Dame, and Texas three; USC just one. Oklahoma has twenty-three combined Vince Lombardi, Jim Thorpe, Dick Butkus, Walter Camp, Johnny Unitas, Doak Walker, Lou Groza, John Mackey, Chuck Bednarik, Bronco Nagurski, Davey O'Brien, Fred Biletnikoff, Ray Guy, Mosi Tatupu, Ronnie Lott, Pop Warner, Dave Rimington, and Maxwell award winners. USC has nineteen, Miami and Notre Dame fifteen, and Nebraska thirteen.

Notre Dame has 96 consensus All-Americans compared to compared to 86 for USC, then Ohio State (84), Michigan (73), Oklahoma (65), Nebraska (52), Texas (48), Alabama (29), Miami (37), and Penn State (34). Among other All-American selections, Ohio State boasts 179, compared to 176 for Notre Dame (seventy-six second team), 153 first teamers at USC, 148 at Oklahoma, 125 at Michigan, 124 for Texas, and 106 at Nebraska, followed by Alabama (104), Penn State (91), and Miami (81).

Michigan loves to tout their impressive win-loss record. They have the most wins (872) and the best record (872–282–36) in history. However, they started playing football

Outland Trophy Winners

1. <u>Nebraska</u> (8): *Larry Jacobson (1971), Rich Glover (1972), Dave Rimington (1981–82), Dean Steinkuhler (1983), Will Shields (1992), Zach Wiegert (1994), Aaron Taylor (1997)
2. <u>Oklahoma</u> (5): Jim Weatherall (1951), J. D. Roberts (1953), *Lee Roy Selmon (1975), Greg Roberts (1978), Jammal Brown (2004)
3. <u>Ohio State</u> (4): Jim Parker (1956), Jim Stillwagon (1970), John Hicks (1973), Orlando Pace (1996)
4. <u>Notre Dame</u> (3): *George Connor (1946), Bill Fischer (1948), Ross Browner (1976)
4. <u>Texas</u> (3): *Scott Appleton (1963), Tommy Nobis (1965), Brad Shearer (1977)
4. <u>Minnesota</u> (3): *Tom Brown (1960), Bobby Bell (1962), Greg Eslinger (2005)
4. <u>Iowa</u> (3): Calvin Jones (1955), Alex Karras (1957), Robert Gallery (2003)
8. <u>Arkansas</u> (2): Bill Brooks (1954), Lloyd Phillips (1966)
8. <u>Auburn</u> (2): Zeke Smith (1958), Tracy Rocker (1988)
8. <u>Brigham Young</u> (2): Jason Buck (1986), Mohammed Elewonibi (1989)
8. <u>Miami</u> (2): Russell Maryland (1990), *Bryant McKinnie (2001)
8. <u>Tennessee</u> (2): Steve DeLong (1964), John Henderson (2000)
8. <u>UCLA</u> (2): Jonathan Ogden (1995), Kris Farris (1998)
8. <u>Maryland</u> (2): *Dick Modzelewski (1952), Randy White (1974)
8. <u>Alabama</u> (2): Chris Samuels (1999), Andre Smith (2008)

One each:

<u>Southern California</u>: *Ron Yary (1967)

<u>Washington State</u>: Rien Long (2002)

<u>Arizona</u>: Ron Waldrop (1993)

<u>Washington</u>: *Steve Emtman (1991)

<u>Air Force</u>: Chad Hennings (1987)

<u>Boston College</u>: Mike Ruth (1985)

<u>Virginia Tech</u>: Bruce Smith (1984)

<u>Pittsburgh</u>: Mark May, 1980

<u>North Carolina</u>: Jim Richter (1979)

<u>Penn State</u>: Mike Reid (1969)

<u>Georgia</u>: Bill Stanfill (1968)

<u>Utah State</u>: Merlin Olsen (1961)

<u>Duke</u>: Mike McGee (1959)

<u>Kentucky</u>: Bob Gain (1950)

<u>Michigan State</u>: Ed Bagdon, 1949

<u>Army</u>: Joe Steffy (1946)

*Team won the national championship

in 1879, which means they have upwards of a ten- to fifteen-year advantage over most of the competition. Their winning percentage is terrific and not to be scoffed at, but much of that was built in the thirty years in which they dominated football while the non-Ivy schools were establishing the sport or playing rugby. USC got off to a particularly late start. While the first official game was played in 1888, it was decades before the game took on more than a "club sport" atmosphere, while Michigan took it seriously and thought of themselves as "national champions." USC played rugby between 1911 and 1915. While they did play Stanford in 1905, until the PCC was formed (1915) and USC slowly made their way toward membership in it (1922), their schedule normally included the likes of Los Angeles High School, the Arrowhead Athletic Club, or small colleges in the L.A. area. USC ranks sixth in overall record, eighth in total wins.

Notre Dame billed itself as a tiny Catholic school, a 1913 version of David defeating Goliath in the form of Army, but they were part of the strong Midwestern football craze going back to before the turn of the century. Their 831-284-42 record is the second best overall, third best in total wins. Interestingly, Texas has 832 wins against 316 losses and 33 ties since 1893. While the 9-0 Longhorns of 1914 contended with Army for the national championship, like most "rural" and Southern colleges they were not well regarded until after World War I.

Victories (through 2008)

1.	Michigan (1879–2008)	872	17. Miami (Ohio) (1888–2005)	639
2.	Texas (1893–2008)	832	20. Army (1890–2004)	631
3.	Notre Dame (1887–2008)	831	21. Minnesota (1882–2006)	626
4.	Nebraska (1890–2008)	817	22. Arkansas (1894–2004)	621
5.	Ohio State (1890–2008)	808	23. Florida (1906–2006)	619
6.	Penn State (1887–2008)	800	24. California (1882–2006)	602
7.	Oklahoma (1895–2008)	791	25. Clemson (1896–2004)	600
8.	Southern California (1888–2008)	766	26. Michigan State (1896–2006)	599
9.	Tennessee (1891–2006)	760	27. Mississippi (1893–2004)	583
10.	Alabama (1892–2008)	750	28. Maryland (1892–2004)	573
11.	Georgia (1892–2006)	702	29. Miami (1926–2008)	544
12.	Louisiana State (1893–2006)	680	30. Stanford (1891–2006)	543
13.	Auburn (1892–2006)	667	31. Illinois (1890–2004)	542
14.	Syracuse (1889–2004)	664	32. Central Michigan (1896–2005)	532
15.	Colorado (1890–2005)	650	33. UCLA (1919–2006)	528
16.	Washington (1889–2006)	646	34. Arizona State (1897–2005)	523
16.	Georgia Tech (1892–2006)	646	35. Texas Christian (1896–2004)	515
17.	Pittsburgh (1890–2004)	639	36. Brigham Young (1922–2004)	456
17.	Texas A&M (1894–2005)	639	37. Florida State (1947–2006)	442

Regular season records are great but do not tell the whole picture, just as is the situation in professional sports and NCAA play-offs. It comes down to the thing the teams play for: national championships. As a secondary aspect of this quest, examination of records always emphasizes whether or not a team won their bowl game. The question might be asked of, say, USC in 2006: Would they rather have gone to the BCS title game and lost or gone to the Rose Bowl and won? Answer: Win the Rose Bowl! Any Trojan fans who compare their emotions after the 2006 Rose Bowl loss to Texas with the 2007 win over Michigan at the same venue know this self-evident truth.

College football is an incomplete, often uneven operation. Over the years, it tends to even itself out; whether some conferences are better than others, or certain teams play stronger schedules, while these affect seasons and even multiple years, over the decades the whole thing works itself out pretty well. In the course of a century, it is not generally felt that LSU (680–736–47 through 2006) has played a significantly harder schedule than Syracuse (664–435–49), although they definitely have over the past two decades.

The bowls have always fascinated the public because it gave them a chance to compare and contrast regions, conferences, and teams. The South earned respect largely on the strength of Alabama's stellar performance in a series of Rose Bowl encounters between 1926 and 1946. Bowls determine national championships, influence final rankings in a greater way than any other games, and cut away much of the overrated hype that is attached to a team's regular season record.

USC is the dominant bowl team, by a relatively substantial margin (31–16) over Alabama (31–22–3), with Penn State sporting an impressive 26–12–2 mark, followed by Oklahoma (24–17–1). When it comes to bowls, Notre Dame, Michigan, and Ohio State would all prefer that historians overlook them. Each is under .500. In the case of Ohio State and Michigan, they are under .500 because they have played USC so often.

The Trojans can attribute an enormous part of their success to the Rose Bowl and geography. When Stanford built their new stadium in 1921, they made a bid for the Rose Bowl to switch locations to northern California. Had they succeeded, it may well have changed the face of college football. Stanford, a major national power at the time, might have built on a big bowl game played in their stadium, thus turning themselves into a tradition on par with Notre Dame, Alabama, and Ohio State.

When the Rose Bowl was built, it meant that Southern California would be the de facto "home team" more often than not. USC has captured nine national championships playing at home. Only Miami (Orange Bowl in 1983, 1987, 1991) and to a lesser extent LSU (Sugar Bowl in 1958, 2003, 2007) and Florida (Orange Bowl, 2008) can lay claim to such an accomplishment. The Rose Bowl is the oldest, most prestigious, most watched bowl game, for any number of reasons. It always was the "best game." In recent years other bowls have equaled it for drama, matchups, and national-title implications. It had down years, but whether the Tournament of Roses Committee admits it or not, the BCS has had the uneven effect of leading its comeback. It has been Southern Cal (24–9) that is the face of the Rose Bowl. No other school has this kind of association or success in any bowl game.

The record of "elite ten" teams in bowl games is as explanatory of why the historical rankings are what they are as any other factor. The simple fact is that if teams such as Michigan (19–20) and Ohio State (18–22) had records approaching USC's in bowl games, they would have many more national championships and might rank ahead of the Trojans overall. They do not, so therefore they don't. Most shocking of all is Notre Dame. Somehow they have positioned themselves in the unenviable position of being a team looking at its bowl history and seeing no friendly ammunition when arguing that they are the greatest of all traditions. Their 14–15 mark is bad enough; the fact that the Irish hold the ongoing NCAA record for consecutive losses (eleven between January 1995 and January 2007) is probably the single greatest factor determining why they have fallen behind USC in the pantheon. That is only the half of it. Notre Dame's *avoidance* of competitive bowls for decades (while the Trojans and Crimson Tide took on all challengers) ices the case in USC's favor.

The fact is that, while in the past two decades Notre Dame has played a consistently difficult schedule, for many years they played a notoriously soft one. USC *never* did that. USC subjected itself to annual struggles not just with the Irish but also with crosstown rival UCLA, who hate them like Palestinians hate Israelis. USC has always dotted its schedule with challenges, often on the road in hostile atmospheres (at Texas, 1955 and 1966; at Alabama, 1970 and 1978, just to name a few).

Notre Dame's "no-bowl" policy after the 1925 Rose Bowl win over Stanford, which was not rescinded until they lost to Texas in the 1970 Cotton Bowl, makes for some interesting scenarios. What if the 1929 Irish had played USC in a Rose Bowl rematch? What if the Sugar Bowl had been instituted by 1930 and in that year the Irish had played Alabama in the South? What if the 1943 Irish had played Navy, Michigan, or unbeaten Purdue in a bowl? What if the Big 10 and PCC had not signed a contract to play each other in Pasadena, and Notre Dame had played Fritz Crisler's Michigan Wolverines in the 1948 and 1949 Rose Bowls?

How would the 1949 Notre Dame national champions have fared against Bud Wilkinson's 10-0 Oklahoma Sooners in the Orange Bowl? Most intriguing of all would have been the matchup between Notre Dame and Alabama in a Sugar Bowl showdown for the 1966 national title. Common sense indicates that at least a few of their champions would have lost some of those bowl games. At least in light of historical legitimacy (the AP polls would not have changed due to prebowl voting), the Irish would not be as prestigious. If one uses their *actual* history, that being the 14–15 record they have when they buckled it up and played the games for real, then the question simply answers itself.

However, there is a flip side to this argument. Notre Dame was not ranked number one entering the 1973 Sugar Bowl with Alabama or the 1978 Cotton Bowl with Texas. Their victories propelled them to the number one slot. Taking away the irritating concept of the AP prebowl votes, had they played a bowl game after the 1948 season they might have won and used that to vault over Michigan in the polls. The 1953 Irish may well have won the title had they gone to a bowl game.

What would have been more intriguing than a true "national championship game" between the 1920 Cal Wonder Team and Rockne's unbeaten Irish in the Rose Bowl? The 1938 squad would have loved a second chance at Southern Cal, who ended their unbeaten season with a 13-0 shutout at the Coliseum, in a Rose Bowl rematch.

All of this is speculation. What we are left with are actual events. In this regard, Notre Dame has both hurt itself and helped itself by virtue of its 55-year policy of bowl avoidance.

The concept that winning bowl games usurps winning regular season games, and that national championships are more important than anything else, manifests itself also when comparing historical final Associated Press polls. Michigan has been ranked in the final Top 25 (Top 20 until a few years ago) fifty-four times, compared to Notre Dame's and Ohio State's forty-eight, Alabama's forty-six, and USC at forty-three. This is impressive but serves to mock the Wolverines slightly. It ends up creating in their fans' collective mind the disappointment felt when all those highly rated (and often overrated) Michigan teams had their maize and blue helmets handed to them by better Pacific-8 and Pac-10 teams in the Rose Bowl.

USC is not at the top of this list. They have had down periods where they were not ranked. But their national championships have served to erase all that memory. Ask any Michigan or Ohio State fan if they would trade their higher AP rank totals with USC's eleven national titles. The answer is not necessary herein. It simply offers itself as that which is obvious.

Michigan is the "champion" of all AP Top 20/25 rankings, too (747), compared to Ohio State (746), Notre Dame (703), Oklahoma (672), and USC (666). This statistic serves the same dubious purpose, again mocking Michigan as always good, always tough, always a winner, more often than not overrated.

A more telling statistic is Michigan's thirty-two number one overall AP rankings. USC (90), Notre Dame (89), Oklahoma (88), and Ohio State (86) are far ahead of them. *Number one* is what the boys play for, not number nine, or number eighteen, or number twenty-three.

USC was ranked number one for thirty-three straight weeks between 2003 and 2006, followed by Miami with twenty (2001–2002), Notre Dame at nineteen (1988–1989), and USC again with seventeen (1972–1973).

Winning streaks and unbeaten streaks are less instructive in search of history than other records. Oklahoma's 47-game winning streak is a record that will be as difficult to break as Joe DiMaggio's 56-game hitting streak of 1941. In the modern era, USC and Miami are second (34 each). California, Georgia Tech, and a series of other programs got hot over relatively short periods of time. Notre Dame has no winning streaks near the top, but their 39-game *unbeaten* skein meant those entering the school as freshmen in the fall of 1946 and graduating in the spring of 1950 *never saw them lose*!

The Irish claim a distinct advantage when it comes to College Hall of Famers (forty-eight to USC's thirty-six as of the 2009 induction). USC returns the favor when comparing *Pro Football* Hall of Famers. 2007 inductee Bruce Matthews gave them fourteen to Notre Dame's nine. Both schools have produced NFL heroes. Notre Dame's Joe Montana is generally considered the greatest quarterback who ever lived. O. J. Simpson was one of the greatest NFL running backs ever. Paul Hornung defined the Packer dynasty. Tim Brown will go to the Hall of Fame when he is eligible. Super Bowl MVPs? Sure, the Irish have Montana, but USC has Lynn Swann and Marcus Allen.

Going Pro

In 2006, Miami led all collegiate programs with fifty-two players on NFL rosters, according to *Sports Illustrated*. The Southeastern Conference had 266 players in the league.

These kinds of records can have anomalies. For instance, in baseball USC has nine Cy Young award winners and one most valuable player. Arizona State has *eight* MVPs, courtesy of Barry Bonds's seven (plus Reggie Jackson, 1973). Michigan similarly offers Tom Brady's two and Desmond Howard's one Super Bowl MVP awards.

USC leads with seventy-four first-round draft picks compared to Ohio State (sixty-seven), Miami (fifty-nine), and Notre Dame (fifty-eight). USC, Notre Dame, and Alabama are tied for the most number one overall draft picks (five each). Miami's six first-round picks in 2004 are the highest number, followed by USC (1968) and Miami (2002) with five. Through the 2009 draft, 485 Trojans have been drafted, compared to 464 from Notre Dame, with Oklahoma trailing in the distance (334). The 1946 draft class at Notre Dame had the highest number of players picked (sixteen), followed by Southern Cal (fifteen in 1953, fourteen in both 1975 and 1977) and Notre Dame (fifteen in 1945).

Records are sketchy and incomplete, but USC appears to have the most professional players (414 to Notre Dame's 395). Nobody else is close. USC had 203 Pro Bowlers entering the 2008 season (compared to Notre Dame's 135 entering the 2007 season). Ohio State had 122. Nobody else is close here, either. USC also became the first college to have 100 alumni Super Bowl players. Miami, the great newcomer of the modern era, trailed with eighty. Forty-eight Trojans have played on the winning Super Bowl team. Notre Dame had thirty-eight.

Finally, it is very important in ranking history to place more emphasis on modern greatness. This creates some problems, rankling a few, but to ignore the logic behind it is to apply uneven standards that *defy* logic. First and foremost, failing to apply the "modern weight" theory leaves one to conclude that Princeton, followed very likely by Harvard or Yale, is the greatest collegiate football tradition ever. One could go on for pages in an effort to prove why this is not so. Rather, the simple fact that *they are not*, which is knowledge universally possessed, is simply stated. Thus, and it is.

Judging sports is a tricky business, but the modern athlete is better . . . and better and better and better as time goes by. Sports like track or swimming offer measurable records in terms of times and distances. In using these measurements there is no comparison between the Olympic heroes of the 1920s and 1930s with those of the 1990s and 2000s. That said, one could easily imagine that, given modern training methods, Jesse Owens would have been able to compete equally with Carl Lewis.

Other sports offer obvious social discrepancies, which among other factors tells us to favor modernity. Basketball in the 1950s versus basketball in the 2000s? Is this even an argument?

Baseball is the most traditional sport, America's national pastime. It is the single sport that allows the historian to make comparisons that do not seem ridiculous. Ty

Cobb or Pete Rose? Honus Wagner or Alex Rodriguez? Christy Mathewson or Tom Seaver? Baseball defined America prior to World War I. It offers a 154-game yearly schedule that was in place until 1961. The "dead ball era" ended in 1920. Comparisons between Babe Ruth, Barry Bonds, and Henry Aaron; between Jimmie Fox and Mark McGwire; between Bob Feller and Nolan Ryan are much easier to contrast with each other than Gus Dorais and Carson Palmer, the best quarterbacks of 1913 and 2002, respectively.

Later quarterback heroes like Davey O'Brien and Sammy Baugh have gained some favorable comparison with their modern counterparts, but whether fair or not the likes of Montana, Brady, and Johnny Unitas get most of the kudos. Few really are willing to say that Bronco Nagurski, Minnesota's bruising fullback of the late 1920s, is as great as Barry Sanders, Oklahoma State's Heisman winner of 1988.

For many reasons, ranking college football tradition requires one to separate the period between 1869 and 1918 from the period between 1919 and the present day. Up until the end of World War I, college football was far too undeveloped, uneven, and regional, and it possessed too many irregularities in terms of rules and play to compare it with the game in the years since. In judging a football team, its success prior to World War I is taken into consideration, but not given as much weight.

The ball was bigger and difficult to throw. The forward pass was virtually unheard of until 1913. There were no field goals, very little punting, and mostly quick kicks. There were no facemasks or helmets or pads to speak of. The rules were changed constantly. The "Yale wedge" was outlawed. Congress got involved. Between 1905 and 1918 many teams played rugby or reduced football to "club sport" status.

It is for these reasons that Michigan, perhaps the most obvious example, does not get as much credit for their premodern record as they might wish they did. Princeton, Yale, Harvard, and Penn are not considered to be among the greatest college traditions despite utter dominance of the first thirty to forty years of the game's existence. Washington, Stanford, Army, Georgia Tech, and Pittsburgh are among those teams that established their traditions on a national basis in those early days and are still recognized today as "major college football programs."

Army was, until midcentury, a tremendous power on a level with Alabama, Notre Dame, and Michigan. They have not maintained that level of excellence but continue to play a relatively heavy schedule.

Over time, as one examines the decades, great runs over long periods of time, and dynasties, the "usual suspects"—Notre Dame, Southern Cal, Oklahoma, Alabama, and the like—continue to show themselves to be the class of collegiate football.

The emphasis on modern achievement shows itself in different ways. This emphasis has its greatest effect on the state of Florida. Florida State was a *girls' school* until after World War II. A Florida high school star named Burt Reynolds was recruited to play football for the Seminoles. He favored Miami but was told that FSU was about "90 perfect female" except for the football team. That was all he needed to hear.

Florida State was mostly mediocre until Bobby Bowden's hiring prior to the 1976 season. They possess none of the age-old tradition of Penn State or Texas, yet their record in the age of integration, network TV, national recruiting, and modern techniques is so outstanding that their two national championships and two Heisman Trophies help rank them far above Army, winners of three national championships and three Heismans.

Their downstate rivals, Miami, were playing football long before Florida State but were a minor operation. Out of *nowhere*, the Hurricanes put on a run beginning in 1983 that is equaled by very few programs, ever. So dominant has Miami been that their record surpasses traditions like LSU, Texas, even Michigan.

Florida State's unique recruitment of Reynolds also points out some truths about sports, in general. Where the great athletes are, so one will find the girls, and vice versa. What comes first is up for debate. High schools that have the best teams more often than not have the prettiest cheerleaders. There are definitely exceptions to this rule, but in college, particularly in the Sun Belt—USC, UCLA, Arizona State, Texas, LSU, Alabama, Florida State, Miami—one of the biggest inducements used in the recruitment of stellar ball players is the pleasant existence of beautiful, tanned coeds.

USC has always used its natural advantages to take it one step further. John Wayne was a Trojan football player. Through him, Howard Jones was able to land jobs for his players as extras, often as Roman Legionnaires, Napoleon's *Grand Armée*, or Biblical flocks in epics of the silent film era. Access to these jobs, which came with the perks of off-campus money and access to attractive actresses, was a recruiting tool that Howard Jones had in Los Angeles but not in Iowa.

The fact that USC—as well as UCLA in basketball, or to a lesser extent Cal State Fullerton in baseball and Stanford in tennis and women's sports—is the best football program and top athletic department in the country owes itself to these among other advantages. They have great weather and are located in the middle of the second biggest city and the largest metropolitan *area* in the nation. High school sports in southern California are second to none. It is natural that high school players want to play near their family and friends in convenient fashion. USC is able to get more kids like that than any program, although it does not stop them from recruiting nationally.

They have benefited from the fact that there is strong media attention; from great professional sports played in the area, with opportunities over the years to see the Dodgers, Angels, Rams, Raiders, Lakers, and other teams play. The Rose Bowl in their backyard creates a great edge for them. The professional teams in L.A. do not simply provide more chances for a local college player to be seen or to hook on as a free agent, but also create opportunity in the area of sports broadcasting. An inordinate number of USC and UCLA athletes have excelled in the sports media.

So it is, too, that the modern era favors the Trojans. What is more impressive, USC's run between 2003 and 2005 or Minnesota's run between 1934 and 1936? Miami's dominance between 1987 and 1991 or Notre Dame's between 1946 and 1949? Oklahoma's teams between 1971 and 1975 or Bud Wilkinson's Sooners of 1953-1957? Pittsburgh's national champions of 1976 or the 1916 Panthers?

USC and Notre Dame have two things going for them: tradition and continuing tradition. They rise above all other programs on the basis of this premise. In looking at the two traditions side by side, often the differences are narrow. Nevertheless, there is enough to formulate definite opinions.

The game has demarcation points: 1919, when the Great War was over; 1946, when World War II was over; 1960, when equipment and coaching improved, TV eventually became colorized, schedules went national; 1970, when segregation finally came to an end; and 1998, when the BCS began. In each instance, the Trojans match, come close enough, or surpass Notre Dame. In the latest modern periods, they overcome them. In the 2000s, they created distance.

Until 1962, Notre Dame had won seven national championships and had five Heisman winners. USC had won four national crowns and had zero Heismans. Since then, USC has won seven national titles and seven Heismans to four titles and two Heismans for the Irish. Notre Dame still has the edge in the win-loss record between the two schools, which is an important point, but USC has unquestionably enjoyed two periods of dominance in the rivalry: 1967–1982 and the 2000s. In the 2000s, in the most modern of eras, USC has roared back into the proverbial "tie" and, in the historical analysis, the *lead* over Notre Dame as the greatest tradition.

It is important to understand, however, that such a moniker, *greatest college football tradition of all time*, has the potential of being only a temporary one, or even a trade-off. This is the level the Trojans have reached as of 2009, the time of this book's publication. They did not hold this position at the turn of the 21st century, or even as late as 2003. It is a position in the hierarchy to be continually fought over, defended, challenged with honor by Notre Dame, Alabama, Oklahoma, Ohio State, and the other great traditions of this fabulous game we call college football.

PART III

The Best of the Best

Chapter 16

Top Single-Season Teams

1. 1972 Southern California
2. 1995 Nebraska
3. 2004 Southern California
4. 2005 Texas
5. 1947 Notre Dame
6. 1971 Nebraska
7. 2001 Miami
8. 1945 Army
9. 1979 Alabama
10. 1956 Oklahoma
11. 1999 Florida State
12. 1987 Miami
13. 1968 Ohio State
14. 1986 Penn State
15. 1988 Notre Dame
16. 1969 Texas
17. 1932 Southern California
18. 1920 California
19. 1948 Michigan
20. 1973 Notre Dame
21. 1991 Washington
22. 1928 Southern California
23. 1924 Notre Dame
24. 1962 Southern California
25. 1992 Alabama
26. 2000 Oklahoma
27. 1966 Notre Dame
28. 1976 Pittsburgh
29. 1934 Alabama
30. 1901 Michigan
31. 1917 Georgia Tech
32. 1929 Notre Dame
33. 1930 Alabama
34. 1936 Minnesota
35. 1944 Army
36. 1946 Notre Dame
37. 1985 Oklahoma
38. 1997 Michigan
39. 1997 Nebraska
40. 1998 Tennessee
41. 2002 Ohio State
42. 2003 Southern California

CHARLES "TREE" YOUNG was an All-American tight end at the University of Southern California in 1972. He is a member of the College Football Hall of Fame and played on the 1979 Los Angeles Rams Super Bowl team. He caught Joe Montana's passes as a member of the 1981 world-champion San Francisco 49ers. A respected Christian pastor in the Seattle area, he was asked in October 2005 who was better, the 1972 Trojans or the 2005 Trojans, who at that time were being spoken of as the greatest college team ever.

"This team [2005] isn't as good as last year's team," said Young, "and they wouldn't score on the 1972 team until late in the third quarter."

At the time, Young's comments appeared incredulous—the overhyped memory of a proud ex-jock. USC pounded through the rest of the regular season schedule. They appeared poised to make all kinds of history as they prepared for Texas in the BCS championship game at the Rose Bowl: 50 points a game, best team ever, first three-straight AP national champions, twelfth school title, thirty-four weeks in a row ranked number one on the way to 40, and a direct assault on Oklahoma's 47-game winning streak.

But when the Trojans were unable to stop Vince Young in Pasadena, Charles Young's words had extra resonance. While the 2005 Trojans may have been the finest *offensive* team ever, it was their 1972 defense that separates that team from all others.

Determining who actually was the best team in a single season is subjective at best. Many college football experts have other choices. Old-timers like the 1947 Notre Dame Fighting Irish. Statistically, Michigan's "point-a-minute" team was unparalleled, scoring 128 against Buffalo, 89 versus Beloit, 49 against Stanford in the first Rose Bowl, all while allowing *zero points all season*.

Hey, how about Brick Muller and California's 1920 Wonder Team; Knute Rockne's 1924 Four Horsemen of Notre Dame; Howard Jones's 1932 "Thundering Herd" Trojans; Red Blaik's 1944 Army team (which averaged almost 60 points a game); or Bud Wilkinson's 1956 national champions, in the latter stages of a 47-game winning streak?

Too old, you say? Prefer the modern era? Well then, let us consider Bob Devaney's 1971 Nebraska Cornhuskers, Bear Bryant's greatest team at Alabama (1979), Jimmy Johnson's Miami juggernaut (1987), or the unbelievable powerhouses at Nebraska in 1995 and Florida State in 1999.

The New Millennium, the BCS era? The 2001 Miami Hurricanes were nothing less than awesome. Charle' Young himself seemed to prefer the 2004 Trojans, at least over the 2005 Trojans, and if the 2005 team was *almost* the best ever, what does that say about the team that beat them, Vince Young and Texas?

In the end, a majority of those who know enough to have an expert opinion pick the 1972 Trojans. They trailed 3–0 for a couple minutes in the season opener at Arkansas, a 31–10 USC blowout. Troy briefly trailed in the first half of the fifth game of the season at Stanford before winning handily. That was it.

"We were never pushed," said backup quarterback Pat Haden.

They scored around 40 points a game; threw one shutout; and beat UCLA (24–7), Notre Dame (45–23), and Ohio State (42–17, Rose Bowl) in easy manner to close out the season. They were ranked first in every poll. Statistically, other teams have looked better. The 1932 Trojans were more impressive on defense. Army (1945), Nebraska (1971 and 1995), Texas, and even USC (2005) scored more points.

The 2004 Trojans won the Orange Bowl by more (36 compared to the 25-point margin over Ohio State). The 1995 Cornhuskers' 62–24 victory over Florida looked as awesome as either of the others. In 1971 Nebraska throttled unbeaten Alabama, 38–6. Was it the schedule perhaps?

Who Is the Greatest Single-Season College Team of All Time?

<u>1972 Southern California Trojans</u>

Keith Jackson, longtime network college broadcaster, considered "the voice of college football":

"[USC was] a remarkable group of athletes. They were never threatened in an unbeaten national championship season."

Dan Jenkins, longtime *Sports Illustrated* college football writer (author of *Semi-Tough* and *Saturday's America*):

"John McKay's 12–0 Trojans destroyed every opponent, and why? They had Anthony Davis, Sam 'Bam' Cunningham, Lynn Swann, Mike Rae, Charles Young and Richard 'Batman' Wood, plus a couple of subs named Pat Haden and J. K. McKay. They scored more than forty points against seven teams, including humiliations of Notre Dame (45–23) and Ohio State (42–17 in the Rose Bowl)."

Michael MacCambridge, editor, *ESPN Encyclopedia of College Football: The Complete History of the Game*:

"Southern California, 1972. Every year, someone gripes that they were robbed, or deserved a shot at number one. But after USC tore through its schedule and dismantled Ohio State in the Rose Bowl, no one complained. The Trojans were that good."

Blackie Sherrod, longtime sports columnist, *Dallas Times-Herald* and *Dallas Morning News*:

"Southern California, 1972." Period!

<u>2005 Southern California Trojans</u>

Kirk Herbstreit, former player; ESPN *GameDay* analyst:

". . . one of the most prolific offenses we've seen. Combine that with [Pete Carroll's] defensive scheme . . . one of the best teams ever to play college football."

<u>2004 Southern California Trojans</u>

Lee Corso, former player, coach; ESPN *GameDay* analyst:

"In a big time game, the Trojans destroyed an excellent Oklahoma team 55–19. They could have scored seventy points that day."

<u>2001 Miami Hurricanes</u>

Edwin Pope, longtime sports columnist, *Miami Herald*:

"This team had everything: great quarterback with Ken Dorsey, a great defense led by Ed Reed. No wonder the 'Canes routed Nebraska in the Rose Bowl to win the national title."

(continues)

Who Is the Greatest Single-Season College Team of All Time? (*continued*)

1995 Nebraska Cornhuskers

Chris Fowler, ESPN announcer:

"*Unbeaten champs who grew more comfortable as the season progressed, destroying Florida 62–24 in the Fiesta Bowl. Scary to watch.*"

1961 Alabama Crimson Tide

Bill Curry, former player, Alabama coach, and ESPN college football analyst:

"*They refused to lose. Gritty, lightning quick, near perfect in their fundamentals.*"

1947 Notre Dame Fighting Irish

Beano Cook, ESPN college football analyst:

"As the 1946 Notre Dame team did, the 1947 Fighting Irish won the national title. And as the 1946 team did, they never trailed once."

1938 Duke Blue Devils

Furman Bisher, longtime sports columnist, *Atlanta Journal-Constitution*:

In 1972, the Pacific-8 Conference was the best in the nation, but it was probably not as powerful top-to-bottom as the Southeastern Conference has been in the 1990s and 2000s. The Pac-8 of the 1960s and 1970s might even have been underrated at the time. Its victories in ten of eleven Rose Bowls between January 1970 and January 1980, often against unbeaten Ohio State and Michigan teams hungry for national titles (that would have come with victories in several of those games), provide a retrospective analysis favoring a conference that got better every year.

Nebraska was the preseason number one in 1972, but UCLA upset them in the opener in Los Angeles. Arkansas was also a preseason national championship contender, supposedly the best team since the 1969 Razorbacks came within a whisker of going all the way. USC dominated them in their home stadium.

Troy beat Illinois on the road, 51–6. Duffy Daugherty claimed that his Michigan State team was the best since his 1966 "Game of the Century" Spartans, and linebacker Brad Van Pelt was touted as "the best player in college football." USC dismantled them, 51–6. The conference offered no challengers.

Many believe the 1995 Cornhuskers might have been better. USC's traditional rivals—UCLA, Notre Dame, and for that matter, Woody Hayes's Buckeyes—were all powerhouses at the time. The Bruins were an excellent team over a period of years: the kind of team that occasionally challenged for the national championship, could beat anybody, won Rose Bowls. They ended Nebraska's 32-game unbeaten streak and were considered an offensive juggernaut on the ground, but against USC it looked like boys playing against men.

Notre Dame was similarly a power in the "Era of Ara." Had the Fighting Irish not subjected themselves to their annual game with USC every year, they very well might have won several more national championships than the three they did come away with between 1966 and 1988.

The same thing can be said of Ohio State. Buckeye fans must have questioned the wisdom of the Rose Bowl arrangement when year after year their "invincible" teams came out west only to get their clocks cleaned in the California sunshine, often accompanied by Woody Hayes punching an *L.A. Times* photographer, cursing out reporters, or finding general immorality and conspiracy in the liberal "Hollywood atmosphere."

In the final 1972 Associated Press poll, Ohio State finished ninth, Notre Dame fourteenth, and UCLA fifteenth. In the final 1995 AP poll, Nebraska's opponents were Florida (second), Colorado (fifth), Kansas State (seventh), and Kansas (ninth). Because their traditional rival, Oklahoma, was down in that period, many forget that the Big 8 (soon to become the Big 12 when the Southwest Conference joined the league) was as strong as they were. Colorado was still in a strong period, and Kansas State was on the rise. All things considered, Nebraska has the edge in terms of strength of schedule component.

Sophomore Anthony Davis scored six touchdowns in USC's 45–23 win over Notre Dame at the Coliseum. This included two kickoff returns for TDs. Statistically, other players have done more. Illinois' Red Grange's 402 total yards against Michigan in 1924 had long been considered a benchmark of single-game greatness, but all things considered—the setting, the opponents, the stakes—A. D.'s 1972 game probably should be looked upon as the most spectacular day any college football player has ever enjoyed.

Nebraska opened the 1995 season with a 64–21 throttling of Oklahoma State in Stillwater. They beat Michigan State 50–10 on the road, Arizona State 77–28, Missouri 57–0, Iowa State 73–14, Oklahoma 37–0 in Lincoln, and Florida 62–24 at the Fiesta Bowl. Like the 1972 Trojans they were never "pushed." Their 35–21 win over Washington State (unranked in the final polls) at home was the nearest thing to a close game, similar to USC's 30–21 game with defending Rose Bowl winner Stanford (which was 30–13 until Stanford scored and converted a 2-point conversion late in the game). The Cornhuskers took slight criticism for scheduling UOP but eased up on the little central California school, 49–7.

Nebraska's victory over Florida was the most impressive bowl performance ever up until that time, an absolute blowout against a 12-0 team. It had more of a "track meet" effect than USC's 42–17 triumph over Ohio State in the 1973 Rose Bowl. The difference between the two games represents a difference in football in that twenty-three-year period. In 1972 the players lifted weights, but it was not nearly the science it had become by 1995. Steroid use may have been around, at least among linemen, as early as 1972 (although this is a bit of a question), but football players trained in the off-season mainly playing basketball; often playing other sports (the 1972 Trojans had a number of unique talents in baseball, track, and basketball); and of course in the weight room, where they used antiquated equipment. Diet was not nearly as understood, either. Big men just packed on the calories with little regard for health.

Nebraska built their program in the 1980s and 1990s on the "strength" of the best weight training facilities in the country; a cutting-edge approach to powerlifting; and, of course, the unspoken secret that everybody knows but few really like to say out loud: steroids.

Nebraska and a few other programs were ahead of the curve when it came to strength training and probably were able to stay that way for the better part of a decade, with direct results manifesting itself in the form of football victories. By 1995, however, whatever they were doing, the rest of the country was copying. If Nebraska was "juiced," so was everybody else to one extent or another. Despite the revelations of the 2000s, everybody still is, despite lip service about testing. The ability to mask its use, or manipulate the system, makes it possible for anybody with a little brains to do just that.

There was a different element to the 1995 Cornhuskers—a new look that for lack of a better demarcation point seems to have first really shown itself at Miami in the 1980s. College football was 100 percent integrated by this point in the South as well as everywhere else. This factor and more sophisticated training methods, plus a combination of size, speed, and the explosive power of a new breed of remarkable black athletes, created for visual spectacles like never before.

Nebraska was a fully modernized team. A decade later, there was no particular sense that the game was much different. They were part of a new optimum in terms of level of play that had seemingly showed human development at its maximum. For this reason it seems reasonable to conclude that, absent enormous breakthroughs in medical science, the game will not see major changes in its "appearance," for lack of a better word, for many years to come.

Nebraska's 1995 opponents were part of a level playing field. USC's in 1972 probably were less so. John McKay built his program out of a series of enormous advantages. An eighteen-year "down period" (by USC's standards) between 1983 and 2001 can best be explained by stating that in four or five key areas, society changed and allowed other colleges, particularly in the South (and most particularly in Florida), to "catch up." USC failed to recognize what was going on. They took for granted the natural advantages McKay benefited from, not understanding that these factors no longer were as prevalent.

In 1972, however, USC's dominance was a combination of these factors, all in their favor. They had unlimited scholarships, stocking their roster three- and four-deep with prep All-Americans just to keep them away from Stanford, UCLA, and Notre Dame. They were well ahead of the national trend in terms of black recruitment and had been for over a decade. A pipeline of African American talent flowed like a river into the Coliseum. They had so much more speed, quickness, athleticism, and strength than the rest of college football as to be scary. Perhaps it is slightly "politically incorrect" to state this, but the fact is their black athletes, most sporting Afro hairstyles of the day, were so big, so fast as to be absolutely intimidating in terms of attitude and physical impact. Ironically, from among all these "scary guys" would emerge at least two Christian ministers, two corporate attorneys, a network broadcaster, entrepreneurs, schoolteachers, and the 2006 Republican gubernatorial candidate of Pennsylvania!

Metropolitan Los Angeles had reached epic population growth. The schools increased funding after the launch of the "space race" with the USSR in the late 1950s. The result was a plethora of high school stars coming out of sophisticated programs in the Southland.

"USC's unlike any other program," legendary Trojan assistant coach Marv Goux once stated. "Because of the location of the school in the middle of the city, with the surrounding population, all those high schools pouring players into us, with the good weather, the media, and the tradition we have, we hardly had to work for players. They just *came*."

The Trojans also benefited from social unrest on other campuses. USC is a conservative, traditional university that maintained its commitment to sports throughout the turbulent 1960s and early 1970s, as opposed to a place like California, where athletes were viewed as second-class citizens. Stanford's student newspaper wrote scathing editorials, accusing USC of not being able to put football in perspective.

"The Trojans aren't the best team in the country," Washington State coach Jim Sweeney said at the time. "The Miami Dolphins are." In 1972, the Dolphins put together the only unbeaten season in the Super Bowl era.

The 1995 Cornhuskers were far more than just a bunch of strong linemen. It was their athleticism and speed that made them so spectacular. Punter Darren Erstad was one of their best athletes. He later became a baseball star with the Anaheim Angels. Running back Lawrence Phillips was troubled yet explosive. Quarterback Tommie Frazier was perfect to run coach Tom Osborne's option-style offense. However, it was a *team*, not just a group of All-Americans. Frazier, who finished second to Ohio State's Eddie George in the Heisman Trophy balloting, was their only consensus All-American. Amid much consternation, Phillips was their only first-round draft choice (St. Louis Rams).

The 1972 Trojans were a virtual spawning ground of NFL talent. Wide receiver Lynn Swann would be a Pro Football Hall of Famer and Super Bowl MVP with the Pittsburgh Steelers. Tight end Charle' Young was a pivotal member of the first 49ers Super Bowl winners. Quarterback Mike Rae was Ken Stabler's able backup on the 1976 Raiders Super Bowl champions. Fullback Sam "Bam" Cunningham was a star with the New England Patriots for a decade. Linebacker Richard "Batman" Wood started in Tampa Bay.

Young was a first-round selection of the Eagles, Cunningham of the Patriots, and tackle Pete Adams of the Cleveland Browns. Ten Trojans were drafted overall, but underclassmen from that team made up the 1973 (nine players drafted, two in the first round; Swann and Steve Riley) and 1975 Trojan drafts (fourteen players including Anthony Davis). The 1977 Super Bowl between Oakland and Minnesota was a Trojan party held at their old "stomping grounds," the Rose Bowl in Pasadena. Seven Trojans and two Vikings were USC alums, many from the 1972 team.

John McKay was the 1972 American Football Coaches Association Coach of the Year. Young made consensus All-American, but like the Cornhuskers, despite all the star power and future pro greatness, he was the only one from a group emphasizing *team*work. No Trojans won major awards.

The 1972 USC Trojans played several "cautious first half" games, including the opener at Arkansas (3–3 at the half) and the Rose Bowl against Ohio State (7–7 at the half).

"McKay got a little scared of Woody Hayes," recalled offensive lineman Allan Graf. "He changed things around, and at the half we weren't doing all that well so he just said, 'Ah, what the heck, let's just go back to what were doing,' and we blew 'em out."

In assessing which of these two teams is the greatest, there are many strong arguments favoring either one. Nebraska fans, jealous of their school's legacy, argue strenuously on behalf of the 1995 team as the best of them all. USC fans are more laid-back and less concerned with this kind of thing. Either way, the choice is a difficult one to make, but in the end USC gets the nod based on intangibles. While there are some pure statistics favoring Nebraska (scoring average, strength of schedule), the fact that USC beat three storied traditions (UCLA, Notre Dame, and Ohio State), all at or near the height of their . . . storied tradition, and in the case of Notre Dame and Ohio State, coached by legends (Ara Parseghian and Woody Hayes), places greater imprimatur with Southern Cal.

USC produced more professional stars, and while separation of the professional from the college game is important, nobody really can deny the best players usually go pro, making for the best professionals. Furthermore, USC played a strict pro-style offense. Tommie Frazier was a fabulous collegian but was never viewed as a legitimate professional quarterback prospect. Despite his athleticism, he was not. Mike Rae did not star in the NFL, but perhaps had he not been benched behind Stabler he would have had more success. Second-stringer Haden led the 1976 Rams to the NFC championship game.

USC produced one Pro Hall of Famer (Swann) and four College Hall of Famers (Swann, Young, Wood, and Coach McKay), with future inductions to Sam Cunningham and possibly Pat Haden.

The 1972 Trojans and 1995 Cornhuskers are not the only teams that make a strong statement when it comes to judging history's greatest squads. Third on the list is another Trojan juggernaut, their 2004 repeat national champions. When it comes to "bells and whistles," Hollywood glamour, and overall star power, no other team comes close. If one believes that "the more modern the better," they fit that bill. As mentioned, though, there does not seem to be a vast difference, if any, when one considers what the game was like in 1995 versus 2004. The only discernible difference seems to be the size of *quarterbacks*. By the mid-2000s, a new breed of signal-caller, likely to stand six-foot-five and weigh 240 or even 250 pounds (Vince Young, Brady Quinn, JaMarcus Russell) had hit the scene.

Other eras undoubtedly looked different. 1905 was a different ball game from 1895. 1915 was substantially changed from 1905. 1925 was a whole new ball game from 1915, and 1935 the same in comparison with 1925. 1945 was the beginning of a modern game, but the postwar era saw vast changes so that in 1955 it was much more modern. Then came the 1960s, when it all changed irrevocably. Still, 1975 was a different era from 1965. Finally, in the 1980s the game began to find its highest plateau.

The 1995 season was different from 1985 in small increments, and by 2004–2005 there was little comparative change.

As great as the 2004 Trojans were, they were really only seen as preparation for the "all-time-champions-in-waiting" 2005 USC juggernaut. The 2004 team had only five players drafted. One (Mike Patterson) went in the first round, with a second first rounder (Mike Williams) who sat out the season after declaring himself the previous year but was denied by the courts. The old days in which a college team might have fifteen or sixteen players drafted, with five or six in the first round, were now most likely over. Juniors could declare early, meaning there would be fewer senior-heavy teams with superstars who had not yet been gobbled up by the pros. For a program that recruits the best football players, this new reality hurts elites such as USC, but Pete Carroll's program has not been set back by it. Instead, they have thrived.

The 2004 Trojans were a young squad. Had Williams played he would have been a junior. Quarterback Matt Leinart won the Heisman Trophy and made All-American for the second straight year. He was only a junior. All-American running back Reggie Bush, a New York finalist for the Heisman Trophy, was just a sophomore. Two Trojans made consensus All-American on the defensive side: lineman Shaun Cody and linebacker Matt Grootegoed.

With the NFL having left Los Angeles after the 1994 season, Southern California filled the vacuum and was being referred to as "L.A.'s pro football team." Many people said there were several professional clubs they could beat, and they were not kidding. As great as USC's tradition was prior to Pete Carroll's arrival in the 2001 season, the atmosphere, enthusiasm, and fever-pitch excitement of USC football in this new era eclipsed anything in its past.

The 2004 team seems to have run the table in the most "perfect" manner ever; they were only the tenth club ever to repeat as AP champions. They also carried the number one ranking all the way from the final regular season poll of 2003, the preseason, each regular season poll, and the final vote after their Orange Bowl blowout of Oklahoma. They held the number one position in each of the BCS rankings when they came out after the seventh week. They featured the Heisman Trophy winner and a finalist. Finally, the 2005 BCS Orange Bowl probably was the most hyped college game ever played up until that time.

The Sooners were also unbeaten and had been second in each poll since the preseason. They had the reigning 2003 Heisman winner, quarterback Jason White. He and running back Adrian Peterson were also Heisman finalists, so there were four players on the New York stage who would face each other a month later.

The Trojans, wearing their home jerseys in that Orange Bowl (as the 1972 USC team had done in their Rose Bowl win over Ohio State), put a 55–19 drubbing on OU. It is considered the greatest single-game performance of all time. The only other game that really compares would be Nebraska's insane pounding of Florida in the 1996 Fiesta Bowl. Again, however, considering the buildup, the BCS component, and the stakes, USC's 2005 Orange Bowl win is, as ESPN's Lee Corso stated, the best game "any team ever played!"

Carroll had such a powerful program that expectations were off the charts in 2004. The 2002 Trojans were the Pacific-10 champions, featuring Heisman Trophy winner Carson Palmer and a 38–17 triumph over Iowa in the Orange Bowl. The 2003 Trojans won the school's first national championship since 1978, annihilating poor old Michigan in the Rose Bowl. They entered the following season ranked number one in every single poll, a very rare consensus. Leinart was the overwhelming Heisman pick from the get-go. With all of this going on, there was considerable talk prior to the season that *this* Trojan team might just be the best of all time.

The reason they are not is that, unlike the 1972 Trojans and 1995 Cornhuskers, they played several tough games on the road to their ultimate destiny. The opener was a donnybrook, played in 90-degree heat against a de facto "home team," Virginia Tech at FedEx Field (the home of the Washington Redskins) in Landover, Maryland. Of the 91,665 fans in attendance, most were Hokie supporters from nearby Blacksburg, Virginia. Troy did not put the 24–13 win away until the fourth quarter. On September 25 they had to pull out all the stops to beat Stanford, 31–28 on the road. Two weeks later they were forced to defend their goal line against four pass attempts by California's Aaron Rodgers in the last minute of a 23–17 victory. At Oregon State the fog was thick as soup in a hard-fought 28–20 win. Their 29–24 triumph over UCLA was too close for comfort. Southern California averaged 36 points a game and played stifling defense (two shutouts), but others have been statistically better on both sides of the ball.

The 2004 team dealt with Hollywood hype like none before, but in 2005 the attention paid to them eclipsed all previous *sports teams* in L.A., including great Lakers and Dodgers champions. Pete Carroll was called the "prince of the city" by local sportstalk host Petros Papadakis. Matt Leinart achieved celebrity status above and beyond the town's actor class. From a recruiting standpoint, it was a "perfect storm." No teenage human being could easily resist the chance to be part of it. By virtue of Texas beating them in the Rose Bowl, two things happened. First, they exposed USC's "secret" Achilles heel: an injured, faulty defense that had lost several seniors to the NFL Draft. Linebacker Lofa Tatupu was helping the Seattle Seahawks to the Super Bowl instead of stopping Vince Young with a minute left in Pasadena as a 2005 senior. Cornerback Eric Wright was not around to break up any of Young's passes or runs, either. Kicked off the team for various acts of misconduct, he became a high draft pick out of UNLV in 2007. Had the Trojans held Texas, history most likely would have overlooked their defensive lapses and accorded them the "all-time best" title, on the strength of their Heisman combination (Leinart and the 2005 winner, Reggie Bush), their Thunder and Lighting running back tandem (Bush and LenDale White), an unprecedented third straight title, plus what would have been ongoing streaks of thirty-five straight wins and thirty-four straight number one rankings.

Alas, the loss to Texas put USC in that "close but no cigar" category occupied by the 1969 Ohio State Buckeyes, the 1983 Nebraska Cornhuskers, and other teams that came within a game of or close to attaining the elusive "best ever" title. With this came the second factor at play, which is the realization that if USC was not the greatest team ever, then the team that beat them might just be.

The unbeaten Longhorns, like Troy, entered the Rose Bowl scoring more than 50 points a game. USC's star power was so bright that Longhorn greatness was diminished, but they were so powerful that even the most hubristic Trojan fan was filled with unease in the days leading up to the game. Under coach Mack Brown, Texas compiled fabulous records every year, but the "brass ring" eluded the program since Darrell Royal's 1969 champions. In 2004, sophomore quarterback Vince Young led them to an 11–1 record, featuring an incredible comeback to beat Michigan (who must have been wondering why the Big 10 ever signed that pact with the Tournament of Roses back in 1946) in the Rose Bowl, 38–37. The win gave Texas a huge burst of momentum heading into 2005.

Texas was second in every poll beginning in the preseason. It was USC one, Texas two every week from beginning to end, just as had been the case with USC and Oklahoma the previous season. As impressive as the Trojans were, Texas continually tried, and often succeeded, in looking better. The media largely missed it. When USC dismantled UCLA in the last regular season game, 66–19, Texas's 70–3 drubbing of Colorado in the Big 12 title game was even gaudier.

Just like 2004, the Heisman award was a Trojan show featuring their latest winner, Reggie Bush, with Matt Leinart on the podium to offer congratulations. Vince Young, the Longhorns' nominee, was not particularly gracious in defeat. He was viewed as a sore loser by some, but in retrospect it seems he knew something nobody else did.

Whether there were more USC fans in the Rose Bowl stands is debatable. Texas traveled well and was louder. When Young crossed the goal line to win it, 41–38, it sounded like the D-day invasion on June 6, 1944. Young's performance equaled previous legendary games played by Red Grange versus Michigan (1924) and Anthony Davis versus Notre Dame (1972). He was matched by Leinart, who was everything he had been billed to be in three All-American seasons that may be the best collegiate football career in history.

But Bush, while spectacular at times, was not as good as he had been in the regular season. His key fumble killed his team. The disquieting fact is that, had the Heisman Trophy been voted on after the game, Young would have received it, hands down.

Old-timers like Beano Cook still point to the 1947 Notre Dame Fighting Irish as the best team ever. In comparing them to their opponents at the time, they might very well be. They never trailed in a game and threw four shutouts. Army fell 27–7, and they beat USC at the Coliseum, 38–7. They did not play in a bowl game, and at the time Michigan—unbeaten and a 49–0 winner over those same Trojans in the Rose Bowl—argued that they were worthy. Fritz Crisler's Wolverines went through their schedule by more impressive scores, and a BCS-style national title game between the two schools would have been a donnybrook.

Notre Dame was a repeat national champion. It was their third in four years. They would barely miss in 1948 and then win it again in 1949. Quarterback Johnny Lujack was their second Heisman Trophy winner in 1947. Tackle George Connor was their other consensus All-American. An unbelievable eight members of that team are in the College Football Hall of Fame (Lujack, Connor, Leon Hart, Ziggy Czarobski, Moose Fischer, Red Sitko, Jim Martin, and coach Frank Leahy).

A core of old-time Nebraska fans, insisting with much merit that the 1971 Cornhuskers were the best of all time, dismisses all arguments favoring other teams. This was legendary coach Bob Devaney's marquee group. Unlike many Nebraska squads that emphasize the team concept, they were filled with star power. This was another repeat champion. In 1970, only a 21–21 tie with USC marred Nebraska's record. They "snuck in" when they beat LSU 17–12 in the Orange Bowl. Texas, Notre Dame, Ohio State, and Michigan had been ranked ahead of them all year, but one by one they fell. Michigan lost to Ohio State, and Notre Dame lost to USC. Then unbeaten Texas lost to Notre Dame in the Cotton Bowl, while Ohio State fell to Stanford in the Rose Bowl.

In 1971 Nebraska was ranked number one in every poll from the first regular season ranking until after the bowls. They tossed three shutouts and demolished Big 12 competition. Then, on Thanksgiving day, they faced unbeaten Oklahoma at Norman in that year's "Game of the Century." Nebraska dominated early, but OU pulled back into the game using trick plays. Nebraska's Johnny Rodgers returned a punt for a touchdown. The Sooners, led by running back Greg Pruitt and quarterback Jack Mildren, moved into a 31–28 lead. Nebraska quarterback Jerry Tagge pulled out all the stops, engineering a game-winning touchdown drive. Running back Jeff Kinney and Rodgers made key plays as Nebraska scored to win it, 35–31.

Unbeaten Alabama faced them in the Orange Bowl. It was Bear Bryant's first integrated team, but the Tide was no match in a 38–6 blowout that could have been worse. Rodgers, defensive end Willie Harper, and tackle Larry Jacobson (the Outland winner) made consensus All-American. Rodgers, a junior, won the Heisman in 1972. Kinney was a first-round selection of the Chiefs. Rich Glover won the Outland Trophy the next year. In judging the difference between the 1971 Cornhuskers and the 1972 Trojans, any edge USC gains is marginal. They played a pro-style offense. In terms of speed, power, and athleticism, there is no real differential.

Lost in the glare of Pete Carroll's great run at USC, not to mention the great teams that have contended and beaten him, are the 2001 Miami Hurricanes. Under three coaches (Howard Schellenberger, Jimmy Johnson, and Dennis Erickson), Miami utterly dominated the 1980s and early 1990s. It was a remarkable run and unique in that it was achieved under different coaches. Few programs have been able to transition well between two coaches (Nebraska: Bob Devaney/Tom Osborne; Oklahoma: Chuck Fairbanks/Barry Switzer; USC: John McKay/John Robinson). Miami did it under three with less downside than any of the others. The Hurricane program has always had a professional element to it. They play in a pro city in an iconic NFL stadium (the Orange Bowl). Their speed, size, and attitude have always more resembled the mercenaries of the pro game, and their coaches reflect this.

Butch Davis took over in 1995. For a few years the program declined. But there is too much talent in Florida to lose for long. The allure of south Florida is often a winning edge in recruiting battles between Miami, Florida, and Florida State. In 1998, the Hurricanes announced their presence back on the national scene when they knocked off unbeaten UCLA at the Orange Bowl in the last game of the year.

Davis had the program back at the top with an 11–1 campaign in 2000, but he, like his predecessors, went for the pot at the end of the rainbow, leaving perhaps the fullest cupboard of all time for Larry Coker in 2001. Lineman Bryant McKinnie and defensive back Ed Reed were consensus All-Americans. Quarterback Ken Dorsey finished third in the Heisman balloting. He won the Maxwell award, with McKinnie taking the Outland.

Kinnie, tight end Jeremy Shockey, defensive
Michael Rumph.

scare before beating Virginia Tech 26–24 at
squad that had no business being at the Rose

ling in 2002, when they (like the 2005 Trojans)
eam, they may well have gone down as the best
ouble-overtime loss to Ohio State in the Fiesta
national championships (not to mention con-
ng string was broken up.
–0 at Yankee Stadium. This was the second
"Red" Blaik. They featured the famed Mr. In-
ion of Heisman winners Doc Blanchard and
ntil the Leinart-Bush run). History oddly con-
a was waging its most desperate battles. While
dets playing a game while their Army brethren
notion. First, many a football cadet of this era
fought in Korea, too). Second, the 1945 team
had ceased.
ne 59–0, might have been better. They averaged
year. The next year Army allowed only 45 total
are given the greater position in the pantheon
n, with all the added pressure, is very difficult.
d two offensive units. The "Lombardo team,"
consisting mostly of freshmen, would come in
perienced "Kenna team," led by senior quarter-
the best game he ever saw his team play, Blaik
afternoon in October when they scrimmaged

ch the national championship.
ne permitted the complete satisfaction of being
his team.
ootball was a source of national pride and played
onfronted by the fact that they were opposed by
we could chop them up piecemeal on the battle-
ducing sports champions on the home front.
was accorded the status of "greatest team ever."
a retrospective on them that certainly did not

Greatest Single-Season Teams—Chronological Order

1901	Michigan	1972	Southern California
1913	Washington	1973	Notre Dame
1920	California	1976	Pittsburgh
1924	Notre Dame	1979	Alabama
1928	Southern California	1985	Oklahoma
1929	Notre Dame	1986	Penn State
1930	Alabama	1987	Miami
1932	Southern California	1988	Notre Dame
1934	Alabama	1991	Washington
1936	Minnesota	1992	Alabama
1944	Army	1994	Nebraska
1945	Army	1995	Nebraska
1946	Notre Dame	1997	Michigan
1947	Notre Dame	1998	Tennessee
1948	Michigan	1999	Florida State
1956	Oklahoma	2000	Oklahoma
1962	Southern California	2001	Miami
1966	Notre Dame	2002	Ohio State
1968	Ohio State	2003	Southern California
1969	Texas	2004	Southern California
1971	Nebraska	2005	Texas

argue against this notion. They were denied a third straight title when Notre Dame's Johnny Lujack stopped Blanchard in the open field during the famed 0-0 tie of 1946. Blaik's teams were a national powerbolt for the remainder of the decade. A cheating scandal ended Army as a true contender in the increasingly competitive college football field of the 1950s. Pete Dawkins did capture the 1958 Heisman Trophy.

Bear Bryant's best team ever was his unbeaten 1979 national champions. Featuring center Dwight Stephenson, considered by many to be the best ever to play that position, they ran the table, capturing a repeat title. Like all of Bryant's teams, they lacked major star power, winning it with discipline and togetherness on both sides of the ball. Unlike the first eight teams—the 1972 Trojans, 1995 Cornhuskers, 2004 Trojans, 2005 Longhorns, 1947 Fighting Irish, 1971 Cornhuskers, 2001 Hurricanes, and 1945 Black Knights—the 1979 Crimson Tide are virtually never mentioned among a discussion of the greatest teams ever, but they should be.

Next on the list, the 1956 Oklahoma Sooners, are a strange story. Bud Wilkinson's team was not really the best in OU history. His 1955 squad, which had powered past

Maryland 20–6 in the Orange Bowl, might have been better with five shutouts. In 1956 the Sooners featured halfback Tommy McDonald and center Jerry Tubbs. They were prevented from going to another bowl by Big 8 policy. The biggest reason they rate where they do is because this was the team that cemented Wilkinson's record 47-game winning streak and it was their second straight title. They finished the season at 40 straight.

Within the OU hierarchy, the 1971, 1973–1975, 1978, 1985, and 1986 teams probably were better. These were modern, fully integrated teams. The 1956 team was still, sadly, all white, but Coach Wilkinson bravely brought black players into his program shortly thereafter. Oklahoma, while not in the Deep South, is still in the *South*west, so it was no easy move. Wilkinson could do it based in great part on the success he achieved before that.

In observing that while the 1956 Sooners are highly ranked by history, yet in actuality are not the best Oklahoma team by a long shot, one arrives at one of the seminal points of the historical rankings process, which is that the older teams cannot really be compared to the newer ones.

The relative greatness of the 1924 Fighting Irish or 1932 USC Trojans is given its due merit, but in truth the game—and society—changed too much in succeeding years to rate the teams of that era with the later ones. Even the segregated 1969 Texas Longhorns must be judged by different criteria than Bobby Bowden's 1999 Florida State Seminoles. California (1920) and Georgia Tech (1917) put up astonishing numbers, but common sense and logic tell us that Notre Dame (1988) or Ohio State (1968) were better.

Chapter 17

Top Single-Season Teams of the Decades

19th century:	1893 Princeton
1900s:	1901 Michigan
1910s:	1913 Washington
1920s:	1924 Notre Dame
1930s:	1932 Southern California
1940s:	1947 Notre Dame
1950s:	1956 Oklahoma
1960s:	1968 Ohio State
1970s:	1972 Southern California
1980s:	1987 Miami
1990s:	1995 Nebraska
2000s:	2004 Southern California

PRINCETON'S BEST TEAM in the nineteenth century was their famed 1893 squad, although great teams at Penn a few years later helped shape the game, spreading its popularity. Once the twentieth century began, however, all bets were off. While the predecessors of the Ivy League—Princeton, Yale, and Harvard—continued strong runs in the 1900s, it was coach Fielding "Hurry Up" Yost's "point-a-minute" 1901 Michigan Wolverines, winners of consecutive national championships accorded by historical ratings services, that make the Wolverines the choice for this decade. The single decisive factor in favor of Michigan is their famed 49-0 pounding of Stanford in the Rose Bowl.

The 1917 national-champion Georgia Tech Yellow Jackets under legendary coach John Heisman put the South on the map before Alabama came along. They shut out seven opponents but oddly are not the best team Georgia Tech had. The once-tied 1916 team, which is not considered a consensus national champion, beat Cumberland by the largest score ever (222-0). In 1918 the 'Jackets won games by scores of 118-0 and 123-0 over military teams. They defeated North Carolina State 128-0. But that 1918 season hardly counts because of World War I and its effect on college rosters. Michigan has been accorded historical national championship status for the truncated 1918 campaign.

The 1913 Washington Huskies are the choice for best single-season team of the 1910s. It is hard not to pick them, even though their schedule was not as strong as Eastern and Midwestern teams. Auburn (8–0) was felt to be their equal that year. So too was Notre Dame, upset winners of Army and suddenly a major powerhouse on the national scene. Harvard (1912) was another contender.

The 1920s offer one of the most competitive fields ever when it comes to choosing the best single-season team of the decade. Whether the 1924 Notre Dame Fighting Irish really were or not takes a back seat to the fact they were the most heralded, famed Irish team perhaps of all time; made the school's and coach Knute Rockne's legend; and created much of the inspiration that changed collegiate football from "boola-boola" and fur coats into Saturday madness.

This was the Irish of Four Horsemen fame (Harry Stuhldreher, Don Miller, Jim Crowley, and Elmer Layden). They beat Army at the Polo Grounds and, in a game that separates them from most pre-1969 Irish teams, went to a bowl. The Irish beat Ernie Nevers and Stanford, 27–10, in the Rose Bowl. This game was a major contest pitting powerhouses from the West and Midwest. Of just as much interest, it matched the great Glenn "Pop" Warner against the new superstar of the coaching ranks, Rockne.

The next best team of the decade was Howard Jones's 1928 national champions, but two factors work against the Trojans. First, some systems rated Georgia Tech number one (not unusual; the Davis ratings saw Penn as the 1924 champs, and there was virtually no such thing as consensus in any single season). The second factor hurting USC was that, after the regular season ended, their natural path to the Rose Bowl was blocked by their own decision not to play in Pasadena. The facts are murky to this day, but a dispute arose, and for the first and last time in their history, Southern California did not accept a challenge. California went in their stead, and after "Wrong Way" Roy Riegels ran . . . the wrong way, they fell to Georgia Tech, 8–7.

Cal's 1920 Wonder Team may well have beaten the 1924 Irish. Coach Andy Smith's Golden Bears, led by superb end Brick Muller, was almost unbeatable; in fact they *were* unbeatable, for fifty games. Perhaps it is political, but Notre Dame's historical reputation compared to Cal's less-than-stellar one, on and off the field, gives the edge to Notre Dame.

In the 1930s, co-national champions Notre Dame and Alabama (1930) or Alabama and Minnesota (1934) all have good arguments to make. The 1930 Irish are considered one of Rockne's greatest teams (not to mention his last; he died in a plane crash after the season). They featured the great quarterback Marchy Schwartz. In 1934, Don Hutson, one of the finest receivers ever, lined up opposite Bear Bryant.

Bernie Bierman's Minnesota Golden Gophers were champions from 1934 to 1936. In the late 1930s great Southern teams competed with varying degrees of success and disappointment when national championships, or chances at them, were denied to Duke, Alabama, and Tennessee by the polls, the California Golden Bears, and the USC Trojans.

Bob Neyland's Volunteers were powerhouses, as were the Alabama teams that transitioned from the era of Wallace Wade to that of Frank Thomas. Wade went on to coach the unbeaten, untied, unscored-on 1938 Duke Blue Devils, who finally were scored on with a minute to go in their Rose Bowl loss to Southern California.

But Howard Jones's 1932 "Thundering Herd" Trojans stand far above all other teams in this decade. They won eight games by shutout, beat Pittsburgh in the Rose Bowl 35–0, and featured three All-Americans (Tay Brown, Aaron Rosenberg, Ernie Smith). All three are in the College Football Hall of Fame, as is teammate Cotton Warburton.

The 1940s were a replay of the 1930s, with numerous contenders. Again, reputation helps Notre Dame, but of course their reputation was built on solid achievement. That said, picking the 1947 Irish over the 1945 Army Black Knights or the 1948 Michigan Wolverines is not an easy sell. The Irish played in no bowl game, just as Army did not. In 1948 Michigan beat USC, 49–0, in the Rose Bowl. USC had tied undefeated Notre Dame, 14–14. Offensively both the 1948 Michigan and 1944–1945 Army juggernauts were more impressive than Notre Dame.

In 1946, a record sixteen Notre Dame players were drafted, and in 1947 the Irish featured an incredible eight Hall of Famers. Quarterback Johnny Lujack won the Heisman Trophy and tackle George Connor was a consensus All-American selection. Lujack, Connor, Leon Hart, Ziggy Czarobski, Moose Fischer, Red Sitko, Jim Martin, and coach Frank Leahy are all in the College Football Hall of Fame.

In the 1950s, the choices come down to 1956 Oklahoma, 1955 Oklahoma, and Oklahoma. Due to prebowl voting, only Michigan State (1952) can claim a worthy national championship between the 1950 and 1953 seasons. After Notre Dame finally ended the Sooners' winning streak at 47 games in 1957, there were solid teams (Woody Hayes's Ohio State Buckeyes in 1957, the famed LSU Tigers of the legendary Billy Cannon in 1958, and Syracuse coach Ben Schwartzwalder's 1959 national champs). But in the 1950s, it was all Bud Wilkinson and OU. His 1956 team, by virtue of winning the title for the second year in a row while running their winning streak to forty, is the pick.

The 1960s offer a more disparate set of choices. Four teams competed for domination: USC, Alabama, Notre Dame, and Ohio State. Who was the best? At first glance, and certainly in the minds of Alabamians, it was Bear Bryant's Crimson Tide. In 1961 they featured quarterback Pat Trammell (who later became a doctor before dying of cancer) and the legendary lineman Lee Roy Jordan. Bill Curry, who later coached the Tide, said this was the best team he ever saw. Their 1966 team, starring quarterback Kenny Stabler and receiver Ray Perkins, was probably Bear's best in the 1960s, but for reasons gone over ad infinitum, they were not the national champions.

USC and Notre Dame battled each other, both rising after down periods. The best teams of the decade were the 1966 Irish and the 1968 Trojans. Neither is the "Team of the Decade" because, as Willie Mays once said when asked, "Whose gonna win the pennant this year?" well, *"Hey man, that's why we play the games."*

Notre Dame beat USC 51–0 in 1966. They featured quarterback Terry Hanratty, end Jim Seymour, center George Goeddeke, tackle Bob Kuchenberg, running back Rocky Bleier, defensive lineman Alan Page, and linebacker Jim Lynch. An insane total of *twelve* Irish players earned some All-American recognition. "Team of the Decade" status is denied them, however, not because they tied Michigan State 10–10, but because Ara Parseghian *played for the tie*!

Great teams *do not play for the tie*!

In 1968, USC was looking to repeat their 1967 national championship with Heisman winner O. J. Simpson, wide receiver Bob Chandler, tackle Sid Smith, tight end Bob Klein, linemen Al Cowlings and Jimmy Gunn, and defensive back Mike Battle. Just as in 2005, when Troy arrived at the Rose Bowl knocking on history's door, their most publicized glamour team was upset by a team that may have been more of a *team*: Woody Hayes's sophomore-laden Ohio State Buckeyes.

The 1969 Buckeyes were supposed to be better. After they beat TCU 62–0, *Sports Illustrated* touted them as the best team ever, but Bo Schembechler and Michigan ended that dream. In later years, Pasadena would more often than not be a graveyard for Ohio State, but on January 1, 1969, Woody was singing "California Dreamin'." Led by quarterback Rex Kern, end Jan White, fullback Jim Otis, defensive lineman Jim Stillwagon, and all-everything defensive back Jack Tatum, the Bucks beat Troy 27–16.

It looked like a Southern Cal day when O. J. ripped off an 80-yard touchdown run. USC led 10–0 before Ohio State took over. Trojan turnovers in the second half did them in, and history shall record that the 1968 Buckeyes were the best of this turbulent decade.

The 1970s offer two of the all-time best: the 1972 Trojans over the 1971 Nebraska Cornhuskers. Four other "close but no cigar" teams will not go down in history as national champions but were better than many that did finish number one: the 1971 Oklahoma Sooners (who lost to Nebraska), the 1973 Alabama Crimson Tide (beaten in the Sugar Bowl by Notre Dame), the 1979 Trojans (tied by Stanford), and the 1979 Buckeyes (whose hearts were broken in the last minute by USC in the Rose Bowl).

Oklahoma (1974) was a flawed probationary juggernaut. Notre Dame (1977) plus 1978 co-national champions USC and Alabama each had losses. What about Notre Dame (1973), Pittsburgh (1976), and Alabama (1979)? Great teams, but not as good as the 1972 Trojans or the 1971 Cornhuskers. In 1973 Notre Dame fielded one of their best teams. In 1976 Tony Dorsett had one of the most incredible seasons any player ever had. In 1979 'Bama was the best of all Bear Bryant teams. As AC/DC once famously stated, "It's a long way to the top, if you wanna rock 'n' roll." It was that kind of decade.

The first five years of the 1980s did not produce a great champion. Georgia, led by freshman running back sensation Herschel Walker, played slightly above their level in winning it all. Clemson was a survivor in 1981. Penn State finally delivered a title for Joe Paterno, but he probably had three or four better teams in the preceding fifteen years. Nebraska was a team for the ages until Miami created a demarcation point in the game's history in 1983, knocking them off in the Orange Bowl. BYU, God bless 'em, won it in 1984, but outside of Utah they are not much remembered.

The decade's second half saw greatness. Of all those teams, Jimmy Johnson's 1987 Miami Hurricanes were the best of the bunch. Quarterback Steve Walsh and wide receiver Michael Irvin were unstoppable. Defensive back Bennie Blades personified the newer, fast DBs of the era. They were the new faces of college football: renegades, attitude, "hip-hop" warriors.

The 1988 Notre Dame Fighting Irish were the second best team of the decade. Three years after losing to Miami 58–7, they held off the Hurricanes by the barest of margins, 31–30 in a classic Notre Dame Stadium confrontation. That game was called the "Catholics versus the convicts" because the Hurricanes featured, uh, a criminal element.

Linebackers Frank Stams and Mike Stonebreaker and defensive back Todd Lyght represented a return to old-school Irish football: hard-nosed defense. Quarterback Tony

Rice and receiver Raghib "Rocket" Ismail represented the new: fast, explosive. After de-railing Southern California at the Coliseum 27–10, coach Lou Holtz's team toppled un-likely Fiesta Bowl opponent West Virginia 34–21 for the national championship.

Brian Bosworth's 1985 Oklahoma Sooners, Paterno's better 1980s Penn State team (1986), and the 1989 Hurricanes round out the other contenders. The best team looked to be Miami in 1986 behind Heisman quarterback Vinny Testaverde, but their 14–10 loss to Penn State in the Fiesta Bowl did to them what Alabama's loss to Texas in the 1965 Orange Bowl, or Texas's 1971 Cotton Bowl defeat at the hands of Notre Dame, *should have* done to them: eliminate the very possibility of *thinking* they were national champi-ons. Instead of sulking over it, Miami (like 'Bama in 1965) just went out there and earned it the next year.

Coming up with the best single-season team of the 1990s is a difficult exercise. Washington (1991) and Florida State (1999) are among the greatest teams of all time. Miami (1991), Penn State (1994), Florida (1996), Michigan (1997), Nebraska (1997), and Tennessee (1998) were all unbeaten champions that could make legitimate arguments they are among the best teams ever. When discussing such a thing, it is unfortunately inevitable that such great teams as these do not get the recognition they deserve, but in a way this is what makes college football so wonderful. It is a game of fabulous teams, outstanding coaches, legendary players. The greatest of the 1990s are the 1995 Nebraska Cornhuskers. They may have been the finest team ever assembled.

The 2000s, at least after a couple seasons, started to look different from the previous decade. Nebraska, Penn State, Miami, and Florida State, sooner or later, experienced a drop from the incredibly high standards they had risen to. Oklahoma, Ohio State, USC, and Texas all made dramatic comebacks to restore their good names in the hierarchy of college football. Virginia Tech and Kansas State, both teams that had knocked on the door, were not able to make it to the next level. Florida, the "third wheel" in the Sunshine State after coach Steve Spurrier's departure to the NFL, climbed back to the top of the mountain.

The best team? Again, it was a team that lost in the end, the 2005 USC Trojans. But losing is not rewarded in this game, so they must step down and give it to somebody else. Their predecessors, the 2004 Trojans, rate as the best team of the 2000s. This is a decade that in its first five years produced three of the best five single-season teams in history. Texas (2005) and Miami (2001) are ranked close behind the 2004 Trojans. Such great teams in such a short time—the combination of traditional powers making comebacks; of USC dominating Notre Dame again after many years of suffering; of the Irish threatening in the years ahead to right those "wrongs," as they see it; as new shifts take place and perhaps some new programs rise to the highest level—all of this makes this decade a new "golden age" of college football. The 2000s have proven to be the best, most competitive decade yet.

Chapter 18

Teams of the Decades

19th century:	Princeton
1900s:	Michigan
1910s:	Washington
1920s:	Notre Dame
1930s:	Southern California
1940s:	Notre Dame
1950s:	Oklahoma
1960s:	Southern California
1970s:	Southern California
1980s:	Miami
1990s:	Nebraska
2000s:	Southern California

THE BEST TEAM of all decades in the nineteenth century was Princeton, hands down. If one were to attach no relativism to the Tigers' record, without regard to modern logic, their numbers would dictate that this is the greatest dynasty in the history of collegiate football.

In the 1900s, Michigan's great teams between 1901 and 1905 resulted in two national championships. They are also given worthy consideration from a number of the historical systems in several other years. That was the period in which the Midwest truly took to football. Minnesota and Chicago had champions, too. Michigan first played Notre Dame in 1887. The series was an irregular affair but scheduled consistently enough to establish a strong rivalry. Finally, in the 1980s it took as a yearly home-and-home arrangement, eventually without interruption.

The Wolverines began playing Ohio State in 1897. While their rivals were still getting their feet wet from a football standpoint, Michigan established themselves as the first national power that, to this day, is still a national power.

The others—Princeton, Yale, Harvard, Penn—are Ivy League "small colleges." Chicago no longer plays football. Minnesota has maintained major college status, but nobody would confuse the Golden Gophers of recent years with a "national power."

Through the Decades

#	Decade	Team	Record		#	Decade	Team	Record
1.	1900s	Yale	100–4–5		9.	1940s	Notre Dame	82–9–6
2.	1950s	Oklahoma	93–10–4		10.	1920s	Notre Dame	81–12–4
3.	1990s	Florida State	109–13–1		11.	1930s	Alabama	79–11–5
4.	1920s	Southern California	88–13–2		12.	1980s	Nebraska	103–20
5.	1910s	Washington	49–4–3		13.	1980s	Miami	99–20
6.	1990s	Nebraska	108–16–1		14.	1960s	Alabama	89–16–4
7.	1970s	Alabama	103–16–1		15.	2000s	Oklahoma	102–18
8.	1970s	Oklahoma	101–12–2					

In the 1910s, the so-called Ivy League maintained a strong presence. Great teams at Army, Notre Dame, Pittsburgh, and Georgia Tech emerged. But the "Team of the Decade" was coach Gil Dobie's Washington Huskies. The logging industry and general wanderlust drew hardy settlers to the Pacific Northwest. Ocean and train travel created a population boom. So, too, did the discovery of gold in Alaska. Seattle became a destination point, just as Omaha/Council Bluffs had when the transcontinental railroad was built. Los Angeles had gotten off to a slow start and would not grow until creation of their water aqueduct. Washington had all the fresh water they needed.

Washington, Washington State, and Oregon all had powerful champions in the 1910s. The Pacific Coast Conference was formed, and the Rose Bowl resumed after a fourteen-year absence. The Huskies lost a game in 1907 and never lost another one until 1917, when the war had taken a major toll. They tied four games in that period, cranking out a 39-game winning streak between 1908 and 1914. The 1913 squad, considered a legitimate national champion (although services have recognized others, too), were the best of the lot. They beat Whitworth 100–0. The schedule also consisted of some athletic clubs, Oregon State, Oregon, and Washington. At seven games it was not as impressive as Midwestern or Ivy League teams, and for this reason historians discount Washington's record slightly. But the temptation to play rugby in the years after President Theodore Roosevelt urged rule changes did not take. During this period Pacific Northwest teams went ahead of many others. When Washington State and Oregon won the first two Rose Bowls after the game was resumed on January 1, 1916, it demonstrated that in fact this region played the best brand of football at that time (better even than in California and particularly better than in southern California). It provides enough evidence to determine that the Huskies were the decade's best team.

It is considered an article of faith that Notre Dame is the "Team of the 1920s" because they took two national championships (1924, 1929) and easily could have won more. Historians have touted Knute Rockne's record in this decade as the greatest of periods. Of course, this also includes the unbeaten 1919 and 1930 campaigns. But based strictly on the 1920s, believe it or not, Southern California (88–13–2) had a better win-loss mark than the Irish (81–12–4). (Oklahoma, at 93–10–4, was far superior in the 1950s, for that matter.)

Nevertheless, the Irish *are* the "Team of the 1920s." It was their popularity that spurred college football's growth more than any other factor. Whether USC had a better record in the decade or not is immaterial to the fact that the world knows full well who Knute Rockne and George Gipp are. They have little knowledge of Elmer "Gloomy Gus" Henderson and Morley Drury, even though the latter was known as the "Noblest Trojan of them all." Howard Jones and his Thundering Herd are stamped into the football memory, to be sure, but much of their reputation is based on their games *against Notre Dame*!

Notre Dame played without a satisfactory stadium. They certainly had home games, but the really big contests were usually reserved for the Polo Grounds in New York City (beat Army 1924), Yankee Stadium (lost to Army 1925; beat Army 1926, 1928, 1929), Soldier Field in Chicago (beat Northwestern 1924; beat USC 1927, 1929; beat Navy 1928; beat Wisconsin 1919), Baltimore (beat Navy 1927, 1929), Philadelphia (beat Penn State 1928), or the L.A. Memorial Coliseum (beat USC 1926; lost to USC 1928). The demand for tickets could not be met in their South Bend facilities until the 59,000-seat Notre Dame Stadium was built in 1930.

Alabama (back-to-back national champions in 1925–1926) and Stanford (co-champions in 1926) were powerhouses, but it is sad that history accords so little attention on California's Wonder Teams of 1920–1924. It is almost as if, when the Vietnam War protesters took over in Berkeley, memory of Cal's *wonder*ful football history was erased as by Stalinist purge. If Cal could have maintained their long, almost glorious football tradition, perhaps the Wonder Teams would be as consistently mentioned as are USC's Thundering Herd or other "wonder teams" at various schools.

They were 46–0–4 and won three national championships and a Rose Bowl. Dan McMillan transferred from USC to Cal, making All-American and eventually the College Football Hall of Fame. They never lost to USC, a situation that got so bad in L.A. that "Gloomy Gus" Henderson was fired despite accomplishing the best record any Trojan coach *ever had* until Pete Carroll.

In all honesty, Cal should be the "Team of the 1920s." They did not fall off the map after finally losing in 1925 for the first time since 1919. Falling to Georgia Tech on the ignominious "Wrong Way" Riegels run in the 1929 Rose Bowl, however, seemed to be the kind of thing that would never happen at Notre Dame. The rivalry with Stanford was red hot, and the Golden Bears were the pride of the Golden West, but in the end Rockne's Irish star shines brighter.

USC earns "Team of the Decade" honors for the 1930s based on the fact that they were a dominant program in the first four years (1930–1933), which included two straight national titles and a 1932 team ranking as one of the greatest in history. Then, after a few down years, the Trojans were a powerhouse again, upending Duke in the 1939 Rose Bowl and Tennessee in the 1940 Rose Bowl. These are two of the greatest upsets ever and had a major effect on persuading the country that the most prestigious

Notre Dame—two decades

1910s	63–7–6		1960s	62–34–4
1920s	81–12–4		1970s	91–22
	144–19–10			153–56–4
1920s	81–12–4		1970s	91–22
1930s	65–20–5		1980s	76–39–2
	146–32–9			167–61–2
1930s	65–20–5			
1940s	82–9–6			
	147–29–11			

Notre Dame—three decades

1910s	63–7–6		1960s	62–34–4
1920s	81–12–4		1970s	91–22
1930s	65–20–5		1980s	76–39–2
	209–39–15			228–41–15
1920s	81–12–4			
1930s	65–20–5			
1940s	82–9–6			
	229–95–6			

Notre Dame—four decades

1910s	63–7–6		1940s	82–9–6
1920s	81–12–4			291–48–21
1930s	65–20–5			

Southern California—two decades

1920s	88–13–2		1970s	93–22–1
1930s	73–25–9		1980s	78–36–3
	161–38–11			171–58–4
1960s	76–25–4			
1970s	93–22–1			
	169–47–5			

Alabama—two decades

1920s	71–22–6		1960s	89–16–4
1930s	79–11–5		1970s	103–16–1
	150–33–11			192–32–5
1930s	79–11–5		1970s	103–16–1
1940s	66–24–4		1980s	85–33–2
	145–35–9			188–49–3

Alabama—three decades

1960s	89–16–4		1980s	85–33–2
1970s	103–16–1			277–65–7

region was the West. Their 14-0 win over Bob Neyland and the Volunteers resulted in the Dickinson/Rockne system naming USC the 1939 national champions. In many ways, the systems were more accurate than the polls, since a majority of them rightly awarded their championships after bowls instead of prior to them. It was the bowls, not the polls, that really separated "the men from the boys."

The late 1930s saw California beat Alabama 13-0 in the 1938 Rose Bowl, earning the fourth and last national championship for a Golden Bear squad coached by Stub Allison, featuring Vic Bottari and Sam Chapman. Chapman later starred for Connie Mack's Philadelphia A's baseball team.

Notre Dame lost momentum with the death of Knute Rockne in a 1931 plane crash that, interestingly enough, caused enough attention to help jump-start creation of the Federal Aviation Administration. The Irish won the 1930 title and were excellent throughout most of the period but captured no other national championships in the decade (the 1938 team received mention, but Notre Dame does not recognize it as historically legitimate). Alabama under Frank Thomas continued to be a dominant power in the Southeastern Conference, with Rose Bowl victories accompanying both their titles (1930, 1934). Of course, Minnesota's three national championship run (1934–1936) is an incredible accomplishment, but they never played in a bowl game in any of those years. Stanford's "Vow Boys" managed three straight wins over the Trojans (1933–1935) and a 1936 Rose Bowl victory over Southern Methodist, 7–0.

Michigan—two decades

1930s	59–20–8
1940s	73–15–3
	132–35–11

USC edges out the competition in this decade based in part on the fact that they were 4-0 in Rose Bowls against the most rugged competition available, with three national titles. Their 1932 team was bigger and faster than any other football team of the era, almost something from the future in terms of power and modern speed. USC was 5-4-1 against Notre Dame in the 1930s.

The easy pick for the 1940s is Notre Dame, winner of four national titles (1943, 1946, 1947, 1949). This despite the fact that Michigan (1948 national champions) and Army (1944–1945 repeat champs) enjoyed the best decades in their respective histories. Ohio State won their first national championship in 1942, a "shot over the bow" against rival Michigan, which until then looked down on the Buckeyes as inferior on the field, in the classroom, and in the alumni world. Minnesota earned two straight titles, and Bruce Smith won the 1941 Heisman Trophy. Stanford under coach Clark Shaughnessy, who masterminded the T-formation, managed their last national title in 1940 with legendary left-handed quarterback Frankie Albert calling the signals.

As great as the college football scene was, World War II overshadowed the decade. Many players' careers were broken up by military service. Programs were disrupted and in some cases took years to return to normalcy, if they ever did. Notre Dame appeared to be a program that figured out how to navigate the war years and, when the boys came marching home, were in perfect position to assume the dominant position. Three Irish players earned Heismans in the decade (Angelo Bertelli, 1943; Johnny Lujack, 1947; Leon Hart, 1949).

The war created new sensibilities, too. Integration began to occur, albeit slowly, in professional sports (Jackie Robinson with the Dodgers in 1947) and the collegiate ranks. This would eventually be the prime reason USC, UCLA, and Ohio State either returned to greatness or ascended to previously unheard of heights.

The war also helped make Catholicism mainstream. Many Catholics served in the military, spreading their love of Notre Dame football to fellow service members. Postwar population shifts created a suburban Catholic fan base, expanding beyond the cities Knute Rockne saw as Notre Dame's natural "subway alumni" fan base. Former Irish star Frank Leahy took over the program, and they were absolutely phenomenal.

Bud Wilkinson's Oklahoma Sooners probably were better in the 1950s (not to mention the last few years of the 1940s) than any program ever was in a single decade. Notre Dame experienced some down years. USC and the PCC went through a ruinous scandal that saw the Trojans go on probation along with California, UCLA, and Washington. It happened at a terrible time, just as UCLA had won their first (and only) national title (1954), Washington was strong, and Cal was still thought of as a power.

A shift to the South and the Southwest occurred in the 1950s. Oklahoma was simply unbeatable, featuring Heisman Trophy winner Billy Vessels (1952). Wilkinson's Sooners mainly did it with teamwork and great defense, the cornerstone of championships. LSU and Auburn broke out from under the considerable shadows that had been cast by Tennessee and Alabama in previous decades.

Choosing USC as the "Team of the 1960s" is subjective, since there are statistics favoring other programs, but in the end the intangibles and a certain amount of common sense favor the Trojans. Alabama's 89–16–4 record is better than USC's 77–25–4. So is Texas's 86–19–2 and Penn State's 80–26–1. However, win-loss record is not the only worthy criteria in college football.

Jim Murray of the *L.A. Times* wrote disparagingly of Alabama's social policies, stating that they needed to win more than the "Magnolia Bowl" if they wanted to be considered for national supremacy. While Murray's point is well taken, Bear Bryant's team was as good as anybody in these turbulent times.

"Alabama football was something we could be proud of," said Taylor Watson, curator of the Paul W. Bryant Museum in Tuscaloosa. "Alabamians don't have much to be proud of, but we could be proud of our football team."

They most assuredly were. The Tide won in 1961, but in 1964 their dreams of greatness were upended. Quarterback Joe Namath, the best player (and probably the best all-around athlete) in the nation, was injured in the seventh game of the season. It eliminated his Heisman Trophy hopes. Notre Dame's utilitarian John Huarte won it. The nature of how America looks at college football changed that year. First, the politics of Alabama could not help but creep into the mind-set of college football fans.

The Alabama-Notre Dame rivalry, which was only partly about football, started when Tide fans resented the fact the Irish were ranked first every week despite Namath and Alabama appearing to be the better team. Namath's injury had Alabamians gritting their teeth because it not only jeopardized their title and bowl chances but of course also denied them what would have been the only Heisman ever won by a 'Bama player.

When USC knocked off the Irish, it was "happy days are here again" in Dixie. The polls went for 'Bama and it all looked good. Then Texas beat them in the Orange Bowl and Arkansas won the Cotton Bowl. Glory was denied. Two years later, the 1966 imbroglio just hardened feelings. They called it the "poll bowls" and the "poll wars." Alabama fans said that Alabama "plays football" while Notre Dame "plays politics." When Ara Parseghian went for a tie against Michigan State, they said that Bear Bryant "played to win, not to tie."

UCLA—two decades		Texas—two decades	
1950s	68–24–3	1960s	86–19–2
1960s	59–39–4	1970s	88–26–1
	127–63–7		174–45–3

Penn State—two decades		Penn State—three decades	
1960s	80–26–1	1960s	80–26–1
1970s	96–22	1970s	96–22
	176–48–1	1980s	89–21–2
			265–69–3

Ohio State—two decades	
1960s	68–21–2
1970s	91–20–3
	158–41–5

Both Texas and Alabama could make a strong claim that they were each the "Team of the Decade." Texas had two unbeaten, untied national championship seasons with Cotton Bowl wins over worthy Navy (Roger Staubach) and worthier Notre Dame (Joe Theismann) teams.

Alabama claims three titles, but of course one is the illegitimate 1964 version. The other comes in a 9-1-1 campaign in which the AP, for one year, reversed its policies as if manipulated by Bear Bryant. The UPI "crowned" Michigan State before they lost to UCLA in the Rose Bowl. The 1966 season is viewed as *The Missing Ring* in Alabama by their fans, and is the name of a fine book on the subject by Keith Dunnavant.

Notre Dame claims the semitainted 1966 crown, although their team was a powerhouse that season. USC won only two national championships (1962, 1967). So why are the Trojans the best team of the 1960s? For this reason: they produced two Heisman Trophy winners (Mike Garrett in 1965 and O. J. Simpson in 1968). Probably the most egregious error in the history of the Heisman balloting was the awarding of the trophy to UCLA's Gary Beban in 1967 instead of O. J. Their two titles came with wins over unbeaten Wisconsin (42-37 in the 1963 Rose Bowl) and Indiana (1968 Rose Bowl). The 1967 team produced a record five first-round draft picks (including Outland Trophy winner Ron Yary) *and most of their best players* returned the next year. Yary was the first overall pick of the 1968 NFL Draft by Minnesota. O. J. was the number one pick in the entire 1969 draft by Buffalo. Two of the best teams they fielded in the 1960s were not national champions.

The 1968 Trojans may well have gone down in history as one of college football's best teams had they not met their match in the form of Woody Hayes's Ohio State Buckeyes on the green plains of Pasadena. The 1969 Trojans, known as the Cardiac Kids, were one of the most exciting teams ever assembled. They won miracle comebacks against Stanford and UCLA. Featuring a defensive front called the Wild Bunch after the Sam Peckinpah Western of that year, they were tied by Notre Dame 14-14 at South Bend. When Texas and Penn State ran the table, it cost the Trojans a national championship. Ohio State, the presumptive champion, was beaten by Michigan. The Wolverines, full of themselves after defeating a team many had called the best ever, were stopped stone cold by the Wild Bunch in Pasadena, 10-3.

USC went to the Rose Bowl four straight years and were one of the first teams to expand their schedule nationally when much of the rest of the country did not. John McKay's team consistently went into Dixie when teams from Dixie stayed in Dixie. Bob Devaney's Nebraska Cornhuskers went 32 games without a loss. The streak started after falling to Troy 31-21 at home in 1969. The only tie: against USC the next season. The rivalry with Notre Dame heated up like never before. The Trojans started or continued rivalries with not one but four all-time great coaches and programs.

USC and college football fans were entertained by intense battles between McKay's charges and those of Notre Dame's Ara Parseghian, UCLA's Tommy Prothro, Ohio State's Woody Hayes, and Michigan's Bo Schembechler. No team had ever put themselves out there against so many of the best teams and coaches in such a short time. In the era of color television, the Trojans became the face of collegiate football. Images of their games on green Coliseum fields, under blue California skies, with pretty cheerleaders and sun-drenched fans, glamorized the collegiate game in a way that had not occurred since Rockne's Irish.

That is why they were the "Team of the Decade."

Nobody can say that Alabama is not the "Team of the 1970s" because they were no longer integrated. After USC traveled to Birmingham and laid waste to them in the first game of the decade, Bryant's team did integrate (they already had Wilbur Jackson in school, and John Mitchell was being recruited).

Record-wise, 'Bama again had the best mark (103–16–1), followed by Oklahoma (101–12–2), Michigan (96–16–3), Nebraska (98–20–4), Penn State (96–22), Ohio State (91–20–3), Southern California (93–22–1), Notre Dame (91–22), and Texas (88–26–1). Based on this, it would certainly appear that Bryant's program was the best of the 1970s. If not the Tide, then Oklahoma, Michigan, Nebraska, Penn State. . . .

Ask any fan of OU, Michigan, Nebraska, Penn State, or Ohio State if, given the totality of the decade, the glory of bowl victories, the Heismans, and the hype, they would trade their better win-loss records of the 1970s for the decade enjoyed by USC.

The answer to that question is thought of, mulled over, analyzed, and answered: yes. The boys play for national championships. Whatever formula exists resulting in national championships above all things, the Trojans—in this decade led by McKay and John Robinson—are usually better at it than anybody else. Forget Michigan and Ohio State. Every year, it seemed, they were 10–0 or some such gaudy record, averaging 40 points per game or more. Then came January, the sight of those cardinal and gold uniforms, and with it defeat. Next. . . .

Penn State? Joe Paterno's team would win and win and win. John Cappelletti's 1973 Heisman Trophy was *Something for Joey*. They personified excellence, but when it came to ultimate glory, they were like the Allies when they tried to win World War II ahead of *shedjuel* under the leadership of Sir Bernard Law Montgomery's ill-fated "Operation Market Garden" between D-day and the Bulge: *A Bridge Too Far* away.

Oklahoma? Most of the time the Sooners looked virtually unbeatable, which they actually were between 1973 and 1975. Unfortunately, they are part of that "close but no cigar" group based on the fact that in 1971 they lost to Nebraska; in 1974 their co-national championship is asterisked by NCAA probation; their 1977 team blew it in the Orange Bowl to Lou Holtz and Arkansas; and the 1978 Sooners watched in frustration while voters decided USC and Alabama were better. The Sooners' probations, their non-academic style, their wild coach Barry Switzer—all of it would have made for a great Dan Jenkins novel, but in the end OU is a notch below.

Oklahoma—two decades		Nebraska—two decades		Nebraska—three decades	
1970s	101–12–2	1970s	98–20–4	1970s	98–20–4
1980s	91–26–2	1980s	103–20	1980s	103–20
	192–38–4		201–40–4	1990s	108–16–1
					309–56–5

Nebraska? Win and win and win and win and win . . . then lose to OU. Next. . . .

Texas? Everybody waited for them to build on the 1969 title and their 30-game winning streak, snapped in the 1971 Cotton Bowl by Notre Dame. They could not reach the promised land. In 1977, led by Heisman Trophy winner Earl Campbell, it looked as if they would get there. When "The Eyes of Texas"—and everybody else—were upon the Longhorns, new coach Fred Akers's team got stage fright in a way Darrell Royal's teams had not.

Notre Dame? Six words and an exclamation point separate the Irish from the honor: the University of Southern California Trojans! Troy just beat them every year. If they did not, then Notre Dame won the national championship (1973, 1977). The battle for ultimate collegiate glory between the Irish and USC—between McKay and Parseghian; between John Robinson and Dan Devine; between Anthony Davis and Pat Haden and Joe Montana—in the end it is the defining reason why USC is again the "Team of the Decade" for the 1970s.

Alabama was good, no doubt. They integrated and America was better for it. The whole South changed, socially, politically, and athletically. In 1971 Alabama was unbeaten before losing to the great Nebraska juggernaut in the Orange Bowl, 38–6. In 1972 they were again undefeated until Auburn knocked them off in the "iron bowl," 17–16. In 1973 they were *again* unbeaten until Notre Dame took them in New Orleans, and they could no longer hide behind the AP's prebowl vote, which did not stop them from hiding behind the UPI's prebowl vote. Their claim of "three national championships" rings hollow. Alabama would be better off not even reminding people of their titles "won" in bowl defeat.

In the mid-1970s, Alabama seemed to go 11–1 every year but fell short to OU, Pittsburgh, and Notre Dame again. In the decade, they played USC four times. They lost twice at Legion Field (42–21 in 1970, 24–14 in 1978). They beat the Trojans twice at the Coliseum (17–10 when they broke out the veer in 1971, then 21–20 when they stood off a furious USC fourth-quarter comeback in 1977). In 1978 they were co-national champions with USC, but even though they were legitimate AP winners, details of that season leave the thinking reader, armed with common sense, logically convinced they should not have been. The facts are these: Alabama was 11–1 with a Sugar Bowl win. USC was 12–1 with a Rose Bowl win. Fair enough, a split title makes sense. Except . . .

On September 23, USC traveled to Birmingham's Legion Field *and beat the Crimson Tide, 24–14!* Alabama came in ranked number one. It was a rematch of the 1970 Sam "Bam" Cunningham game, but the event was marked more by what it *was not*. It was not a day of racial firsts and breakthroughs. Instead, integration had by 1978 come so seamlessly in all phases of Southern life that news reports do not even mention its significance.

Alabama was filled with just as many fast, skilled black athletes as the Trojans. The long-held "quiet advantage" McKay used to propel his program back to the top no longer existed. Still, USC put it to 'Bama on that steamy Saturday, behind Charles White's 199 yards. After the bowls, the AP voted for Alabama, the UPI for USC. It was not an *illegitimate* national championship like the Tide's 1964 and 1973 claims.

That said, USC was robbed by the Associated Press. Rarely in the pre-BCS era have the voters been given the opportunity to judge the number one teams based on the fact that they actually played each other. When one team—USC—goes to the other guys' place and beats them soundly in front of their fans, and the season ends with no other discernible advantage in record weighing the difference, common sense dictates that the team who beat the other is the deserving champion. The UPI got it right; the AP did not.

'Bama fans make the fair argument that they defeated unbeaten, top-ranked Penn State in the Sugar Bowl. USC beat 10–1 Michigan in Pasadena. The logic works this way: Michigan was a less impressive opponent because, despite great regular season records, they always lost in the Rose Bowl. Yeah, they always did lose . . . *to USC*! That is like discrediting Ty Cobb's batting championships because he always beat out "Shoeless Joe" Jackson, Eddie Collins, and Tris Speaker, who, if the argument is extended, were not so good because they never won the batting championships . . . that Cobb always won, often with a .400 average.

Hey, man, Charlie White and Troy smoked 'Bama in their house. They should have won the AP title as well as the UPI version. In 1979 unbeaten and untied Alabama won it outright.

The Trojans had off years in the 1970s that Alabama did not have (except for 1970). They were only 6–4–1 in both 1970 and 1971, but when they shined, they shined brighter than anybody. The 1972 team is the finest in the history of the game.

The 1974 national championship Trojans are probably the most exciting college team in history. Anthony Davis's performances against Notre Dame in both 1972 and 1974 rate as two of the three greatest days any collegian ever had. Year after year, they beat Notre Dame in L.A. and South Bend.

Pitt may have been the 1976 national champion, but USC, after losing to Missouri in the season opener in John Robinson's first year, won eleven straight. Many pundits felt that had the two teams played, USC would have prevailed. The 1976 Trojans (11–1) were named national champions by no fewer than six services after smoking Michigan in the Rose Bowl. Alabama, Ohio State, Oklahoma, or Michigan would have stuck it in their media guide trying to promote the idea that it was, as it could have been in USC's case, their twelfth national title. USC does not try to legitimize it, since the true consensus national champion of 1976 was Pitt. A game behind Tony Dorsett's Panthers and Ricky Bell's Trojans? Wow!

Then there is 1979. That year's USC team is likely, with the possible exception of the 2005 Trojans, to be the finest team *not* to win a national title. USC's Charlie White won the Heisman Trophy in 1979. Anthony Munoz blocked for him. So did Lombardi Award winner Brad Budde. Quarterback Paul McDonald was an All-American. They beat unbeaten Ohio State, the number one team in the nation, to win a thrilling Rose Bowl, 17–16. Yes, Alabama went all the way, beating Arkansas 24–9 in the Sugar Bowl to finish 12–0 with Bryant's last national championship. Bravo.

The 1979 Trojans (11–0–1) were also named national champions by the College Football Researchers Association after Ohio State fell to them in the manner by then well accustomed to. No, the school does not count this as their *thirteenth* title, either, even though the team was supposed to be the best ever, and a fair number of people still believe they were the finest in USC history. Alabama was the legitimate number one team. Therefore, while Alabama claims three titles and two are legit, they really should have only one. USC earned three with a Heisman (plus the 1978-1979 "Heisman teammate" duo of White and Marcus Allen, the 1981 winner).

Add to that the glamour of TV; the height of Notre Dame matchups with Parseghian, Devine, and Montana; the continued battles with UCLA's Pepper Rodgers, Terry Donahue, and John Sciarra, Washington's Don James and Warren Moon, Stanford's Jim Plunkett and Bill Walsh, California's Steve Bartkowski and Chuck Muncie, Arizona State's Frank Kush and Mark Malone, Oregon's Dan Fouts, Ohio State's Woody Hayes and Archie Griffin, Michigan's Bo Schembechler and Rick Leach, Michigan State's Duffy Daugherty and Kirk Gibson, Nebraska's Bob Devaney and Johnny Rodgers, Oklahoma's Chuck Fairbanks, Lee Roy Selmon, and Barry Switzer, Arkansas' Frank Broyles and Joe Ferguson, and Pitt's Tony Dorsett; plus LSU at "Death Valley"; Texas A&M in the South (twice); and of course Bear Bryant and the whole state of Alabama . . . the fact is that in this new "golden age" of college football they were a team with greater mystique and panache, who took on bigger challenges, traveled more widely, and performed more spectacularly than any other. The Trojans are the 1970s' "Team of the Decade."

In the 1980s, Miami wins it hands down: three national championships and two other years (1986, 1988) in which they just missed. Vinny Testaverde won the 1986 Heisman Trophy, and the team reeled off a 36-game regular season winning streak while starting their historic 58-game home winning skein. In the Pac-10, a new power shift took place. UCLA beat USC three years in a row (1982-1984) and won three Rose Bowls. Washington rose under coach Don James. Arizona State beat Michigan 22-15 in the 1987 Rose Bowl. Overall, the conference fell with the demise of USC but continued general dominance over the Big 10.

Penn State won two national championships (1982, 1986) and Notre Dame one (1988) while falling just short of a second one (1989). New coach Lou Holtz took over a program that had seen down times under Gerry Faust. In the late 1980s and early 1990s he returned them to the top of the college football mountain. They began a run of eleven straight wins over USC in 1983.

Nebraska's 1983 team looked like it was going to go down in history as the best ever until coach Tom Osborne went for 2 against Miami in the Orange Bowl. He failed and the 'Huskers lost 31-30, but it was a courageous move by Osborne. There were no overtimes in those days. Had he tied the game Nebraska would have won the national

Florida State—two decades		Washington—two decades	
1980s	87–29–5	1980s	84–33–2
1990s	109–13–1	1990s	82–35–1
	196–42–6		166–68–3

championship but lost its claim to be "history's best team." He decided not to go the route of Ara Parseghian in 1966 and looked noble in defeat.

The 1990s come down to two teams: Nebraska and Florida State. Nebraska, winner of three national titles (1994, 1995, 1997) gets the nod over Florida State with two (1993, 1999). When Bobby Bowden defeated Tom Osborne in the 1994 Orange Bowl, 18–16, Osborne faced great criticism from the "Cornhusker nation" because, despite great records since taking over from Bob Devaney in 1973, he consistently lost the "big one" in the form of bowl defeats or Oklahoma games. Chief among his most disappointing efforts were the 1984 Orange Bowl loss to Miami and now, one decade later, the loss to Florida State. His heroic "go for 2" against the Hurricanes was by then worn thin. 'Husker fans wanted the national championship that Devaney had delivered two years in a row (1970–1971).

After that, however, Osborne's team made him into a legend. His 1994–1995 champions may be the best two-year run ever. In 1997 he split the title with unbeaten Michigan. The Wolverines were very good, but most feel had the teams played, Nebraska would have prevailed.

The 2000s belong to Pete Carroll and USC. The numbers are staggering: thirty-four wins in a row (2003–2006), 45–1 (2002–2006), 51–2 (2002–2006), 82–8 (2002–2008), two straight national championships, thirty-three straight weeks ranked number one, perhaps the best-ever two year run (2003–2004), the best three-year run (2003–2005), inches removed from an unprecedented third straight title (2005), and a shot at Oklahoma's 47-game winning streak. All of this comes replete with a number one draft choice (Carson Palmer, 2003), fourteen first-round selections, three Heisman Trophy winners (Palmer, 2002; Matt Leinart, 2004; Reggie Bush, 2005), five straight national-best recruiting classes (2003–2007), eleven NFL draftees in each of the 2007 and 2009 drafts, and 26 All-Americans in seven seasons. There is no competition for the honor, so dominant has Troy been in the new century.

They ran their winning streak to seven against both UCLA and Notre Dame. They won seven straight Pac-10 titles, went to seven straight BCS bowls (6–1, an NCAA record), won four Rose Bowls, finished in the top four for seven consecutive years, and won 11 games another NCAA-record seven straight seasons (2002–2008). They did it all in the BCS era, which is like adding an extra national title to their record. Had the BCS not existed in 2005, USC would have beaten Penn State something like 75–2 in the Rose Bowl, leaving unbeaten Texas to complain that they never had their shot at the title.

Entering 2009, Carroll was 82–8 in seven seasons and 88–15 overall, but wait. Of those fifteen losses, only one has been by more than seven points (27–16 at Notre Dame in 2001). Eleven of them have been on the road or in a bowl game. In 2001 he lost to Kansas State (home, 10–6), Oregon (road, 24–22), Stanford (home, 21–16), Washington (road, 27–24), and Utah (Las Vegas Bowl, 10–6).

In 2002 he lost to Kansas State (road, 27–20) and Washington State (road, 30–27 in overtime). In 2003 he lost to California (road, 34–31 in three overtimes). In 2006, he lost to Texas (Rose Bowl, 41–38). In 2006 he lost to Oregon State (road, 33–31) and UCLA (road, 13–9). In 2007 he lost to Stanford by a point and Oregon by seven on the road.

In 2008 he lost at Oregon State by six. That is fifteen losses by a total of 65 points. Take away the Notre Dame defeat and it is fifteen losses by fifty-four, an average of less than 4 points per loss!

In other words, with luck and a few good bounces, Pete Carroll's record could be *102–1*! If so, he could have seven or eight national championships, not two. If his 2001 team had won all those close games, finishing 10–1 at the end of the regular season, they might have gotten the nod over once-beaten Nebraska to play against Miami in the BCS Rose Bowl. Once-beaten Oregon was barely edged out as it was.

In 2002, both losses were by the slimmest of margins, so obviously if Troy were 12–0 (with the toughest schedule in the nation that year), they would have finished ahead of both Miami and Ohio State in the BCS standings going into the Fiesta Bowl.

In 2003, once-beaten USC was ranked number one by the Associated Press anyway in a season with no unbeatens. The 2006 Rose Bowl loss spoke for itself. All that need be said about USC in the 2000s is that the 2006 team was 11–2; won the Pac-10 title; beat Brady Quinn and Notre Dame by 20 points; beat Michigan (undefeated going into the "Game of the Century" with Ohio State) 32–18; were the junior year of a 2003 recruiting class considered the best of all time; had the number one recruiting class in the country for the fifth straight year; were led by a quarterback who would enter the following season the leading contender for the Heisman Trophy and a backup who was the former *Parade* magazine National High School Player of the Year; were the odds-on early favorites to win their third national championship of the decade in 2007; and . . . *were the worst USC team under Carroll between 2002 and 2008*!

If all of that were not enough, when the season ended, Arkansas' freshman quarterback sensation Mitch Mustain, a potential Heisman-caliber star, transferred to USC! Carroll and Southern California entered the elite status of Knute Rockne's Irish of the 1920s, Frank Leahy's Notre Dame teams of the 1940s, and Bud Wilkinson's record at Oklahoma in the 1950s. Rockne (with the exception of the 1925 Rose Bowl win over Stanford) and Leahy had done it without the hassle of an end-of-the-season bowl challenge. Wilkinson's Sooners reeled off 47 straight and two titles, one without a bowl game to muck up the works. The BCS system, in place since 1998, had created a higher standard, but USC owned it.

In January of 2007, Ohio State thought they were making a bid for "Team of the Decade" when they carried their unbeaten record into the BCS championship game against Florida at University of Phoenix Stadium in Glendale, Arizona. The subsequent poundings they received at the hands of the Gators and LSU (2008 BCS title game) eliminated the very hint that Ohio State deserved to be mentioned in the same breath with Carroll's Trojans. Entering 2009, Florida, with two national championships and a Heisman (Tim Tebow, 2007), are their closest competition.

Through the Travail of Ages

1900s

Yale	100–4–5
Michigan	83–8–3
Harvard	69–8–8

1910s

| Washington | 49–4–3 |
| Notre Dame | 63–7–6 |

YALE		MICHIGAN		WASHINGTON		NOTRE DAME		HARVARD	
1900	12–0	1900	7–2–1	1910	6–0	1910	4–1–1	1910	8–0–1
1901	11–1–1	1901	11–0	1911	7–0	1911	6–0–2	1911	6–2–1
1902	11–0–1	1902	11–0	1912	6–0	1912	7–0–0	1912	9–0
1903	11–1	1903	11–0–1	1913	7–0	1913	7–0–0	1913	9–0
1904	10–1	1904	11–0	1914	6–0–1	1914	6–2	1914	7–0–2
1905	10–0	1905	12–1	1915	7–0	1915	7–1	1915	8–1
1906	9–0–1	1906	4–1	1916	6–0–1	1916	8–1	1916	7–3
1907	9–0–1	1907	5–1	1917	1–2–1	1917	6–1–1	1917	3–1–3
1908	7–1–1	1908	5–2–1	1918	1–1	1918	3–1–2	1918	2–1
1909	10–0	1909	6–1	1919	5–1	1919	9–0	1919	9–0–1
100–4–5		**83–8–3**		**52–4–3**		**63–7–6**		**69–8–8**	

1920s

Southern California	88–13–2
Notre Dame	81–12–4
California	73–16–7

Alabama	71–22–6
Stanford	67–22–6
Illinois	55–19–3

SOUTHERN CALIFORNIA		NOTRE DAME		CALIFORNIA	
1920	6–0	1920	9–0	1920	9–0
1921	10–1	1921	10–1	1921	9–0–1
1922	10–1	1922	8–1–1	1922	9–0
1923	6–2	1923	9–1	1923	9–0–1
1924	9–2	1924	10–0	1924	8–0–2
1925	11–2	1925	7–2–1	1925	6–3
1926	8–2	1926	7–2–1	1926	3–6
1927	8–1–1	1927	7–1–1	1927	7–3
1928	9–0–1	1928	5–4	1928	6–2–2
1929	10–2	1929	9–0	1929	7–1–1
88–13–2		**81–12–4**		**73–16–7**	

(continues)

Through the Travail of Ages (*continued*)

ALABAMA		STANFORD		ILLINOIS	
1920	10–1	1920	4–3	1920	5–2
1921	5–4–2	1921	4–2–2	1921	3–4
1922	6–3–1	1922	4–5	1922	2–5
1923	7–2–1	1923	7–2	1923	8–0
1924	8–1	1924	7–1–1	1924	6–1–1
1925	10–0	1925	7–2	1925	5–3
1926	9–0–1	1926	10–0–1	1926	6–2
1927	5–4–1	1927	8–2–1	1927	7–0–1
1928	6–3	1928	8–3–1	1928	7–1
1929	6–3	1929	9–2	1929	6–1–1
71–22–6		**67–22–6**		**55–19–3**	

1930s

Alabama	79–11–5	Notre Dame	65–20–5
Tennessee	79–17–5	Minnesota	57–18–6
Pittsburgh	75–14–7	Michigan	59–20–8
Southern California	73–25–9		

ALABAMA		TENNESSEE		PITTSBURGH		SOUTHERN CALIFORNIA	
1930	10–0	1930	9–1	1930	6–2–1	1930	8–2
1931	9–1	1931	9–0–1	1931	8–1	1931	10–1
1932	8–2	1932	9–0–1	1932	8–1–2	1932	11–0
1933	7–1–1	1933	7–3	1933	8–1	1933	10–1–1
1934	10–0	1934	8–2	1934	8–1	1934	4–6–1
1935	6–2–1	1935	4–5	1935	7–1–2	1935	5–7
1936	8–0–1	1936	6–2–2	1936	8–1–1	1936	4–2–3
1937	9–1	1937	6–3–1	1937	9–0–1	1937	4–4–2
1938	7–1–1	1938	11–0	1938	8–2	1938	9–2
1939	5–3–1	1939	10–1	1939	5–4	1939	8–0–2
79–11–5		**79–17–5**		**75–14–7**		**73–25–9**	

NOTRE DAME		MINNESOTA		MICHIGAN	
1930	10–0	1930	3–4–1	1930	5–1–2
1931	6–2–1	1931	7–3	1931	5–3–1
1932	7–2	1932	5–3	1932	7–1
1933	3–5–1	1933	4–0–4	1933	4–2–2
1934	6–3	1934	8–0	1934	8–1
1935	7–1–1	1935	8–0	1935	6–2
1936	6–2–1	1936	7–1	1936	6–1–2
1937	6–2–1	1937	6–2	1937	8–2
1938	8–1	1938	6–2	1938	6–3
1939	7–22	1939	3–4–1	1939	4–4–1
65–20–5		**57–18–6**		**59–20–8**	

1940s

Notre Dame	82–9–6	Army	59–17–7
Michigan	73–15–3	Alabama	66–24–4

NOTRE DAME		MICHIGAN		ARMY		ALABAMA	
1940	7–2	1940	7–1	1940	1–7–1	1940	7–2
1941	8–0–1	1941	6–1–1	1941	5–3–1	1941	9–2
1942	7–2–2	1942	7–3	1942	6–3	1942	8–3
1943	9–1	1943	8–1	1943	7–2–1	1943	(no team/WW II)
1944	8–2	1944	8–2	1944	9–0	1944	5–2–2
1945	7–2–1	1945	7–3	1945	9–0	1945	10–0
1946	8–0–1	1946	6–2–1	1946	9–0–1	1946	7–4
1947	9–0	1947	10–0	1947	5–2–2	1947	8–3
1948	9–0–1	1948	9–0	1948	8–0–1	1948	6–4–1
1949	10–0	1949	6–2–1	1949	9–0	1949	6–4–1
82–9–6		**73–15–3**		**59–17–7**		**66–24–4**	

(continues)

Through the Travail of Ages (*continued*)

1950s

Oklahoma	105–9–6	Tennessee	72–30–4
Michigan State	68–17–1	UCLA	68–24–3

OKLAHOMA		MICHIGAN STATE		TENNESSEE		UCLA	
1950	10–1	1950	8–1	1950	11–1	1950	6–3
1951	10–1	1951	9–0	1951	10–1	1951	5–3–1
1952	8–1–1	1952	9–0	1952	8–2–1	1952	8–1
1953	9–1–1	1953	9–1	1953	6–4–1	1953	8–2
1954	10–0	1954	3–6	1954	4–6	1954	9–0
1955	11–0	1955	9–1	1955	6–3–1	1955	9–2
1956	10–0	1956	7–2	1956	10–1	1956	7–3
1957	10–1	1957	8–1	1957	8–3	1957	8–2
1958	10–1	1958	3–5–1	1958	4–6	1958	3–6–1
1959	7–3	1959	5–4	1959	5–4–1	1959	5–4–1

105–9–6	**68–17–1**	**72–30–4**	**68–24–3**

1960s

Alabama	89–16–4	Ohio State	68–21–2
Texas	86–19–2	Notre Dame	62–34–4
Penn State	80–26–1	UCLA	59–39–4
Southern California	76–25–4		

ALABAMA		TEXAS		PENN STATE		SOUTHERN CALIFORNIA	
1960	8–1–2	1960	7–3–1	1960	7–3	1960	4–6
1961	11–0	1961	10–1	1961	8–3	1961	4–5–1
1962	10–1	1962	9–1–1	1962	9–2	1962	11–0
1963	9–2	1963	11–0	1963	7–3	1963	7–3
1964	10–1	1964	10–1	1964	6–4	1964	7–3
1965	9–1–1	1965	6–4	1965	5–5	1965	7–2–1
1966	11–0	1966	7–4	1966	5–5	1966	7–4
1967	8–2–1	1967	6–4	1967	8–2–1	1967	10–1
1968	8–3	1968	9–1–1	1968	11–0	1968	9–1–1
1969	6–5	1969	11–0	1969	11–0	1969	10–0–1

89–16–4	**86–19–2**	**80–26–1**	**76–25–4**

OHIO STATE		NOTRE DAME		UCLA	
1960	7–2	1960	2–8	1960	7–2–1
1961	8–0–1	1961	5–5	1961	7–4
1962	6–3	1962	5–5	1962	4–6
1963	5–3–1	1963	2–7	1963	2–8
1964	7–2	1964	9–1	1964	4–6
1965	7–2	1965	7–2–1	1965	8–2–1
1966	4–5	1966	9–0–1	1966	9–1
1967	6–3	1967	8–2	1967	7–2–1
1968	10–0	1968	7–2–1	1968	3–7
1969	8–1	1969	8–2–1	1969	8–1–1

68–21–2   **62–34–4**   **59–39–4**

1970s

Alabama	103–16–1	Ohio State	91–20–3
Oklahoma	101–12–2	Southern California	93–22–1
Michigan	96–16–3	Notre Dame	91–22
Nebraska	98–20–4	Texas	88–26–1
Penn State	96–22		

ALABAMA		OKLAHOMA		MICHIGAN		NEBRASKA		PENN STATE	
1970	6–5–1	1970	7–4–1	1970	9–1	1970	11–0–1	1970	7–3
1971	11–1	1971	11–1	1971	11–1	1971	13–0	1971	11–1
1972	10–2	1972	11–1	1972	10–1	1972	9–2–1	1972	10–2
1973	11–1	1973	10–0–1	1973	10–0–1	1973	9–2–1	1973	12–0
1974	11–1	1974	11–0	1974	10–1	1974	9–3	1974	10–2
1975	11–1	1975	11–1	1975	8–2–2	1975	10–2	1975	9–3
1976	9–3	1976	9–2–1	1976	10–2	1976	9–3–1	1976	7–5
1977	11–1	1977	10–2	1977	10–2	1977	9–3	1977	11–1
1978	11–1	1978	11–1	1978	10–2	1978	9–3	1978	11–1
1979	12–0	1979	11–1	1979	8–4	1979	10–2	1979	8–4

103–16–1   **101–12–2**   **96–16–3**   **98–20–4**   **96–22**

(continues)

Through the Travail of Ages (*continued*)

OHIO STATE		SOUTHERN CALIFORNIA		NOTRE DAME		TEXAS	
1970	9–1	1970	6–4–1	1970	10–1	1970	10–1
1971	6–4	1971	6–4–1	1971	8–2	1971	8–3
1972	9–2	1972	12–0	1972	8–3	1972	10–1
1973	10–0–1	1973	9–2–1	1973	11–0	1973	8–3
1974	10–2	1974	10–1–1	1974	10–2	1974	8–4
1975	11–1	1975	8–4	1975	8–3	1975	10–2
1976	9–2–1	1976	11–1	1976	9–3	1976	5–5–1
1977	9–3	1977	8–4	1977	11–1	1977	11–1
1978	7–4–1	1978	12–1	1978	9–3	1978	9–3
1979	11–1	1979	11–0–1	1979	7–4	1979	9–3
91–20–3		**93–22–1**		**91–22**		**88–26–1**	

1980s

Nebraska	103–20	Alabama	85–33–2
Miami	99–20	Washington	84–33–2
Penn State	89–21–2	Southern California	78–36–3
Oklahoma	92–26–2	Notre Dame	76–39–2
Florida State	87–29–5		

NEBRASKA		MIAMI		PENN STATE		OKLAHOMA		FLORIDA STATE	
1980	10–2	1980	9–3	1980	10–2	1980	10–2	1980	10–2
1981	9–3	1981	9–2	1981	10–2	1981	7–4–1	1981	6–5
1982	12–1	1982	7–4	1982	11–1	1982	8–4	1982	9–3
1983	12–1	1983	11–1	1983	8–4–1	1983	8–4	1983	7–5
1984	10–2	1984	8–5	1984	6–5	1984	9–2–1	1984	7–3–2
1985	9–3	1985	10–2	1985	11–1	1985	11–1	1985	9–3
1986	10–2	1986	11–1	1986	12–0	1986	11–1	1986	7–4–1
1987	10–2	1987	12–0	1987	8–4	1987	11–1	1987	11–1
1988	11–2	1988	11–1	1988	5–6	1988	9–3	1988	11–1
1989	10–2	1989	11–1	1989	8–3–1	1989	7–4	1989	10–2
103–20		**99–20**		**89–21–2**		**91–26–2**		**87–29–5**	

ALABAMA		WASHINGTON		SOUTHERN CALIFORNIA		NOTRE DAME	
1980	10–2	1980	9–3	1980	8–2–1	1980	9–2–1
1981	9–2–1	1981	10–2	1981	9–3	1981	5–6
1982	8–4	1982	10–2	1982	8–3	1982	6–4–1
1983	8–4	1983	8–4	1983	4–6–1	1983	7–5
1984	5–6	1984	11–1	1984	9–3	1984	7–5
1985	9–2–1	1985	7–5	1985	6–6	1985	5–6
1986	10–3	1986	8–3–1	1986	7–5	1986	5–6
1987	7–5	1987	7–4–1	1987	8–4	1987	8–4
1988	9–3	1988	6–5	1988	10–2	1988	12–0
1989	10–2	1989	8–4	1989	9–2–1	1989	12–1
85–33–2		**84–33–2**		**78–36–3**		**76–39–2**	

1990s

Florida State	109–13–1	Tennessee	98–22–3
Nebraska	108–16–1	Washington	82–35–1
Florida	102–22–1		

FLORIDA STATE		NEBRASKA		FLORIDA		TENNESSEE		WASHINGTON	
1990	10–2	1990	9–3	1990	9–2	1990	9–2–2	1990	10–2
1991	11–2	1991	9–2–1	1991	10–2	1991	9–3	1991	12–0
1992	11–1	1992	9–3	1992	9–4	1992	9–3	1992	9–3
1993	12–1	1993	11–1	1993	11–2	1993	9–2–1	1993	7–4
1994	10–1–1	1994	13–0	1994	10–2–1	1994	8–4	1994	7–4
1995	10–2	1995	12–0	1995	12–1	1995	11–1	1995	7–4–1
1996	11–1	1996	11–2	1996	12–1	1996	10–2	1996	9–3
1997	11–1	1997	13–0	1997	10–2	1997	11–2	1997	8–4
1998	11–2	1998	9–4	1998	10–2	1998	13–0	1998	6–6
1999	12–0	1999	12–1	1999	9–4	1999	9–3	1999	7–5
109–13–1		**108–16–1**		**102–22–1**		**98–22–3**		**82–35–1**	

(continues)

Through the Travail of Ages (*continued*)

2000s

Oklahoma	79–14	Ohio State	70–18
Texas	75–14	Southern California	69–19

OKLAHOMA		TEXAS		OHIO STATE		SOUTHERN CALIFORNIA	
2000	13–0	2000	9–3	2000	8–4	2000	5–7
2001	11–2	2001	11–2	2001	7–5	2001	6–6
2002	12–2	2002	11–2	2002	14–0	2002	11–2
2003	12–2	2003	10–3	2003	11–2	2003	12–1
2004	12–1	2004	11–1	2004	8–4	2004	13–0
2005	8–4	2005	13–0	2005	10–2	2005	12–1
2006	11–3	2006	10–3	2006	12–1	2006	11–2
2007	11–3	2007	10–3	2007	11–2	2007	11–2
2008	12–2	2008	12–1	2008	10–3	2008	12–1
102–19		**97–18**		**91–23**		**93–22**	

Chapter 19

Dynasties

1. Southern California under John McKay & John Robinson (1962–1982) . . . greatest
2-decade run ever . . . 5 nat'l titles, 4 Heismans . . . could have been no. 1 in unbeaten '69,
'79 seasons . . . probably best team in '76 . . . would have been no. 1 if not lost Rose Bowl
in '69 . . . 23-game ('71–'73), 28-game ('78–'80) unbeaten streaks . . . '72 team was greatest
of all time . . . '74 Troy most exciting team ever . . . 5-0 ('78–'82) and 12-2-2 ('67–'82) vs.
Irish during great Notre Dame stretch . . . McKay likely would rate with Bear Bryant, Bud
Wilkinson had he not gone pro after '75 season . . .

1962	11–0 John McKay		1973	9–2–1
1963	7–3		1974	10–1–1
1964	7–3		1975	8–4
1965	7–3		1976	11–1 John Robinson
1966	7–4		1977	8–4
1967	10–1		1978	12–1
1968	9–1–1		1979	11–0–1
1969	10–0–1		1980	8–2–1
1970	6–4–1		1981	9–3
1971	6–4–1		1982	8–3
1972	12–0			

2. Alabama under Bear Bryant (1958–1982) . . . 4 legit nat'l champs plus 1 AP title
('64 with bowl loss) and one UPI title ('73 with bowl loss) . . . could have been no. 1 in
unbeaten '66 season, '77 1-loss season . . . 26-game win streak ('60–'62) . . . greatest team
concept ever . . . Bryant was greatest college football coach who ever lived . . .

1958	5–4–1	1965	9–1–1	1971	11–1	1977	11–1
1959	7–2–2	1966	11–0	1972	10–2	1978	11–1
1960	8–2–1	1967	8–2–1	1973	11–1	1979	12–0
1961	11–0	1968	8–3	1974	11–1	1980	10–2
1962	10–1	1969	6–5	1975	11–1	1981	9–2–1
1963	9–2	1970	6–5–1	1976	9–3	1982	8–4

3. Notre Dame under Knute Rockne (1919–1930) . . . defined college football . . . 3-time nat'l champs . . . could have been no. 1 ('19, '20, '26) . . . Four Horsemen ('24) beat Army (Polo Grounds), Stanford (Rose Bowl) . . . Rockne was game's best coach until '60s . . .

1919	9–0	1922	8–1–1	1925	7–2–1	1928	5–4
1920	9–0	1923	9–1	1926	7–2–1	1929	9–0
1921	10–1	1924	10–0	1927	7–1–1	1930	10–1

4. Oklahoma under Bud Wilkinson (1948–1958) . . . 47-game winning streak, 48-game unbeaten streak ('53–'57) . . . 31-game winning streak ('48–'50) . . . greatest decade in history . . . 2 nat'l champs plus AP, UPI titles with bowl loss ('50) . . . could have been nat'l champs ('49, '54) . . . 1 Heisman . . . Wilkinson was ultimate coach . . .

1948	10–1	1952	8–1–1	1956	10–0
1949	11–0	1953	9–1–1	1957	10–1
1950	10–1	1954	10–0	1958	10–1
1951	10–1	1955	11–0		

5. Notre Dame under Frank Leahy & Terry Brennan (1941–1955) . . . dominated college football, solidified Irish legend forever . . . 4 nat'l titles, 3 Heismans . . . could have won titles ('41, '48, '53) . . . 6 unbeaten seasons ('41, '46, '47, '48, '49, '53) . . . 39-game unbeaten streak ('46–'50) . . . ended Army reign with 0–0 tie at Yankee Stadium ('46) . . . '47 Irish were one of greatest teams ever . . . epitomized postwar American glory days . . . Leahy was embodiment of Notre Dame class . . .

1941	8–0–1	Frank Leahy	1949	10–0
1942	7–2–2		1950	4–4–1
1943	9–1		1951	7–2–1
1944	8–2		1952	7–2–1
1945	7–2–1		1953	9–0–1
1946	8–0–1		1954	9–1 Terry Brennan
1947	9–0		1955	8–2
1948	9–0–1			

6. Miami under Howard Schnellenberger, Jimmy Johnson, & Dennis Erickson (1983–1992) . . . redefined modern game . . . 4 nat'l titles, 2 Heismans . . . 36-game regular season winning streak ('85–'88) . . . unbeaten at home ('84–92) . . . almost won '86, '87, '88, '92 titles . . . '87 'Canes were one of best in history . . . galvanized talent in state of Florida . . .

1983	11–1	Howard Schnellenberger	1988	11–1
1984	8–5	Jimmy Johnson	1989	11–1 Dennis Erickson
1985	10–2		1990	10–2
1986	11–1		1991	12–0
1987	12–0		1992	11–1

7. Penn State under Joe Paterno (1968–1986) . . . 31-game unbeaten streak ('67–'70) . . . 2 nat'l titles, 1 Heisman . . . beat Miami (1/'87 Fiesta Bowl) . . . came close in '68, '69, '73, '78 . . .

1968	11–0	1973	12–0	1978	11–1	1983	8–4–1
1969	11–0	1974	10–2	1979	8–4	1984	6–5
1970	7–3	1975	9–3	1980	10–2	1985	11–1
1971	11–1	1976	7–5	1981	10–2	1986	12–0
1972	10–2	1977	11–1	1982	11–1		

8. Nebraska under Tom Osborne (1993–2001) . . . 3 nat'l titles, 1 Heisman . . . lost '01 BCS title game . . . just missed '93 title . . . '95 'Huskers were 2nd best team in history . . . beat Florida 62–24 in 1/95 Fiesta Bowl . . . '93–'97 'Huskers were as good as any team ever . . . reestablished dominance over Oklahoma in pre-BCS era . . .

1993	11–1	1996	11–2	1999	12–1
1994	13–0	1997	13–0	2000	10–2
1995	12–0	1998	9–4	2001	11–2

9. Oklahoma under Chuck Fairbanks & Barry Switzer (1971–1988) . . . 37-game unbeaten streak ('72–'75) . . . repeat nat'l champs ('74–'75) . . . '85 nat'l title . . . 1 Heisman . . . just missed '71, '77, '87 nat'l titles . . . '71 loss to Nebraska in "Game of Century" . . . dominated Nebraska after that . . .

1971	11–1 Chuck Fairbanks	1980	10–2
1972	11–1	1981	7–4–1
1973	10–0–1 Barry Switzer	1982	8–4
1974	11–0	1983	8–4
1975	11–1	1984	9–2–1
1976	9–2–1	1985	11–1
1977	10–2	1986	11–1
1978	11–1	1987	11–1
1979	11–1	1988	9–3

10. Southern California's Thundering Herd under Howard Jones (1928–1939) . . . rivalry with Irish nationalized college football . . . 25-game winning streak, 27-game unbeaten streak ('31–'33) . . . 4 nat'l champs ('28, '31, '32, '39) . . . '28 team was possibly best ever up to that year . . . '31–'32 repeat champs threw 14 shutouts, allowed 65 points . . . 16–14 win over Irish ('31) one of greatest all-time games . . . '32 team was greatest in history until then . . . integrated games vs. UCLA (Jackie Robinson, Kenny Washington, Woody Strode) before packed Coliseum crowds in '30s helped change society . . .

1928	9–0–1	1932	11–0	1936	4–2–3
1929	10–2	1933	10–1–1	1937	4–4–2
1930	8–2	1934	4–6–1	1938	9–2
1931	10–1	1935	5–7		

11. Ohio State under Woody Hayes (1968–1975) . . . 1 nat'l title ('68), 2-time Heisman winner (Archie Griffin '74–'75) . . . almost won '69, '70, '75 titles . . . beat O. J. Simpson & USC in memorable '69 Rose Bowl . . . loss to USC in '75 Rose Bowl thriller for ages, frustration vs. Pac-8 in Pasadena marked era . . . . rivalry with Trojans' John McKay and Wolverines' Bo Schembechler are what make college football great . . .

1968	10-0	1972	9-2
1969	8-1	1973	10-0-1
1970	9-1	1974	10-2
1971	6-4	1975	11-1

12. Notre Dame's "Era of Ara" under Ara Parseghian & Dan Devine (1964–1978) . . . USC rivalry marked "golden age" of college football, every game but 2 affected nat'l title, all-time TV ratings . . . Parseghian-John McKay (USC) matchups were titanic struggles for nat'l supremacy . . . 2 nat'l titles, 1 Heisman . . . just missed in '64 . . . beat USC 51-0 ('66 in L.A.) . . . 10-10 tie with Michigan State ('66) was "Game of Century" . . . 24-23 win over 'Bama in '73 Sugar Bowl one of greatest games ever . . . '77 "green jerseys" game vs. USC was Joe Montana's "coming-out party," propelled nat'l title . . . trounced Earl Campbell & Texas ('78 Cotton Bowl) . . . Devine-John Robinson (USC) rivalry just as heated in late '70s . . .

1964	9-1 Ara Parseghian		1972	8-3
1965	7-2-1		1973	11-0
1966	9-0-1		1974	10-2
1967	8-2		1975	8-3 Dan Devine
1968	7-2-1		1976	9-3
1969	8-2-1		1977	11-1
1970	10-1		1978	9-3
1971	8-2			

13. Florida State under Bobby Bowden (1993–2000) . . . .Top 5 every year . . . greatest sustained run . . . 2 nat'l titles, 2 Heismans . . . 3 BCS title games . . . just missed ('96, '98, '00) . . . Miami, Florida rivalries were apex of college football, shifted focus to Sunshine State . . .

1993	12-1	1997	11-1
1994	10-1-1	1998	11-2
1995	10-2	1999	12-0
1996	11-1	2000	11-2

14. Southern California under Pete Carroll (2002–2008) . . . ushered in new golden age . . . repeat nat'l titles, 3 Heismans, 2 straight nat'l-title games defined higher standards of greatness in BCS era . . . 34-game winning streak ('03–'06) . . . 48-1 ('03–'06), 51-2 ('02–'06), 82-8 ('02–'08) . . . Troy's 55-24 annihilation of Oklahoma ('05 BCS Orange

Bowl) considered greatest single performance ever . . . '04 Trojans one of three best teams in history . . . '05 Troy was best of all time until last-19-seconds-of-game loss to Texas in '06 Rose Bowl (best game ever played) . . . just missed first-ever "three-Pete" AP titles, chance to come within less than season of Oklahoma's 47-game winning streak . . . easily could have been '02, '05, '06 nat'l champs . . . 5-0 vs. Irish ('02–'06), 4 straight vs. Bruins ('02-'05/66–19 in '05) . . . BCS game, Top 5 each season ('02–'06) . . . no. 1 recruiting class 5 straight yrs. . . absent NFL, L.A.'s "pro team" . . . 7 straight top 5 finishes . . . NCAA-record 7 straight 11-win, BCS seasons (6-1 in BCS bowls) . . . only 1 loss more than TD, could have been 102-1 ('01-'08) . . .

2002	11–2	2005	12–1	2008	12–1
2003	12–1	2006	11–2		
2004	13–0	2007	11–2		

15. Texas under Darrell Royal (1963–1970) . . . 2 nat'l titles ('63, '69), UPI title with bowl loss ('70) . . . 30-game winning streak ('68–'71) . . . beat Irish in thrilling '70 Cotton Bowl . . . "wishbone" changed face of offensive football . . . '69 15–14 "Game of Century" win over Arkansas was all-time classic . . . defined football as representative of Lone Star State . . .

1963	12–1	1967	11–1
1964	10–1–1	1968	11–2
1965	10–2	1969	12–0
1966	11–1	1970	11–2

16. California's Wonder Teams under Andy Smith (1920–1924) . . . 3 straight nat'l titles ('20-'22) . . . longest 50-game unbeaten run in modern history (46-0-4) . . . 1st team to recruit, get transfers . . . revolutionized approach to game . . . opening of Memorial Stadium helped usher in huge new stadiums . . . destroyed Ohio State in '21 Rose Bowl . . . turned national focus to West in post-WWI era . . .

1920	9–0	1923	9–0–1
1921	9–0–1	1924	8–0–2
1922	9–0		

17. Army under Red Blaik (1944–1950) . . . 2 straight nat'l champs ('44-'45) . . . 2 Heismans, Doc Blanchard and Glenn Davis (Mr. Inside & Mr. Outside) . . . '45 Black Knights one of all-time greatest . . . '44 team was better (56 points a game) . . . 32-game ('45-'47), 28-game ('47-'50) unbeaten streaks . . .

1944	9–0	1948	8–0–1
1945	9–0	1949	9–0
1946	9–0–1	1950	8–1
1947	5–2–2		

18. Minnesota under Bernie Bierman (1933–1941) . . . last three-straight nat'l champs ('34–'36), 1st AP champs ('36) . . . AP repeat nat'l champs ('40–'41) . . . 1 Heisman . . . unbeaten 3 yrs. ('33, '34, '35) . . .

1933	4-0-4	1936	7-1	1939	3-4-1
1934	8-0	1937	6-2	1940	8-0
1935	8-0	1938	6-2	1941	8-0

19. Alabama under Wallace Wade & Frank Thomas (1924–1937) . . . established Southern football with Rose Bowl wins ('25, '30, '34) . . . missed '37 nat'l champs in Rose Bowl loss to California . . . back-to-back '25–'26, '30, '34 nat'l champs . . . '34 Tide featured Don Hutson and Bear Bryant . . . 24-game unbeaten streak ('24–'27) . . .

1924	8-1 Wallace Wade	1931	9-1 Frank Thomas
1925	10-0	1932	8-2
1926	9-0-1	1933	7-1-1
1927	5-4-1	1934	10-0
1928	6-3	1935	6-2-1
1929	6-3	1936	8-0-1
1930	10-0	1937	9-1

20. Tennessee under Bob Neyland & W. H. Britton (1926–1940) . . . one of most dominant teams ever . . . received some nat'l-title recognition in '38 (11-0) but missed '39 title with Rose Bowl loss to USC . . . 33-2 from '37–'40 . . . along with 'Bama, Texas A&M, Tulane, Duke gave national recognition to Dixie before WWII . . .

1930	9-1 Bob Neyland	1936	6-2-2 Bob Neyland
1931	9-0-1	1937	6-3-1
1932	9-0-1	1938	11-0
1933	7-3	1939	10-1
1934	8-2	1940	10-1
1935	4-5 W. H. Britton		

21. Michigan's "point-a-minute" teams under Fielding "Hurry Up" Yost (1901–1905) . . . made football popular beyond Ivy League in early 20th century . . . established Michigan grid tradition that lives today . . . 2 straight nat'l champs ('01–'02), received some nat'l-title recognition ('03–'05) . . . along with Chicago, Minnesota made Midwestern football . . . beat Stanford 49-0 in 1st '02 Rose Bowl . . . '01 Wolverines considered best team ever until then . . .

1901	11-0	1904	11-0
1902	11-0	1905	12-1
1903	11-0-1		

22. Michigan under Fritz Carlisle (1940–48) . . . nat'l. champs ('48), easily could have been in '47 (unbeaten with 49-0 Rose Bowl win over USC) . . . nat'l. struggle for supremacy with Notre Dame . . . established Midwest football dominance in early years of Big 10-PCC Rose Bowls . . .

1940	7-1	1943	8-1	1946	6-2-1
1941	6-1-1	1944	8-2	1947	10-0
1942	7-3	1945	7-3	1948	9-0

23. Washington under Gil Dobie (1908–1916) . . . focused attention on Pacific Northwest as pre-WWI football capital . . . at least 1 nat'l. title ('13) . . . 39-game winning streak ('08–'14) . . . 63-game unbeaten streak ('07–'17) is longest ever . . .

1908	6-0-1	1911	7-0	1914	6-0-1
1909	7-0	1912	6-0	1915	7-0
1910	6-0	1913	7-0	1916	6-0-1

24. Michigan under Bo Schembechler (1970–1980) . . . best nontitle run . . . Wolverines dominated regular season but disappointed in Rose Bowls . . . finally won Rose Bowl over Washington ('81) . . . sustained excellence . . . embodied tough, interior game . . . Schembechler vs. Woody Hayes (Ohio State), vs. John McKay/John Robinson (USC), vs. Don James (Washington), vs. Dan Devine (starts sustained rivalry with 28-14 win at Notre Dame in '78) were epic battles in best settings ("Big House," "Horse Shoe," Rose Bowl, South Bend) that define game's appeal . . .

1970	9-1	1974	10-1	1978	10-2
1971	11-1	1975	8-2-2	1979	8-4
1972	10-1	1976	10-2	1980	10-2
1973	10-0-1	1977	10-2		

25. Stanford under Pop Warner (1924–1930) . . . legendary coach had his best teams . . . '26 nat'l. champs . . . along with Cal, Notre Dame considered best programs prior to start of USC-Notre Dame rivalry in '26 . . . embodied nat'l. shift to warm weather West in Roaring '20s . . . Ernie Nevers was one of game's legends . . . building of Stanford Stadium ('21) marked sports popularity, harbinger of Rose Bowl, Coliseum, Olympics in Calif. . . . failed attempt to get Rose Bowl in Palo Alto instead of Pasadena marked shift from NoCal to SoCal . . .

1924	7-1-1	1928	8-3-1
1925	7-2	1929	9-2
1926	10-0-1	1930	9-1-1
1927	8-2-1		

26. Pittsburgh under Jock Sutherland (1929–1938) . . . '37 nat'l. champs but Rose Bowl losses to USC ('30, '33) diminished prestige of Eastern football . . . AP awarded Pitt in '37 but sentiment leaned toward California after beating 'Bama in Rose Bowl . . .

1929	9–1	1934	8–1
1930	6–2–1	1935	7–1–2
1931	8–1	1936	8–1–1
1932	8–1–2	1937	9–0–1
1933	8–1	1938	8–2

27. Georgia Tech under John Heisman (1915–1919) . . . won by series of most lopsided scores in history during war years . . . '17 nat'l. champs . . . award named after their legendary coach . . . unbeaten 3 straight yrs. ('15–'17) . . .

1915	7–0–1	1918	6–1
1916	8–0–1	1919	7–3
1917	9–0		

*   *   *

Why is USC's run between 1962 and 1982 a greater two-decade dynasty than Bear Bryant's Alabama juggernauts of 1958 to 1982, despite the fact that Alabama's record in the 1960s and 1970s is 192–32–5, while USC's is "only" 169–47–5?

Because USC has:

- Five legitimate national championships, all with Rose Bowl victories attached to them
- Four Heisman Trophy winners
- National rivalries with Ara Parseghian and Dan Devine (Notre Dame); Tommy Prothro, Pepper Rodgers, and Terry Donahue (UCLA); Woody Hayes and Earle Bruce (Ohio State); and Bo Schembechler (Michigan)—all of which were dominated by Troy
- Five first-round draft picks in 1968
- Three number one overall draft picks
- Eleven draft picks (1968), ten (1970), ten (1973), fourteen (1975), fourteen (1977), and eleven (1983, seniors from the 1982 team)
- Six players and one assistant coach from this era in the Pro Football Hall of Fame
- Two players from this era who were Super Bowl Most Valuable Players
- Two players from this era who were NFL Players of the Year
- Thirteen players, one head coach, one assistant coach, and one athletic director of this era in the College Football Hall of Fame

- Far more All-Americans than Alabama, not to mention winners of other major awards such as the Outland Trophy and the Lombardi Award
- Seven players in the 1977 Super Bowl, including five on the world-champion Oakland Raiders
- Could have been national champions in 1976 and 1979; the 1968 team was thought to be one of the best ever until they lost the Rose Bowl, and the 1979 Trojans are felt to be one of the best *never* to win the title
- In 1978 they beat Alabama at Legion Field and split the national title with the Tide, but USC should have been the consensus winner

Alabama (1958–1982) has four legitimate national championships with bowl victories; two illegitimate ones (with bowl losses); one title they shared with the Trojans that should have been all USC's; zero Heisman Trophies; and eight bowl losses in a row (1967 season to 1974 season). For almost half that period of time they were segregated; they played mostly segregated opponents; and when integrated USC traveled to Legion Field in 1970, the Trojans beat Alabama up and down the field.

The question is asked, and thus answered.

Alabama's racial history is one that their fans would really like to forget. In truth Bear Bryant is a hero in the end because of the way he ended the practice, but in the glare of national scrutiny, when bidding for such terms as "Team of the Decade" or "greatest dynasty of them all," it must cost them valuable points.

It is also true that while USC carried on a yearly rivalry with Notre Dame on the field, Alabama's rivalry with the Irish was fought with placards and letters to the editor, at least until the 1973 Sugar Bowl. It is, however, a popular myth that USC played a tougher conference schedule than Alabama in the 1960s and 1970s. The Pac-8 and Pac-10 (beginning in 1978) produced some of its best teams during this time, but there were weak sisters (California, Washington State).

Winning Streaks (Includes Bowls, No Ties)			
Modern era (1919–2008)			
1. Oklahoma	47 (1953–57)	7. Oklahoma	28 (1973–75)
2. Southern California	34 (2003–06)	7. Michigan State	28 (1950–53)
2. Miami	34 (2000–03)	11. Nebraska	26 (1994–96)
4. Oklahoma	31 (1948–51)	12. Southern California	25 (1931–33)
5. Texas	30 (1968–71)	12. San Diego State	25 (1965–67)
6. Miami	29 (1990–93)	12. Michigan	25 (1946–49)
7. Alabama	28 (1991–93)	12. Army	25 (1945–46)
7. Alabama	28 (1978–80)		

Unbeaten Streaks (Includes Bowls and Ties)

Modern era, 1919–2008

1. California	50 (1920–25)	16. Southern California	28 (1978–80)
2. Oklahoma	48 (1953–57)	16. Oklahoma	28 (1973–75)
3. Notre Dame	39 (1945–50)	16. Army	28 (1947–50)
4. Oklahoma	38 (1972–75)	16. Minnesota	28 (1933–36)
5. Southern California	34 (2003–06)	20. Southern California	27 (1931–33)
5. Miami	34 (2000–03)	21. Nebraska	26 (1994–96)
7. Nebraska	32 (1969–72)	21. Alabama	26 (1960–62)
7. Army	32 (1945–47)	23. Southern California	25 (1931–33)
9. Alabama	31 (1991–93)	23. San Diego State	25 (1965–67)
9. San Diego State	31 (1968–70)	23. Michigan	25 (1946–49)
9. Penn State	31 (1967–70)	23. Army	25 (1945–46)
9. Georgia Tech	31 (1950–53)	27. Alabama	24 (1924–27)
9. Oklahoma	31 (1948–51)	28. Southern California	23 (1971–73)
14. Texas	30 (1968–71)	29. Notre Dame	23 (1988–89)
15. Alabama	29 (1978–80)		

There were weak sisters in the Southeastern Conference, but by and large it was as strong then as it is now, which is saying something. Based upon a review of the final poll rankings between 1962 and 1982, the parallel years of the essential dynasty period of USC and Alabama, the SEC scores a wide margin of victory.

The raw numbers, which tend to favor Alabama, speak to the core philosophies of the two programs and their place in the collegiate football realm. The Alabama fan looks at USC and sees a lot of flash, plenty of "Hollywood sparkle" in the form of flamboyant players (like Anthony Davis) winning big-time awards like the Heisman Trophy, earning well-publicized All-American honors, then signing million-dollar first-round bonus contracts with the NFL.

AAWU-Pacific-8/10 vs. Southeastern Conference (1962–82)

Ranked in Associated Press polls

AAWU-Pac-8/10		SEC	
No. 1	5	No. 1	5
Top 10	22	Top 10	39
Top 20	53	Top 20	66

Ranked in Associated Press Polls

1962
PAC: 1. USC
SEC: 3. Mississippi; 5. Alabama; 7. LSU

1963
PAC
SEC: 5. Auburn; 7. Mississippi; 8. Alabama

1964
PAC: 8. Oregon State; 10. USC
SEC: 1. Alabama; 7. LSU

1965
PAC: 4. UCLA 10. USC
SEC: 1. Alabama; 7. Tennessee; 8. LSU

1966
PAC: 5. UCLA
SEC: 3. Alabama; 4. Georgia

1967
PAC: 1. USC; 7. Oregon State; 10. UCLA
SEC: 2. Tennessee; 8. Alabama

1968
PAC: 2. USC; 14. Oregon State; 20. Stanford
SEC: 4. Georgia; 8. Tennessee; 12. Alabama

1969
PAC: 5. USC; 10. UCLA; 16. Stanford
SEC: 8. LSU; 11. Tennessee; 12. Auburn; 13. Mississippi; 15. Florida

1970
PAC: 8. Stanford; 15. USC
SEC: 4. Tennessee; 7. LSU; 10. Auburn; 20. Mississippi

1971
PAC: 10. Stanford; 19. Washington; 20. USC
SEC: 4. Alabama; 7. Georgia; 9. Tennessee; 11. LSU; 12. Auburn; 15. Mississippi

(continues)

Ranked in Associated Press Polls (*continued*)

1972

PAC: 1. USC; 15. UCLA; 19. Washington State

SEC: 5. Auburn; 7. Alabama; 8. Tennessee; 11. LSU

1973

PAC: 8. USC; 12. UCLA

SEC: 4. Alabama; 13. LSU; 19. Tennessee

1974

PAC: 1. USC

SEC: 5. Alabama; 8. Auburn; 15. Florida; 17. Mississippi State; 20. Tennessee

1975

PAC: 5. UCLA; 14. California; 17. USC

SEC: 3. Alabama

1976

PAC: 2. USC; 15. UCLA

SEC: 10. Georgia; 11. Alabama; 20. Mississippi State

1977

PAC: 10. Washington; 13. USC; 15. Stanford

SEC: 2. Alabama; 6. Kentucky

1978

PAC: 1. USC; 14. UCLA; 17. Stanford; 20. Arizona State

SEC: 1. Alabama; 16. Georgia

1979

PAC: 2. USC; 11. Washington

SEC: 1. Alabama; 16. Auburn

1980

PAC: 11. USC; 13. UCLA; 16. Washington

SEC: 1. Georgia; 6. Alabama; 19. Mississippi State; 20. Florida

1981

PAC: 10. Washington; 14. USC; 16. Arizona State

SEC: 6. Georgia; 7. Alabama; 19. Mississippi State

1982

PAC: 5. UCLA; 6. Arizona State; 7. Washington; 15. USC

SEC: 4. Georgia; 11. LSU; 14. Auburn; 20. Alabama

Notable Streaks

Regular season winning streaks

Oklahoma	45 (1953–1957)
Southern California	38 (2003–2006)
Miami	36 (1985–1988)

Home winning streaks

Miami	58 (1985–1994)
Southern California	33 (2001–2007)

Consecutive bowl appearances

Nebraska	36 (1969–2003)
Michigan	32 (1975–2006)
Florida State	25 (1982–2006)
Alabama	25 (1959–1983)

Major bowl streak

Nebraska	*17 (1982–1998)

*NCAA record 17 consecutive "major" bowls (January 1, 2), 1982 (Orange) to 1998 Orange.

Pre-World War I era winning streaks (1900–1918)

Washington	39 (1908–1914)
Pittsburgh	32 (1913–1917)
Michigan	28 (1901–1903)

Pre-World War I era unbeaten streaks (1900–18)

Washington	*63 (1909–1916)
Michigan	*56 (1901–1905)
Georgia Tech	*33 (1914–1918)

*Records are sketchy prior to World War I. This is not considered the modern era because in some cases rugby was played instead of football.

Miscellaneous winning streaks

Concord (California) De La Salle High School	151 (1991–2003)
Mt. Dora College	54 (1996–1999)
Morgan State College	54 (1931–1938)
Mt. Union College	46-game unbeaten streak
Toledo	35 (1969–1972)
Hillsdale College	34 (1954–1957)

Chapter 20

The Greatest Games Ever Played

Top 20 Greatest Single-Game Individual Performances

1. Anthony Davis (Southern California) vs. Notre Dame, 1972
2. Vince Young (Texas) vs. Southern California, 2006 Rose Bowl
3. Red Grange (Illinois) vs. Michigan, 1924
4. Johnny Rodgers (Nebraska) vs. Oklahoma, 1971
5. Matt Leinart (Southern California) vs. Oklahoma, 2005 BCS Orange Bowl
6. Joe Montana (Notre Dame) vs. Houston, 1979 Cotton Bowl
7. Ron VanderKelen (Wisconsin) vs. Southern California, 1963 Rose Bowl
8. Anthony Davis (Southern California) vs. Notre Dame, 1974
9. Doug Flutie (Boston College) vs. Miami, 1984
10. Tim Brown (Notre Dame) vs. Southern California, 1986
11. Joe Montana (Notre Dame) vs. Southern California, 1977
12. O. J. Simpson (Southern California) vs. UCLA, 1967
13. Joe Montana (Notre Dame) vs. Southern California, 1978
14. C. R. Roberts (Southern California) vs. Texas, 1956
15. Johnny Lujack (Notre Dame) vs. Army, 1946
16. Ty Detmer (Brigham Young) vs. Miami, 1990
17. Vince Young (Texas) vs. Michigan, 2005 Rose Bowl
18. Tommie Frazier (Nebraska) vs. Florida, 1996 Fiesta Bowl
19. Charles Woodson (Michigan) vs. Washington State, 1998 Rose Bowl
20. Knute Rockne/Gus Dorais (Notre Dame) vs. Army, 1913</nl>

Greatest Single-Game Individual Performance

At the L.A. Memorial Coliseum on December 2, 1972, Southern Cal sophomore Anthony "A. D." Davis scored six touchdowns, two on kickoff returns, totaling 218 yards on three runbacks averaging 72.7 yards, to lead the number one Trojans to a 45–23 blowout of Notre Dame. USC was well on their way to the national championship and general consensus (as well as Keith Jackson's analysis) as the "greatest team of all time." Two years later Davis repeated the effort versus the Irish (earning him the sobriquet "the Notre

Dame Killer"). Two other games stand, possibly equaling A. D.'s 1972 game as the finest single-game performance of all times. In 1924, Illinois' Red Grange had a phenomenal game versus Michigan that not only electrified college football but also is credited with kick-starting the NFL when his entrance into the league generated enormous crowds. Vince Young's performance for Texas in the 2006 Rose Bowl certainly contends, as well.

Top 40 Greatest Single-Game Team Performances

1. Southern California 55, Oklahoma 24 (2005 BCS Orange Bowl)
2. Nebraska 62, Florida 24 (1996 Fiesta Bowl)
3. Notre Dame 51, Southern California 0 (1966)
4. Army 48, Notre Dame 0 (1945)
5. Nebraska 38, Alabama 6 (1972 Orange Bowl)
6. Michigan 49, Southern California 0 (1948 Rose Bowl)
7. Georgia Tech 222, Cumberland 0 (1916)
8. Alabama 66, California 0 (1973)
9. Southern California 55, Notre Dame 24 (1974)
10. Oklahoma 77, Texas A&M 0 (2003)
11. Michigan 55, Iowa 0 (1970)
12. Miami 58, Notre Dame 7 (1985)
13. Florida 52, Florida State 20 (1997 Sugar Bowl)
14. Arkansas 31, Oklahoma 6 (1978 Orange Bowl)
15. Ohio State 62, Texas Christian 0 (1969)
16. Texas 66, UCLA 3 (1997)
17. Oklahoma 35, Louisiana State 0 (1950 Sugar Bowl)
18. Michigan 49, Stanford 0 (1902 Rose Bowl)
19. Southern California 42, Ohio State 17 (1973 Rose Bowl)
20. Illinois 39, Michigan 14 (1924)
21. Notre Dame 49, Southern California 19 (1977)
22. Texas 41, Southern California 38 (2006 Rose Bowl)
23. UCLA 45, Illinois 9 (1984 Rose Bowl)
24. Miami 46, Texas 3 (1991 Cotton Bowl)
25. Southern California 35, Pittsburgh 0 (1933 Rose Bowl)
26. Alabama 61, Syracuse 6 (1953 Orange Bowl)
27. Nebraska 40, Notre Dame 6 (1973 Orange Bowl)
28. Alabama 34, Southern California 14 (1946 Rose Bowl)
29. Alabama 34, Nebraska 7 (1967 Sugar Bowl)
30. Louisiana State 41, Notre Dame 14 (2007 Sugar Bowl)
31. Notre Dame 38, Texas 10 (1977 Cotton Bowl)
32. Alabama 35, Ohio State 6 (1978 Sugar Bowl)
33. Alabama 34, Miami 13 (1993 Sugar Bowl)
34. Southern California 50, Arizona State 0 (1988)

35. Washington 31, Southern California 0 (1990)
36. UCLA 41, Nebraska 28 (1988)
37. Brigham Young 48, New Mexico 0 (1984)
38. Miami 37, Nebraska 14 (2002 BCS Rose Bowl)
39. Oklahoma 63, Kansas State 0 (1974)
40. Arizona State 19, Nebraska 0 (1996)

Top 30 Greatest Games Ever Played

1. Texas 41, Southern California 38 (Rose Bowl/Pasadena, Calif.); January 4, 2006
2. Southern California 21, UCLA 20 (Los Angeles Coliseum); November 18, 1967
3. Nebraska 35, Oklahoma 31 (Tinker Field/Norman, Okla.); November 25, 1971
4. Texas 15, Arkansas 14 (Razorback Stadium/Fayetteville, Ark.); December 6, 1969
5. Notre Dame 10, Michigan State 10 (Spartan Stadium/East Lansing, Mich.); November 19, 1966
6. Southern California 16, Notre Dame 14 (Notre Dame Stadium/South Bend, Ind.); November 21, 1931
7. Southern California 7, Duke 3 (Rose Bowl/Pasadena, Calif.); January 2, 1939
8. Southern California 42, Wisconsin 37 (Rose Bowl/Pasadena, Calif.); January 1, 1963
9. Southern California 34, Notre Dame 31 (Notre Dame Stadium/South Bend, Ind.); October 15, 2005
10. Notre Dame 0, Army 0 (Yankee Stadium/New York City); November 9, 1946
11. Notre Dame 24, Alabama 23 (Sugar Bowl/New Orleans, La.); December 31, 1973
12. Miami 31, Nebraska 30 (Orange Bowl/Miami, Fla.); January 1, 1984
13. Notre Dame 31, Miami 30 (Notre Dame Stadium/South Bend, Ind.); October 15, 1988
14. Ohio State 31, Miami 24 (BCS Fiesta Bowl/Tempe, Ariz.); January 3, 2003
15. California 25, Stanford 20 (Memorial Stadium/Berkeley, Calif.); November 20, 1982
16. Southern California 55, Notre Dame 24 (Los Angeles Coliseum); November 30, 1974
17. Notre Dame 7, Oklahoma 0 (Tinker Field/Norman, Okla.); November 16, 1957
18. Boston College 47, Miami 45 (Orange Bowl/Miami, Fla.); November 23, 1984
19. Notre Dame 31, Florida State 24 (Notre Dame Stadium/South Bend, Ind.); November 13, 1993
20. Ohio State 41, Michigan 38 (Ohio Stadium/Columbus, Ohio); November 18, 2006
21. Southern California 18, Ohio State 17 (Rose Bowl/Pasadena, Calif.); January 1, 1975
22. Georgia Tech 8, California 7 (Rose Bowl/Pasadena, Calif.); January 1, 1929

23. Southern California 20, Notre Dame 17 (Los Angeles Coliseum); November 28, 1964
24. Boise State 43, Oklahoma 42 (Fiesta Bowl/Glendale, Ariz.); January 1, 2007
25. Illinois 39, Michigan 14 (Memorial Stadium/Champaign, Ill.); October 18, 1924
26. Southern California 27, Notre Dame 25 (Los Angeles Coliseum); November 25, 1978
27. Oklahoma 29, Ohio State 28 (Ohio Stadium/Columbus, Ohio); September 24, 1977
28. Notre Dame 49, Southern California 19 (Notre Dame Stadium/South Bend, Ind.); October 22, 1977
29. Southern California 42, Alabama 21 (Legion Field/Birmingham, Ala.); September 12, 1970
30. Dartmouth 3, Cornell 0 (Memorial Field/Hanover, N.H.); November 16, 1940

Chapter 21

All-Time All-American Team

The Greatest Players

OFFENSE

Pos.	Player	College
QB	Matt Leinart	Southern California
RB	O. J. Simpson	Southern California
RB	Tony Dorsett	Pittsburgh
WR	Tim Brown	Notre Dame
WR	Johnny Rodgers	Nebraska
TE	Mike Ditka	Pittsburgh
OL	Ron Yary	Southern California
OL	John Hannah	Alabama
OL	Orlando Pace	Ohio State
OL	Dean Steinkuhler	Nebraska
C	Dwight Stephenson	Alabama

DEFENSE

Pos.	Player	College
DL	Tony Casillas	Oklahoma
DL	Lee Roy Selmon	Oklahoma
DL	Bob Lilly	Texas Christian
DE	Hugh Green	Pittsburgh
DE	Warren Sapp	Miami
LB	Junior Seau	Southern California
LB	Cornelius Bennett	Alabama
LB	Brian Bosworth	Oklahoma
DB	Ronnie Lott	Southern California
DB	Jack Tatum	Ohio State
DB	Charles Woodson	Michigan

SPECIAL TEAMS

Pos.	Player	College
K	John Lee	UCLA
P	Reggie Roby	Iowa
KR	Anthony Davis	Southern California
FB	Bronco Nagurski	Minnesota

OFFENSIVE PLAYER   Matt Leinart, Southern California
DEFENSIVE PLAYER   Brian Bosworth, Oklahoma
COACH   Paul "Bear" Bryant, Alabama

Top 65 Greatest Players

1. Matt Leinart, Southern California
2. Brian Bosworth, Oklahoma
3. O. J. Simpson, Southern California
4. Orlando Pace, Ohio State
5. Johnny Rodgers, Nebraska
6. Tony Dorsett, Pittsburgh
7. Dean Steinkuhler, Nebraska
8. Hugh Green, Pittsburgh
9. Warren Sapp, Miami
10. Charles Woodson, Michigan
11. Lee Roy Selmon, Oklahoma
12. Jack Tatum, Ohio State
13. Desmond Howard, Michigan
14. Earl Campbell, Texas
15. Jim Plunkett, Stanford
16. Archie Griffin, Ohio State
17. Herschel Walker, Georgia
18. Roger Staubach, Navy
19. Ricky Williams, Texas
20. Bubba Smith, Michigan State
21. Mike Ditka, Pittsburgh
22. John Hannah, Alabama
23. Harold "Red" Grange, Illinois
24. Ronnie Lott, Southern California
25. Dwight Stephenson, Alabama
26. Dave Rimington, Nebraska
27. Ty Detmer, Brigham Young
28. Doug Flutie, Boston College
29. Ron Dayne, Wisconsin
30. Barry Sanders, Oklahoma State
31. Ross Browner, Notre Dame
32. Ted Hendricks, Miami
33. Steve Emtman, Washington
34. Mike Reid, Penn State
35. Jim McMahon, Brigham Young
36. Randy White, Maryland
37. Jim Stillwagon, Ohio State
38. Jim Thorpe, Carlisle
39. Dick Butkus, Illinois
40. Lee Roy Jordan, Alabama
41. Don Hutson, Alabama
42. Tommy Nobis, Texas
43. John David Crow, Texas A&M
44. Doak Walker, Southern Methodist
45. Brick Muller, California
46. Deion Sanders, Florida State
47. Sammy Baugh, Texas Christian
48. Jim Brown, Syracue
49. Ernie Nevers, Stanford
50. John Elway, Stanford
51. Vince Young, Texas
52. Davey O'Brien, Texas Christian
53. Paul Hornung, Notre Dame
54. Bronco Nagurski, Minnesota
55. Glenn Davis, Army
56. George Gipp, Notre Dame
57. Tom Shevlin, Yale
58. Leon Hart, Notre Dame
59. George Webster, Michigan State
60. Marchy Schwartz, Notre Dame
61. Tom Harmon, Michigan
62. Bo Jackson, Auburn
63. Charley Trippi, Georgia
64. Tim Tebow, Florida
65. Reggie Bush, Southern California

Index

Numbers in italics refer to pages in the photo section.